Schubert in the European Imagination

Eastman Studies in Music

Ralph P. Locke, Senior Editor
Eastman School of Music

Additional Titles on Nineteenth- and Early Twentieth-Century Music

*Analyzing Wagner's Operas: Alfred Lorenz
and German Nationalist Ideology*
Stephen McClatchie

Berlioz: Past, Present, Future
Edited by Peter Bloom

Berlioz's Semi-Operas: Roméo et Juliette
and La damnation de Faust
Daniel Albright

*"Claude Debussy As I Knew Him" and
Other Writings of Arthur Hartmann*
Edited by Samuel Hsu,
Sidney Grolnic, and Mark Peters
Foreword by David Grayson

*Debussy's Letters to Inghelbrecht:
The Story of a Musical Friendship*
Annotated by Margaret G. Cobb

*Explaining Tonality:
Schenkerian Theory and Beyond*
Matthew Brown

*French Organ Music from the Revolution
to Franck and Widor*
Edited by Lawrence Archbold
and William J. Peterson

*Historical Musicology: Sources, Methods,
Interpretations*
Edited by Stephen A. Crist and
Roberta Montemorra Marvin

*Musical Encounters at the 1889 Paris
World's Fair*
Annegret Fauser

The Musical Madhouse
(*Les Grotesques de la musique*)
Hector Berlioz
Translated and edited by
Alastair Bruce
Introduction by Hugh Macdonald

*The Poetic Debussy: A Collection of
His Song Texts and Selected Letters*
(Revised Second Edition)
Edited by Margaret G. Cobb

*Schubert in the European Imagination,
Volume 1: The Romantic and
Victorian Eras*
Scott Messing

*Schumann's Piano Cycles and the
Novels of Jean Paul*
Erika Reiman

*Substance of Things Heard: Writings
about Music*
Paul Griffiths

*Wagner and Wagnerism in Nineteenth-
Century Sweden, Finland, and the Baltic
Provinces: Reception, Enthusiasm, Cult*
Hannu Salmi

A complete list of titles in the Eastman Studies in Music Series,
in order of publication, may be found at the end of this book.

Schubert in the
European Imagination
Volume 2

Fin-de-Siècle Vienna

SCOTT MESSING

UNIVERSITY OF ROCHESTER PRESS

The University of Rochester Press gratefully acknowledges generous support from the Manfred Bukofzer Publication Endowment Fund of the American Musicological Society.

First published 2007

University of Rochester Press
668 Mt. Hope Avenue, Rochester, NY 14620, USA
www.urpress.com
and Boydell & Brewer Limited
PO Box 9, Woodbridge, Suffolk IP12 3DF, UK
www.boydellandbrewer.com

ISBN-13: 978–1–58046–213–6
ISBN-10: 1–58046–213–8
ISSN: 1071–9989

Library of Congress Cataloging-in-Publication Data

Messing, Scott.
  Schubert in the European imagination / Scott Messing.
     v. cm. – (Eastman studies in music, ISSN 1071–9989; v. 40–)
  Includes bibliographical references and index.
  Contents: v. 1. The romantic and Victorian eras.
  ISBN 1–58046–233–2 (hardcover : v. 1 : alk. paper) 1. Schubert, Franz, 1797-1828. 2. Gender identity in music. 3. Music in art. 4. Music in literature. I. Title. II. Series.
  ML410.S3M46 2006
  780.92–DC22

2006013868

A catalogue record for this title is available from the British Library.

For Chuck

Contents

Illustrations

Music Examples

Figures

Acknowledgments

In the long process of researching and writing this study, I was extremely fortunate to have benefited from the cooperation of a variety of institutions and the counsel of many colleagues and friends. I am pleased to recognize their generosity.

Two organizations have kindly given me permission to reproduce manuscript materials and musical excerpts by Arnold Schoenberg: the Arnold Schönberg Center, Vienna, and Belmont Music Publishers, Los Angeles. Copies of artworks and reproduction rights come from Art Resource, New York (figure 3.4), Wien Museum, Vienna (figures 3.2, 6.1, and 6.2), Hans Schneider, Tutzing, Germany (figure 2.1), and the Bildarchiv of the Österreichische Nationalbibliothek, Vienna (ÖNB/Wien, figures 1.1 and 3.5, and dust jacket). ÖNB/Wien is also the source for figure 2.2 as well as the picture of the sixteen-year-old Schubert from the *Illustrirtes Wiener Extrablatt*, which is used in volume one of this book. Figure 3.1 was made available courtesy of the Hatcher Graduate Library of the University of Michigan. Further relevant acknowledgment appears with the appropriate figure or music example.

An earlier version of chapter 3 was published as "Klimt's Schubert and the Fin-de-Siècle Imagination," in *Music and Modern Art*, ed. James Leggio (New York: Routledge, 2002). Parts of chapters 4 and 6 appeared in my "Franz Schubert and Viennese Modernity," in *Wien 1897: Kulturgeschichtliches Profil eines Epochenjahres*, ed. Christian Glanz (Frankfurt am Main: Peter Lang, 1999).

The following individuals from the indicated libraries and organizations graciously provided timely answers to my many questions: Charles Barber and Melissa Bush, Hargrett Rare Book and Manuscript Library, University of Georgia Libraries; Patricia Baughman, Music Division, Library of Congress; John Benicewicz, Art Resource, New York; Richard Carlin, Executive Editor of Music and Dance, Routledge, New York; Camille Crittenden, formerly of the Archive of the Arnold Schoenberg Institute, Los Angeles; Peggy Daub, Special Collections Library, University of Michigan; Eike Fess, Arnold Schönberg Center, Vienna; Lynne Heller, Archiv der Universität für Musik und darstellende Kunst, Vienna; Dana Ledger and Katharina Schubert, Leo Baeck Institute, Jerusalem; Christa Prokisch, Jüdisches Museum der Stadt Wien, Vienna; Peter Prokop and Silke Pirolt, Österreichische Nationalbibliothek Bildarchiv; Charles Reynolds, University of Michigan Music Library; Victoria Walker, Fine Arts

Library, Michigan State University; Helmut Selzer, Wien Museum; Bryan Skib, Hatcher Graduate Library, University of Michigan; Anne Wirth, Belmont Music Publishers, Los Angeles; and Georg Zauner, Hans Schneider Verlag. I appreciate the kind assistance shown me by personnel at the wonderful institutions in Vienna where I conducted much of my research: the Wien Museum (formerly the Historisches Museum der Stadt Wien), the Österreichische Nationalbibliothek, the Österreichisches Theatermuseum, the Universitätsbibliothek der Akademie der bildenden Künste, and the Wiener Stadt- und Landesbibliothek.

The following individuals thoughtfully responded to my often esoteric queries: James Briscoe, Alessandra Comini, Scott Frank, Maureen Healy, Charles M. Joseph, Jolanta T. Pekacz, the late David Raksin, Carl B. Schmidt, James Steakley, Rita Steblin, and John Wiley. Christopher H. Gibbs made many salutary observations. I am especially grateful to Walter Frisch, Carol Slater, David Smyth, and Glenn Watkins, who read early drafts of chapters.

Unless otherwise indicated, I am responsible for all translations, but I have been incalculably lucky to have colleagues at Alma College who were unstinting in their guidance through the frequently abstruse byways of turn-of-the-century language use. I owe a substantial debt to John Arnold, Julie Arnold, Gunda Kaiser, Jennifer Starkey, and Ute Stargardt for their bravura expertise and generous consideration in answering every one of my questions.

The faculty and staff of the Alma College Library, past and present, were unceasing in helping me locate materials, however remote or rare. I am grateful to faculty colleagues Peter Dollard, Priscilla Perkins, Jennifer Starkey, Steven Vest, and Carol Zeile; and staff members Susan Beckett, Viki Everhart, and especially Susan Cross, who was responsible for completing interlibrary loan requests whose number I am no longer able to total. David Reed and the staff of the Office of Information Technology furnished many types of technological assistance. My longtime colleagues and friends in the music department, Will Nichols and Ray Riley, have been unerring in their support for my research.

I am thankful that my institution, Alma College, has been munificent in providing the wherewithal to enable me to undertake this study. In addition to my receiving a sabbatical leave for the academic year 2003–2004, I have benefited from many faculty grants that allowed me to travel to archives and libraries as well as to obtain essential materials and documents.

The University of Rochester Press has always shown enthusiasm for my research, dating back to the reprint of my *Neoclassicism in Music.* Sean Culhane and Timothy Madigan were early supporters. I am especially thankful to Ralph Locke for his encouragement of this project from its initial submission to its completion. Suzanne Guiod has been a canny and thoughtful editorial mind throughout my labors. Sue Smith contributed greatly during the final preparations of both volumes of this project.

Finally and most of all, I am beholden to my beloved parents, who, in addition to their unconditional love, have served as the most useful of clipping services in spotting the merest mention of Schubert.

Introduction to the Project and to Volume 1

Excerpted from the Introduction to Volume 1

The subject for this work arose from modest beginnings. In 1994, I was searching for a suitable topic in connection with applying to attend a National Endowment for the Humanities Summer Seminar at Columbia University on German modernism led by Walter Frisch. Three years earlier, I had published an article on the circumstances surrounding Vienna's commemoration of the hundredth anniversary of Beethoven's birth, an event that became embroiled in the controversy over the so-called music of the future.[1] With Schubert's centennial falling in 1897—an auspicious year of musical, cultural, and political change in Vienna during which Brahms died, Mahler arrived, the Secession was founded, the Café Griensteidl was closed, Karl Lueger became mayor, and national agitation over new language ordinances prompted the resignation of the prime minister—I thought there might be something intriguing to discover with regard to the intersection of these and perhaps other markers as well. I quickly came to the realization that Schubert was a central figure for Viennese public life at the turn of the century. This was hardly a revelation, but what struck me was the extraordinary array of individuals who invoked the composer. The ways in which they appropriated particular aspects of Schubert's image for their own creative ends suggested a fascinating tension between a received history and the artistic responses to it, which in some cases were designed to challenge the very tradition that had spawned them.

As I pursued my research, I was intrigued by the appearance of Schubert's name in the works of so many of the avatars of Viennese modernism. There seemed to be a recurring thread in their treatment of Schubert that bound their captivation with relationships between men and women to their handling of traits that issued from the composer's legacy as a feminine type. Was it the case, then, that gender, a pillar of recent historiography of nineteenth-century European culture, hovered ineluctably behind Schubert's reception at the turn of the century?[2] As I embarked on my exploration of this subject, the at times contentious debate about the composer's sexuality was a particularly vivid topic *du jour* whose repercussions produced a variety of studies, many having to do with documentary evidence of the composer's life and new approaches to interpreting his music.[3] My scholarly interests, however, were stirred by the question of provenance. I have long believed that there is value to be had in discovering the sources for the terminology that becomes part of our common lexicon and in trying to make sense of how well-known expressions produce an apparently shared understanding. I had arrived at this position in part through an analysis of the origins and development of the term neoclassicism as a fin-de-siècle phenomenon that pitted French and Austro-German aspirations against each other in a polemical battle for cultural hegemony, although Schubert did not figure in that volume to the extent that Beethoven, Wagner, and Schoenberg did.[4] This study persuaded me that an examination of the genesis and evolution of a term that comes to represent a larger cultural phenomenon could indeed illuminate an understanding of history, especially when such an exploration reveals that the path to familiarity has been neither linear nor benign.

The interests that sparked my work on neoclassicism impelled me to wonder about the circumstances and forces that had forged the concept of a feminine Schubert during the nineteenth century. To be sure, my fascination was initially incited by the ways in which gender resonated with the inhabitants of fin-de-siècle Vienna, not least because this place and time was also of great interest to historical and cultural studies. The paucity therein of material about the composer suggested that here might be an untapped area of research, linking those disciplines with the field of musicology.[5] Moreover, from the standpoint of the latter, the fin de siècle is the least well served period when it comes to previous documentary and bibliographic resources on Schubert.[6] As I dug into the question of origins, however, I came to realize that the history of Schubert and gender required its own lengthy exegesis in order to reveal sufficiently its unfolding in nineteenth-century Europe prior to considering its manifestations in fin-de-siècle Vienna. It is to this matter that the present first volume is dedicated.

In retrospect, uncovering the first use of the term "neoclassicism" was probably never in the cards, but fortunately there was such a starting point for tracing the relationship between Schubert's reception and gender. Robert Schumann's essay of 1838 in which he coined the expression Mädchencharakter was and is well known.[7] Chapter 1 of the first volume seeks to demonstrate that the essay of 1838 was the culmination of a decade of Schumann's Schubert reception whose prose and musical manifestations converged in ways that reveal an intricate and subtle treatment of gender. The Mädchencharakter that Schumann invested in Schubert was not simply a clever locution designed to represent a singular womanliness whose appropriate site was the home and whose artistic expression was an untroubled Hausmusik. Rather than creating an alignment of uncrossed binary categories of masculine and feminine natures, Schumann offered an interpretation of Schubert that sought to bridge discrete gender classifications and to which the romanticism of the first volume's subtitle is apposite.[8] The nineteenth century is plainly laced with far more contradictions than a single term can encompass. That troubling condition, however, was not one to which individuals or institutions necessarily deferred as the century proceeded, especially when it came to a comprehension of gender. Quite the contrary, the roles assigned to men and women and, by extension, the representations of their very character were increasingly becoming segregated with an imperturbable fixity that, however much it may have belied reality, was evermore a state to which the sexes were encouraged to aspire by societal authorities and artistic experts. Even as Schumann was formulating his unique conception of Schubert in word and tone, the custodians of culture who were to rely on his authority had already begun to erect precisely those distinct boundaries that his reception of Schubert seemed designed to smudge if not completely eradicate.

Schumann's appropriation of Schubert is fascinating in and of itself, but it is even more important for a study of the composer's reception because the *Mädchencharakter* essay remained one of the most influential sources for subsequent writers during the second half of the nineteenth century at a time when Schubert's reputation evolved from its formative stages and attained a level of prestige that finally assumed iconic status. Chapter 2 charts this development principally in the biographical, historical, and critical literature centered in Austria and Germany. There, Schumann's authority was first embraced as a decisively influential component in a larger cultural enterprise that elevated Schubert's reputation even as it located his *Mädchencharakter* within an ever more explicit gendered domain, thereby leeching it of much of the nuance and complexity with which Schumann had invested it.

Among musicologists, not surprisingly, the literature on the nineteenth-century reception of Schubert has tended to focus on the relationship of his output, whether as individual works or as representatives of genres, to the compositions of subsequent figures.[9] Also, the scholarship that considers responses beyond musical ones has continued to expand since Christopher H. Gibbs, who has contributed as much as anyone to an understanding of the composer's influence in the nineteenth century, noted in 1997 that "there has been relatively little study of Schubert's critical reception."[10] My interest in concentrating on gender is that this particular category was so powerful that it redounded in creative works of the imagination that had nothing to do with music. I hold that, beyond contemporary criticism, one of the most telling indications of the power with which Schubert's *Mädchencharakter* acted upon the popular consciousness was its ubiquitous manifestations among writers and artists who were keenly tuned to the creative potential of this image but who translated its qualities through media other than musical composition or critical commentary. The remarkable plentitude with which a feminine Schubert was performed and heard by characters in nineteenth-century fiction and painting beyond Austria is the subject of chapters 3 and 4. It is an extraordinarily rich array of texts and images that have hitherto remained untouched by musicologists even as an analysis of these works demonstrates the pervasiveness of the image of Schubert as a feminine type.

These chapters reveal a synchronous development in the second half of the nineteenth century in which the emergence of the composer's reputation and its linkage to his *Mädchencharakter* became inextricably intertwined with concepts about the disparate social roles of men and women, particularly among the middle classes and especially as those roles applied to the functions and interactions of the sexes within domestic settings. Here the vastness of the scholarly literature is breathtaking, so much so that the often repeated idea of gendered dualities cannot so easily be relied upon as either an analytic tool or a historical verity, any more than the existence of a uniform and undifferentiated middle class can be taken at face value.[11] The long list of dichotomous divisions along gendered lines of masculine and feminine—culture/nature, public/private, reason/intuition, intellect/feeling, active/passive, and so on—has received its due scrutiny by scholars. For example, nineteenth-century women (including those who might be counted as middle class) were essential to consumer economies whereas men in turn occupied significant roles in the home. Nonetheless, however problematic the notion of "separate spheres" for men and women may have been as a lived reality, there is still a clear record that those who sought to mold nineteenth-century thought and behavior conceived of the distinction between the sexes as a concept required by civilization and as an ideal toward which its citizens must strive.

For a composer whose reputation was principally founded upon musical genres that both the public and professionals in the nineteenth century construed as most suitable for private performance, the enticement to locate Schubert within domestic spaces and to attach to him the attributes of their female occupants may have seemed both irresistible and inevitable. Yet the story is not without its complications. Regarding the evidence that the sites for such music-making were located in households of a certain economic standing, I am mindful that current scholarship also does not necessarily accept a monolithic middle class without local variation, even as I am sympathetic to the thesis that, accepting the differences and contradictions among Victorian, bourgeoisie, and *Bürger*, individuals from one country would have recognized similarities in the functions prescribed for men and women in other societies. This situation is apparent in the evidence regarding the gendered reception of Schubert, and there are distinctions to be made with regard to both time and place. (Schubert's reception in England after 1850 is a special matter that warrants its own discussion in chapter 5.) Despite these variants, however, the relationship between Schubert and gender acquired an authenticity precisely during the period in which men and women were evermore maneuvered into immutable categories with their roles cast by societal sanction, their natures prescribed by scientific authority, and their archetypes refashioned by their artistic progeny.

Introduction to Volume 2

The present volume pursues an examination of Schubert's reception in fin-de-siècle Vienna, particularly among its modernist spirits. As detailed in the first volume, the gendered nature of Schubert's music permeated nineteenth-century European texts and images in which characters performed and listened to the composer's works. As pervasive as these representations were, however, nowhere was the gendered treatment of Schubert more imaginatively reconceived and radically transformed than among those individuals who have come to be connected with that loaded expression in which time, place, and culture so influentially converge: fin-de-siècle Viennese modernism.

The chronology of the fin de siècle has all the fluidity of a representative artwork of the period. For example, when much of the material in the groundbreaking exhibition *Traum und Wirklichkeit: Wien, 1870–1930* of 1985 was moved from Vienna to Paris, the new show acquired the title *Vienne, 1880–1938: Naissance d'un siècle*. In beginning my book about neoclassicism with a survey of events and documents from 1884, I was employing a device common among cultural historians for selecting a particular year as a striking stratagem for introducing the larger issues that confronted Europe at the turn of the century. As with my work, many such studies have drawn their evidence from Paris, although Frederick Morton famously chose Vienna in the ten months between July 1888 and April 1889 because "they seemed representative of [the] watershed when the Western dream started to go wrong dramatically and the very failure was flooded with genius."[1] Among the major figures considered in this volume, birth dates range over fifteen years, although the actual output of these individuals is centered in the two decades that abut 1900. Peter Altenberg was born in 1859, and his first book appeared in 1896, whereas Hugo von Hofmannsthal published his first poem in 1890 when he was only sixteen, making him Schoenberg's exact contemporary. Thus, classifying as a generation those individuals who take up the bulk of the discussion in this volume relies less upon cataloguing their specific ages than upon recognizing that their responses to Schubert bespoke a shared sensitivity to the tradition of the composer's reception bequeathed by the nineteenth century.[2]

Recognizing that, for all their totemic value, specific years are artificial markers for histories of culture, there is more than good fortune in the coincidence of important signposts in Schubert's reception occurring in tandem with significant events in Austrian history. The fifty years prior to World War I are in fact both the period when Schubert's reputation assumed an unassailable position alongside the most illustrious composers of the past and the era in which the political fortunes of the Austro-Hungarian Empire underwent substantial changes. The arch of these two parallel developments, however, is more than a matter of chronological happenstance. They intersect to such a compelling degree because, alone in the pantheon of great composers of serious music established by the time the century came to a close, Schubert was the only one actually to have been born in Vienna. This stature as the capital city's most cherished musical native son placed him in a unique position: his reception carried with it the capacity to articulate a broader cultural identity during a period when the meanings of "Austrian" and "German" were being subjected to momentous political remodeling.

It is in this context that issues of nationalism arise.[3] These are the first issues that the present volume appraises, using two pivotal episodes in the formation of Schubert's Viennese reputation and evaluating their impact in relation to larger contemporary historical events. Chapter 1 considers the statue of the composer in the city's Stadtpark, first planned in 1862 and unveiled a decade later. The civic aspirations symbolized by the 1865 submissions to the design competition for a monument to Schubert (a date framed by years in which the publication of the composer's first documentary biography and the premiere of the *Unfinished* Symphony took place) collided the following year with the shock of the Prussian victory over Austria-Hungary at the battle of Königgrätz, derailing Habsburg pretensions to hegemonic control over German-speaking Europe. Assessing the creation and reception of the Stadtpark statue is especially relevant to an era when the monuments to the honored dead conveyed ever more symbolic weight in the shaping of national identities.

Chapter 2 examines the circumstances surrounding the 1897 municipal commemoration of the centennial of the composer's birth, coinciding with local elections that culminated in the mayoralty of Karl Lueger, the leader of the rightist Christian Social Party. Certainly the list of events from that year—as I indicated in the introduction to the first volume—make it a significant chronological watershed. Studies of the visual arts in Vienna, for example, take the founding of the Secession in 1897 as a transformative occurrence, while political affairs also make this year remarkable.[4] In particular, the proximity of Schubert's birth date, January 31, and the celebrations surrounding it to a crucial municipal election encouraged the Viennese press to respond in ways that crystallized competing nationalist views and prejudices. Although the relationship between these events has been mentioned in passing in the musicological literature, my detailed examination of the newspaper and journal reports on the Schubert celebrations, most vividly represented by the exhibition at the city's Künstlerhaus, is designed to shed light upon the polemical manipulation of the composer's image, and its merging of political and cultural interests.[5] The year 1897 may have been the most representative year for radical change in Viennese political life during the fin de siècle (at least until the outbreak of World War I), but the appropriation of Schubert had first required decades in which the composer's reputation could develop to the level where he could be hailed as the city's favorite son even as he was simultaneously fought over as both a representative of exclusionary pan-German nationalism and a liberal icon of transcendent universal values.

That the matters discussed in chapters 1 and 2 occurred during a period when Schubert's *Mädchencharakter* was undergoing its popularization, if not its unalterable enshrinement, carries fascinating ramifications for the analysis of the composer's Viennese reception. Whether in regard to the attempt in 1872 to achieve an artistic balance between idealization and reality by rendering the composer's figure in marble at a time when the city was in dire need of heroic images, or in regard to the war over his cultural identity as German or Austrian amid coruscating nationalist rhetoric in 1897, the semblance of Schubert as a feminine type could have problematic implications. While these are discussed in the first two chapters, the treatment of the composer's gendered character is the paramount theme in the subsequent consideration of those representatives of Viennese modernism who sought to conceive Schubert's reception anew.

Modernism is a term whose time span has a fugitive quality, which was recognized by its exponents as being essential to understanding its meaning. Although modernism did not need to wait for advocates to articulate its character, in the Vienna of the 1890s the very attempt to assay a definition came close to giving the word a fixity that was contradictory to its nature. "Staying put is meaningless," declared one of modernism's most avid promoters, Hermann Bahr, in "Die Moderne," his touchstone essay of 1890. In its motility, the very condition of being modern was paradoxical; it existed "only in our desire . . . not in our spirit."[6] At its most extreme, the artistic imagination was so evanescent that it might not even result in anything tangible. Writing to Arthur Schnitzler in 1894, two years prior to the publication of his first book, Altenberg described his mode of writing as something utterly free and lacking any deliberation: "I never know my subject beforehand, I never think after. I take paper and write." Altenberg indicated that he hated "retouching." Instead, he just tossed his work away, remaining indifferent to whether it was good or bad. "Whether I write or not is all the same to me."[7] Yet, the immediacy, impermanence, and separateness of the new, of youth, of the present were themselves ironically destined to become part of memory, and fleeing the past required that one first had to be aware of it. In 1892, Bahr could already see himself as one of "the old ones" when compared to a second wave of modernism exemplified by the eighteen-year-old Hofmannsthal.[8]

The self-reflective character of modernism, as Hofmannsthal himself noted in an essay the following year, presented the individual with creative paths in which "you engage in an anatomy of your own psyche or you dream."[9] Being modern required that one seek truth elsewhere than in the homogenous and patently false uniformity of epigonal historicism. History, at least the version promulgated for much of the nineteenth century, came to be no longer seen as a dynamic process of collective development as in the natural sciences and philosophy. It was not composed of logical and coherent patterns with the capacity to illuminate the future as well as the past by offering instructive models to those in the present. In the arts and literature, what had once been honored as tradition now was seen as "burdened with a system of conventions that, trivialized through overuse and exploitation, had been rendered unresponsive to the more immediate and intuitive dimensions of human experience."[10] The creative imagination was not at the service of uncovering universal truths. As Altenberg described himself to Schnitzler, "I am a little hand mirror, a dressing table mirror, not a world mirror."[11]

Remnants of the past could have relevance, but only as autonomous elements invested with meaning by each individual's experience. Indeed, it was the very anachronism of such relics that gave them meaning. Ludwig Hevesi, the literary mouthpiece for the Secession artists, thought as much when he reviewed Gustav Klimt's *Schubert am Klavier* (*Schubert at the Piano*) in 1899. The painting was modern because Klimt had appropriated an ostensibly familiar detail—the "naive, trusting profile" of the composer's head—and designed around it a scene whose manipulation of shape, surface, and light approximated a "visible music" that produced a volatile "electric vibration" coursing through one's nerves.[12] Like the Secession artists whom he valorized, Hevesi himself came to be viewed as a representative of the age: "He was, along with others, an opponent of tradition, a rediscoverer of the tradition of tradition."[13] Modernism thus transgressed the artifice of a formalized, homogenous, and uniform past, not by ignoring it, but rather by selectively reformulating its separate components through the distanced lens of the creative imagination. In a characteristically enigmatic and aphoristic observation, Hofmannsthal noted in 1893: "Old furniture and young nervousness are modern." Writing in the same year, Bahr went so far as to distinguish Viennese modernists from their German counterparts by their self-conscious manipulation and reconfiguration of their forebears' work.[14] A decade later, Hevesi could claim that the newness of Klimt's style would nonetheless have pleased Schubert's friend Moritz von Schwind, an artist who had famously rendered the composer at the piano forty years earlier, while Hevesi himself could be considered "fundamentally at heart never seriously hostile to the good old days."[15]

Of all those placed in the shrine of serious music during the fin de siècle, Schubert's unique stature as the one individual who was born and spent his entire career in Vienna aided in making him an irresistible figure for the modernist imagination. Moreover, the desire to refashion his image, at least the image that was a cherished tradition in the public mind, would have been even greater because its creation had been of such recent vintage. Indeed, the one feature that may be said to be constant in Schubert's reception by Viennese modernists was their contravention of the popular representation of the composer (and, by extension, the culture that had acquiesced to it) through the reshaping of its most revered attributes, including those that took the form of gendered or nationalist symbols.

The discussion of the Schubert commemorations of 1897, including newly commissioned paintings for the Künstlerhaus exhibition, leads into chapter 3's examination of the first of several individuals' reception of the composer. Klimt's *Schubert at the Piano* was executed for the music room of the industrialist Nikolaus Dumba, Vienna's most ardent collector of Schubertiana and a recurring figure in the preceding two chapters. As one of the most celebrated of Klimt's works during his lifetime, the painting, although destroyed in 1945, has received due consideration by art historians. Treating the work as both a part of and a response to the composer's larger cultural appropriation, however, provides a new perspective that reanimates the topic of gender in fin-de-siècle Vienna. In chapter 4, I examine Schubert's reception by writers who were collectively grouped under the rubric Jung-Wien, concentrating upon the works of Schnitzler and Hofmannsthal. My thesis is that the tradition of Schubert's *Mädchencharakter* had become so deeply ingrained in the cultural consciousness of the nineteenth century that writers, in this case those associated with Viennese modernism, could expect that their readers had a familiarity with its components and could then manipulate those features in ways that at times proved to be a critique of the very culture that had created and accepted the image of a feminine Schubert in the first place.

At the heart of Jung-Wien's reception of Schubert was the nexus of meaning that arose from overlapping concepts of the composer as both *Mädchencharakter* and the empire's most characteristic musical icon. A nation rendered feminine by traits embodied in Schubert's life and works conveyed associations that were celebrated by some modernists even as contemporary self-anointed wardens of tradition viewed them with appreciable alarm. The cultural stakes became even higher at the turn of the century as new medical theories of both the body and the mind, many of them emanating from Vienna, produced notable fissures between considerations of sex and gender. Together, the appearance and the absence of the composer in this medical literature and its popular pseudoscientific offshoots form the topic of a separate chapter. My interest here is to evaluate this evidence in the context of the changing tradition of Schubert's reception at the turn of the century. Whether it may have relevance for more recent debates about the composer's sexuality is tangential to this study.

In acknowledging that there remains a tension between the documentary evidence, the arguments that scholars have shaped from it, the analytical commentary about the music that they have drawn from it, and the warmth of recent rhetoric that has issued from interpretations of it, I am not making claims for a more objective methodological approach. I recognize that severing a consideration of Schubert's place in the fin-de-siècle science of sexuality from both what we can know of his life and what in his music passionately engages us today does not elevate the topic to a rarefied status beyond interpretation. Schubert's reception is a subject to which Anton Kaes's formulation is still relevant, even though he was speaking about literature rather than music: "All cultural production has a social dimension: it articulates what a society lacks and desires. It delivers in the make-believe world of fiction what cannot be had or said in reality. In order to reactivate this social dimension of a literary text, one must reconstruct the question(s) that the work answers and addresses."[16] Schubert's relationship to the medical literature and its rhetorical progeny at the turn of the century serves as another node of knowledge in understanding the ways in which the era confronted changing notions of sex and gender.

Nowhere is the unmistakable frisson underlying the vicissitudes of sexuality more apparent than in the work of Peter Altenberg. Owing to Altenberg's persistent avowal that Schubert was his favorite composer, a particularly rich amount of evidence warrants a discussion of this writer in a separate chapter. More than anyone else affiliated with fin-de-siècle Viennese modernism, Altenberg appropriated the shards of Schubert's reception, which supplied him with the means to create a separate identity that nonetheless mirrored his own self.

The last chapter returns the discussion to a Viennese composer: Arnold Schoenberg. My design in concluding with this individual is manifold. The examination of Schubert's relationship to Schoenberg has been limited largely to an analytical body of work concerning the latter's String Quartet no. 3.[17] My intent is to trace Schoenberg's response to Schubert starting with the same prewar period that frames my investigation of Schoenberg's literary and artistic contemporaries. As the fin-de-siècle composer from the Austro-German tradition who left a body of polemical and theoretical prose as extensive as his music, Schoenberg brings this project full circle from its examination, at the beginning of the first volume, of Robert Schumann, whose reception of Schubert was likewise constructed through aesthetic and compositional interstices. Moreover, a consideration of Schoenberg allows a broadening of the study of Schubert's reception from the perspectives of gender and nationalism to the issue of the confrontation with tradition itself. In substituting his own formulation of Schubert for the banality of familiar, shopworn conventions and stereotypes, Schoenberg was binding the older composer to an illustrious and selective list of Austro-German figures whose significance he sought to redesign so that his own work could establish him as their natural legatee. For Schoenberg, Schubert would stand as a more radical figure, shorn of the tuneful *Gemütlichkeit* that had so conspicuously attended the construction of the composer as a gendered type during the nineteenth century.

To be sure, against the compelling reasons for including a figure like Schoenberg in this work, there must be set certain disadvantageous aspects of method and period. For all the pertinence of his writings, Schoenberg was first a composer, and his reception of Schubert thus necessitates a measured consideration of his compositions. As a consequence, this chapter perforce uses a musical terminology whose details may sometimes elude the lay reader. Hopefully, its employment in this instance does not derail the purpose of this study, which at base is to produce an accessible cultural history. Regarding chronology, although events following World War I surface throughout this book, particularly with regard to Schoenberg, I take the war years as the approximate terminus of the fin de siècle. Certainly, this decision accommodates several of the Viennese figures under discussion; Klimt died in 1918 and Altenberg the following year. An evaluation of Schoenberg's reception of Schubert has the effect of injecting what I consider to be plausible doubt rather than maddening paradox; I intend this to be cautionary rather than contradictory and so to challenge the easy sense that, considered as the final act of the "long" nineteenth century, the end of the fin de siècle can be so readily defined.

Chapter One

Political Culture and Schubert's Stadtpark Monument

Among the many local eulogies crafted in fond memory of Schubert upon his death in Vienna in 1828, one can find expressions of sympathy in which Germans and Austrians were equally in debt to his achievement:

> You singers of German lands, who will have buried you,
> Who sings as deeply and delicately of the grace of women as he does?
> Who will sing of heroes, of fidelity and honesty,
> That his songs resound down through all time?
> Oh Austria, your hills, oh Danube, your shores,
> Nevermore will a sound greet you, created by his hand.[1]

This poem by Andreas Schumacher is just a lyrical version of Josef Christian von Zedlitz's more prosaic sentiment: "The deceased belongs to the few great talents whose names will do honor to the enduring glory of the Austrian fatherland, whose works will contribute to the enduring joy of all Germany."[2] As a composer whose reputation would come to rest most securely upon vocal works that set the language common to Austrians and Germans, Schubert could be allotted equally to the heritage of citizens who shared a corresponding culture, despite the separation due to political and geographical boundaries. As Schubert's star became permanently fixed in the European musical firmament over the course of the second half of the nineteenth century, such attitudes as those voiced on the occasion of his passing became a ubiquitous feature of the cultural landscape, especially in Vienna, the city of his birth. By the end of the century, however, competing sensibilities had also arisen, articulated in local panegyrics to the composer in which now, with equal fervor but each omitting the other, Austria and Germany were each seen as the mutually exclusive beneficiaries of his genius.

In order to explain what informed this subtle but nonetheless seismic shifting of cultural allegiances, this and the following chapter take as their centerpieces two seminal events in Schubert's Viennese reception during the second half of the nineteenth century: the creation of the Stadtpark monument to the composer, first conceived in 1862 and unveiled a decade later, and the municipal celebrations of 1897 in commemoration of the centennial of the composer's birth. They are set against and intertwined with events that reshaped both the political and cultural terrain of Austria and its capital. (Modern scholars often use the term Cisleithania, that is, the crown lands west of the Leitha River, to refer to the western part of Austria-Hungary, inasmuch as that part of the empire had no official designation after 1867. Certainly, however, the name "Austria" was a commonly used expression among its inhabitants in the ensuing fifty years and, as such, can serve adequately for the present discussion.) The trajectory of Schubert's reputation during the second half of the nineteenth century coincides with a paradigmatic shift in the fortunes of the nation in which he spent his entire life. If the 1860s can with some justification be considered the decade in which the composer's stature took its first measurably significant steps forward, flourishing during the next half century and culminating in the certainty of his greatness, these years also constituted the decade during which his native land sustained an assault on its position among the continental powers that would conclude with its annihilation as an imperial dynastic entity at the end of World War I.

A reminder of several pertinent historical markers may serve as a worthwhile preface. To scan the titles of studies devoted to the history of the country that gave birth to Schubert is to come away with the impression, unintended to be sure, that the half century leading up to the dismemberment of the Habsburg Empire in 1918 was a period of inexorable if not inevitable atrophy.[3] Of course, the matter is far too complex to be reduced to such a generalization, although one might be excused for appreciating its pithiness inasmuch as chronological précis so often tend to emphasize the monarchy's compromises and setbacks rather than its outstanding triumphs. Such is the case regardless of where one places the beginning of the temporal frame; whether in 1866 with the military defeat at the hands of Prussia, which quashed Habsburg ambitions for hegemony over German-speaking Europe, or one year later with the accord between the Austrian and Hungarian parts of the realm, which created the dual monarchy under dynastic rule (with Franz Joseph I as emperor of the former and king of the latter), a compromise for which, as one writer has succinctly noted, "most historians, like most contemporaries, have scarcely a good word to say."[4]

Although there is hardly any sympathy for the view that ineluctable eclipse can be charted in every facet of the empire during the fifty years prior to World War I, there is a scholarly consensus that, for German Austrians in the monarchy, and especially for those in Vienna, there was an emerging sense that they were in danger of becoming merely another minority, albeit the principal one, whose historically privileged status was under increasing threat. As one historian has observed, "the political problem for Austro-Germans after 1867 was how to retain the German character of the Monarchy with only one-third of the population."[5] This challenge to the German character of Austria in general and Vienna in particular remained an expanding feature of public life in the second half of the nineteenth

century, whether one considers the rise and fall of liberalism from the inauguration of constitutional reforms in 1860 and 1861 to the demise of the liberal
majority in provincial governance in 1879, or one looks at the burgeoning
nationalist movements of the ensuing two decades—not excepting their more
baleful pan-German, irredentist, and anti-Semitic incarnations that came so conspicuously to dominate civic discourse in the capital by the century's end.

With German Austrians experiencing an increasing sense of the evanescence
of political authority, maintaining the cultural sovereignty that had guaranteed
their historic stature assumed a commensurate magnitude and urgency. Under
such circumstances, the reception of a composer—himself the beneficiary of an
emerging reputation that would come to rest principally upon works written in
the German language, and more importantly the only serious musical figure of
widespread prominence actually to have been born in Vienna—was not likely to
remain immune from the confrontation over national identity that roiled the
city during the fin de siècle. The political fissures that increasingly divided
German Austrians who had traditionally thought of themselves as the empire's
true *Staatsvolk* meant that there was a growing competition over the interpretation of the culture that had hitherto legitimized their superiority. As a consequence, the appeal to the authenticity symbolized by their most treasured icons
meant that no event was likely to occur without assuming a larger significance,
even to the point of its meaning being fought over by what finally devolved into
rancorous factions.

One notable sign that the 1860s marked a crucial furtherance in Schubert's reputation was the appearance of the first documentary biography of the composer.
In the succinctly entitled *Franz Schubert*, which was completed at the end of 1864
and published the following year, its author, Heinrich Kreissle von Hellborn,
acknowledged that a vast trove of material had not been available to him when
he wrote his original "biographical sketch" three years earlier. For the later volume, in addition to incorporating the reminiscences of Schubert's contemporaries, Kreissle made a serious effort to document the growing stream of
performances and publications of the composer's music throughout Europe,
especially during the previous decade. The final such example he cited was,
however, still an unfinished local enterprise: the design and construction of a
monument to Schubert in the city's Stadtpark. Laid out according to a plan by
Joseph Selleny, the Stadtpark had been opened to the public on August 21,
1862. Along with the Volksgarten, it was one of two green areas incorporated
into the construction plan for Neu-Wien endorsed by Franz Joseph, who came
to the throne of the Austrian empire in the wake of the revolutions that had
echoed through continental Europe in 1848. On December 25, 1857, the
emperor gave the order for the expansion of Vienna, and his decree permitted
the demolition of the old fortifications and the redevelopment of the glacis
encircling the city. Two years later, on September 1, Franz Joseph approved the
building plan for the new Ringstrasse surrounding the inner city, and during the

next two decades most of the public structures along the west side of this broad avenue were completed.

The design of the Ringstrasse has been much discussed in the context of the political and cultural aspirations of both the emperor and the liberal municipal government that was elected in 1861. Although the symbolism of its public buildings has received the most commentary, the Ringstrasse's attendant green spaces were very much a part of this scheme. Commenting on the Stadtpark, a city council protocol of May 23, 1862, concluded that "the garden should have a simple, unpretentious beauty."[6] That may have been its intended character, but it served other purposes as well. Its patrons came principally from "the upper middle classes, officials, officers, shopkeepers, as well as members of the *Grossbürgertum*," that is, many of the constituents who had helped to bring the liberals to power.[7] Furthermore, even as the majority of the new buildings were constructed along the west side of the Ringstrasse in proximity to the imperial Hofburg, the placement of the Stadtpark on the avenue's southeast side had the effect of separating its wealthier residences from those of the working-class occupants in the outlying Landstrasse district.

The buildings along the Ringstrasse reflected a merging of public function and monumental form, and their attendant sculptures demanded a commensurate symbolism. Quite apart from representing liberal aspirations, however, the first honorees were reminders of imperial power: three equestrian statues commemorating past military figures. The year 1860 saw the dedication of Anton Fernkorn's monument to Archduke Karl (the victor over the French at the Battle of Aspern in 1809 and an icon of dynastic prestige as a Habsburg family member) on the Heldenplatz in front of the Hofburg, as well as the commencement of work on two others in honor of Prince Eugene of Savoy (also on the Heldenplatz) and Field Marshal Karl Philipp Prince Schwarzenberg (on the square that bore his name). Like the public squares of the Ringstrasse, the Stadtpark was intended to provide locations for sculpture. Its intimate and informal nature, however, inspired monuments to the arts rather than to the heroic deeds of war. Schubert was a likely first choice for more than one reason.

However spotty his reputation was throughout Europe, by 1862 Schubert was Vienna's most prominent native-born composer, and as such a monument to him served the twin symbolic needs of promoting a localized patriotism embodied in Schubert as the *echter Wiener* and valorizing a broader cultural nationalism that could embrace him as the creator of the *deutsches Lied*. In this respect, imperial and liberal strategies were in agreement. In 1862, the Habsburg dynasty still held aspirations to be the dominant German-speaking power in Europe (the inscription on the pedestal of the monument to Archduke Karl bears Franz Joseph's dual dedication "to the heroic leader of the Austrian army, to the steadfast fighter for Germany's honor"), while civic leaders drew their authority from groups for whom the German language and culture were sovereign forces. Given this viewpoint, however, the commemoration of the country's generals during the 1860s was beset by bad historical timing. If the Archduke

Karl's monument of 1860 had been unveiled one year earlier to celebrate the fiftieth anniversary of the archduke's victory over Napoleon, the occasion would have coincided with Austria's defeat in Lombardy by the Italians who had enjoyed the support of France. The completion of the other two equestrian monuments, in 1865 and 1867 respectively, unluckily framed the Battle of Königgrätz (also known as Sadowa), as a result of which Prussia replaced Austria as the political power in German-speaking Europe. This outcome ended, at least for two decades, the local vogue for mounted effigies of the country's generals. (By comparison, Prussian fortunes were better served. In 1867, two years after the foundation stone for the monument honoring the 1864 victory over Denmark had been laid in Berlin's Königsplatz, Kaiser Wilhelm I ordered that it also honor "the glorious struggle of the year 1866."[8] Vienna's civic leaders were doubtlessly aware that for decades German cities had honored their cultural heroes with commemorative statues: Luther in Wittenberg [1821], Gutenberg in Mainz [1837], Schiller in Stuttgart [1839], Dürer in Nuremberg [1840], Goethe in Frankfurt am Main [1844], Beethoven in Bonn [1845], Herder in Weimar [1850], and Lessing in Brauenschweig [1853].)

Selma Krasa's analysis of the changing program of public sculpture in Austria after the mid-century—"one based on the recollection of great deeds from the past rather than on dreams of power relating to the future"—also accommodates the initiative for constructing a monument to honor Schubert, Vienna's greatest musical native son.[9] At the same time, the nature of the composer's music, as promulgated by critics, historians, and biographers (including Kreissle) during the previous quarter century, was uniquely suited to the purpose of the Stadtpark's "simple, unpretentious beauty." Most decisively, however, the choice of Schubert was championed by a dedicated and well-financed private organization, the Wiener Männergesang-Verein. By the 1860s, the Verein had become closely associated with the promotion of Schubert's works, although that relationship was not particularly emphasized when it was founded in 1843. Schubert's name does not appear among the composers whose works were performed by the Verein during its first five years of existence, and only Kreissle stands out as an obvious Schubertian among the singers, although Josef von Spaun and Josef Teltscher—both friends of Schubert—appear on a list of patrons.[10] Rather, the contemporary popularity of German song festivals seems to have been a principal motivation for the Verein's creation. To be sure, Schubert's music was subsequently performed and celebrated. Concerts in commemoration of the composer's death occurred on November 18, 1847, November 19, 1850, and November 22, 1853, although Mozart and Mendelssohn were accorded like honors.[11] Indeed, Mendelssohn's *Antigone* and *Oedipus* were the big works in the Verein's repertoire in the 1840s and 1850s, with the former work's "Hymn to Bacchus" Chorus a particular favorite.

The addition of certain key individuals to the Verein's membership provided the catalytic impetus toward Schubert's elevation. When the Verein performed at the dedication of a memorial plaque at the composer's birthplace on October 7, 1858, it had just hired as its new choirmaster Johann Herbeck, who, apart from his wide-ranging tastes (he conducted music ranging from Berlioz, Rubinstein, Liszt, and Wagner to Handel, Pergolesi, and even Lassus), proved to be a Schubertian whose dedication culminated in 1865 with his celebrated levering of the manuscript of the *Unfinished* Symphony (D. 759) from the proprietary hands of the composer's friend, Anselm Hüttenbrenner. Listed as a first tenor in 1865, Nikolaus Dumba, to whom we will often have occasion to return, appeared in the Verein's records in 1856 as a sustaining member, his occupation, recorded as that of a *rentier*, reflecting a status that had profited from contemporary investment rather than from aristocratic inheritance. Indeed, Dumba's social and economic position as much as his adoration for Schubert's music would play a critical role in the creation of the composer's monument.

As the Stadtpark was nearing completion, the Verein seized upon the opportunity afforded by the city planners. In March 1862, it received permission to erect a statue of Schubert on what was called the Zelinka hill, named after Andreas Zelinka, Vienna's liberal mayor. On June 6, the Verein accepted by acclamation the proposal made by its director, Franz Schierer, and Herbeck that a fund be created for the erection of the monument. The money had to be raised from private donations, not public funds. This endeavor was no easy task as was demonstrated by the difficulty encountered with regard to the collection undertaken for a monument in honor of Schiller, whose centennial in 1859 had incited a wave of commemorative events across German-speaking Europe. The Verein, however, enjoyed a roster of well-off members and patrons such as Dumba. On August 9, 1862, the organization mustered 1,200 voices from thirty-four singing societies for an event to raise funds for the monument. More than 10,700 florins had been collected by 1864, and one year later that amount had more than doubled, allowing the project to go forward.[12]

Even if the Stadtpark had a different purpose from the Ringstrasse buildings and their attendant commemorative figures, it was nonetheless a public site, and its statuary had to perform a commensurate symbolic function. The divergence between the park's natural intimacy and the civic import of the larger urban design of which it was a part was not ameliorated by the figure of Schubert, whose reception up to that point did not immediately conjure up a representation of heroic monumentality. Contemporary planners therefore recognized that it was going to be a daunting venture to create an image of the composer that was at once specific and universal. The commission that was established by the Verein on May 24, 1865, to judge proposed sketches for the statue acknowledged this challenge: "Between Schubert's personality as it remains in many memories and that prodigious prince of song appreciated by the world, there lies a gulf that sculpture hardly has the capacity to bridge. The more his statue effects the portrait-like and individual, the less it suits the idea that the musical world has of Schubert."[13] By the following year, there had developed a general awareness of the challenge facing the organizers of the project. For one writer in the *Zeitschrift für bildende Kunst*, a Leipzig art journal, the problem was insurmountable, not only because there was an irreconcilable clash between the composer's body and spirit, but because his figure was at odds with the very rules of sculptural design. The unnamed critic observed: "The general difficulties in creating a monumental portrayal of a modern person are well known and have been emphasized innumerable times." Moreover, in the specific case of Schubert, the obstacles reached the level of impossibility, because the "characteristically unattractive roughness" of the composer's outer appearance was not only in conflict with "his deeply inward, delicately strung inner life" but also with "the stylistic laws of sculpture."[14]

The Verein had good reason to advocate a rendering of the composer that expressed the inner man rather than one that too accurately mimicked the actual individual. Schubert's remains had been exhumed on October 13, 1863, and the physical description provided by the attending experts did not particularly facilitate an idealized artistic representation of the composer. Kreissle famously reported that those present were unable to hide their surprise that the composer's skull had a "delicate, almost womanly structure," and he indicated:

> The outer appearance of our composer was anything but attractive. His round, plump, somewhat swollen face; the low forehead; the pouting lips; bushy eyebrows; the stumpy nose; and the curly hair gave his head a moorish appearance, which also corresponds to the present bust in the Währing Cemetery. His stature was below medium size, rounded back and shoulders, the arms and hands plump, the fingers short.[15]

This itemization of somatic characteristics, hardly a suitable inspiration for a monumental rendering in marble, assembled features that were not only feminine but also conveyed the look of a "negro," the notorious translation of "mohrenartiges" in contemporary English adaptations of Kreissle's biography.[16] As has been detailed in chapter 2 of the first volume of this study, this combination of traits that were other than masculine and Caucasian was especially meaningful during a decade in which evolving notions about both Schubert's appearance and his music embodied similar mental and physical characteristics that were knitted together under the influence of fields ranging from evolutionary biology and anthropology to more dubious pseudosciences such as craniometry.

The commission created by the Verein recognized that the physical representation of Schubert had to accommodate both local memory—many Viennese who had known the composer were still alive—and an emerging historical figure who was best imagined through his music. The statue thus had to be a symbol of both the real and ideal, no simple feat given that the monumental form and cultural function of contemporary public sculpture as embodied in three equestrian military heroes seemed irreconcilably at odds with the image of the composer that had developed from the hagiography of the previous decades.

The commission in fact operated under the first principle that "there is to be erected to the memory of Franz Schubert a simple monument, which corresponds to the simple and unpretentious man to be honored."[17] To that end, the Verein sought the advice of Moritz von Schwind, who had been the composer's close friend during his last years and was himself a highly regarded artist. On October 23, 1865, Schwind responded to the Verein's request for his judgment of earlier portraits of Schubert. He praised in particular the 1825 watercolor by Wilhelm August Rieder, a much-admired work that caught the composer sitting casually with his right arm draped over the back of a chair, his right hand holding a book, and that was to be the most lasting influence on subsequent fin-de-siècle iconography.[18]

Armed with financial wherewithal and expert opinion—two criteria essential for any public project in mid-century industrial Europe—the next task of the Verein was to settle on a suitable sculptor. In 1865, invitations were sent to four artists, although only three—Karl Kundmann, Max Wiedemann, and Vincenz Pilz—proffered designs. (Reinhold Begas declined.) On September 11, the jurors, assembled at the Museum of Art and Industry, announced the rejection of all three submissions. According to one contemporary account, Pilz's design had the composer dressed in antique drapery on a pedestal surrounded by a group of singers and an idealized female form offering up the laurels of victory. In the view of another observer, this depiction was utterly foreign to the real Schubert.[19] It seems at odds with the values of unpretentiousness and simplicity that the committee had sanctioned, and it may have figured in its rejection. At the other end of the design spectrum, Wiedemann's conception drew criticism for its realistic treatment. On May 25, 1866, the *Neue freie Presse* reported: "The naturalistic disarray of the hair, the stand-up collar, the shamelessly rounded belly 'like a full moon'—everything is glued together piecemeal, connected through no feeling for nature." Those features made the composer appear "like an outwardly well-dressed clerk, who, in a pensive attitude, keeps between his thumb and index finger a pinch of snuff, with which he will reward his nose as soon as the right thought comes to him."[20] In a similar vein, the newspaper also considered Kundmann's decision to depict the composer sitting with his legs crossed at the calves to be "a mortal sin against the spirit of sculpture," and indeed such figures were uncommon sights in mid-century Vienna.[21] Echoing sentiments about the gulf that separated the symbolic purpose of public memorials from the actual features of Schubert's "moorish" appearance, the anonymous critic for the *Zeitschrift für bildende Kunst* observed the daunting difficulties of producing a monumental portrayal of a contemporary individual whose soulful inner life was so at odds with his unattractive outward form:

> This plump curly head with glutton's lips and bespectacled snub nose; who wants to create him full size for us, who can, without doing damage to the spirit of sculpture and particularly to the genius of the godlike singer, who for us is the embodiment of everything tender and intimate, the mind of the German Lied itself?[22]

The solution for this critic was to abandon the idea of a full-size statue and to settle upon a bust. He pointed out that, given the features of the composer, the task would still be challenging but this at least was a feasible proposition. This opinion was by no means unique. In contemplating the project in the winter of 1868, Franz Grillparzer, Vienna's most prominent man of letters, who died the year the statue was unveiled, did not consider that Schubert, whom he knew, was especially well suited to a visual rendering beyond the creation of a bust. While Grillparzer thought it would be interesting to know how a man who transformed his thoughts into music looked, he mused that a life-size reproduction was not appropriate and would require the addition of cloaks that the subject would never have worn. (Grillparzer jokingly thought his own possible monument should be cast as a mounted figure, because he did not think he could bear to stand for so long.)[23] The jury itself went so far as to suggest that a fountain take the place of a monumental figure.

Ultimately, the locally trained Kundmann assumed the task (see figure 1.1), although he could hardly be said to have been a famously experienced sculptor at that time. At the age of twenty-eight, he was just beginning to attract public regard. In 1864, he completed the well-received statue *The Good Samaritan*, which led the following year to the prominent commission for four statues of army leaders to adorn the weapons museum in the Arsenal. (The designer for that building was Theophil Hansen, the architect of both the Parliament building and the Musikverein, and subsequently the designer of the pedestal on which Kundmann's statue was to be placed. When Schubert's remains were transferred to the Central Cemetery in 1888, Hansen and Kundmann again collaborated on the memorial.) Kundmann's output later included effigies of Apollo with the muses for the Burgtheater and the statue of Athena in front of the Parliament building.

Kundmann did not have obvious prototypes for creating a grand, massive monument to the embodiment of musical intimacy; the Verein in fact compelled him to submit a new plaster model in January 1868, drawings of which were often reproduced at the time to give the public a sense of his new conception.[24] The most celebrated contemporary example of a full-bodied statue in commemoration of a composer was the Beethoven monument in Bonn, completed in 1845. Kundmann surely was familiar with it, since his teacher, Ernst Julius Hähnel, had designed it. Indeed, Kundmann quoted the older work by using the identical props of quill and manuscript and placing them in the same hands. Nothing else of the Bonn figure, however, seems to have been suited to Schubert's nature. In contrast to Beethoven's direct and purposeful stance, Kundmann placed Schubert in a relaxed sitting position that recalls Rieder's watercolor.[25] One also wonders whether Kundmann might have been aware of the strikingly similar pose given to Schubert in 1863 by his Viennese colleague Joseph Machold in a drawing for a monument that depicts Weber, Mendelssohn, Schubert, and Handel. Schubert, labeled "liebes" on the sketch, is in a sitting position with his pen poised above his music. Machold's work was apparently

Figure 1.1. Karl Kundmann, Schubert's monument in the Vienna Stadtpark. Undated heliogravure (Vienna: Gesellschaft für vervielfältige Kunst). Author's collection. ÖNB/Wien, Bildarchiv, NB 510616-B.

well known at the time when Kundmann embarked on the design of his statue. That year, the *Wiener Zeitung* described a monumental silver goblet dedicated to German song and based on Machold's design, whose octagonal form featured between its panels the heads of Bach, Handel, Haydn, Mozart, Beethoven, Weber, Mendelssohn, and Schubert. Constant von Wurzbach described it in 1867 as among Machold's "newest and most important works." Throughout the 1860s, "Machold-Albums" with photographs were common in Vienna.[26]

The sitting position chosen by Kundmann is not the only element that suggests the passive nature of the composer. Fin-de-siècle opinion held that Kundmann had captured his subject at the moment of artistic conception, "musing dreamily, as though about to put down a musical thought with his upraised pen."[27] In the history of aesthetics, creative and specifically musical inspiration (*Begeisterung*) had possessed an inexplicably transcendent quality if we are to judge by Johann Georg Sulzer's definition of it in 1774, but the next century had to tailor its representations of the compositional process to suit the example of Beethoven, whose genius was invariably characterized by arduous struggle and heroic triumph. Friedrich Nietzsche, for one, had rejected the notion of artistic inspiration as a kind of unexpected transmission sent from above, the kind of creative process embodied in Kundmann's conception of Schubert. Nietzsche instead specifically chose Beethoven as his model:

> Artists have an interest in the existence of a belief in the sudden occurrence of ideas, in so-called inspirations; as though the idea of a work of art, a poem, the basic proposition of a philosophy flashed down from heaven like a ray of divine grace. In reality, the imagination of a good artist or thinker is productive continually, of good, mediocre and bad things, but his *power of judgement*, sharpened and practised to the highest degree, rejects, selects, knots together; as we can now see from Beethoven's notebooks how the most glorious melodies were put together gradually and as it were culled out of many beginnings. He who selects less rigorously and likes to give himself up to his imitative memory can, under the right circumstances, become a great improviser; but artistic improvisation is something very inferior in relation to the serious and carefully fashioned artistic idea. All the great artists have been great workers, inexhaustible not only in invention but also in rejecting, sifting, transforming, ordering.[28]

Nietzsche's argument appeared in 1878, six years after the dedication of the Stadtpark monument. This was presumably a coincidence, although his reference to Beethoven's notebooks reflects his awareness of contemporary musical events, in this case Gustav Nottebohm's study of the composer's sketches that also happened to appear in 1872, the same year as the unveiling of Schubert's statue. In light of the Beethovenian standard, a contemporary sculptural realization of Schubert was ill suited to the display of laborious and dramatic effort. Given the height of Kundmann's monument when placed on Hansen's pedestal, the composer appears more than ever as a figure looking skyward, awaiting the divine impulse to pass, complete and without arbitration, onto the page.

This image of intuitive quietism has an almost sacred element about it, and indeed the seemingly reflexive act of creativity suggested by Kundmann's Schubert owes something to the artistic rendering of religious figures like the apostles Matthew and John—the latter appearing as the transcriber of the book of Revelation—who were often depicted as unreasoning conduits for holy thought, their quills hovering in spiritual anticipation.[29] Furthermore, in addition to this visual tradition, more than one contemporary Viennese public address in honor of the composer was cast in religious terms. When the Hesperus Arts Society placed a memorial wreath at Schubert's grave on January 30, 1858, Friedrich Steinebach provided a prologue, a variation of the Christmas story, in which the seven muses visit the infant Schubert to bestow upon him his creative gifts so that, like Jesus, his kingdom would not be of this world. Likewise, when the same organization again commemorated the composer on March 21, 1863, Josef Weyl's speech portrayed the angel Schubert convincing God the Father to let him bring his song to the world: "Where dark suffering menaces the poor sons of mankind, there my song, to the sound of the harp, should tenderly reconcile all enemies."[30]

Certainly musical creativity as a metaphor for worldly and stalwart purpose was alien to the emerging myths about the composer, as was understood by one anonymous Viennese observer writing for Leopold Zellner's *Blätter für Musik, Theater und Kunst* at the time of the statue's dedication in 1872:

> The monument is conceived purely artistically and, in a victory over all difficulties that here presented themselves, Schubert's form, hard to idealize, is realized through a sitting position, eliminating that impressive heroism which would have had to be granted to him when standing. Kundmann wanted to portray the now so happily executed idea of representing the master at the moment of inspiration, and how poor Schubert thereupon might have looked! But now he sits on a rock, his head freely raised as if in apprehension, the right hand just lifting the stylus, supported by a tree stump, and in the other hand an open notebook that he has laid on a knee, an inspired and yet in itself meaningful and distinctly reserved character, which upon examination evokes the most pleasing impression. The face resembles a portrait only it does not show that plumpness which we see in pictures of Schubert. The figure of white marble is otherwise extremely well done in speaking of the softness and the natural flow of form. The base, as well as the pedestal, with its steps of reddish granite, shows three splendidly executed bas-reliefs in white marble in between such slender columns. On the front side an aspirant Sphinx, on whose hand sits divine imagination with its lyre, has to represent the mystery of art. The two other reliefs must express instrumental and vocal music and show a feminine genius encircled by charming child-forms who sing and play instruments.[31]

In the view of this writer, Kundmann was clearly faced with a dual challenge. A sculpture of the composer was hard to realize because on the one hand his musical output did not lend itself to the Beethovenian model of "impressive heroism" while, on the other hand, the corporeal Schubert did not present the most suitably handsome model to be rendered in marble. Another observer at the monument's unveiling, Franz Pylleman, recognized this artistic quandary. Kundmann had been directed to produce a statue that was a portrait, but to obey the most important aesthetic laws of sculpture was no easy task given the subject's actual short and corpulent form. Nonetheless some degree of verisimilitude had to be adhered to because "Vienna would not recognize a hollowed-out, imaginary Schubert draped in antique garb."[32] The result was consequently a modified idealization of the composer that was emerging from the contemporary reception of him. By the time these assessments of the monument were written, texts such as Kreissle's biography loomed large as authorities for the ways in which Schubertian discourse took place. After all, it was Kreissle who, having produced a mass of documentation that portrayed a composer whose appearance was as unremarkable as his career, nonetheless offered the much-repeated sophistry: "Schubert is, perhaps, a single instance of a great artist whose outer life had no affinity or connection with art."[33]

The need to sever the superficiality of the composer's existence from the greatness of his music was reflected in the sculptor's challenge of reconciling that genius with the problematic character of the composer's physical appearance, whose details were only too easily exploited by those disposed to find fault with Kundmann's monument. To be sure, no Viennese event, however hallowed, could take place without at least one satiric gloss. In *Der Floh*, a weekly journal of humor, one wit caught the sense of the city's having ignored the composer in his lifetime, acerbically wondering: "Why does Schubert's monument show him sitting? Since the Viennese have let him sit while he was alive, now they still cannot be inconsistent after his death."[34] In his critique of the composer's statue in 1873, the feuilletonist Ferdinand Kürnberger took the cliché of Schubert's tubbiness to extreme lengths. He reckoned that, despite the composer's sitting position, no amount of classical drapery could successfully conceal Schubert's paunch. This "mad, unruly, and absolutely unreasonable" belly was an insurmountable obstacle protruding between the tip of his nose and the point of his toe. The sculptor was like a Columbus attempting to set afloat a foundering design by hitting upon the clever idea of hiding Schubert's belly in a seated lap and beneath a robe. There was no other way to harmonize "the ideal Greek belly with the German beer belly."[35] Other critics outside of Austria were also dubious about the final result. The psychologist Gustav Fechner cited the statue as a striking example of the impossibility of resolving the conflict between the outer appearance of its subject and the monumental character and purpose of a sculptural object. Fechner suggested that the best recourse would have been for donors to dedicate an endowment to the composer's memory.[36]

Despite such naysaying, the Stadtpark monument more often was seen to fit snugly into a representation of Schubert in which the sculptural elements of idealization were in accord with the nature of the composer's creative achievement. For the majority of observers, the recumbent figure, forever frozen in artistic communion with an unseen divinity, succeeded admirably in severing his image from both unattractive physical reality and unsuitable heroic stature. The anonymous evaluation cited above even has a distant but distinct echo of Robert Schumann's essay of 1838 in the *Neue Zeitschrift für Musik*, whose coining of the term *Mädchencharakter*, as detailed in chapter 1 of the first volume of this study, did so much to shape the nineteenth-century reception of Schubert. Not only does the monument's form rid its subject of "imponirenden Heroismus," but also in both material and manner it evokes a characteristic "Weichheit." The symbols on Hansen's pedestal are equally telling: they depict "weiblichen Genius" encircled by "reizenden Kindergestalten." The language is significantly reminiscent of Schumann's oft-quoted words: "Schubert ist ein Mädchencharakter an jenen gehalten, bei weitem geschwätziger, weicher und breiter; gegen jenen ein Kind, das sorglos unter den Riesen spielt." ("Compared with him [Beethoven], Schubert is a feminine [girlish] character [ein Mädchencharakter], much more voluble, softer and broader; or a guileless child romping among giants.")[37]

Along similar lines, one of Vienna's most skillful feuilletonists, Ludwig Speidel, found a remarkable synergy between the music of the composer and the milieu of the Stadtpark. Designed specifically for women and children, and for the swan who swam in its waters, this bucolic refuge was the ideal site for Schubert, whose works evoked the same avian, feminine, and childlike symbols, a familiar trio by 1872:

> Where the swan trails its beautiful rings in the pool and well-dressed women murmur through the verdancy and happy children play and shout with joy—here is rightfully the memorial site of the composer, who sang notwithstanding all the songbirds of the world, who rivaled the swan by the beauty of rhythm, who revealed all the secrets of the female soul and who conveyed a pure childlike spirit throughout his life.[38]

For Speidel, Schubert was the incarnation of the Viennese soul. As such, his songs ran the gamut from depth to frivolity and even on occasion to shallowness, while his dances were full of both womanly grace and jaunty movement. Of course, the composer lacked Beethoven's powerful logic and vehement thematic activity. Schubert's principal charm lay instead in his harmony, which belonged to "his feminine, mellifluous manner, to his Viennese nature." As to Kundmann's conception, Speidel found the flowing robes that covered the composer's short legs to be an effective artistic gambit.

Eduard Hanslick, Vienna's leading music critic, drew a similar connection between site and sitter. Schubert's monument conformed beautifully to its tree-shaded, green bay, "its most colorful bouquets of flowers and sweetest perfumes of acacias" serving as nature's emissaries. This synergy was appropriate only to a composer who betrayed no traces "of a lively interest in politics, of intense literary engagement, or of an inclination to philosophical meditation as with Beethoven." (The mention of that composer may also have inclined Hanslick to offer a soupçon of criticism. For all of his melodious magic and charming youthfulness, Schubert, "in recalling the consummate breadth of Beethoven," evinced in his instrumental works a lack of "the coherent power" necessary for an ambitious and tightly organized structure whose organic quality arose from a central focus.)[39]

The observers of the statue's unveiling were not alone in having recourse to such imagery, although without exhibiting Hanslick's jaundiced opinion about Schubert's shortcomings as a composer of instrumental music. At a festival concert given on the occasion of the dedication of the monument on May 15, 1872, a recitation of Eduard von Bauernfeld's verse by the actor Joseph Lewinsky furnished the opportunity for the writer to honor his late friend in characteristic language:

> He shows us clearly, how rich,
> How inexhaustible his spirit proves to be;
> For he does not only rule the Lied,
> But also the instrumental forces,
> Guided by his master hand,
> Open up to us the romantic land,

> And his naive nature flows forth,
> Fresh, glorious, new, thoughtful,
> Trio, Quartet and Symphony,
> Blow through from the breath of poetry—
> So chaste, so delicate, what he creates,
> So tender, and yet full of pure power—
> The others try and fail—
> In short, our countryman was a genius.[40]

Bauernfeld's terms may have narrowly skirted the vocabulary of the Schubertian *Mädchencharakter*, but Joseph Weilen's poem, composed for the monument's unveiling and recited by the actor Louis Gabillon, was marked by unmistakably explicit feminine traits. It concludes: "And only when you approached death's door, / as a dying girl's pale mouth / reveals a secret life to her mother, / so you framed these dying words / of your secret love and desire: / 'I wish to be buried next to Beethoven!' "[41] As noted earlier, the introduction of Beethoven into any discourse on Schubert always threatened to place the latter in a subservient position. With Kundmann's Schubert the touchstone for comparison, subsequent Viennese monuments to Beethoven instead offered godlike portrayals. Kaspar Zumbusch's 1880 statue of the composer stares down upon the viewer from a public square near the Stadtpark, one that is notably outside of its quiet confines, and its pedestal is supported by the figures of Hercules and Victory. Max Klinger's monument created for the Secession exhibition of 1902 includes an eagle paying homage at Beethoven's feet.[42]

For the Viennese architectural theorist, Camillo Sitte, Schubert's Stadtpark monument incarnated the ideal interplay of environment, function, and meaning. In his influential treatise on city planning, *Der Städtebau* (1889), in which he offered an alternative plan to the disposition of structures along the northwest avenue of the Ringstrasse, Sitte observed that the symbolic nature of the site and the purpose of its buildings dictated the selection of its commemorative statuary. For example, the Parliament building, as "an artistic symbol of the imperial spirit . . . should govern the choice of monuments that would be gradually assembled in it," while the plaza of the Rathaus should have "monuments erected here [that] could appropriately be given over to the memory of persons who have been famous in the history of the City."[43] Further south along the Ringstrasse, Sitte approved of the statues in the area bordered by the new palace buildings that provided monuments to Prince Eugene, Archduke Karl, and Empress Maria Theresa. By contrast, Sitte recognized that "the location of idyllic parks in the environs of a city's principal plazas results in a clash between nature and stylistic monumentality."[44] With the Stadtpark appropriately located on the opposite side of the Ringstrasse from Vienna's public buildings, its space demanded statuary equally suitable to its purpose. Given the function of the site, the selection of the composer had been especially successful: "The excellently oriented Schubert Monument has a snug, appropriate place in the foliage of a city park."[45] Further, more than one local observer echoed this opinion. Like Hanslick, Speidel extolled its location in a green bay, framed by bushes and trees, and surrounded by "vivid lawns and laughing flowerbeds." Recalling Kundmann's designs for the Arsenal by way of comparison, one local official, Franz Hottner, considered the Stadtpark monument no less than "an epoch-making artwork for Vienna. All the heroic figures immortalized in the weapons museum without exception fall short of the Schubert statue." According to Robert Schauffler, Sigmund Munz remembered that he and Johannes Brahms frequently stopped in front of it, and that the composer "praised it as the ideal artist's monument."[46]

Here was a harmonious union of the naturalistic intimacy of the green space and the character of Schubert's music embodied in turn by Kundmann's design. Both the symbolic meaning of the statue and its bucolic setting were unsullied by the edifices of state power, and contemporary reproductions of the monument invariably placed behind it a thick bower of leafy trees that appeared to embrace and shelter the composer even as it isolated his form from the public world of commerce and government. Indeed, whether they appeared in newspapers or were sold as separate etchings, these popular images gave the impression of a figure ensconced in an environment that was utterly alien to man-made civilization as characterized by the modern industrial cityscape. (The intimacy of the Stadtpark was to have one unforeseen consequence in the fin de siècle. Although surely not intended, there is a certain measure of irony in the presence of Schubert's monument in the one open place in the city where, as one turn-of-the-century writer noted, both local and visiting homosexual men were accustomed to encountering each other.)[47]

The Wiener Männergesang-Verein could scarcely have realized in 1862 that the decade that would intervene between its proposal to create a monument to Schubert and the statue's unveiling in 1872 would also see the eclipse of its country's leadership in German-speaking Europe. Austria's defeat by Prussia at the battle of Königgrätz in 1866 was the most palpable sign that the empire's ambitions for political hegemony were beyond its grasp. Prior to that realization, German Austrians were able to conceive of themselves as German in matters of culture and language but as Austrian in the diplomatic, economic, and military components that defined a sovereign state, without there being a threat to either identity. As Andrew Whiteside has observed, so long as German nationality embodied a "cultural and ethnic concept" rather than a political philosophy of the state, German Austrians were not confronted with the "problem of divided loyalties. Politically, the Germans of the Habsburg Empire were Austrian, and Austrian statehood did not contradict German nationality."[48] At least during the first half of the nineteenth century, one could remain an Austrian patriot without contravening one's belief in the primacy of German culture.

The concept of German nationality grounded in culture and language rather than in the relationship between politics and the state had emerged after the

French Revolution and the subsequent dismemberment of the old European order during the Napoleonic Wars. *"Deutsches Reich* and *deutsche Nation* are different things," Schiller had pithily written in "Deutsche Grösse," an unfinished poem: "It lives in the culture and in the character of the nation, independent of its political fate."[49] In his *Reden an die deutsche Nation* of 1808, Johann Gottlieb Fichte likewise regarded the nation and the state as separate entities. A higher culture united German peoples through shared customs and language rather than through "any man of German spirit seated at the helm of government."[50] This philosophical and literary tradition furnished the foundation for equating an Austrian identity with German cultural hegemony when, in wake of Schubert's death in 1828, local paeans to the composer appeared even as Prince Metternich's government enjoyed considerable influence in German-speaking Europe. The literary eulogies by Schumacher and Zedlitz quoted at the beginning of this chapter accorded the composer a primacy without political confines, invoking both German territories and an Austrian homeland. These views, along with Johann Gabriel Seidl's celebration of Schubert's legacy—"the German Lied remains undisputedly his domain"—conveyed a meaning that owed far more to a conception of nationalism grounded in language and culture than it did to Otto von Bismarck's formulation of the German state, which even in the 1850s pointedly excluded Austrian participation.[51]

Three decades after the composer's death, a local ceremony such as the laying of a memorial wreath at the composer's grave could still produce a characterization of Schubert that was more of an appeal to *Volk* than to *Staat*. Friedrich Steinebach's speech of 1858 concluded with the sanguine apotheosis of "ein echtes deutsches Sängerblut." This might still have been construed as a metaphor for uniting people with a common linguistic patrimony rather than dividing them on the grounds of politics or geography, especially as earlier in the speech Steinebach portrayed the paternal Beethoven kissing the child Schubert on the forehead and intoning, "Wake up, you shall be my heir."[52] The appeal to blood might thus be made in cultural terms, without necessarily implying the presence of the state. Steinebach presented composers of two generations whose common German character symbolized a familial union, a natural idea for a writer who had chronicled both a history of the reforming Austrian emperor Joseph II and Vienna's commemoration of Schiller's centennial in 1859. Steinebach's language in fact recalls an earlier poetic tribute to camaraderie by Theodor Körner—a German from Dresden transplanted to Vienna whose patriotic verse was set by Schubert—written shortly before he was killed in battle in 1813: "a god unites us, a fatherland, a true, German blood."[53]

A decade after Steinebach, even in the wake of the defeat at Königgrätz, a Viennese writer of an older generation such as Bauernfeld might still invoke these past associations. When the foundation stone for the Schubert monument was laid on October 12, 1868, the actor Louis Gabillon recited Bauernfeld's poem:

> Enough! The artist lives! Leave the songs,
> The earnest rhythms roar forever and ever,
> And the noble sounds of the fatherland!
> You may be proud, you deeply moved multitude,
> Your Schubert, behold, was also a part of you—
> He was, even as no equal ventures at his side,
> Was, what we all are: German and Austrian![54]

Bauernfeld had been a close friend to Schubert during the composer's final years, but this poetic apotheosis was less biography than it was a reflection of an older conception, which saw no contradiction between local patriotic pride and a national German culture that transcended governmental and geographic frontiers. If this verse echoed an earlier time, in 1868 it contained sentiments that could be embraced by the German-speaking Viennese who were a key constituency of contemporary Austrian liberalism, which had included Bauernfeld among its advocates during the revolutionary months twenty years earlier. The characterization of Schubert as a composer whose legacy could bridge the figurative cultural boundaries, if not the literal political borders, between the two countries was certainly one that liberal-minded German Austrians might find appealing. Bauernfeld had excellent credentials for authoring such a reception of Schubert. In 1848, he had a hand in writing the petition against the government and supporting "close adherence to German interests and German policies" while declaring "eternal love and loyalty to the illustrious imperial house."[55] Two decades later, however, there was an unavoidable sense of nostalgia in attempting to accord Schubert the status represented by Bauernfeld's poem.

The military catastrophe in the summer of 1866 had badly shaken the members of institutions like the Wiener Männergesang-Verein and the Schubertbund, who optimistically relied on the unifying power of music and words to mitigate through art and language the insane acts of governments. As relations between Austria and Prussia deteriorated during the spring, the Verein recognized the urgency of promoting ventures that could accommodate both local patriotism and transnational pride:

> The political situation of the fatherland was in fact never suitable for harmonizing with minds appreciative of singing and songs, but everyone hoped for the best and so was agreed on the premise that the impending brotherly rift with the German alliance will yet ultimately still be settled peaceably.[56]

Despite its members' deep concern over the gloomy political news, the Verein determined that, as part of an agrarian exhibition being held in the Volksgarten, it would organize a May concert whose proceeds would be devoted to the Schubert monument fund. By the end of the month, the performance was still being planned even as a diplomatic solution to war seemed less possible:

Meanwhile the dark clouds that overshadowed the horizon of our fatherland gathered themselves, always more perilously threatening, and it stood to expect at any moment the beginning of hostilities against Austria in both the south and the north. The Verein held the view about these circumstances that its duty even at this time was to contribute according to its abilities to the mitigation of the difficult effects of ruinous war, and it resolved to give a festival concert in the Volksgarten with the best patriotic objectives.[57]

The concert took place on June 21, four days after Franz Joseph's declaration of war against Prussia, and it is a measure of the Verein's optimistic and liberal-minded purpose that the repertoire consisted of both Austrian and German music from the past and the present. Whereas Schubert (with the *Rosamunde* Overture, "Ave Maria," "Das Dörfchen," "Wohin?" and the March in B Minor) was the most performed composer, all three of the brothers Strauss were also represented. In addition, Mendelssohn's "Lied ohne Worte" in A flat, Weber's "Schwertlied," and marches from Wagner's *Tannhäuser* and *Lohengrin* were interspersed with titles appropriate to the coming conflict: K. M. Kunz's "Hymne an Odin" and Anton Rubinstein's "Kriegslied." The concert concluded with Herbeck's honorific "Festgesang über die alte Weise 'Prinz Eugenius,' " which had first been performed at the dedication of the monument to Prince Eugene. Such patriotic compositions enjoyed only momentary celebrity, but that did not prevent both sides from exploiting the conflict by churning out music with jingoistic titles. In the weeks surrounding the decisive battle, the Berlin publishers Bote and Bock advertised many such works for male quartet or piano that were designed for rapid and easy domestic consumption by the readers of the *Neue Berliner Musikzeitung*, founded and edited by Gustav Bock. (This journal was particularly vocal in harnessing culture to the Prussian cause. It announced that, in emulation of the army, Berlin's private theaters had placed themselves on a war footing by reducing the honoraria of laid-off performers who were rehired. In looking back upon the campaign, it appreciatively took note of a Milanese music journal's opinion that Prussia won its victory because of the greater literacy of its soldiers rather than because of its superior technology.)[58]

The outcome of the battle at Königgrätz was decided on July 3, and the Verein's subsequent minutes reveal an organization that continued to cling to the healing integration of German art. Speaking on October 13, Dumba summed up the year's events:

[Dumba] thereby attached reports about the position of the membership, of the Verein's assets, and of the Schubert monument fund and, looking back on the sad events of the previous summer, which even had a detrimental effect on the operations of the Verein, closed with the words: "We gather ourselves around our German banner and we do not forget that our Verein, which is a pure, thriving child of German culture and understanding, was founded on and will uphold the enthusiasm for German art, and that this forms the mighty hopeful bond that connects us to the great German fatherland and can be split by no power on earth!"[59]

In the face of military disaster, some German Austrians in Vienna tried to maintain the older notion of an integral culture. In such circumstances, Schubert could serve as a unifying force for Austrian cultural aspirations since he could be celebrated as the creator of the German Lied while being hailed as the city's greatest musical native son. If the Prussians had their Beethoven, then Austria could assure itself a place at the cultural table with the presence of a composer for whom the German language was inseparable from the music of his most characteristic genre. Franz Mair addressed the Schubertbund when it convened on November 10 at its yearly gathering:

> [Mair] emphasized that, even though our fatherland might henceforth be detached from Germany, Austria's German singers will never cease feeling, singing, and acting German! He went further: "With pride we can speak of and point to the greatest Germans in music, Mozart, Haydn, and Schubert: they were Austrian Germans!—We take courage in this horrible time and they allow us to find comfort and consolation for our damaged feelings for the fatherland in our circle of singers, where harmony is master; because life is serious enough, only art is brighter! May the Schubertbund grow and flourish, may its members always be mindful of its motto: 'loyal to knowledge, free in song!' "[60]

By maintaining their faith in German culture, Viennese promulgators of Schubert could make the composer their emblematic local representative even as succeeding historical events thrust the new German state into a position of political leadership. Thus, an event like the Franco-Prussian War could be a cause for pride among German Austrians. On November 25, 1870, two months after the first German victories, the Wiener akademische Gesangverein performed E. S. Engelsberg's chorus, "Der Kriegsgefangene," and the minutes for the meeting of the Schubertbund on March 9, 1871, two months after the new Reich was proclaimed, referred to a composition by Karl Raimund Kristinus, "Wir werden Deutsche bleiben," with the motto: "Within our bodies, there still beats a German heart that will not fall silent so quickly."[61] Such sentiments spoken and sung in Vienna did not constitute a compromise with patriotism; rather, they were a reaffirmation of the superiority of a culture shared by German Austrians. Their contemporary counterparts in Germany, by contrast, enjoyed the luxury of expressing a musical lineage that conveyed both cultural and political symbolism, while excluding a native Viennese such as Schubert. War hysteria in 1870 could elicit from the Neue Zeitschrift für Musik the view that, in such important and solemn circumstances, a great cultural movement now prepared itself with the help and through the influence of the music of Beethoven, Weber, and Wagner. Whatever debt German music may have owed to Austrian composers, the writer argued, they nonetheless symbolized a kind of "Austrian naiveté and gaiety, a Viennese Gemütlichkeit," characteristics that hardly suited a nation preparing for combat.[62]

The musical culture of the new Germany apparently did not need Schubert as much as the old Austria did, nor was every Viennese resident so optimistic.

Grillparzer, who mistrusted nationalist political movements, was compelled to accuse the Prussian victors of 1866: "You claim that you have founded a *Reich*, but all you have done is to destroy a *Volk*." (In the wake of the German triumph in the Franco-Prussian War, Nietzsche leveled a similar critique, warning against the utter destruction of the German *Geist* in favor of the German *Reich*.)[63] Grillparzer recognized that, despite its traditions, the rhetoric of nationalism could not withstand the changes in the political landscape of German-speaking Europe during the second half of the nineteenth century. The tectonic shifts in both the internal and external civic life of Austria were bound to incite competing uses for the terminology.

After the military debacle of Königgrätz and the creation of the dual monarchy in 1867, different ethnic constituencies within the empire competed ever more loudly for rights and benefits, while other developments placed increasing pressure, both real and imagined, on German Austrians: their decline as a percentage of the population even in the Austrian part of the empire, the rise of pan-German political movements in the decades following Austria's dual alliance with Germany in 1879, and the contemporary defeat of the liberals, whose authority in Vienna was eventually replaced by the rightist Christian Social Party.[64] Of course, the country's most significant institutions, including those of Viennese culture, remained predominantly German in orientation and governance. Consequently, it is difficult to parse the usage of words like *Deutscher*, *Österreicher*, and *Wiener* as they took on more varied shades of meaning. The treatment of such terms was by no means limited to discussions of Schubert. Austrian historians at mid-century had far more difficulty in articulating theories of national identity (based on the dynastic past of the Habsburgs) than did their counterparts in Germany, whose arguments were confidently buttressed by the diplomatic and military triumphs that had led to the creation of the modern German state. Brahms's uncertain attitude toward the title of his recently completed *German Requiem* in 1867—"I would very happily also omit the 'German' and simply put 'Human'"—may have reflected in part a desire to avoid any appearance of sympathy for the Prussian victors.[65] This suggestion seems plausible, given that the remark came from a German-born composer whose ties to Vienna were becoming increasingly strong at the time.

If this was an instance of linguistic ambivalence, one can find more blunt usage of the terminology even in connection with a figure like Schubert, whose reception up to this time had lacked overt political connotations. Thus in 1868, one finds invocations to the Lied and its creator that fail to allude to Schubert's local origins. The day before Bauernfeld's poem was read at the laying of the foundation stone for the composer's memorial, a commemorative concert in the Redoutensaal was preceded by Carl Rick's prologue, in which German song took primacy of place: "The Lied, the German *Männerlied*! Who can hear it sung and not wish to swear in formation to his colors?" Rick ended with an aggressively haranguing tone. Schubert, as the icon of Alt-Wien, is noticeably absent from his conclusion:

[Pure folksong] will extinguish the world's fire and will thunder in warfare:
That is the German fatherland—Who here dares an objection?
Many sacred greetings, celebrate his jubilee! You still indomitable hero!
You dove-eyed, brave eagle! You resounding Nibelungs!
Grant us again the priestly convocation with a thousand tongues!
Let your melody roar—let your Lieder roar![66]

One cannot easily reconcile these symbols with the rather more benign imagery conveyed in the next day's speech by Dumba at the ceremony for the laying of the foundation stone: "He was a pure Viennese; a living, bright spirit, a rich, warm heart and spirit marked him in life—in his art he was a rich, inexhaustible spring."[67]

A knowledge of the author's background can shed light on the messages implicit in the appearance or absence of terms that were becoming increasingly freighted with political meaning. If the poet Carl Rick was a literary nonentity, Dumba was emerging as one of Vienna's most distinguished Schubertians. In 1817, his father had come from Macedonia to Vienna where he founded a lucrative company, trading goods such as cotton and sugar with the Ottoman Empire. The younger Dumba was eighteen at the time of the 1848 revolution, and his father sent him to Athens so that he would not join any student organization that might be drawn into the violence. At the home of the first Austrian ambassador to the recently created Greek state, Dumba's cultural tastes, including music, were nurtured. The combination of financial success and aesthetic sensitivity resulted in an acquired wealth that, after his return to Vienna, was given over to the support of the arts and to a series of political appointments after 1870.[68] At his palatial residence on the Parkring, Dumba accumulated nearly two hundred manuscripts of Schubert's music, which he willed to the city of Vienna upon his death.

Throughout his life, Dumba's capacity to channel his fondness for the composer into civic good deeds, as in the case of his crucial support of the Stadtpark memorial, was of a piece with his advocacy of liberal causes, as we shall see in chapter 2. For Dumba, a paean in honor of Schubert was bound to articulate an image of the composer that located him as a product of the same beneficent Viennese culture that had nurtured the speaker who honored him. When Dumba spoke at the installation of the Stadtpark statue on May 15, 1872, he signaled the idea that the monument to the composer served as the kind of representation that had previously been provided by the empire's military figures. "This statue is also worthy of being ranked among those which grace our city and which honor the memory of Austria's heroes and victors. He is also a victor, a conqueror: he has conquered the hearts of the civilized world, and the conquered so eulogize him with thankful hearts."[69] For the liberal philanthropist Dumba, culture rather than politics now furnished the symbolic identity for the nation.

A similar interpretation can be gleaned from Ludwig August Frankl's poem, spoken by Gabillon at Schubert's reinterment in the Central Cemetery on

September 23, 1888, and remarkable for the fact that the word *deutsch* never appears:

> Ah, songs of the lark, as far as the stars!
> Yes, they who made heroes mighty,
> They came here to us from foreign lands,
> Only Schubert is Vienna's native son.
> Thus our twin! We may declare proudly,
> A feeling for him, blood of our blood,
> He sang, in oh so brief a lifespan,
> What endures forever: simple and joyous.[70]

Frankl, born in 1810, was old enough to have remembered Schubert's milieu (if not actually to have known the composer) and, like Bauernfeld, his elegant chronicles of Alt-Wien were inclined to be sympathetic toward liberal causes. Four decades earlier, his poem "The University" in support of the student revolutionaries, written while on sentry duty, had been popular enough to receive nineteen different musical settings.[71]

That anyone could write a panegyric to Schubert that failed to mention *deutsch* even once, however, reflects the fact that, by 1888, a reaction against the rising chorus of pan-German political sentiment in Vienna would have been sufficient to cause a member of an older generation to bypass a word that no longer had just a cultural connotation and instead to characterize the composer as wholly and uniquely Viennese. Perhaps it was no coincidence that, only one month before Frankl's poem was declaimed, Georg von Schönerer had been convicted of assaulting the editors of the *Neues Wiener Tagblatt*. Schönerer was the most notorious representative of that poisonous amalgam of pan-German nationalism and radical anti-Semitism that was exerting an increasing influence in Viennese politics in the fin de siècle. In such a climate, the old cultural terminology was under great pressure. The signature pan-German verse by Aurelius Polzer that began with the once familiar adjectives, "German and loyal, so complete and pure," now continued: "not Jewish, not Czech, not clerical and not Latinized: concise and good, completely unadulterated."[72]

German Austrians who advocated separation from empire and religion were an extremist minority; their irredentism consisted of either "a sentimental attachment to Germany or at best a sulky protestation against the growing influence of the Slavs which menaced German hegemony."[73] The authority of the Habsburg monarchy as a dynastic institution rooted in the Catholic faith was never seriously at risk. Nonetheless, the mistrust and hatred incarnated in crude non-German stereotypes, especially those targeted at urban, bourgeois Jews in Vienna, were increasingly exploited for both political and cultural gain by radically violent pan-German factions and by the more successful populist Christian Social Party. The advocates of traditional Austrian liberalism may have believed in the primacy of German culture and language, but they also recognized the capacity of any individual regardless of origin to become part of civic and social life through education. In the final two decades of the nineteenth century, however, the accession to power of new political organizations was becoming increasingly based upon a treatment of the German Austrian character that was calculated to be exclusionary. The coincidental celebration of Schubert's centennial in 1897 provided an ideal occasion for competing parties to interpret the composer's legacy for their own ends.

Chapter Two

1897: The Politics of a Schubert Year

The gradual rise in Schubert's stature during the second half of the nineteenth century reached its fin-de-siècle apogee in 1897 with the hundredth anniversary of the composer's birth. This date furnished the occasion for commemorative musical performances such as the concerts in Hamburg and Munich featuring the *Unfinished* Symphony conducted by Gustav Mahler and Richard Strauss respectively.[1] Although many European cities observed January 31 with performances of Schubert's works, the celebrations in Vienna were particularly extensive, consisting of a series of four concerts involving the city's principal musical organizations and a massive exhibition at the Künstlerhaus of artworks and documents related to the composer's career. As it happens, 1897 is also a fertile time for assessing the culture of turn-of-the-century Vienna, since several significant events took place during that year whose protagonists responded to Schubert in ways that have hitherto not been sufficiently examined from the standpoint of the composer's reception history. Thus, a group broke with the main artists' society, the Künstlerhausgenossenschaft, to found the Secession, whose first president, Gustav Klimt, was shortly to embark on a painting of the composer, an examination of which reveals a complex interplay of public and private responses. On January 20, the Café Griensteidl—the celebrated haunt of Vienna's leading literary lights—closed its doors for the last time, coincidentally just twelve hours after Franz Joseph spoke at the official opening of the Schubert exhibition. It was precisely writers such as Peter Altenberg and Arthur Schnitzler who manipulated popular images of the composer for their own modernist ends. These examples of Schubert's reception are taken up elsewhere; this chapter examines the relationship of the centennial celebrations in 1897 to the sea change in Viennese politics. The unprecedented citywide commemoration of the composer was framed by elections that consolidated local and regional authority in a single party, the Christian Socials, and consigned liberalism as it had been known in nineteenth-century Austria to political oblivion.

On January 20, 1896, coincidentally one year to the day prior to the opening of the Schubert centennial exhibition at the Künstlerhaus, the left-leaning newspaper *Montags-Zeitung* ruefully conceded: "The word liberalism, which only twenty years ago in Austria inflamed the best in people, now seems taboo."[2] This observation came in the wake of the liberals losing their majority in Vienna's city council as a result of elections in the previous year, but it was also a recognition that the last time they had been in power at the national level was in the 1870s. It was, in fact, as a consequence of the elections of 1879 that the liberals lost their majority in the Reichsrat (Parliament), and their representation would be further reduced in the elections of 1897 after the commemorations of Schubert's death had come and gone during the first two months of the year. As liberal prestige in Austria waned during the last two decades of the nineteenth century, new and increasingly fractious political movements and parties developed to fill the widening void, although in 1897 their competing interests, symbolized by "electioneering of an almost terroristic nature," threatened to make effective governance at times a near impossibility.[3]

Austrian political history in the fin-de-siècle period is beyond the scope of this study, but it bears mentioning that the two national controversies that brought down prime ministers in 1895 and 1897—dates that frame the Schubert centennial—involved controversies concerning the equal representation of languages other than German in local education and governance. (The Cilli affair of 1895 gets its name from the south Styrian town that became the lightning rod for ethnic insistence that a local school should provide classes with equivalent instruction in Slovene and German. In 1897, language ordinances designed to recognize Czech and German parity in the transaction of provincial governmental business in Bohemia again precipitated a change in national leadership.) As noted in the previous chapter, German Austrians were in the minority throughout the empire, but their historic positions of authority in the capital meant that their obstructive tactics could serve as an effective political weapon in their desire to protect long-standing cultural assumptions from the claims of other ethnic constituencies. Thus, nationalism remained at the center of public discourse in Vienna, and aspects of it invariably crystallized at moments when the citizens were called upon to exercise their civic duty at the ballot box. (In 1897, for the first time, every male citizen above the age of twenty-four could vote.) In this regard, several scholars have pointed out that the ascendant rightist political groups, the pan-Germans and the Christian Social Party, shared with the ruling liberals who came before them an unshakable faith in the hegemonic nature of Germanness.[4] Unlike the ideology of their predecessors, however, the rightists' credo was exclusionary, particularly when it came to harnessing a belief in German cultural superiority to a newly racist reconsideration of anti-Semitism. To be sure, the irredentist pan-Germans, most vividly (if hardly exclusively) represented by Schönerer, who sought closer ties to the new German empire than any Habsburg would countenance, never achieved meaningful political power. At the same time, however, the Christian Social Party and its leader Karl Lueger proved far more adept at wielding the rhetoric against *Judenliberalismus*, bringing the party sufficient dominance in Vienna that even Franz Joseph would finally be compelled to approve Lueger as the city's mayor on April 16, 1897, after refusing to do so on four previous occasions.[5]

Such a belligerent political environment could not fail to overlook the centennial of the birth of the only major composer to be born in the city, especially when his stature rested principally upon vocal works in German. Indeed, Schubert's centennial would seem to have been ready-made for the ruling party, whose local governance invested it with the warrant to plan the commemoration. For civic authorities, Schubert's birthday had to have been an irresistible occasion, inasmuch as similar festivals in nineteenth-century Europe had developed into symbols of cultural significance. Vienna had witnessed its share of these events, but in the case of composers, its collective memory was not an entirely happy one. The Beethoven centennial of 1870 had been an embarrassment inasmuch as Joseph Joachim, Clara Schumann, Franz Liszt, and Richard Wagner—all combatants in the skirmishes over the music of the future—had refused to attend once they learned the names of the others who had been invited.[6] The city fathers were not about to endure a similar disappointment a quarter century later.

For the exhibition at the Künstlerhaus, overseen by the officially designated municipal committee of the Schubert-Ausstellung der k. k. Reichshaupt- und Residenzstadt Wien, the only solicitation for outside assistance came in the form of a request appearing at Easter 1896 in newspapers in Austria, Germany, Switzerland, and France for loans of artworks related to the honoree's career. The parochial emphasis extended to the concerts of the city-sponsored music festival, whose performers and ensembles were exclusively Viennese with the qualified exception of the pianist Karoline Geisler-Schubert, the composer's grandniece, who resided in England. (Her ancestry, however, did not shield her from Robert Hirschfeld's sour description of her performance of the G-Major Sonata as "colorless.")[7] Aside from the official events, numerous local organizations and individuals supplied their own commemorations. Press reports indicate that on January 31 there were no fewer than five performances of the *Unfinished* Symphony, three of which featured only the first movement. During the same week, the composer's songs were pressed into varied service, ranging from a Musikverein recital by Hermann Winkelmann with orchestrations courtesy of Eduard and Josef Strauss to a *Schubert-Abend* at the St. Annahof Restaurant featuring the band of the First Infantry Regiment of Bosnia-Herzegovina playing a fantasy on Schubert Lieder by Adalbert Schreiner, entitled *Eine Immortellenkranz für Franz Schubert*. More cerebral fare could be had from free lectures delivered by the music historian Eusebius Mandyczewski, chief editor of the complete edition of Schubert's works, and the music theorist Heinrich Schenker, at that time largely known as a reviewer and critic.

As a consequence of this cultural activity during the first month of 1897, the Viennese press had no end of opportunities to discuss and dissect Schubert's life and work for whatever purpose was in their editorial interests, including reasons that were not strictly speaking aesthetic. In fin-de-siècle Vienna, the newspapers were the primary arena in which political debate intersected with Schubert's reception. The twentieth-century technology that made mass media possible was still in its infancy; in the Vienna of 1897, the press made as much of the electrical illumination that allowed the Schubert exhibition to remain open in the evening as it did of the inauguration of the city's electric tramway or the demonstration of Louis Lumière's motion pictures. Aside from party rallies, newspapers provided the only route to reach a mass audience, an avenue that was all the more important in that year since millions of male voters became enfranchised through newly enacted electoral changes. These publications conveyed passionate positions through cultural and political commentary, and in many cases they were identifiable as house organs of the political parties.

Even if we allow for the existence of something we might consider today as objective journalism, a century ago the reporting of almost any event, however politically neutral it may have appeared, could be signaled to readers through the lens of a publication's party sympathies by the use of language that was often obvious, even crudely so. One caution in using Vienna's newspapers as a resource for analyzing Schubert's reception is that neither the press nor its audience constituted an undiversified entity in terms of opinion.[8] Although recognizing relationships between party and paper certainly makes the task easier, especially as conspicuous liberal and antiliberal forces dominated both politics and publishing, such connections were neither uniform nor inseparable. A publication's allegiances could be monarchical rather than parochial, or religious (ranging from Roman Catholic to Jewish) rather than nondenominational. Its contents might be geared toward a reader's economic or social status, in which case it might still exhibit political ties, as with the *Arbeiter-Zeitung* and the Social Democrats. Other newspapers could just as readily calculate their appeal to the prosperous Viennese *Bürgertum* without necessarily incorporating an explicit political agenda. Yet, even in these instances, at a time when the relationship between identity and culture was a consuming interest for both the governing and the governed, otherwise nonpartisan publications could extract political meaning from an event such as the Schubert centennial, especially given its symbolic resonance at all levels of society from local to imperial.

The consideration of party attachments among Vienna's newspapers is also relevant with regard to both their contributors and their audience. Not all readers of a particular publication necessarily shared its beliefs on every political matter, and the writers were a decidedly mixed group ranging from anonymous and bribable hacks to well-known and distinguished journalists. Besides, as opposed to an essay about the composer's career, a concert review permitted and even encouraged critics to maintain a preoccupation with principally musical concerns of genre and form rather than to dwell upon the real or imagined political meaning that might underlie either the performance or its content. Several factors, however, abetted the manipulation of Schubert's commemoration by the Viennese press. Much of the repertoire was sufficiently familiar that it did not demand the degree of interpretive or technical explanation required of a review of new music. Indeed, Hirschfeld went so far as to complain about the unimaginative programming of the festival's performances.[9] In addition, the concerts that constituted the Schubert festival were only part of a larger celebration that was bound to elicit a different kind of reportage given that the inaugural event, the opening of the Schubert-Ausstellung, featured speeches by both the emperor and the Christian Social mayor, Josef Strobach. Finally, the position of Schubert's birthday in the electoral calendar made it too attractive for the parties not to invest it with political significance. Thus, an analysis of some two dozen newspapers in the months surrounding the Schubert centennial reveals that certain consistent viewpoints often spread through every section of a particular publication, whether they took the form of a news report, an editorial column, a literary feuilleton, an arts review, or even a satirical cartoon.

Characterizing those ideas in terms of political orientation is sometimes a challenge even when considering newspapers with well-established party loyalties. On the one hand, the terms liberal and *linksliberal* had been familiar in Austrian civic discourse for many decades. The newspapers that articulated the cause of liberalism were as readily identifiable as the representatives elected to the nation's institutions of governance, although, as noted earlier, liberalism's demise was a theme that even its sympathizers were compelled to accept. On January 20, 1897, the day of the Schubert exhibition's official opening, the *Wiener allgemeine Zeitung* noted that the leading role that the liberals had occupied a quarter century earlier had since been taken over by the Social Democrats.[10] (Along with its house organ, the *Arbeiter-Zeitung*, the Social Democrat Party was home to Austrian Marxism, but it too suffered defeat at the hands of the Christian Socials in the 1897 elections for the Niederösterreichischer Landtag, the Lower Austrian Diet.)

At the other end of the political spectrum, newspapers did not employ a single term to characterize the opposition to liberalism, acknowledging that its membership embraced more than one philosophy or party. For example, extreme pan-German nationalism, represented most infamously by Georg von Schönerer in the 1880s, was by no means interchangeable with the Catholic conservatism of Karl Lueger's ruling Christian Socials in the 1890s, even if today they are less distinguishable because of their shared anti-Semitism. In reporting the legislative debates of 1897, the press usually had recourse to the word *Rechts* to identify the voices that were raised against liberal positions, but elsewhere newspapers of whatever political stripe relied on other terminology. In February, a reader of the left-leaning *Die Zeit* did not require the identification of party affiliation in order to understand the meaning embedded in the report on the Ball of the City of Vienna—whose symbolic honoree was Schubert—at which the emperor had asked after Lueger's health: "Since the ball, it must have been clear to the most obstinate liberal that the anti-Semites have managed to outflank the Liberal Party with their art of governance."[11]

If any term appeared with consistency in the fin-de-siècle Viennese press to label the forces arrayed against liberalism, it was *antisemitisch*, and its occurrence was equally common in newspapers whether their support fell to the political left or right. The most persistent themes in Viennese public discourse in 1897 related to nation and race, and to the attendant construction and exploitation of "others," most significantly but not exclusively the city's Jewish population. There is a large literature on the history of Austria's Jews in fin-de-siècle Viennese politics and culture.[12] This scholarship is in general agreement that there were many types of anti-Semitism, expressing diverse economic, religious, and racial prejudices. The manipulation of such prejudices by the parties was equally varied, just as there was no monolithic right wing to which all newspaper publishers pledged a uniform journalistic fealty. The pan-German nationalist press in particular, however, boasted political opportunists. Karl Hermann Wolf's *Ostdeutsche Rundschau* supported the Christian Socials in the 1895 elections, much to Schönerer's anger. Yet in the heat of another campaign two years later—even as the paper approvingly described Mayor Strobach, the first member of the Christian Social Party to occupy that position, as an "Oberantisemit"— it was reproving the party for its growing intimacy with the interests of Vienna's high clergy by warning that, while "christlich" could accommodate "antisemitisch," it should not be equated with "catholisch."[13]

The anti-Semitism articulated by Lueger, the leader of the Christian Social Party and Strobach's successor in 1897, was generated by a subtler political mind in comparison to the overt racist hatred displayed by individuals like Ernst Schneider or Ernst Vergani, whose extremist rhetoric usually remained in inverse proportion to the actual power they wielded within the governing hierarchy. The Christian Socials in fact were canny enough to take advantage of the population's anxiety over ethnic and religious stereotypes while still voicing loyalty to the empire. The historian Theodor Gomperz recognized these machinations when he wrote to his wife on September 8, 1896: "What do you say to the cunning exploitation of patriotic-dynastic feelings by Lueger's side and his consorts?"[14]

Yet if the ruling party could not count on the abject loyalty of every representative who was an irredentist pan-German, when it came to the expression of anti-Semitism as a necessary component of an exclusionary conception of German Austrian culture—whether in the contest over an election or in the celebration of a beloved musical kinsman—a reader of Vergani's *Deutsches Volksblatt* in January 1897 would have found little difference between its treatment of either Jews or Schubert and that of the *Reichspost*, founded in 1893 in part to ensure that there was a newspaper with a more dependable Christian Social viewpoint. Moreover, for readers who were amenable to the lure of such rhetoric, the distinctions between Luegerian anti-Semitism and its more baleful cousins were scarcely discernable.[15] Likewise, among antiliberals, the Austrian incarnation of German nationalism may have created divided allegiances among those expressing admiration for either Habsburg or Hohenzollern, but even the extremist pan-Germans shared with the governing Christian Socials the position that the liberal press was run by a cabal of Jews, a common refrain whose cynical uses were not diminished by the reality that many of Vienna's newspapers that advocated liberal causes had, in fact, Jewish owners or editors.[16] Thus, whereas Schönerer and his allies physically attacked workers in the offices of the *Neues Wiener Tagblatt* in 1888, Lueger drafted several contemporary speeches in which he named that newspaper along with the *Neue freie Presse* and the *Wiener Tagblatt* as examples of "the liberal press, sometimes also called the Jewish liberal, or Jewish Press, [which] is the most impudent press on this earth, that it was and is the ally and accomplice of all robberies and thefts that have been committed against the Christian people. In Vienna, only fools and those on the same moral level support it; all decent and intelligent people reject it with disdain."[17] Similarly, Vergani remained too loose a journalistic cannon to be unequivocally embraced by the Christian Social leadership, but on January 31, 1897, his newspaper joined the loyalist *Reichspost* and *Freiheit!* in a page-one presentation of the party proclamation "An das christliche Volk in Oesterreich," which was signed by Lueger and in which liberalism and Judaism were treated as insidious twins. That this screed happened to appear on Schubert's birthday was not a prerequisite for the political treatment of the celebrations in the composer's honor, but the timing provided too ripe an opportunity for the press not to turn a cultural icon into a campaign poster child. (Whether musical or political, any event had the potential to be received in a similar fashion and could even be made conspicuous by its absence. Whereas in January the rightist press ignored Mahler's resignation from his post in Hamburg and his imminent arrival in Vienna, the news was first reported only by liberal papers like the *Neues Wiener Journal* and the *Neues Wiener Tagblatt*.)

In this milieu, the struggle for the symbolic ownership of Schubert reflected the tensions in Viennese public life, and the increasing acrimony of debate was as much a feature of its journalism as of its government. Tributes to Schubert proved to be well suited for manipulation by party factions and their proxies in the press, who desired to exploit the consuming issue of nationalism once Schubert's entry into the ranks of great composers at the century's end had been accomplished via his dual identification as prince of the German Lied and Vienna's greatest musical native son. In the midst of a heated local election, which was destined to be one in a series of transformative events in the empire's political history, the struggle over what properly constituted Schubert's identity was bound to resonate in newspaper reports of the city's celebrations dedicated to the composer. Even in publications where Schubert's reception was leavened by the ingredients of class or religion, the commentary often betrayed a political character, especially when it was generated by a disputatious viewpoint. Given the sheer size of Vienna's journalistic output in 1897, there was no shortage of the sort of opportunism created by the presence of so many contributors of widely varied abilities and motivations to papers with a diverse constellation of political agendas. Then as now, the press recognized that the lure of controversy could snag commercial benefits even if a subject like Schubert did not appear to be freighted with scandal.

Given the discussion of the development of Schubert's *Mädchencharakter* during the nineteenth century in the first volume of this study, the composer might not seem to be an obvious subject for political and journalistic manipulation, at least not in comparison to other figures of the central European musical tradition like Beethoven and Wagner, whose reception has been the topic of recent scholarship.[18] However, Schubert's status as the only great composer actually born in Vienna had made him a uniquely treasured cultural icon by the century's end. At the same time, the fact that his reputation had emerged principally from vocal works in which language was an essential component heightened his attraction for pan-German ideologues. The synchronous evolution in late nineteenth-century Austria of political extremism and mass print media produced a set of circumstances in which the composer's image became inexorably drawn into the rhetorical vortex wherein issues emanating from the competition among the empire's nationalities played progressively leading roles in civic discourse.

So powerful and compelling was the intersection of Schubert's fame with the increasingly fractious developments in Viennese public life that only an individual who had lived well before the journalistic zealotry exhibited in 1897 could blithely ignore the radicalization of culture. Inasmuch as the one commentator who remained aloof from partisan estimations of Schubert was the oldest contributor to newspaper reports about the centennial celebrations, there is a generational component buttressing the sense that using the composer as a tool for political debate was a relative novelty in the history of his reception. Schubert's unlikely candidacy as a political emblem seems to be supported by a perusal of the response to the commemorations of the composer by Vienna's most distinguished music critic, Eduard Hanslick, in one of the city's most venerable newspapers, the *Neue freie Presse*. Reading Hanslick's two feuilletons—one after the opening of the Schubert-Ausstellung on January 20 and the other a review of the composer's operas *Der vierjährige Posten* and *Die Verschworenen*—one might conclude that Schubert was in fact a figure immune to opportunistic manipulation. The biographical details that other writers exploited for partisan purposes were, in Hanslick's hands, without obvious political meaning:

> Schubert's entire significance was only recognized after his death. How little trouble old Vienna took to perform and publish Schubert's works is a sad chapter, indeed a series of sad chapters, which we in the festive and conciliatory mood of today's celebration do not want to reopen. The sin of omission by Schubert's contemporaries can neither be glossed over nor denied; nevertheless we should be reminded of two mitigating circumstances.[19]

For other writers, as we shall see, Schubert's mistreatment by contemporary society would prove to be an irresistible starting point for political interpretation.

Hanslick veered away from this gambit, observing instead that Schubert's neglect was extenuated by two phenomena: the brief time during which his music
was published and the contemporary popularity of the Italian aria.

Hanslick's lack of interest in pursuing the political implications of the composer's centennial appears to have a generational explanation. The disjunction
between generations has been a central tenet in the analysis of fin-de-siècle
Viennese culture, most famously promulgated by the historian Carl Schorske in
his influential *Fin-de-Siècle Vienna* (1979), and it has duly influenced the scholarly
consideration of the era's journalism. The stridency that one finds in the rhetoric in 1897 was a quarter century in the making. As Jill Mayer has observed in
her analysis of the nationalities issue in the Austrian press during this period, "a
relative scarcity of references to ethnicity or national conflict in all of the peri-
odicals in 1877 became in some of them a scream of outrage and despair by
1887. A decade later the discourse surrounding nationality had hardened into
firm political camps."[20] A like-minded view of Viennese music criticism is offered
by Sandra McColl's study of the years 1896–97: "In short, the use of the music
feuilleton for the purpose of the advancement of civil-political opinions is a special characteristic of some critics in the younger generation."[21] Although the
period covered by McColl includes the Schubert centennial, she mentions the
event only in passing, but, to the extent that the critics who did report on it can
be identified, they were invariably younger than Hanslick.

It may be no coincidence, then, that the one notable observer of the composer's commemoration who remained aloof from naked political partisanship
should also be Vienna's most durable writer on music, having produced criticism for the *Wiener Zeitung* prior to the revolution of 1848, then for *Die Presse*
beginning in 1855, and finally for the *Neue freie Presse* from its inception in 1864.
Hanslick had, in fact, been in retirement for two years when he reported on the
events of 1897, and the paper for which he wrote had become the journalistic
mainstay of cultural centrism. Having written music criticism for more than half
a century, Hanslick possessed the capacity for a broad historical perspective, but
he apparently did not see the relevance of giving the composer's celebration the
sort of overt political meaning that characterized the responses by his younger
contemporaries, particularly those who contributed to newspapers that positioned themselves at the more extreme ends of the cultural spectrum and that
catered to a readership other than the comfortable members of Vienna's well-
established *Bürger* class. For Hanslick, it was sufficient to conclude that the
Schubert exhibition recorded "a uniquely rich artistic life embodied in a great
part of Austrian cultural history."[22]

The complete absence of radical partisanship from Hanslick's reviews was
exceptional among press responses to the events of the Schubert festival. In view
of the alliances between Viennese political parties and the press in 1897, there
were instead journalists with widely differing skills and agendas who were avidly
engaged in exploiting the composer's image for whatever political interests
were in accord with those of their sponsors. Besides, the business need to sell

newspapers did not easily allow reporters to take a longer historical view, especially given that the centennial of Schubert's birth was a date surrounded by transformative events in the empire's civic life that shifted power away from liberalism and toward the political right. The same forces that brought about the triumph of the ideas espoused by the Christian Social Party also altered the nature of Austrian journalism.

The battle over nationalism was fought just as bitterly in the press as in the arenas of government. The tumultuous changes also infiltrated considerations of class and religion so that publications whose central focus was ostensibly devoted to such matters also viewed Schubert's social rank and faith through the prism of contemporary politics. Given the connection between the Social Democrats and the *Arbeiter-Zeitung*, its music critic Josef Scheu interpreted Schubert as victimized by social inequity and financial privation, a fate with which any contemporary trade unionist might have empathized: "Because he did not deal with a fixed income, and never at the outset and only later found a very stingy publisher, it is only natural that his economic situation was never in order, and that he found himself frequently in dire straits."[23] Scheu emphasized those aspects of the composer's life that would likely have appealed to the paper's working-class readership: that he came from a poor teacher's family, that he never felt comfortable as a student at the Stadtkonvikt, that he was never motivated by money, and that he was prey to "adroit commercial exploitation."

This sad litany extended to every biographical detail, whether it was the issue of compensation by the Esterházys for their daughter Caroline's music lessons or the gift of one hundred florins from the Gesellschaft der Musikfreunde, a paltry sum given the composer's genius. Likewise, Julius Pap's report in the same paper on the opening of the exhibition at the Künstlerhaus offered a jaundiced view of the main gallery's artworks that again articulated class-conscious differences:

> When one enters the exhibition's main hall, whose walls are for the most part bedecked with portraits of contemporaries, these familiar old Austrian portraits with their vacantly insipid faces, the bureaucratically stiff collars in high-necked coats, and the atrociously sweet manner of painting, then Schubert and his delightful songs do not so much well up in our spirit as does the wearisome picture of the epoch to which he belonged.[24]

By contrast, reading Ludwig Basch's reaction in the *Illustrirtes Wiener Extrablatt*, one would have had difficulty recognizing the same room: "Every figure [in the painting by Julius Schmid] is individualized, the character of each particular face is singled out, and the accessories are treated with great care."[25]

The *Extrablatt* was not designed for detailed political commentary, and whatever coverage it gave to such matters was muted and moderate. Its title instead indicates that it was one of the few newspapers that used images extensively; every front page was dominated by an illustration. On the day of the opening of the Schubert-Ausstellung, it displayed a picture of the composer based on Rieder's 1825 portrait, and its caption read in part: "The folk spirit of Vienna rings and sings forth from the songs which our Franz Schubert—the simple, modest child of a Viennese land forgotten by the world—has left behind."[26] Here was a description of the composer with which the newspaper's large read-ership might well identify, as this clientele consisted of citizens whose back-ground was perhaps not quite so sophisticated as that of other publications and whose interests were drawn less toward dense political commentary and more toward vivid pictorial imagery. Thus, the issue that appeared on the composer's birthday was filled with visual Schubertiana: drawings of his father, of the houses where he was born and died, and even of his skull. Yet the character of the paper's audience might also be judged by the fact that the front page had noth-ing to do with Schubert but rather was an artist's rendering of the discovery of one Marie Slawik, the victim of a sensational murder in the working class Favoriten district.

The *Extrablatt* had in Karl Storck a music critic much like Basch. Born in 1873, Storck became a prolific writer of works notable for their popular tone and many illustrations, and his best-selling *Geschichte der Musik* helped to perpetuate many of the most durable clichés about Schubert's life and works. One of these appears in the very title of his contribution to the newspaper, "Der Schubert Franzl." Appealing to the parochial interests of his readers, Storck took Schubert's geographic particularity (and consequently his cultural uniqueness) to extreme lengths:

> Among the greatest of all the masters of music who lived, created, and achieved immor-tality in Vienna, Franz Schubert was the only Viennese born in Vienna. By birth, Gluck was from the Palatine, Beethoven a Rhenish Prussian, Mozart a son of Salzburg, Haydn a lower Austrian from the Hungarian border. Only Schubert's cradle was in Austria, he was a child of Vindobona. And not only as regards the accident of being born in a Viennese suburb. He was a Viennese as regards his temperament, his talent, his view of life, his whole being, and his life's destiny. If Vienna by rights can be considered as the city of music, especially as the city of three-quarter time, then Franz Schubert is its human incarnation.[27]

For the benefit of local residents who were unable to attend the celebrations, the *Extrablatt* was also the only newspaper to provide a visual record of the ceremo-nial events that took place on Schubert's birthday. At a time when technological limitations made such images difficult and expensive to produce, an illustration entitled "The Homage of the Singers" shows members of the Niederösterreichischer Sängerbund arriving in front of the Schubert monument in the Stadtpark at 11 AM with banners flourished, hats doffed, and wreaths laid in honor of the composer.[28]

If some newspapers construed events in terms of class, others for whom reli-gion was an overarching concern viewed Schubert through the prism of their respective orthodoxies. Thus, given the close affiliation between the Catholic

Church and *Das Vaterland*, Alfred Schnerich described therein both the composer's life and his music as models of the faith: "Whether their artistic worth is
greater or lesser, Schubert's sacred works are an expression of a deeply religious
Catholic soul, as indeed the master lived, faithful to the beliefs of his fathers—
and also much too early for us."[29] Carl Staubach, writing on the same matter in
the more radical pan-German *Deutsches Volksblatt*, which had enshrined the
Christian Social proclamation denouncing *Judenliberalismus*, made certain that
his readers knew that the dying Schubert had received the final sacrament: "On
November 19, at three in the afternoon, death, whose power he so movingly
depicted in music, gently took him away, after he received the last rites as a good
Catholic Christian."[30]

Not surprisingly, the paper failed to mention that Schubert had written music
for Vienna's synagogue, a connection that did not elude *Die Neuzeit*, the weekly
publication of the city's Jewish association, the Israelitische Kultusgemeinde. For
its anonymous reporter, a tour of the Schubert-Ausstellung summoned forth the
words of Heinrich Heine: "Lovely ringing moves softly through my soul." For
this organ of Vienna's Jewish community, the era of two generations ago that the
exhibition evoked was neither the quasi-police state offered up in the liberal
press nor the site of class warfare supplied by the Social Democrats. Rather, the
newspaper's Jewish readers were reminded that there was a time in Austria when
their grandfathers were protected by the religious tolerance of Josephinism and
were permitted to "attend to [their] livelihood quietly and industriously." The
implication was presumably that in fin-de-siècle Vienna such ideals were under
stress, and indeed the paper took note that, although many Jews who were connected with Schubert (Heine among them, via the composer's settings of his
poems) were represented in the exhibition, it had failed to include the cantor
Salomon Sulzer, who had come to the city in 1826 and who "had delighted so
very many with the performance of Schubert songs through his soulful voice and
artistic interpretation."[31]

As with religion and class, so too did the dominant political issue relating to
gender—the movement for universal suffrage—find a niche in Schubert's reception at this time. The novelty of a female string ensemble, the Soldat-Röger
Quartet, elicited predictable responses especially when, at a performance on
January 21, the musicians programmed Beethoven rather than Schubert.
Writing for the *Neue musikalische Presse*, one critic wondered: "Did the ladies
really want to emancipate themselves from the Schubert festival? To avoid the
obligatory, constantly replayed Schubert compositions, we think there might be
enough of a selection, if only the spirit were willing."[32] Papers that appealed to
conservative readers responded in a similarly bemused and patronizing tone.
The illustrated weekly *Die vornehme Welt* reported that the four musicians "were
able to play their instruments agreeably, if also here and there not 'manly'
enough," while Richard von Kralik observed in *Das Vaterland*: "The devout
fidelity of the performance is here mixed with a sweet gentleness and grace,
which would truly have been missed if even only half of the performers had

belonged to the weaker sex."[33] Only Richard Heuberger, writing for the liberal *Wiener Tagblatt*, took a position that advocated a degree of equity at least in the field of music education. Heuberger asked rhetorically why this should not be obtained by women at official institutions: "I mean in no way a female strings department but an instructional class without discrimination by sex. The fear that a woman could not get sufficient respect is in my opinion totally untenable. For those who only pay attention to the shape of the garment and not the art, one may just leave them be. For them nothing is lost."[34]

On January 31, with the temperature gradually dropping below freezing throughout the day, a series of official events took place in commemoration of Schubert's birth. The ostensible solemnity of the occasion, however, provided no immunity against the rhetorical manipulation of even its seemingly uncontroversial elements. Editorial gibe and satiric riposte, familiar weapons in the city's local press, were at the service of political interests whose otherwise combative and even unpleasant character was perhaps leavened only by the mordant irony that distinguished fin-de-siècle Viennese literary tact. The festivities began at 9 AM with a ceremony led by the Schubertbund in front of the composer's birthplace on the Nussdorferstrasse. The event was threatened, however, owing to a law that forbade public parades while the Landtag was in session. According to the *Deutsche Zeitung*, the composer's disciples were not deprived of bestowing their musical greetings owing to the appreciative intervention of the owner of the birthplace, who was "German in body and spirit."[35] This characterization might be considered innocuous were one unaware that the publication advertised itself as "Vienna's twice daily anti-Semitic German national newspaper." In anticipation of the same event, the like-minded *Wiener neueste Nachrichten* made its Jewish target explicit when it suggested that any difficulties would be due to the interference of a police official, who was fingered by the paper as a minion of the Baron Rothschild.[36]

At 10 AM, members of the Schubertbund performed the Mass in F Major (D 105) at the parish church in the Lichtental suburb where the composer had been baptized, followed an hour later by a commemoration at Schubert's Stadtpark monument led by the Musikkapelle of the 71st Imperial Infantry Regiment and the Niederösterreichischer Sängerbund, as reported in the *gemütlich* tones of the *Extrablatt*:

> The hundredth birthday of Schubert, the prince of song, was undertaken in a most festive way by Vienna's choral society. The commemorative festival procession of the Niederösterreichischer Sängerbund before the monument of the great homegrown composer in the Stadtpark formed an extremely imposing part of the festival program. The song-loving interpreters of Schubert's Lieder passed before the monument in stately procession and brought the master their greetings of homage. The ensigns flourished their banners and the singers uncovered their heads. The ground from which the statue rose displayed a rich, handsome wreath. Almost every one of the Verein who marched past laid a laurel wreath near the feet of the immortal

composer. The festival procession lasted almost an hour, favored by the cold, clear weather.[37]

After this ceremony, two performances were on offer. At 12:30 PM, the first of the four festival concerts at the Musikverein featured Hans Richter conducting the combined forces of the Hofoper orchestra and the Männergesang-Verein. For the majority of the people, who could not afford a ticket to Vienna's most prestigious concert hall, however, the city fathers provided free admission to a 3 PM *Volksconcert* at the Arcadenhof of the Rathaus, "weather permitting."

By selecting a location at the seat of the municipal government, the ruling members of the Christian Social Party had designed this event to attract potential voters whose economic and social status did not easily accommodate the price of admission to the Musikverein. The political tone was further underscored by the appearance on the Rathaus balcony of Mayor Strobach and other officials (presumably including Lueger, then the deputy mayor). The ruling party perceived the value of appealing to a mass audience, and newspapers indicate the planned participation of 2,300 singers from eighty-four organizations. Lueger in particular understood that male singing societies were useful conduits for spreading cultural nationalism. When he was made an honorary member of the Wiener Liedertafel in 1885, he had thanked its members for their efforts to preserve the unique identity of the German Lied: "The infinite richness that the German people, and especially the German Austrians, manifest in this cultural area attests the depth of feeling that permeates the soul of our people."[38]

Unfortunately for the Christian Socials, Schubert's birthday fell at an inconvenient time of the year as regards the weather, and the exposed location of the Arcadenhof gave the liberal press the opportunity to critique the decision made by the party in power. The inhospitable temperature prompted the *Wiener Tagblatt* to give a head count of only eight hundred, well below other estimates and leaving the Arcadenhof half-filled, while the *Neues Wiener Tagblatt* sniffed: "a concert under a free sky and two and a half degrees below zero!"[39] In the *Wiener Abendpost*, Hirschfeld remarked contemptuously of the event: "It was more of a fumigation than an intoxicant. Or did the Sängerbund—which marched out with banner and bugle to offer three little choruses to the 'folk' in the Arcadenhof of the Rathaus—believe that it had thereby somehow done well by Schubert's genius or by the populace or by the promotion of art in general?"[40] Hirschfeld also supplied the humorous verse to accompany a cartoon in the *Neue musikalische Presse* entitled "Meteorological Schubert Festival," which had a satiric bite to match the frigid weather:

> The people want to hear their Schubert,
> There to the savior they'd draw near:
> "We give to you a *Volksconcert,*
> But only if the weather's clear!"
> They know nothing of winter's pain

It's May they'd prefer to reckon,
They call it a free concert [ein Frei-Concert]
Because it's a concert in the open [ein Concert im Freien].[41]

With the Rathaus in the distance, the picture depicts five Viennese—their shoulders hunched against the cold and their impoverished condition suggested by one young man holding a boot with a hole in its sole—reading a kiosk announcement of the concert emphasizing "free admission" and "only in good weather." (See figure 2.1.) Elsewhere in the same paper, an unnamed writer offered a similar if less whimsical critique: "Until recently the thought of a *Volksconcert*, like the one planned by the Festival Committee, might hardly have come up. That it was considered at all was good; that the *Volksconcert* should also be an outdoor concert (on January 31!) was bad and almost insulting to the 'people' who now and then are still thought of as only those unable to pay."[42] Even the *Extrablatt* had to work hard to cast the event in the best light: "Indeed, the cold milieu of the enterprise was not especially convenient, and the poor acoustics of the Arcadenhof also impaired the performance in places—despite which an inner contact was established between the inspired singers and the thankful listeners. The people were warm and regretted the brevity of the concert."[43]

The opportunity to expose a gaffe by the ruling party even resulted in the exceptional circumstance of a similar response by the pan-German nationalist newspapers, the archenemies of the liberal press, which often shared political viewpoints with the Christian Socials, especially on matters of race, but which on this occasion took advantage of the chance to tweak the noses of the municipal authorities on account of their choice of venue. The *Deutsches Volksblatt* observed: "The not very friendly, far too wintry temperature, however, made enduring the outdoors not very pleasant, and so then it came about that the Arcadenhof scarcely had produced the same number of people as there were singers appearing in the courtyard."[44] The equally maverick *Ostdeutsche Rundschau* also took note of the low turnout and concluded: "If one agrees overall with the view that this way of honoring Schubert is on the whole one of failure, then one here must be particularly critical that the *Volksconcert* only was a pittance, a morsel, which one condescendingly throws to hungry people. . . . But the city has the satisfaction of having done 'something' for its people."[45] Of course, the politicians who bankrolled and published these newspapers were competing for the votes of the same poor, lower-class Viennese to whom the Christian Socials (and the Social Democrats) wished to appeal and who were to swell the electoral ranks later that year. Among critics of the ruling party's apparently cynical programming for the Schubert concerts, only the Marxist *Arbeiter-Zeitung* predictably spread its censorious net to contrast the *Volksconcert* with the economic inaccessibility of the four Musikverein concerts by criticizing their exorbitant ticket prices.[46]

The press critique of the *Volksconcert* is the exception proving the rule that the liberal and anti-Semitic newspapers, which constituted the majority of Vienna's

Figure 2.1. Robert Hirschfeld, "Scharfe Ecke: Meteorologische Schubert-Feier," *Neue musikalische Presse* 6, no. 5 (1897): 17. Reprint, Tutzing, Germany: Hans Schneider, 1987.

publications, were otherwise arch antagonists, especially in the matters of nation and race that dwarfed all other considerations. Similarly, the previously cited reports on the Schubert exhibition that expressed different viewpoints from these combatants were minority opinions in a press dominated by the confrontation between besieged liberalism and its conservative opponents (whether pan-German or Christian Social). The volatility of these issues is manifest in the stories prompted by the exhibition's official opening, at which the words of both the emperor and the mayor supplied the stimulus for political commentary, which was only thinly veiled by the consideration of an honoree who was at once Vienna's most distinguished indigenous composer and the master of German song.

The cue for this construction of Schubert had already appeared in the Easter appeal for loans to the exhibition and was cast in a language that signaled the composer's stature in the cultural life of his hometown:

> On January 31, 1897, it will be one hundred years since Franz Schubert was born. His native city of Vienna considers it a sacred duty to commemorate this anniversary of its immortal son with a festival, which should be an example of devotion and appreciation for the noble singer who has been interred for nearly seventy years in his native soil.
>
> This festival shall consist of the performance of Schubert's masterworks by Vienna's outstanding musical organizations and in an exhibition, in which may be incorporated all that the life and works of the great composer are capable of illustrating.[47]

"Vaterstadt Wiens unsterbliche Sohn" proved to be a popular representation of Schubert that acquired official standing when it was given the imprimatur of the state in a speech by Franz Joseph at the opening of the exhibition: "Today your invitation is so much the more agreeable for me to answer, since it concerns a genuine Austrian celebration. Certainly Franz Schubert, the representative of purer art, the creator of the noblest song, has long belonged to the entire civilized world. But we can proudly call him ours, Vienna especially can call him one of its greatest sons."[48] This description of Schubert—an innately Austrian composer whose music nonetheless possessed features that were accessible to all—must have been compelling for the monarch at a moment when multi-ethnic voices throughout the empire were being raised in favor of greater autonomy even as local parties were exploiting racial stereotypes for political gain.

The implicit natural coexistence between the ability of a self-selected few to discern the greatness of Austrian music as symbolized by Schubert and the rightness of their governance was a rhetorical gambit that was not restricted to imperial designs. A similar effort, as we shall see, was exerted by the mayoralty of the ruling Christian Social Party. It was equally serviceable at the federal level, as one may discern from a speech made at a private Schubert festival on January 29, hosted by the governor of lower Austria, Erich Graf von Kielmansegg, and his wife in the great hall of the Niederösterreichische Statthalterei, whose walls were decorated with frescoes by Schubert's friend Leopold Kupelwieser. Doubtless the exclusive audience was as wealthy as it was powerful, since the governor and his guests were entertained by Vienna's most distinguished chamber ensemble, the Hellmesberger Quartet, which played the Quintet in C Major (D. 956, op. posth. 163). Prior to the performance, the Deutsches Volkstheater actor Adolf Weisse spoke:

> Art is thus no stranger to this room:
> With good reason!—Because whoever cherishes the welfare of the people,
> Ought not to disdain the favor of the muses,
> Which forever deeply inspires the spirit of the people![49]

Those who were by rights present "in this place sanctified by law" were also the ones who possessed a lively appreciation of art. Weisse concluded that, although Schubert was not recognized in his own time and consequently endured "a life of disillusion and pain," only posterity, represented by the small circle of those present, was able to "banish the earlier guilt" and bestow due homage upon the composer, since they shared with him a like-minded nobility; his was artistic and bestowed by genius, theirs was civic and conferred by wealth and privilege.

At the most benign level, newspaper reports of the exhibition's opening reprinted Franz Joseph's speech and offered their own innocuous variant. The weekly *Oesterreichische Volks-Zeitung* described Schubert as the country's greatest musical native son, "who so magnificently helped to propagate the glory of Austria and Vienna," and a week later came more of the same: "Schubert is the greatest and the most Viennese of all Viennese artists."[50] Likewise the *Wiener allgemeine Zeitung* opined: "Nowhere is his name able to resound so heartwarmingly, so lovingly as from the lips of the Viennese. Franz Schubert was as a man of Viennese blood and with his ländler he became the creator of the Viennese dance; in his music is mirrored a good part of being Viennese, and even today, when it has become the common property of the entire world, it has not renounced the soil from which it grew."[51]

Such reports, more often than not the product of anonymous reporters, were common enough, but with a crucial election on the horizon every event acquired political meaning, and many newspapers exploited the event for their own ends depending on whether their sympathies leaned toward the left or the right. Certainly, publications that were militantly *linksliberal* emphasized those aspects of Franz Joseph's speech that characterized Schubert's art as both inherently Austrian and hospitably universal, and as familiar as it was unifying. At the *Wiener Sonn- und Montags-Zeitung*, Johann Georg von Wörz treated the composer as an idealized symbol of *Heimat* whose music transcended political boundaries:

> From high to low, from the art world to the layman, united without differentiating musical or even political parties, the sublime, celebratory festival has displayed our Franz Schubert in the entire fullness of his originality, charm, and warmth of heart—a delightful panorama of the vast, prolific domain of his creative work. The festival is over, but his compositions will remain the pride of the Viennese, the delight of civilized

mankind, the everlasting glory of its creator. Thank goodness the artistic ideal has once again proved its heavenly power to unite, to ennoble, to bless all people, and those intent on making the world better have not yet succeeded in robbing people of this ideal and making it an object of contempt. Thanks to all who nourish and tend the pure fire of the altar of art, because they are the benefactors of mankind.[52]

If Schubert was the incarnation of Austria, liberal sensibilities were fond of suggesting that the universal appeal of his music reached beyond parochial limitations, an observation that an enlightened Habsburg could also make. Thus the *Neues Wiener Journal* reported:

The first citizen of the empire, the towering figure of the monarch, rendered posthumous honor to one of the greatest sons of Vienna. In that act was a solemn, uplifting moment. The highest authority in the empire paid homage to genius. Where sensibility and understanding still exist in spiritual aspirations, in the dignity of art, it will be understood with deeper, more heartfelt satisfaction, as an emperor knows how to honor art in one of its most noble apostles. And Franz Schubert was an apostle of art.

If in general art is indeed international, then certainly in most cases it is music, which sends out its waves of sound into the world, over all mountains and across all highways, and yet one might say and one should and must say, that Schubert's art is truly, purely Austrian.

In his works exist the good Austrian spirit; he borrows its singularity and its true worth. This spirit also was manifest in the short but rich speech of our emperor. The idea was strengthened and invigorated by the greatest power in the empire who offered his homage so unreservedly to these ideal artworks. Such imperial words exerted their power. Not only was Schubert honored, but with him also Austrian art, and this it truly accomplished, which it deserved.[53]

Conspicuous by its absence is any mention of the word *deutsch*, a remarkable omission in discussing a composer known principally for his songs. That lacuna was common to liberal newspapers, which also shared a contempt for the burgeoning radicalism of exclusionary Germanness exemplified by the political right, hence the disinclination to characterize the composer's art as *deutsch*. One of the most explicitly liberal editorial views came from the *Wiener Tagblatt* run by Moritz Szeps, which embraced the spirit of the emperor's speech while asking rhetorically why music should have enjoyed such an extraordinary development in Austria. Yes, there was a natural disposition and special sympathy for music among the people, but this was not sufficient explanation. Schubert's era had been one of political oppression that had circumscribed literary and artistic creativity: "The time of our grandfathers rises before us in which free feelings were barely endurable without fearful restrictions and tortuous surveillance, except in the domain of music." Schubert's art, however, was impervious to censure: "The sound waves of thought, which the composer put into his melodies and symphonies, could never be impeded by any worldly or spiritual policemen."[54]

In juxtaposing the emperor and his inspirational speech with the world of the readers' grandfathers, the newspaper suggested that the political oppression of the latter was a thing of a past era, that is, prior to Franz Joseph's accession to the monarchy in 1848. The use of the Schubert-Ausstellung to convey such a view of the present was not mere patriotic puffery. Coming from a self-styled "democratic organ" that tirelessly engaged in attacking anti-Semitism in Viennese politics and culture as well as pan-German nationalism, the report on the opening of the exhibition supplied an opportunity to voice an optimistically liberal position. The civilized world could admire not only Schubert but also the city and nation that had produced him in what was then a politically repressive milieu and that now celebrated him in the enlightened environment of the present. Thus, the *Wiener Tagblatt* reached the conclusion, without once again invoking *deutsch*, that the composer was "a great master, a splendid man, the creator of the most noble song, as our emperor so suitably characterized him with only a word, a wonderful genius, who belongs to the entire civilized world, but who is also ours, an Austrian, a Viennese, a glory and a pride and a joy for Austria and Vienna. Franz Schubert held sway as a free spirit in a free domain."[55]

For newspapers with liberal sympathies, Schubert's music was inherently Austrian and Viennese even as it expressed universal values. This representation appeared in stark contrast to reports on the celebration in publications of the political right. In them, the composer's *deutscher Genius* was an exclusionary metaphor, implicitly leaving certain groups outside the circle of high culture. The Austrian concept of Germanness had not always been so insular or vitriolic. Pieter Judson has argued that mid-century liberalism in Austria sought to develop common social and cultural norms that might be emulated by all its citizens, regardless of class or race, so long as they embraced Germanness as their hierarchical model.[56] However, during the three decades preceding 1897, a constellation of diplomatic, demographic, and economic pressures had begun to encroach on German Austrian identity, supplying the opportunity for political advantage to those parties that were adept at converting cultural anxiety into ethnic hostility.

Such rhetorical manipulation took many forms in contemporary rightist publications and was not limited to political editorials (although even those that were not fond of the Habsburg dynasty were too canny to assault the person of the emperor by disputing his words). In the poem "Zu Franz Schubert's hundertstem Geburtstag," Guido List effortlessly merged Christian and Germanic symbols. The appearance of the Christ child serves as an antecedent to the birth of Schubert, but the composer's arrival occurs through the agency of Wotan, king of the gods in Norse mythology:

> In the lowly hut, where only want presides,
> Where sorrow darkens the steward's office,
> Where gray anxiety serves as the only attendant,
> There God's spirit mingled with man's blood.
> And so it happened in Vienna in the Danube valley,

> Exactly one hundred years ago today;
> From Wotan, father of the gods, the bowl of grace,
> Gushed forth, consecrating land and grove,
> Ohter, the messenger of the gods, so ordered,
> To travel through the world changing form,
> To announce God's peace in great song,
> He took the human shell to Vienna.[57]

The verse appeared in the *Ostdeutsche Rundschau*, whose founding had been financed by the radically anti-Semitic Schönerer. Its editor was Karl Hermann Wolf, a shrewd member of Parliament whose long career in the furtherance of pan-German nationalism was honored by the Nazi Party at his funeral in 1941, when the State Opera choir sang Schubert's *Litanei auf das Fest aller Seelen* (D. 343). Likewise, the author of the poem, Guido List, produced a succession of books that were to supply the foundation for many of the later political arguments about an Aryan "master race" (including the polemics of Hitler). His invocation of deities in his paean to Schubert was of a piece with the titles of other contemporary writings of his such as *The Wala's Awakening* (1894) and *The Valkyries' Initiation* (1895).[58]

Similar in effect was Wilhelm Schriefer's poem "Zu Schubert's hundertjährigem Geburtstag" in the *Deutsches Volksblatt*, which might lead its readers to wonder whether Schubert was, in fact, Austrian at all:

> The homage, which we pay you
> At today's centennial celebration in joyful Vienna,
> To which you have given the honor to call you its son,
> And to which your songs are dedicated,
> Vienna, which must truly be envied by Germany,
> Because of you, until the end of time,
> Because all the world resounds with your voice,
> Yet you sang German—a German genius![59]

The *Deutsches Volksblatt* had been founded in 1888 by Vergani, a pan-German nationalist whose 1892 pamphlet, "The Situation of the Jews in Vienna," was a touchstone for racist anti-Semitism. Not surprisingly, then, on the day before Schubert's birthday in the newspaper's front-page essay "A German Prince of Song" (briefly cited earlier), Carl Staubach arrived at a conclusion that confirmed the composer's religious credentials while blithely ignoring his citizenship:

> On November 19, at three in the afternoon, death, whose power, he so movingly depicted in music, gently took him away, after he received the last rites as a good Catholic Christian. . . . Inspired, the German nation looks up to its great son, because it owes to him the undisputed honor of being the richest in song of all the peoples of the earth. And so long as our German word and German mind resound in song, then the memory of Franz Schubert will also live on in the heart of his nation.[60]

In their poems, List and Schriefer at least admitted the existence if not the significance of the empire's capital city. The apotheosis of Albert Weltner's "Drei Freunde"—whose title refers to the composer's friendships with Bauernfeld and Schwind—does not even pay lip service to Schubert's nationality, but rather conveys a sense of his Germanness that is spiritually umbilical:

> But the third, whom we call Schubert,
> In whom the German Lied is incarnated,
> From whom German hearts are only separated,
> When the German mind dissolves into the eternal nothingness.[61]

This verse appeared in the *Deutsche Zeitung*, whose editor, Theodor Wähner, was a member of the city council and a German nationalist and, unlike Schönerer, maintained close ties to the Christian Social Party. For the readers of these lines, the term *deutsch* would have lost its older liberal connotations, as the newspaper advertised itself as the only twice daily anti-Semitic German national newspaper in Vienna.

Even when a subtle writer on music like Theodor Helm (who produced a valuable study on Beethoven's string quartets) contributed to the *Deutsche Zeitung*, Schubert's stature could suffer from the acknowledgment of his local roots. Apart from his Lieder making the German nation the richest of all peoples in song, the composer's origins also revealed his shortcomings: "As a pure Viennese, Schubert betrays here and there in his larger works a certain flippancy and happy-go-lucky nature, he lets himself go, he does not always understand how to economize with his immense musical richness." In describing the composer's inability to "keep house," Helm cast a gendered implication that he made explicit elsewhere in the article. Schubert was Beethoven's "wife," conceived in that word's most idealized sense. Helm judged that this was a familiar expression for many of his readers, with the two composers "complementing each other with surprising frequency."[62]

Given the relationship between the rightist political allegiances of some newspapers and their invocation of Schubert's Germanness, one suspects that similar sentiments might have been shared by some music journals, especially when the composer's Viennese pedigree was ignored. In the *Deutsche Kunst- und Musikzeitung*, the self-styled official organ of Austria-Hungary's singing societies, its editor Otto Keller played up this aspect of the composer in his conclusion to a prologue read for the Arion Singing Society: "Your name will never vanish from the German; your song will resound for all time, in every place, and your art will find esteem as long as the German speaks the German word."[63] A similar prologue appeared in the same publication, this time written by Oscar Merz for the Wiener Sängerbund. Merz characterized his listeners as a little band of the faithful for whom the composer, now transformed into an unlikely Siegfried slaying the dragon, was their great leader ("Führer").[64]

The exclusion of the composer's native land was an effective tactic for a local publication, but an opinion actually emanating from Germany could nudge the rhetoric one step further by characterizing Schubert's treatment by the country of his birth as indifferent and inept. The *Neue Musik-Zeitung* (published in Stuttgart and Leipzig by Carl Grüninger) offered a view of the composer that omitted his Austrian lineage but counted him among the great German poets, scientists, and composers. It was precisely Schubert's songs that brought him close to the hearts of the German people, but the paper did not hedge about portraying the composer as a prophet without honor in his own land: "Schubert, who could get no position in Austria despite his wonderful compositions, was thereby compelled to get by for a while as a piano teacher."[65] The article concluded by opining that the money spent on the Schubert monument in the Stadtpark would have been of greater use to the composer during his lifetime.

If this was petty criticism, a more sinister allusion is discernible in the report on the exhibition that appeared in the *Reichspost*, the Vienna newspaper with the most reliably Christian Social viewpoint:

One circumstance allowed today's opening of the exhibition to be of particular delight. Missing entirely from there was a certain presumptuous "intelligentsia" with its affectation and wheedling, with its weak-kneed little men and overdressed little women. And it also took place without them, just as in the future many others will take place without them.[66]

It might be difficult to determine who were the objects of such ridicule were it not for the political sympathies of a newspaper that advertised itself as the "independent daily newspaper for the Christian people of Austria-Hungary." Compacted into its second sentence are several of the most cold-blooded images of anti-Semitism. Rightist publications like the *Reichspost* permanently linked Jews with what they viewed as the cultural pretensions and liberal politics of competing newspapers such as Szeps's *Wiener Tagblatt*. Further, their readers could be counted on to equate "presumptuous intellectuals" with those adhering to modernist tendencies in arts and letters. Although it is true that a number of liberal writers and publishers were in fact Jewish, as in the case of Szeps, anti-Semitic journalists painted with as broad and crude a brush as possible. One needs to look no further than the weeks around the city's Schubert commemoration to discover such representations. The closing of the Café Griensteidl on the same day as the emperor's speech provided an irresistible opportunity for the *Wiener neueste Nachrichten* to report: "On the last night one saw hardly a single Christian there, and in one corner a pair of Jewish rascals traded slaps in the face with each other—presumably because they could not agree thereon which of them might be the insolent one."[67] One month later, the *Deutsches Volksblatt* made certain that the most celebrated writers did not escape an anti-Semitic tarring. Thus, Arthur Schnitzler was a "Literatur-Jude" and Hermann Bahr was a "Halbjude."[68]

In addition to associating Jews with the literary modernism of Jung-Wien, the *Reichspost* report also exploited brutal stereotypes of speech and physiognomy that had been an increasing part of the public discourse of anti-Semitism throughout the nineteenth century. The Jewish voice whined and—as in the example from the *Wiener neueste Nachrichten*—babbled argumentatively. Likewise, the body of the Jew was misshapen in some characteristically observable way that was endemic to the race: if not small and weak-kneed, then bowlegged or club-footed. Immigrant Jews from eastern Europe were especially vulnerable to these sorts of caustic descriptions, even among Viennese liberals whose motivations might not be counted as racist. Like the anonymous reporter who noted the absence of any Christian face at the closing of the Café Griensteidl, the historian Gomperz, himself Jewish, wrote to his wife in 1884 about the denizens of the coffeehouses along the Prater: "I don't exaggerate when I say that not a single non-Jew could be seen, that is, nothing but bent, deformed Yiddish-speaking figures of each [one and the other] kind."[69] Such stereotypes belied the complex sources and motivations of fin-de-siècle anti-Semitism and could spring equally from anecdotal observation or artistic imagination. (The most extreme contemporary literary example of such poisonous rhetoric is Oskar Panizza's *The Operated Jew* of 1893, which portrays a protagonist whose "soft bawling" is nearly unintelligible and who submits to having his bones broken and then reset in order to correct his posture.)[70] The grotesque allure of such images flew in the face of the fact that a healthy athleticism was as much a preoccupation of Austria's Jews as of any other segment of the population. (At the first modern Olympics in 1896, a Jewish Austrian took a gold medal in swimming. In the following year, the nation's first Jewish sports organization was created in the wake of the exclusionary membership rules handed down by the Austrian branch of the German Gymnastic Association.)[71] For anti-Semites, such realities doubtless made their racist rhetoric all the more vicious and necessary.

In the culture of fin-de-siècle Vienna, political parties of the right closely associated nationalism and anti-Semitism, and they eagerly appealed to both sentiments. Indeed, the Christian Social Party had come to power in 1896 in part by taking advantage of hostility toward Jews and Slavs, and, with another election on the horizon in 1897, every event acquired a political meaning. Newspapers that espoused an exclusionary concept of Germanness were often anti-Semitic, and the most extreme among them never tired of injecting racial ridicule if the opportunity presented itself, however improbable or ludicrous the context. Those articles that constructed Schubert as a pure German not coincidentally appeared in publications that elsewhere attacked Jewish-liberal cabals. There was no obvious way to work anti-Semitism into prose intended to celebrate the composer's centennial. Rather, the connection was made via an implicit analogy: as the essence of Schubert's music was German, it had to exclude that which was foreign to its true German nature. The most graphic use of this logic appeared in the *Deutsches Volksblatt* on January 31, Schubert's birthday. The first two pages carried a proclamation by the ruling Christian Social Party, "An das christliche Volk in Oesterreich!" signed by its leader, Lueger. The meaning was blunt: the group warned against the political influence of capitalism and *Judenliberalismus* whose "natural daughters" were the apparently Jewish Social Democrats. The Christian Social Party proudly called itself anti-Semitic, and argued that it alone could protect the innate German values of the populace by its defense against these outsiders. Its conclusion was equally direct: "By this means as well, the gleaming ethical-moral life will again be elevated to that level, which the social and economic welfare of the people requires, and which makes possible the restoration of the public life animated by the true Christian-German spirit of our Austrian fatherland."[72]

The appeals to inborn Germanness, Christianity, and anti-Semitism had been a potent mixture in 1896 when the Christian Socials won control of the provincial Niederösterreichischer Landtag. It was to prove equally successful in the wake of the elections of 1897, whose results finally compelled the emperor to accede to Lueger's appointment as mayor after refusing to do so on four earlier occasions. The connection between this political screed and a centennial homage to Schubert might appear distant were it not for the article on the composer, "Ein Gedenktag," that followed immediately after this proclamation. The two articles begin with remarkably similar language (italics added):

["Ein Gedenktag"] He had been born into poor confined circumstances. *His entire life was a hard, unbroken struggle with fate's envy* and he never was what one tends to call "blessed with earthly wealth"[73]

["An das christliche Volk in Oesterreich!"] In a few weeks the election begins for the new House of Representatives. *The fate of Austria's hereditary people will depend upon the outcome of this historic struggle.*

The description of Schubert's fateful battle against an uncaring society was calculated to mirror the present fight of the Austrian people. The honor bestowed on the composer in 1897 was due solely to the new political regime that understood his true nature. In a remarkable analogy, Schubert was a son of both the people and the party:

We joyously welcomed [the fact] that it was granted to the new council of the city of Vienna to bring about this Schubert celebration. The party that now governs in city hall has often been reproached for possessing no sense or understanding of ideals, of the greatest good of mankind. It is of course hardly necessary to confront seriously such charges, whose slimy sources are envy and hate. Yet it was good that, in this "art- and image-hostile" era, the city of Vienna would already have offered our party the occasion to show that in its battle, it has not forgotten that duty which imposes peace upon the victor. And how could the present government not fulfill this duty in relation to

Schubert. Schubert was a son of the people as well as the party that leads Vienna's government, represents the city to the outside world, and arises from the people. His songs were the language of the people, and, to those who understand this language, they sound twice as beloved and familiar.[74]

Like Schubert before it and by extension the Viennese citizenry it currently governed, the ruling party was engaged in a struggle against enemies who were left unnamed save for their filthy origins. If the latter suggests the cant of anti-Semitism, then the invocation of an "art- and image-hostile era" equally conveys an assault on modernism. The regime could characterize itself as a morally superior force operating beneficently in a contemporary epoch whose culture—in the hands of ethnic outsiders—was inimical to true art.

While liberal voices in the fin-de-siècle Viennese press sought to present Schubert as a universal genius whose art transcended fractious regionalism— their view buttressed by a contemporary understanding that was empathetic in contrast to the neglect visited upon the composer when he was alive—their rightist opponents argued that the true comprehension of Schubert's uniquely German nature was spoiled by those very same modern liberal impulses, which were in turn far more sinister than any slight that had been suffered by the composer. As recurrent as this theme was among daily newspapers (and their political clients) with nakedly antiliberal and anti-Semitic positions, the same sentiments were not completely alien to more narrowly themed cultural publications. For Anton August Naaff, the editor of the conservative literary and music journal *Die Lyra* as well as a contributor to Vergani's *Deutsches Volksblatt*, the forces that sought to prevent the recognition of Schubert's stature as a purely German artist were the same ones arrayed against public appreciation of his most important Austrian successor, Anton Bruckner. Evaluating Schubert's centennial celebration in 1897, a year after Bruckner's death, Naaff attacked contemporary writers on both composers by employing a language with which antiliberal readers could identify. Naaff described Bruckner's critics as an "iron ring"—an expression that had characterized the rule of Eduard Taaffe, the empire's prime minister from 1879 to 1893, who had forged a successful political coalition in part through concessions to the Czech majority in Bohemia at the expense of the region's ethnic Germans—that consisted of representatives of "the capitalist liberal press and party." (Naaff himself was an ethnic German from Bohemia.) He excoriated their ideas as "half-baked, boorishly wrong-headed, and grossly ridiculous." For Naaff, these same critics stood as a barrier to honoring the German essence of Schubert:

> Has our time therefore been better and fairer toward its most characteristic Schubert successor? Truly was Bruckner's path made so hard and difficult, so unsympathetic, so heartless; indeed, a great part of our present authoritative musical community behaves quite maliciously, snobbishly obdurate, and most one-sidedly unjust against almost all younger artists who, springing from the people, truly aspire unflinchingly to the high

goal of an ideal German peoples' art, and who have no wish to bow before the hollowly glittering idols of international sham affectation, social advantage, and their critical temple criers! Today living and striving are truly made more cunningly difficult for such genuine German native artists than it once was in the old Vienna of Schubert, in which it was perhaps fundamentally somewhat more careless, but certainly not so malevolent nor so pigheadedly partisan as now! In view of the centennial festival of our greatest Viennese master of song, it is above all the first and most holy duty of our art-loving German people to draw from such examples and comparisons the right lessons for contemplation and change, and to create strong feelings and designs for necessary revision and improvement so that the truly German, noble, native art and artistry may not become and remain the squashed, tormented, starving stepchild as up to now always obliged to a certain household clique.[75]

One might surmise that, for Naaff, the account of a liberal critical establishment that treated Bruckner so shabbily was also a thinly veiled description of Jewish interests, and that cosmopolitan liberalism, so often condemned by rightist publications as Jewish, was a corrupt obstacle to the just consideration of Schubert's true German character. To be sure, an expression like "Tempelrufer" might have more than one implication, but a Viennese reader, particularly someone who was sympathetic to the cant of the anti-Semitic press, would surely have been well disposed to the implication that the objects of Naaff's scorn embraced Jewish as well as liberal agents, especially when juxtaposed against the ideal of a pure German art. (In its approval of the contemporary decision by the anti-Semitic majority in the Landtag to remove Jews from the ranks of government stenographers, both the *Deutsches Volksblatt* and the *Reichspost* used the term "Tempel-Reinigung," a reference to Jesus's expulsion of the moneylenders from the temple.)[76]

The linking of anti-Semitism and exclusionary German nationalism, and the casting of modernism as the cultural vessel of the liberal and the Jew, remained popular and potent tactics of both rightist publications and political factions. The newspapers that vigorously supported the Christian Social Party in particular described Schubert in very different terms from those used by both their liberal competitors and the habitués of the Café Griensteidl. Those same papers that represented Schubert as a pure German were quick to describe both the writers of Jung-Wien and the liberal press in anti-Semitic terms. One particularly noteworthy intersection of the composer's legacy with contemporary politics that juxtaposes Schubert and anti-Semitism comes obliquely from the music critic of the liberal *Neues Wiener Tagblatt*, Max Kalbeck, known today primarily as the early biographer of Brahms. Both shared a love of Schubert and loaned manuscripts to the composer's centennial exhibition. Kalbeck visited the Schubert-Ausstellung at Brahms's urging, perhaps to report back to the composer who may have been too ill to venture outside during the bitterly cold winter. Recent research using Kalbeck's diary reveals a writer interested in more than music and art.[77] He closely followed events in Vienna's civic life, expressing sympathy for liberal causes and open hostility to rightist politics. In this light, Kalbeck's article is revealing:

It certainly acquires this rosy view, as though our lives henceforth should have remained an unending Schubert festival: "the flowering does not want to end." So a step back sometimes signifies a step forward. Likewise the decision of the Vienna authorities to treat the Schubert festival as a community affair has been perceived with joy everywhere as a delightful return to a milder key. The music savants of Vienna's most worthy city council surely had to know, when they accompanied it with a "Judenknecht," that Schubert in fact composed a Psalm 92 for the synagogue choir of the Israelitische Kultusgemeinde of the original Hebrew community. They judiciously took from that no offense and did not themselves protest against *Mirjams Siegesgesang*, which was paraded on the program of the Schubertbund, although again contrary to expectation this time it was not the Jews but the Egyptians who, driven into the water, should have drowned in the Red Sea.[78]

For Kalbeck, the *gemütlich* character of the festival was incongruously at odds with the anti-Semitic rhetoric of Vienna's civic leaders. He emphasized that, in celebrating Schubert, they had conveniently forgotten that the composer had written a work for the synagogue and could thus be considered a "slave to the Jews."

The term "Judenknecht" was deliberately chosen. According to several newspapers, including Kalbeck's own, it had been shouted at a session of the Landtag on January 20, the same day that the Schubert-Ausstellung opened and during a particularly acrimonious debate over whether too many government stenographers were Jewish. Christian Social Party members supported restrictions, and a liberal representative who accused them of anti-Semitism was loudly derided as a "Judenknecht." Newspapers identified the shout only as coming "auf Rechts," that is, from the political right of the assembly. Kalbeck's paper, however, named the source as none other than the city's mayor, Josef Strobach, and his identity was confirmed by a satiric poem appearing in *Der Floh*, a weekly journal devoted to political humor, under the title "Aus dem Schandtag" ("On the Day of Shame"):

> Herr Strobach perpetually in a fluster,
> In the Landtag the other day did bluster,
> The charming words: "slave to the Jew,"
> Which I might verify it's true,
> He was the author of this rant ·
> So wonderful and elegant
> And of such lofty eloquence
> Who is head of Austria's residence![79]

Kalbeck's readers would certainly have known that Strobach was the official who had represented the city government at the opening of the Schubert-Ausstellung earlier that same day. The first Christian Social mayor of Vienna, "fat Strobach" was regarded by his political opponents as a figurehead for Lueger, his successor and the party's leader. His public comments on Jews were alternately praised and criticized by newspapers and colleagues depending on their political allegiances. His position in the Landtag debate elicited praise from Ernst Schneider, one of the assembly's most virulently anti-Semitic members:

We encourage the removal of equal rights for Jews, the confiscation of Jewish goods, and the expulsion of Jews. Thank God that for once we finally have a different mayor. We are proud of that (applause from the right) and this example of the city of Vienna will become a shining example for all of Austria's crown lands and for all countries of the world. There will come a time, where Jews will say: "Do I have to leave the city?" They should go wherever they wish, at best, into the water to drown. (Cheering from the right.)[80]

For Schneider, the ruling government's treatment of Jews was a model to be emulated by other regimes. Only a few hours had separated this tirade from Strobach's speech at the Schubert-Ausstellung in which that same government promoted itself as a model for honoring the composer by using language that aped the words of the emperor: "Franz Schubert's native city, on the occasion of the hundredth anniversary of the birth of this great composer, has brought about the design of the present exhibition along with other festivities in order to convey to the eyes of today's living generation the memory of the time in which the famous Austrian and great son of the city of Vienna, Franz Schubert, produced and created his immortal works."[81] Given that the Landtag debate occurred within hours of the exhibition's opening, one cannot help thinking that a deliberate connection was intended. With Vienna controlled by the political right, the ruling party could take equal pride in its celebration of the composer and in its treatment of Jews. This latter feature is recalled in Kalbeck's reference to Schubert's *Mirjams Siegesgesang* (D. 942, op. 136) where he notes with withering contempt that this time it was the Egyptians and not the Jews who were drowned in the sea.

In 1919, looking back on the era before the war, that relentless literary inquisitor Robert Musil described the ideology that had been known in Austria as German-national as "nothing but a deadly, rampant tumor."[82] In hindsight the devastation wrought by the war may have sharpened Musil's recognition of the more malignant qualities of rightist values, although this chapter has argued that more than two decades earlier there was no shortage of voices raised in opposition to them. Nonetheless, the political victories of the Christian Social Party at the turn of the century show that the organization and its literary proxies were remarkably adept at winning over public sentiment through the manipulation of civic ceremonies and cultural events. However pernicious their principles may appear in retrospect, there is no gainsaying the fact that their methods were successful. The Schubert centennial celebrations are certainly evidence of this, but the example of the composer is far from being an isolated instance of shrewd political maneuvering by the ruling party. Indeed, the highly effective treatment of the ceremonies of 1897 by Vienna's rightist forces provided the immediate model for Christian Social conduct with regard to a more significant commemoration in the following year: the fiftieth anniversary of Franz Joseph's accession to the throne. One historian's analysis of Lueger's masterful commandeering of the jubilee's events correctly places the mayor's stratagem in a continuum of rightist machinations in connection with imperial celebrations. The conclusions—that "the symbol of the emperor . . . was contested and redefined by political factions endeavoring to present their own interpretations of the Habsburg past, present, and future to potential voters," and that "the Christian Social Party used the commemorations . . . to attack their rivals and to wrap their own party in the black-yellow flag of Austrian patriotism"—are ones that would serve equally well were Schubert's name to be substituted for that of Franz Joseph.[83] In fin-de-siècle Vienna, the cultural significance of the composer was such that the political manipulation of his centennial furnished a remarkably useful testing ground for the tactics that were to be employed on the figure of the emperor one year later.

The advocates of the ascendant right used language that was often crude but highly effective to denounce their opponents, calculating that local chauvinism could be exploited by appealing to both anti-modernist mistrust and anti-Semitic fear. A treasured cultural icon like Schubert was relegated to supplying just so much more corrosive grist for this rhetorical mill. Against this project was pitted a more liberal vision in which the composer's music manifested both Viennese particularity and artistic universality. The voices of reconciliation, however, proved to be unavailing. In such an environment, any occurrence, however innocent, could take on a more telling significance. A week after the Schubert festival ended, the Ball of the City of Vienna—the social event of the Fasching season—took place. Its symbolic honoree was Schubert: every woman in attendance received a *Damenspende*, an album of fifteen zincplate engravings, each one representing a Schubert song rendered by a different contemporary artist. The ball, however, acquired political significance when the emperor inquired after Lueger's health. Rightist newspapers interpreted the exchange as a signal that Franz Joseph was finally prepared to accept Lueger's legitimate right to assume the mayoralty. In contrast, liberal papers accused the ruling Christian Social Party of a conspiracy to exclude prominent Jews from the ball.[84]

Outside of the imperial family, no individual, however distinguished his career, was immune to attacks from the rightist press. Even Nikolaus Dumba, whose service to Vienna's public institutions was as esteemed as his championship of Schubert, was not immune to criticism. Scarcely a week after the conclusion of the commemorative events, during which Dumba had played such an indispensable role that the city council eulogized him "with warmest appreciation and full recognition for his patriotic contribution," the *Deutsches Volksblatt* carped over his donation of two hundred florins to help Jewish orphans, the precise amount that the rightist coalition had just voted down by only one vote: "Now the result is that currently it easily rains money out of the pockets of the liberals for Jewish 'humanitarian organization purposes.' Much good may it do the Jews!"[85]

The flagrant stratagems by the political right and its journalistic proxies to appropriate Schubert for their own ends were so obvious in 1897 that the situation often provided fodder for typically Viennese satire. As illustrations of the maneuvering by anti-Semitic interests, the journal *Wiener Caricaturen* wickedly offered "a few Schubert songs with modernized texts, dedicated to the majority in the city council." "Ständchen" (from *Schwanengesang*, D. 957, no. 4) actually begins with its original first line, "Softly beseech my songs," only to turn quickly to this advice: "Never again buy from Jews, and do read the *Volksblatt*." "Wohin?" (no. 2 of *Die schöne Müllerin*, D. 795, op. 25) goes even further, making fun of both the rhetoric of the Christian Social Party's leader and the witlessness of the party's gullible constituencies:

> I heard Lueger blabber
> At a local inn,
> And listened with pleasure.
> It was a major din.
> I don't know what he meant,
> Only once did I understand:
> He bitched about the Jews,
> Then I gave him a hand.[86]

The often rancorous struggle between the political right and left was exemplified by a cartoon in *Der Floh* (see figure 2.2), in which, despite the musical ministrations of hovering cherubs, a dyspeptic Schubert looks down upon factions clubbing each other with ballot boxes. The composer muses sarcastically: "It's wonderful how the dear Viennese rejoice that I was born a hundred years ago!"[87] Likewise, the same journal ridiculed the Christian Social Party's manipulation of Schubert for its own political advantage by having the composer paraphrase the words of his own "Ständchen":

> Through the night my songs
> Softly beseech of thee:
> What does fat Strobach want,
> I ask you, to have of me?
> Hear, how the people fight,
> Oh, they sicken me!
> How they brawl, how they swear—
> Oh, so repulsively.
> That now they wish to honor me,
> Such hypocritical infamy,
> Because I was silent for so long
> In the kingdom of blessed harmony.[88]

Figure 2.2. "Eine Schubert-Phantasie," *Der Floh* 29, no. 6 (1897): 5. ÖNB/Wien.

This satire illustrates the utter disjunction between appearance and actuality, *Schein* and *Sein*, a symptom of fin-de-siècle culture that has often been observed, not least by Vienna's own inhabitants. In the case of Schubert, the most fanciful and even vicious rhetoric emanated from the same sources that competed to embrace the most benign image of the composer for equal political gain. As we shall see, these irreconcilable juxtapositions proved to be irresistible targets for the contemporary critiques devised by literary modernism.

Chapter Three

Gustav Klimt's Schubert

With its 1,248 items, the Schubert-Ausstellung of 1897 was to that date the most visible public sign of the unique stature that Schubert had attained in fin-de-siècle Austrian culture. In giving his career the full art historical treatment, the exhibition served as the culmination of a process of cultural recognition that had come later to Schubert than to any other nineteenth-century composer, even as it cemented some of the most enduring myths about him. Contemporary photographs of the installations in the Künstlerhaus confirm that Schubert's career was intended to receive the sort of valedictory treatment that characterized Vienna's permanent repository of official art, the Kunsthistorisches Museum, which had opened six years earlier. (See figure 3.1.)

Even as Schubert's reputation was abetted by a hagiography that was prey to cheerily saccharine fictions of a melodically gifted but structurally challenged *Hausmusiker*, he still remained the most illustrious composer who was born, lived, and died in the capital city. As such, a public demonstration of his stature could represent an essentially Viennese character even as his music offered a universal appeal. As chapter 2 has shown, the cultural significance of the Schubert centennial exhibition was matched by imperial gravitas when, at the official opening on January 20 at 11 AM, Franz Joseph gave a brief speech: "I therefore may simply greet with complete approval this enterprise, which here has collected evidence in loving memory to the great master, and herewith declare the Schubert exhibition open."[1] With this greeting, a civic function was layered onto the exhibition's aesthetic purpose. The emperor's proclamation was then echoed by Josef Strobach, the newly installed Christian Social mayor and party figurehead for Karl Lueger, who made the official opening in the presence of the Habsburg ruler also a symbolic watershed for the recently elected party of the political right. The dignitaries then spent an hour touring the exhibition, shepherded through its rooms by Karl Glossy, the director of the Historisches Museum der Stadt Wien.

"There certainly are a lot of things! Where did they all come from?"[2] Franz Joseph's remark to his guide suggests a monarch whose artistic taste was more

Figure 3.1. "Von der Franz Schubert-Ausstellung in Wien," *Über Land und Meer* (Stuttgart) 39 (1897): 397. Lithograph after a photograph by Rudolf Lechner, Vienna.

easily swayed by quantity than by quality. Yet this magnitude had been built into the design of the exhibition. There was no stinting of either human effort or financial support. The planning committee headed by Glossy had published a solicitation for loans during the spring of 1896 in thirty European newspapers, and the city subsequently spent an estimated 15,000 florins.[3] In the end, the emperor's response mirrored the exhibition's success with both the public and the critics. The original closing date of February 28 had to be changed to March 2 to accommodate the popular demand. By February 8, more than 10,000 people had visited the Künstlerhaus, and the relative novelty of electric lighting allowed it to remain open on Sundays until six in the evening. Members of Vienna's artistic and musical communities also admired the exhibition. Ludwig Hevesi, who was to become the unofficial spokesman for the Secession, reported on its virtues for the *Fremden-Blatt*, and his musical counterpart at the *Neues Wiener Tagblatt*, Max Kalbeck, was urged to see it by Brahms, who had loaned half a dozen manuscripts to the exhibition. (Kalbeck also contributed two scores.)[4]

To be sure, not every observer was delighted with the emphasis that official Vienna had placed on the art historical features of Schubert's career. Hirschfeld complained about the greater importance given to the exhibition than to performances, noting the absence from the planning committee of any qualified music professional such as Mandyczewski (or, one suspects, Hirschfeld himself, given that he supplied the recitatives for the performance of Schubert's Singspiel *Der vierjährige Posten* at the Hofoper on January 30).[5] Although Mandyczewski was possibly the most recognizable music authority on Schubert in 1897, due to his stature as the chief editor of the complete edition of the composer's works (in fact, he was in Leipzig to receive an honorary degree for this effort when the main events of the Vienna centennial were taking place), his only public contribution to the commemoration came in the form of a lecture. Given on February 7, it was one of a series connected with twelve free "people's concerts" sponsored by the Wiener Volksbildungsverein (Popular Education Association) in the city's outlying districts, in this case the ninth, and apparently designed as an inexpensive alternative to the official festivities; reports appeared in newspapers like the *Arbeiter-Zeitung*, which had a large working-class readership. (Hirschfeld had earlier given a lecture in the third district, on January 31.)[6] One might possibly glean the lecture's contents from Mandyczewski's two-page biographical sketch of Schubert, which he wrote for Breitkopf & Härtel, the publishers of the complete edition. Perhaps as a backhanded criticism of the exhibition, and certainly in his professional capacity as the edition's guiding hand, Mandyczewski argued that Schubert's music represented the most meaningful account of his life.

One did not have to be a musical elder statesman, however, to offer the perspective that a commemoration with an art historical exhibition as its official centerpiece displayed a misplacement of civic effort. Heinrich Schenker, whose method of music analysis was to have an indelible influence on twentieth-century theory, was at the time known as a music critic. His reviews of performances had appeared in newspapers in Vienna and elsewhere for half a dozen years, and his name had just appeared in a list of teachers in the 1898 supplement to *Fromme's musikalische Welt*, when, in a postmortem commentary on the Schubert festival of the previous year, he took issue with the hyperbolic commemoration that had taken place in Vienna:

> Hardly one hundred years have passed over the name Franz Schubert and already a thousand misunderstandings and prejudices, for as well as against him, are attached to the image of his character and life. What has happened to him has also been the case with older masters; it is wrong for biographers and contemporaries, as a necessary means of comparison or as simple common sense, to collect every last tidbit. The master certainly transcended his fellow creatures and biographers with his genius, and this inexplicability gave to those who do not understand a pretext for every interpretation of his life and work, about which there should be no talk.[7]

The display of "every last tidbit" could only refer to the Künstlerhaus exhibition of Schubertiana. Within Schenker's polemic against the composer's hagiographers, there may also lurk an element of social criticism. On January 31, 1897, in a centennial commemoration of Schubert's birthday, Schenker gave a public talk at no. 3 Gemeindeplatz that was advertised in the *Oesterreichische Volks-Zeitung*, a newspaper known for its sympathy with the working classes.[8] It, too, was one of the free lectures delivered under the auspices of the Volksbildungsverein and took place in the largely working-class third district, suggesting that Schenker's audience was drawn from people other than the wealthier Viennese who could afford to attend the sumptuous concerts sponsored by the city's elite music organizations. One might reasonably assume that the lecture's contents were similar to elements in Schenker's essay published that same year. Like Mandyczewski, Schenker found little in Schubert's biography that could illuminate the composer's genius.

Such caviling, however, remained an otherwise minor blemish upon the widespread critical and popular success of the Künstlerhaus exhibition. Although most of its items came from private collections, the city also commissioned several artworks for the occasion. One such canvas came from the venerable and well-known history painter Karl Joseph Geiger, who had been an important contributor to the decoration of the buildings along the Ringstrasse. Along with Gustav Klimt and Franz von Matsch, he was responsible for the ceiling paintings for the Burgtheater. Aside from his local eminence, Geiger was an obvious choice to contribute to the exhibition, given that he had experience with the visual rendering of composers and their works. His output includes watercolors inspired by Haydn's *The Seasons*, Weber's *Der Freischütz*, Mozart's *Don Giovanni*, and Schubert's *Die Verschworenen*; a sepia drawing entitled *Beethoven Surrounded by His Creations*; and a series of etchings, *To the Glory of Austria*, portraying the nation's great poets, artists, and composers, including Schubert.[9] Thirty of Geiger's drawings appeared in *Oesterreichische Volksweisen in einer Auswahl von Liedern: Alpen-Melodien und Tänzen* (1882), a collection originally assembled by Anton von Spaun, a friend of Schubert as was his older brother Josef. According to one newspaper report, Geiger furnished a series of watercolors on songs of Schubert.

The artist's grandest effort, however, was a symbolic homage to the composer, *Die Huldigung Austrias und Vindobonas vor Franz Schubert's Namen* (*The Homage of Austria and Vindobona before Franz Schubert's Name*).[10] (See figure 3.2.) Framed by a bucolic scene of trees and flowers that recalls so many descriptions of the arcadian setting of Kundmann's monument in the Stadtpark, a Botticellian trio of women give honor to the composer. As Geiger's title indicates, two of the figures represent Austria and Vindobona, the name of the Roman camp built on the site of Vienna, who offer up a victor's laurel wreath and a garland of roses. The personification of music, lute in hand, sits beneath a plaque bearing the composer's name and dates, which, with a reticence typical of the fin-de-siècle view of Schubert's personality, is placed so discreetly in the corner so as to seem almost beside the point. (Elements of the painting may owe their inspiration to another of Kundmann's monuments to the composer: the one in the Central Cemetery completed around 1890. The relief depicts the muse, now with her lyre, holding a laurel wreath above a bust of the composer placed, as in Geiger's

Figure 3.2. Karl Joseph Geiger, *Die Huldigung Austrias und Vindobonas vor Franz Schubert's Namen (The Homage of Austria and Vindobona before Franz Schubert's Name)*, 1897. © Wien Museum, Vienna.

painting, in the upper left. The bust is presumably the one Kundmann himself executed around 1870 as he was working on Schubert's monument in the Stadtpark. It can be seen in figure 3.1 in the lower left corner.)

The most arresting commission, however, was installed as the central image greeting visitors to the exhibition: Julius Schmid's *Ein Schubertabend in einem Wiener Bürgerhause* (*A Schubert Evening in a Middle-Class Viennese House*). (See figure 3.3.) The painting was a huge success with everyone from the emperor to the press, and it was often duplicated at the turn of the century. Coming upon a reproduction in a bookseller's window in 1898, the Prague music historian Richard Batka declined to pass judgment on its aesthetic quality and instead evaluated it in terms of its economic and social value. He noted the accompanying advertisement announcing copies for sale at twenty marks (or an additional four marks if one wanted China paper), which he considered a reasonable price for such a fine, large object. On those grounds, it was a worthwhile decoration for one's room. Batka opined that, if only somebody would put it into an album with copies of works by Kupelwieser, Schwind, and others who had portrayed Schubert, one would then have a really worthwhile book for the table of any German family ("ein wertvolles Buch für den deutschen Familien=tisch").[11]

If Batka was loath to appraise the artistic qualities of Schmid's painting, its style prompted Robert Hirschfeld to consider it as more faithful to the spirit of the composer's era than the more factually accurate and better known group portrait by Schwind, Schubert's contemporary:

> As with the entire exhibition, so also has Schmid's group portrait, number one in the catalog, proved to be a success. The shading guides our senses into Schubert's artistic epoch; the figures . . . are grouped informally around Schubert himself and with a light, sure hand. The synthetic combination, the premeditation of the painter of history is not at all perceptible. We get the impression of truth, fidelity, and naturalness, without historical reality forcing and thrusting itself forward at the cost of the *gemütlich* atmosphere. Schwind's famous group portrait *Ein Schubert-Abend bei Spaun* is from Schubert's time and yet by all preferences more awkward than the modern picture that constructed a Schubert evening from documents and portraits. Schmid's painting has already become a beloved image of the Viennese.[12]

The traits of Schmid's conception that Hirschfeld valued were very much in keeping with the characteristics of Kundmann's monument that were well received by the local population. The painter did not pretend to replicate the exactitude of the past, but rather he offered a semblance of actuality that evinced a natural aura more in tune with Schubert's spirit. To portray the scene with a realism based upon the historical record would have ruined the composer's image, just as would have been the case if Kundmann had reproduced those unattractive but supposedly accurate features detailed by Kreissle. The artifice of myth held greater meaning than documentary authenticity. (Hirschfeld himself was massaging the facts when he indicated that Schwind's group portrait came from Schubert's time, since, although the two were close

Figure 3.3. Julius Schmid, *Ein Schubertabend in einem Wiener Bürgerhause* (*A Schubert Evening in a Middle-Class Viennese House*), 1897. Reproduced from an engraving in Richard Heuberger, *Franz Schubert* (Berlin: "Harmonie," Verlagsgesellschaft für Literatur und Kunst, 1902).

friends, the artist had created his work from memory in 1868.) Even Hevesi, whose association with the Secession artists might have made him ill-disposed toward Schmid's style, pronounced the work "a meritorious picture."[13] Critics viewed the painting as a tour-de-force in the application of light and shadow, even as its style was shortly to become overwhelmed by modernist tendencies that would consign Schmid's work to obscurity. (Among half a dozen different Viennese exhibitions, large and small, celebrating the composer's bicentennial in 1997, the painting was conspicuous by its absence. A show at the Österreichisches Theatermuseum did, however, include several of Schmid's sketches.)

As an example of fin-de-siècle genre painting, Schmid's work was the culmination of a tradition, begun in Schubert's own lifetime, of portraying the composer at a cozy soirée among his close friends. As the nineteenth century proceeded, however, the subject acquired the trappings of historicism as more individuals were crowded into ever more fancifully imagined *Schubertiaden* that strained the sense of a lived intimacy. Thus, Leopold Kupelwieser's watercolor (1821) of the composer among sixteen friends engaged in a charade depicting the exile from paradise was supplanted by Schwind's drawing in which forty-three individuals listen to Schubert accompany the singer Johann Michael Vogl. If Schmid at least reduced Schwind's crowd to twenty-nine, his painting now boasted proportions that were in keeping with the votive nature of its commission. As such, for all its similarity to the subject of its predecessors, the painting is less indebted to the relatively modest Biedermeier aspirations of artworks by Schubert's contemporaries. Rather, it is peopled with listeners in an environment that recalls Franz von Bayros' *Ein Abend bei Johann Strauss* (*An Evening with Johann Strauss*) of 1894, in which an equally prosperous audience—Brahms and Kalbeck among them—enjoys the music of the Waltz King.

Although many of the loans came from collectors outside of Austria, the principal donor was local. The industrialist Nikolaus Dumba's extensive collection of Schubertiana reflected a long-standing affection for the composer's music. Dumba loaned the exhibition no less than fifty-four music manuscripts as well as contemporary portraits and even a pair of Schubert's spectacles.[14] Such largesse was not his first foray into a visual commemoration of the composer. As noted in chapter 1, he was a principal player in the Wiener Männergesang-Verein's commission for Karl Kundmann's statue of the composer in the city's Stadtpark. Dumba delivered the speeches when the foundation stone was laid on October 12, 1868, and when the monument was unveiled on May 15, 1872. By the time of the composer's centennial, Dumba's palatial residence at no. 4 Parkring boasted more than one splendid item in homage to Schubert, ranging from the large Japanese chest with cloisonné paneling, which housed his collection of manuscripts in "six hermetically sealed, colossal cartons," to the designs for the well of the oak staircase. At the time of the composer's centennial, one report noted:

> On the ceiling of the chamber one sees a large panoramic view, a type of *Kinderfries*, in which the various tendencies of Schubertian music are symbolized. Four great medallions in the corner and four smaller ones in the interstices illustrate the main characteristics of the songs. The history painter [Friedrich] Schilcher executed the ceiling picture in 1868.[15]

For his service to the Schubert celebrations, Dumba was made an honorary member of the Männergesang-Verein and the city council warmly acknowledged his selfless contributions (although, as noted in the previous chapter, the council's anti-Semitic members might well have been nonplussed over Dumba's donation to aid Vienna's Jewish orphans after the rightists had voted down any financial support only days after the city's commemoration of Schubert).

Dumba's patronage of the exhibition supplies an initial link between Gustav Klimt and the composer, since it was Dumba's commission to have the artist paint the two supraportes (spaces above the doors) to his music room that resulted in Klimt's *Schubert at the Piano*.[16] (See figure 3.4.) The few letters

Figure 3.4. Gustav Klimt, *Schubert am Klavier* (*Schubert at the Piano*), 1899, destroyed 1945. Historisches Museum der Stadt Wien. Photograph: Erich Lessing/Art Resource, New York City.

exchanged by the artist and his patron indicate that planning for this commission had taken place at the same time as the exhibition was held, although they do not make clear whether the specific choice of image was due to Dumba's urging or to Klimt's recognition that it would undoubtedly please its owner. Certainly so canny a habitué of Vienna's art market as Klimt would have taken note of the city's overindulgent celebration of its most famous musical native son, whose public commemoration was without precedent, and was as much a matter of images as of sounds. Klimt's letter to Dumba on February 9, 1897, promising sketches for the supraportes, is framed by the dates of the Schubert exhibition, and on April 21 the painter again wrote to his patron that in three days he would deliver the complete sketches for the music room.[17] All they needed was a little color in order to give an even better impression. In visiting Dumba's Parkring apartment, itself only a few blocks from the Künstlerhaus, Klimt could not have failed to notice that Dumba had hung immense banners of Habsburg black-and-yellow and Austrian red-and-white from the pediment of the house in celebration of the composer's birthday.[18]

Klimt in any case may not have required such an obvious prompt to choose Schubert as a subject. His nephew Rudolf Zimpel recalled that Schubert was the artist's favorite composer. Zimpel was in a position to speak authoritatively, inasmuch as he inherited the piano that Klimt used as a model for the one in his painting.[19] Klimt did not play an instrument, but one anecdote suggests that Schubert was the composer who leaped into the artist's mind given the right occasion. Bertha Zuckerkandl recalled an afternoon in June 1902 when she served as hostess for a reception in the Prater in honor of the sculptor Auguste Rodin, who was visiting an exhibition of his works at the Secession:

> Klimt and Rodin had seated themselves beside two remarkably beautiful young women—Rodin gazing enchantedly at them. Klimt had created an ideal of this type—the "modern" woman, with a boyish slimness and a puzzling charm. The expression "vamp" had not yet enriched our vocabularies, but it was Klimt who first invented or discovered the ideal Garbo or Dietrich long before Hollywood had stamped those figures upon the dreams of young men all over the world. And, that afternoon, slim and lovely vamps came buzzing round Klimt and Rodin, those two fiery lovers. Alfred Grünfeld sat down at the piano in the big drawing-room, whose double doors were opened wide. Klimt went up to him and asked: 'Please play us some Schubert.' And Grünfeld, his cigar in his mouth, played dreamy tunes that floated and hung in the air with the smoke of his cigar. Rodin leaned over to Klimt and said: "I have never before experienced such an atmosphere—your tragic and magnificent Beethoven fresco; your unforgettable, temple-like exhibition; and now this garden, these women, this music . . . and round it all this gay, childlike happiness. . . . What is the reason for it all?" And Klimt slowly nodded his beautiful head and answered only one word: "Austria."[20]

As a journalist whose salon was frequented by Vienna's leading modernists, Zuckerkandl was well positioned to understand Schubert's significance for Klimt. Along with Hevesi and Hermann Bahr, both staunch propagandists for the Secession, she understood the importance of drawing a connection between Vienna's most illustrious musical native son and contemporary culture's most notorious painter. For her, "the landscapes of Gustav Klimt, the greatest Austrian painter of this time, are Schubert's songs translated into the language of form and colour."[21] The comparison was in fact characteristic of the defenders of modernism. Bahr had made exactly the same connection between a Schubert song and the landscapes of Klimt's fellow Secession founder, Carl Moll.[22]

Klimt's selection of Schubert to be played at that June party may seem just a little too neatly convenient, especially since he had recently used the composer as his subject. Yet, regarding the date, had the painter simply been interested in dropping names, he had a more obvious choice, since the Secession exhibition dedicated to Beethoven, in which his frieze was a prominent element, had run from April 15 to June 15 of that year. Furthermore, Klimt's apparent fondness for Schubert in 1902 was part of a much broader cultural canvas in which contemporary Viennese who were not obviously connected to the field of music turned to the composer with seemingly nostalgic affection. Ludwig Boltzman, professor of theoretical physics at the University of Vienna, was a guest lecturer at the University of California, Berkeley, during the summer of 1905. Invited one evening by his dinner host, Phoebe Hearst, to begin a postprandial concert, he performed a Schubert sonata.[23] In a letter of June 10, 1917, Ludwig Wittgenstein received news from his sister Hermine telling how Schubert's music assuaged their mother's unhappiness at the departure of their brother Kurt (a cellist who took his own life in the following year) for six weeks of military training: "Mama doesn't show her agitation at all, only it is revealed in her sorrow, which she cannot conceal. However, for the moment she is playing four handed with Kurt a splendid Schubert quartet. Thank God that in every emergency there is something that is a blessing!"[24] By all accounts, Schubert was Wittgenstein's favorite composer, and more than one acquaintance was impressed by his ability to whistle a repertoire that included some forty or fifty Lieder. Wittgenstein chose the composer's name for one of his celebrated runic apothegms on language: "I feel as if the name 'Schubert' fitted Schubert's works and Schubert's face."[25] (Given that the members of the Wittgenstein family, one of the wealthiest in turn-of-the-century Vienna, shared a deep love of music—which ranged from father Karl arranging a private performance of Brahms's Clarinet Quintet for its composer in 1892 to the illustrious piano career of brother Paul, who lost his right arm in World War I—one wonders whether an eight-year-old Ludwig might have been taken to the Schubert exhibition by his mother, herself an accomplished pianist.)

Considering the saturation of events in the city that commemorated its greatest musical native son, Klimt could not have been unaware of the symbolic significance that the composer held for Austria's cultural identity at that particular historical moment. For a nation that just a generation earlier had suffered military defeat and financial panic, its significance now lay in its creative progeny, thus raising its cultural icons to a status formerly held by civic leaders. The convergence of politics and culture symbolized by the emperor's presiding over the opening of the 1897 exhibition was replicated a week after its closing when in February, Franz Joseph attended the Ball of the City of Vienna at which every female guest received a *Damenspende*, a volume of fifteen zincplate engravings by as many artists, each one inspired by a different Schubert song: "a Schubert album whose binder is made of white leather with colored borders and metallic covers. On the front cover one finds a medallion with a relief of Franz Schubert's head encircled by a lyre and a laurel wreath. At the bottom of the cover are embossed the dates 1797–1897. The back side of the binder carries the crest of the city of Vienna in enamel with the dedication as a *Damenspende*."[26] Adding to the prestige of the event, the quality of the volume lent its contributors a further celebrity.

The fact that several of these artists—Rudolf Bacher (*Thränenregen*), Maximilian Lenz (*Erlkönig*), Adolf Böhm (*Abschied*), and Koloman Moser (*Irrlicht*)—were contemporaries of Klimt and would become his colleagues in the newly created Secession two months later, only makes his absence from the collection all the more conspicuous. Certainly Klimt's style at that time could not have disqualified him. Indeed, Moser's *Irrlicht* has the flowing, curvilinear manner typical of Jugendstil art, and its *femme fatale* subject was sufficiently common to have rendered it uncontroversial even for the women of Vienna's aristocracy. (In 1903, Klimt quoted both the style and substance of Moser's design in his painting *Irrlichter*.) Indeed, Klimt's absence from the album might be regarded as something of a cultural snub, given his stature during the preceding decade. He had received the Golden Cross of Merit in 1888 for his contribution to the decoration of the ceiling paintings above the staircase of the Burgtheater, his painting of the old Burgtheater won him the Emperor's Prize in 1890, and in the following year he was commissioned to decorate the lobby of the Kunsthistorisches Museum. One suspects that Klimt, having been overlooked as a contributor to this Schubert album, found the prospect of executing a work on a similar subject, in the form of Dumba's commission, all the more attractive.

Whatever the modernist aims of the members of the Secession, an artist like Klimt remained keenly aware of the practical exigencies of marketing and selling his work. The support of someone such as Dumba, not only a celebrated patron of the arts but an influential figure in local government, was an achievement worth publicizing in the Secession's house organ, *Ver Sacrum*. In its third issue, published in March 1898, the journal announced that Klimt was occupied with Dumba's music salon as well as engaging in preparatory work for another choice commission: the ceiling paintings designed to decorate the assembly hall of the university.[27] (Perhaps as a concession to modernism, the journal published in a later volume only the companion piece to *Schubert at the Piano*, *Music II*, which hung over the other door of Dumba's salon. With a curvilinear background whose style evokes contemporary Jugendstil design, and with a subject that includes a cryptic mask and sphinx, *Music II* is a more obvious emblem of its time.)

Given the prominence of his patron's involvement with the Schubert-Ausstellung, the exhibition's emphasis on artworks, and its success with both the public and the critics, it is reasonable to conclude that Klimt may even have gone to the Künstlerhaus. (The Künstlerhaus was the bastion of official contemporary art from whose committee Klimt and his colleagues resigned, leading to the founding of the Secession in April 1897. One cannot help but suspect that the Secession's Beethoven exhibition of 1902 was in part intended as a modernist challenge to the Schubert-Ausstellung five years earlier.) Certainly the many points of contact between Schmid's picture and Klimt's painting strongly indicate that the former may have served as a model. Beyond the general equivalence of their subjects—a *Hauskonzert* whose central figure is the composer as pianist—several similar details provide evidence of Klimt's acquaintance with Schmid's work. The huge chandelier in Schmid's painting is a near replica of one that hung in Dumba's music room. It is an elegant coincidence, which nevertheless echoes the popular practice of portraying elite Viennese society at confident ease. Klimt had originally intended that there be a chandelier, suggested by the crystalline and gold flecks that are noticeable along the top of an oil sketch, probably from 1898.[28] In the final version, they are not discernible, thus allowing attention to be drawn to the prominent light source, the candelabra on the piano, itself an echo of Schmid's painting. A second room is evident in both works, and Klimt appears to have borrowed the detail of a disembodied male head placed within its doorway. The head is visible just over the shoulder of the woman on the left, but its relatively small size appears to place it in the distant room. The visual logic, however, is confounded by the absence of three-dimensional depth of the surrounding walls.

That refutation of real space, and the concomitant unease it produces, is likewise applicable to the candles on the right. The black square that frames them recalls the darkened picture behind Schmid's chandelier. In both cases the opaqueness exaggerates the light, but Klimt has made it impossible to define the space unequivocally. We cannot be certain whether the candles sit on a shelf in front of a darkened picture or whether a mirror reflects them from across the room. If it is the former, the flatness of the wall contradicts the depth shown by a shelf, and, if the latter, nothing other than the candles is reflected in the mirrored surface. By refuting the rational order of light and space of his model, Klimt has also subverted its meaning. Gone is the nostalgic evocation of Biedermeier comfort; its inhabitants continue in the pursuit of the aesthetic life of musical performance, but the security of their private world has now been undermined by the style of an artist for whom societal smugness was the bane of contemporary culture.[29]

Although the painting's subject appears to be the scion of a familiar pictorial tradition, Klimt's reconfiguring of its individual elements dislodges it from any real fealty to the kind of specious convention that modernism abjured. An analysis of the figures is likewise revealing. The glowing beauty of the woman on the left stands in stark contrast to her left arm, which, if one were to imagine the fingers hidden by the pianist's wrists, creates a limb of freakishly distended proportions. As to the representation of the composer, Klimt research has suggested that the profile was copied from Kupelwieser's 1821 watercolor, which was owned by Dumba and loaned by him to the exhibition.[30] The resemblance is close, arguably more so than in Schwind's celebrated drawing showing the composer in profile at the piano, although by Klimt's time, the frequent reproduction of both works had produced the archetypal "Kupelwieser-Schwind head," as Hevesi described it.[31] Neither Klimt's initial pencil designs nor the oil sketch hint at the composer being the individual sitting at the piano.[32] Certainly we may hypothesize that, if Klimt intended from the outset to use Kupelwieser's watercolor as the direct source for his pianist, then the figure's profile might well have been the last item to be added to the final painting, although that does not explain another alteration regarding the people surrounding the composer.

Aside from the profile of the pianist, the most obvious compositional difference between the oil sketch and the finished painting is the grouping of individuals around the seated figure: three women and one man have replaced four women. One possible reason for this change is that, having decided to use Schubert as the seated figure, Klimt added another man to represent the singer Vogl, not present in Kupelwieser's watercolor but prominent in Schwind's drawing.[33] A comparison of Klimt's figure to other portraits of Vogl yields only the vaguest of similarities, but Klimt's habit of working from another source does not appear to have obfuscated the resemblance, certainly not in the case of Schubert. The same may be said of the result when Klimt copied from life, as we will see in turning to the figure of the woman on the left. In viewing the painting, two contemporary critics considered her to be older than the two singers. Hevesi distinguished between the woman and "the two singing girls," and Arthur Roessler described "two younger girls, a woman listening to the blessed sounds, and the darkly discrete form of a man."[34] Although both critics were friends of Klimt, it is not certain whether they were aware of one particular biographical detail that supported their analyses. Klimt scholars agree that the sitter for the woman on the left was the model Mizzi Zimmermann, who had two children by the artist. Their affair seems to have begun around 1899, the year in which her first son is said to have been born.[35] Although exact dating is not possible, it appears that Mizzi Zimmermann had a maternal status in Klimt's private life that dovetails with contemporary views that the left-hand figure was indeed an older woman.[36]

Older man and woman joined by two younger females singing to Schubert's piano accompaniment: Klimt's final choice of figures may not derive from members of some sentimentally imagined *Schubertiade* but from a real family, the Esterházys, the Hungarian aristocrats for whom Schubert served as music teacher in 1818 and 1824. Beginning with Kreissle's second book on the composer's life completed at the very end of 1864, Schubert's biographers had detailed the singing abilities of the two Esterházy daughters: "The whole family was musical. The count was a bass, the countess and her daughter Caroline sang alto, and the older countess Marie delighted in a 'wonderful' high soprano."[37] This biographical detail was surely known to anyone having even a passing acquaintance with Schubert's career, because it provided the background to one of the central anecdotes about the composer's life: his purported love for the younger daughter, Caroline. As detailed in chapter 2 of the first volume of this study, the story had furnished the material for a seemingly unending string of bathetic fables, which makes it all the more certain that one did not require an intimate knowledge of the extant documentary evidence to be aware of it. Moreover, there was a visual counterpart to these narratives in Schwind's placement of Caroline's portrait in the center of his drawing. When Schmid took Schwind's work as his model, he retained the detail of a central painting, but he eliminated its subject by masking it with the chandelier, which at the same time paradoxically illuminates every other figure in the room. Yet anyone who beheld Schmid's painting when entering the Künstlerhaus exhibition, and who had an acquaintance with the anecdotes surrounding Schubert and the young countess (especially through Bauernfeld's verse as quoted by Kreissle), might have guessed that an invisible Caroline was the subject of the central portrait, since the only figure who ignores Schubert's playing is in fact Bauernfeld himself, who gazes backward at the now obscured image.[38]

Whatever attempts at discretion motivated some nineteenth-century interpretations of Schubert's encounter with Caroline Esterházy, they were rearguard actions by the turn of the century. The story after all had propriety built into it: every version—whether sentimental fiction or earnest biography—recognized that this was a composer whose failure in love was entirely in keeping with contemporary interpretations of his music. The Schubertian *Mädchencharakter* still exerted its cloying influence sixty years after Schumann introduced it. For the more adventurous representatives of fin-de-siècle modernism, however, the narrative's very lack of sensuality was an element that could be manipulated into a critique of Viennese culture.

Schubert's encounter with Caroline Esterházy was part of anyone's knowledge of the composer at the turn of the century, not least of all Klimt, an artist who was about to embark on a painting of the composer a year after his city's overindulgent celebration of the centennial of his birth. Whether or not Schubert was Klimt's favorite composer, one might reasonably conclude that the artist was aware of the story's celebrity. The widespread familiarity with that narrative's details in fin-de-siècle Viennese culture might explain Klimt's choice of the final grouping around the composer, abetted by the juxtaposition with events in the artist's private world. Accepting that Klimt was aware of the tradition of Schubert's love for the young countess because of the context in which he created his portrait of the composer for Dumba, the most dedicated collector of Schubertiana, more than one liaison in Klimt's private life from that period might have incited him to choose the subject of Schubert making music with the Esterházys.

If the singing girls in *Schubert at the Piano* represent Caroline and Marie, their presence echoes the prominence of the Flöge sisters in Klimt's life. Helene Flöge was married to Klimt's brother Ernst, and her sister Emilie was Klimt's companion for more than twenty years as well as his artistic muse. He portrayed her four times, first as an innocent seventeen-year-old in a white dress in 1891, the year his brother married her sister. Two years later, Klimt again portrayed her, standing next to a traditional symbol of beauty and grace, a flowering oleander, which recalls the painting *Two Girls with Oleander* (ca. 1890/92) even as the latter anticipates the two girls shown in profile in *Schubert at the Piano*.[39] Klimt's relationship with Emilie Flöge has led to speculation among the artist's biographers. Wolfgang Georg Fischer concluded that it was a platonic friendship, whereas Christian Nebehay withheld judgment, having found it a curious circumstance that four hundred postcards exchanged between the two, starting in 1897, revealed "not a single tender word" from the artist.[40] Although it might be wishful thinking to suggest that photographs of Emilie in profile resemble either of the singing girls, Klimt's relationship with Emilie reflects that of Schubert with Caroline Esterházy, at least in contemporary Viennese consciousness.[41] Caroline could stand in for Emilie Flöge even as Schubert could serve as the painter's proxy, in both cases the relationship symbolizing the artist inspired to create works of genius by a girl whose idealized femininity obscured the reality of the sexual tensions embedded in modern life.

The fact that Klimt's attachment to Emilie Flöge was going on at the same time as the completion of *Schubert at the Piano*, however, does not necessarily mean that the social conventions that rendered Caroline Esterházy unattainable also placed Emilie Flöge at a distance. The nature of her liaison with Klimt appears to have been sufficiently well known for one of the painter's obituarists, Hans Tietze, to theorize that the greatness of Klimt's art lay in the apparent disparity between his considerable libidinous desire and his fear of emotional attachment. By the time of Klimt's death, this condition was discernible as a long-standing symptom of Viennese life, which the artist shared with Schubert's contemporary Franz Grillparzer, "one for whom the only salvation seemed to be flight into solitude; he too living a bourgeois life in total contrast to the range of his inner urges."[42] (Tietze's allusion to Grillparzer's intimate relationships in 1919 would have evoked various contradictory associations, depending upon the reader's familiarity with fin-de-siècle literature. At one extreme, the poet's engagement to Kathi Fröhlich had entered into the mythology of popular accounts of Biedermeier Vienna, most notably in Joseph August Lux's *Grillparzers Liebesroman* of 1912. As will be detailed in chapter 5, however, Grillparzer's relationship with men was the subject of a quite different interpretation in Hans Rau's *Franz Grillparzer und sein Liebesleben* of 1904. The appearance of reminiscences by Schubert's acquaintances in issues of the *Jahrbuch der Grillparzer-Gesellschaft* in 1901 and 1906 supplied Otto Erich Deutsch with the evidence that Therese Grob was Schubert's enduring love.) This description calls to mind contemporary characterizations of Schubert in the face of his encounter with Caroline Esterházy. If the economics of the composer's career were bohemian, the emotional distance he maintained from the countess had the unmistakable air of middle-class respectability. Caroline's nobility made her unreachable, whereas in fin-de-siècle society, social transactions were facilitated by the status of women whose Schubertian characteristics made them so desirable. If Emilie Flöge was kept at a distance in 1898 for reasons other than class, that situation was relevant to another of Klimt's amorous entanglements at precisely the time when *Schubert at the Piano* was executed, suggesting that Schubert's encounter with Caroline gave a special meaning to the final disposition of the painting's figures.

Like Schubert among the Esterházys, Klimt felt at home in the family circle of his fellow Secession artist, Carl Moll. Through him, Klimt met Moll's stepdaughter, Alma Schindler (whose father Jakob Emil had himself been a distinguished painter, and who was later to marry in succession Gustav Mahler, Walter Gropius, and Franz Werfel), and the subsequent rise and fall of their romance was tracked in detail in her diary precisely at the time when *Schubert at the Piano* was created. When Alma, born in 1879, began her diary at the beginning of 1898 (coincidentally at the same age as Caroline Esterházy in 1824 when Schubert purportedly fell in love with her), she was very much the unremarkable sort of young woman one might have encountered in contemporary Jung-Wien literature. Her candid self-analysis of February 9 recalls Schnitzler's characterization of the fictional Berta Garlan, whom we shall encounter in chapter 4:

> If only I were a somebody—a real person, noted for and capable of great things. But I'm a nobody, an indifferent young lady who, on demand, runs her fingers prettily up and down the piano keys and, on demand, gives arrogant replies to arrogant questions, likes to dance . . . *just* like millions of others.—Nothing pleases me more than to be told that I'm exceptional. Klimt, for instance, said:
> You're a rare, unusual kind of girl, but why do *you* do this, that and the other, just like anyone else?[43]

Alma had an enormous desire to be considered something other than ordinary, and in Klimt she encountered an individual who was well practiced in flattering women. Her diary entries over the next year, however, reveal that she too had a certain degree of adeptness at flirtation. Thus on March 31, while visiting the first Secession exhibition with Moll, she encountered Klimt, who, after a prolonged conversation, disappeared without warning. Alma, however, contrived to leave the building without her stepfather:

> Suddenly I heard hasty steps behind me, *guessed* that it was Klimt but just kept walking, and hid behind my umbrella.—So it went on, but then he took a few strides and ended up beside me:
> You can hide behind your umbrella and walk as fast as you like, but you still can't escape me, he said. Will you get into trouble if I walk beside you?
> I said not, although I was inwardly uncertain. So he walked with me and was delightful company. He said he wanted to escort me home, but I declined and got on the bus (the wrong one), had to get out at the next stop and walked home alone. Mama wasn't put out at all. Why didn't I walk home with him? It would have been such fun![44]

If such flirtatious machinations have the ring of familiarity, it is because they were as typical of Vienna's real social rituals as they were characteristic of its literature. Gustav Nottebohm, whose groundbreaking research on Beethoven and Schubert—including thematic catalogues of both composers—does not exactly make him a likely candidate for observing the ephemera of contemporary mating habits, took note of just such a roundelay. Writing to the composer Robert Volkmann on August 10, 1861, he described how two young men pick up two young women on the street. He even drew a diagram to explain it: "Now, what do you say, is that not ingenious? But perhaps the man who writes such serious quartets has little sense and liking of such things. But one should not be one-sided."[45]

Throughout 1898, Alma's diary recorded the mutual attraction between Klimt and herself, played out in a series of escalating encounters worthy of a Schnitzler drama, until on January 30 of the following year she wrote of her happiness at Klimt's confession that he loved her. On February 14, he proposed that she visit his studio on her own. Alma described the subsequent exchange as an astonishingly Schubertian moment, replicating the mythologized words of the composer's alleged confession to Caroline Esterházy, only with the sex of the protagonists reversed. Kreissle had been the first to record the subsequently much-repeated recollection of the tenor Karl von Schönstein, a guest of the Esterházy family when Schubert was serving as the girls' music teacher, in which the unhappy composer had responded to Caroline's jesting reproach for his failure to dedicate any music to her: "What would be the good of it? Everything I have ever done has been dedicated to you!"[46] In the gendered turnaround of Alma's diary, Klimt was now the coy interlocutor and Alma was the frustrated respondent: "A tremor went through my whole body. I don't remember what I answered . . . He asked me to dedicate a song to him, and I said: They're all dedicated to you."[47] Rather than Caroline the talented young singer, it was Alma the budding Lieder composer from whom Klimt requested a dedication.

The emotional intensity of their encounters continued, despite concerns voiced by Alma's mother Anna, who was shrewd enough to intuit that the artist thought of her daughter as a mere plaything and who, with characteristic maternal calculation, told Alma about Klimt's relationship with his sister-in-law, Emilie Flöge. On March 15, Alma described how Klimt spilled a glass of schnapps on her white dress, and attempted to clean it with a glass of warm water: "He took my skirt on his knee, and himself washed the stain out of my petticoat. Both his legs and mine were hidden under the skirt, and inevitably they touched. Although I kept withdrawing—for I consider such behaviour vulgar—I did so with reluctance and was overcome by such a strange, sweet sensation."[48] Here was the archetypal fin-de-siècle collision between bourgeois respectability and physical desire. Alma recognized that writing about such feelings was "madly sensual" even as she expressed her barely repressed jealousy over the impropriety of Klimt's maintaining his liaison with his sister-in-law, whom she elsewhere referred to as the "other woman."

Judging his next move, two days later Klimt contrived to get Alma alone during a private viewing at the Secession, apparently the only time he ever succeeded in such a maneuver, with the expressed intent of showing her his latest painting: "Klimt took me personally to look at his 'Schubert.' It's indisputably the best picture at the exhibition."[49] Although Alma for once did not divulge the conversation, this singular act—regarded as one moment in a pattern of seduction—might at least suggest that Klimt's motivation for this private showing of *Schubert at the Piano* was to reveal a symbolic narrative that had particular resonance for their relationship. The often repeated tale of the composer's love for the young countess would have served well as an allusion to the painter's desire for his colleague's stepdaughter, whose distinguished lineage was determined by her artistic paternity as opposed to a young countess's noble birth. If Klimt intended it as such a gesture, Alma apparently did not grasp the implication. In the wake of the disastrous ending to their liaison, she thought the painting was wonderful, but she failed to appreciate the deliberate incongruity between Klimt's style and the Biedermeier character of Schubert's received image that had been stitched into the Viennese popular consciousness over half a century. She observed: "Schubert sits at the piano, surrounded by ultramodern young ladies singing. The whole thing bathed in dim candlelight—hence in fact alien to Schubert's melody, which is so primary [natural] and healthy. It's Schumann's music that's the more sickly and ultraromantic, hence also the more modern."[50]

Alma remained conflicted, her diary entries alternating between dispassionate objectivity and hyper-romantic yearning. The Molls departed the following week for Italy, where her stepfather warned her to stay away from Klimt. When it came to women, however, Klimt was certainly more adept than the Schubert who was imagined in the reception of the time. Klimt followed the family to Italy, and on April 29 Alma recorded how he entered her room and kissed her: "It's indescribable; to be kissed for the first time in my life, and by the only person in the whole world that I love." Two days later, the act was repeated. "He held me and kissed me again. We were both terribly agitated. Later he stood behind me and said: There's only one thing for it: complete physical union."[51] Within the week, however, the trajectory of their relationship was disrupted when Moll learned what was happening. With all the parties back in Vienna, the two artists spoke about the matter on May 14. Klimt, alarmed at his colleague's reaction, wrote an astonishing thirteen-page confessional letter to Moll on May 19 in which Klimt denied any serious emotional or physical attraction to Moll's stepdaughter.

Both the contents of this letter and Klimt's encounter with Alma reveal noteworthy echoes of the details that were so familiar in contemporary Schubert biography. On the one hand, according to Kreissle, Caroline "esteemed [Schubert], and appreciated his genius, but did not return his love, and probably never guessed its extent and fervency," going so far as to tease him about his failure to dedicate any music to her and thus prompting Schubert's unexpected reply.[52] The image of the composer sublimating his passion through creative inspiration was ready-made for Klimt, who was eager to convince Moll that his affection also had initially been that of an artist deeply moved by the aesthetic contemplation of feminine beauty. "She appealed to me in just the way that a beautiful child does appeal to us artists. I saw her again at [your] home, found her more lovely than ever, and was amazed that neither you nor anyone else had ever painted her."[53] The letter served its purpose: by reducing Alma to a childlike stature and at the same time reminding Moll of the creative comparability to himself, Klimt effectively diffused the situation with his colleague.

Klimt, having in mind Schubert's relationship with Caroline Esterházy as a consequence of his choice of subject for a painting whose sketches date from 1898, may have found that its details supplied a resonance with his own momentary dalliance with Alma Schindler. Threatened by a professional break with Moll, his colleague and friend, Klimt could turn the Schubertian narrative to his own advantage. Like Schubert, Klimt was an artist inspired by youthful female beauty. Neither in the case of the composer nor in the case of the painter was this attraction meant to result in carnal love. Rather than admit that, Klimt reduced Alma to a mere child who was incapable of inciting his lust. Precisely because of her innocence, she was a suitable artistic subject, not a desirable sexual object. Klimt could deny to Moll that his stepdaughter might have been the latter by appealing instead to their mutual creative ambitions. Such a position echoed fin-de-siècle Schubert biographies wherein the composer was compelled to treat the young countess as the source of artistic inspiration, devoid of any physical attraction that risked becoming more than an artist's objective contemplation of beauty. Of course, Klimt could not will away the kiss that Alma recorded in her diary nor the suspicions that might have spiraled in the wake of his well-known reputation with women. His letter therefore furnished more than one excuse for his behavior. He suggested that he himself was the naive participant who was initially unable to accept that "this beautiful, blossoming young child" could be attracted to an older artist. Rather, it was Alma who, for all her youth, revealed qualities that were less than innocent:

> Alma is beautiful, clever, witty/she has in abundance all that a discerning man could look for in a woman/I am sure that wherever she sets foot in the world of men/she is mistress, sovereign. . . . Is it really so easy to feel indifferent towards her/doesn't everyone love her? Isn't everybody bound to care for her? Do you not find it understandable that in her presence there are moments/when one's thinking become [sic] erratic, confused?[54]

Klimt's written act of contrition concluded with the suggestion that his moment of weakness might even have been due to hereditary madness. Before the letter ended, Klimt had transformed Alma from an artless child to a woman with sufficient calculation to hold a man in her thrall. She became a female who recalls Fritz Wittels' archetypal *Kindweib* (whom we will encounter in chapter 6), that peculiarly Viennese type of adolescent *femme fatale* with her combination of youthful innocence and erotic sensuality.

In Kreissle's narrative, Caroline Esterházy never guessed at the depth of Schubert's love. In Klimt's letter, Alma Schindler apparently need not have guessed. According to Klimt's argument, she believed theirs was a mutually understood and ultimately cordial affection. Judging by Alma's diary, however, consuming passion was precisely what engaged the couple, and one entry reveals her to have been upset and angry over the artist's shocking duplicity. Indeed, she became aware of the situation on May 15, four days before Klimt's letter to Moll, and she drew a cross after the date:

> Now I know what it is to be betrayed. Yesterday Carl spoke with Kl. In a cowardly manner he beat a retreat, betrayed me, admitted that he'd acted without premeditation, proved himself a weakling. Now I know what it is to be disconsolate. He's betrayed me. I cannot write for tears.[55]

Klimt's choice of Schubert among the Esterházys as the subject for his painting made perfect sense in 1899. Having himself narrowly averted a situation in which he might be accused of a passionate attraction toward the stepdaughter of a friend and colleague, and excusing his actions as those of the ruminative artist, Klimt turned to a composer whose life and works betrayed none of the features of brutish masculinity that he so quickly wished to avoid once his relationship with Alma Schindler became known. That he had sacrificed her feelings in order to maintain his standing with a fellow Secession artist scarcely seems to have had an impact upon him. *Schubert at the Piano* thus became a reflection of what Klimt had construed his relationship with Alma to be: the artist inspired to create by his contemplation of female beauty, which on the surface was as innocent and naive as the nostalgic evocation of a lost Biedermeier world, but which in reality masked considerably more volatile Dionysian appetites.

Klimt's subsequent career effectively parsed the roles given to women: the Caroline-like Emilie Flöge provided a lifelong companion of similar artistic temperament while continued sexual encounters with lower-class models pro-duced a string of children.[56] Klimt's last and most famous portrait of Emilie in 1902 appears calculated to avoid the fleshly excesses of his anonymous Danae and instead invests her gown with the sensuous extrusions of Jugendstil design. Her pose—her hand on her hip and her elbow thrust outward from her torso— is unique among Klimt's paintings of upper-class Viennese women. It instead recalls a tradition that brings to mind representations of aristocratic young men, such as Bronzino's *Portrait of a Young Man* or Nicolò dell'Abate's *Portrait of a Man with a Parrot*, the latter hanging in the Kunsthistorisches Museum. The implicit androgyny of Emilie Flöge's portrait may not have been lost on Klimt's younger contemporary and admirer Egon Schiele, who appears to have used her pose as the model for his portrait of the fifteen-year-old Erich Lederer in 1913.[57] Klimt himself may have originally intended a much younger singer than those whom he ultimately portrayed in *Schubert at the Piano*. A pencil study from about 1898 shows a singing girl, perhaps sitting at a piano, whose profile appears to be more waiflike than those of any of the women in the final version.[58]

Schubert at the Piano was first shown at the Fourth Secession Exhibition from March 13 to May 31, 1899, and along with *Der Kuss* (*The Kiss*) it became Klimt's most frequently reproduced work. For the writer Anton Lindner, the painting was far removed from the line of "Franzl" images extending over three-quarters of a century from Kupelwieser and Schwind to Schmid. Indeed, its style had far more to do with contemporary literature and music than with the art of the past, although Lindner reckoned that this was not necessarily the painter's objective:

> To these [earlier Schubert portraits] Klimt's alluring effort stands in unintended con-trast. Only just now and then the slight feeling might seize us, that this modern

Schubert may have looked a little too deeply into our contemporary spirit; as though he had occasionally seen some acts of an Arthur Schnitzler drama, experienced some verse by Hugo von Hofmannsthal, studied some gloss by Hermann Bahr, and finally perhaps also appropriated with receptive humility a few measures of Hugo Wolf's neo-Viennese and post-Wagnerian dissonances. But that can be no fault of Klimt, the master.[59]

The critic's suspicion that fin-de-siècle Vienna might find a resonance between Klimt's Schubert and modernist culture was confirmed by the fact that two of its most representative authors, Peter Altenberg and Hermann Bahr, proudly displayed copies of the painting on their walls. (Lindner himself was certainly conversant with modernist sensibilities; as editor of the *Wiener Rundschau*, in 1900 he was responsible for the publication of Hedwig Lachmann's German translation of Oscar Wilde's *Salome*, which Richard Strauss subsequently used as the libretto for his opera.) Another measure of the painting's renown was its appropriation for the lucrative postcard market. In 1905, Fritzi Ulreich aped its general outline while leeching it of all its compositional subtleties. (See figure 3.5.) The background is lost in an undifferentiated obscurity, and rather than the complexities of light being dealt with, the candles are merely masked behind one of two female listeners.

Perhaps because of the very popularity of *Schubert at the Piano*, it became a victim of Vienna's crabbed literary genius, Karl Kraus, in the inaugural issue of his influential journal *Die Fackel* in 1899. In his polemic, Kraus did not address the subject of the painting; Schubert at least was spared. Instead, his apparent target was Dumba's commission for his fashionable Parkring residence, an action that Kraus considered to be merely a thinly disguised attempt by a wealthy patron to affect an acquaintance with what Dumba imagined was artistic modernism simply by purchasing it. Although the painting itself was not so bad, Kraus ridiculed Dumba as someone who in his old age had turned to decorating his home in a Secessionist style. Having bought his sophistication through the acquisition of Klimt's painting, Dumba needed "only to hang it a little more in the dark." Kraus found the idea of Dumba as a Secessionist to be amusing. Furthermore, Kraus ridiculed Dumba for selecting Klimt to decorate the music room, as if the creations of this artist were no different from his patron's more typical tastes, which ran toward the work of two deceased painters who were much in vogue during the previous decade: Ferdinand Julius Laufberger, a professor at the Kunstgewerbeschule who had been Klimt's teacher, and Hans Makart, who had decorated the study of Dumba's residence. (Kraus's readers would surely have recalled that the high point of Makart's fame came in 1879 with his designs for the public procession commemorating the silver anniversary of the imperial couple.) Noting the recent impact of the Belgian painter Fernand Khnopff, Kraus concluded with a typical Viennese pun: "And now, so that the story is not left without a punch line [*Pointe*], he [Klimt] has become a pointillist. And naturally the purchaser must also take part in all of it. So Herr von Dumba became a modernist."[60]

Figure 3.5. Fritzi Ulreich. *Schubert am Klavier* (*Schubert at the Piano*), 1908. Undated photographic reproduction for a postcard. Author's collection. ÖNB/Wien, Bildarchiv, PCH 18566-A/B.

Even worse than Dumba's patronage and the crass commodification of culture it reflected was the description of the painting by Bahr, one of Kraus's most despised literary rivals. Kraus dubbed Bahr the self-anointed "Aristotle of our 'time,'" thus indulging in a typical pun on *Zeit* (Time), the newspaper for which Bahr served as theater critic. In his paean to *Schubert at the Piano*, Bahr had declared it to be "the most beautiful picture ever painted by an Austrian," and his exultant style contains just the sort of lyrical and opaque hyperbole that Kraus loathed.[61] It must have galled Kraus to see Bahr's assertion that the painting "says what we cannot say with our miserable words," and then to read:

> With this Schubert and the singing girls, which has something of a bourgeois and yet almost religious quality, I am left feeling an indescribable—I should say—gay melancholy, in the same consoling sadness that is possessed by the little hills in the meadow. I don't want to quarrel with anyone, I don't want to convert anyone; I have only said what I feel about this painting. Beauty does not give itself to proof, certainly we will not follow art with the intellect: let us tell what it has granted us, and let us be grateful.[62]

For Kraus, this sort of writing would have demonstrated an obfuscation of language against which he would rail for nearly four more decades. His contempt for Bahr was manifest:

The confused drift of this gentleman, who still pretends to bring culture to Austria and continually performs his poetic crowning, will, before he ends up in the longed-for greater daily editorial office, be exposed more often and painfully in these pages [of *Die Fackel*]. . . . One still remembers how, written in a ludicrous German and printed on handmade paper, he ceremoniously declared in the pubescent sentiments of a Kalksburger grammar-school student:[63] in fourteen days Europe will talk about this book. The word took wing, but the book has long ago sunk below the surface. Now the same gentleman flatly declares a painting by Klimt in the Secession (the "Schubert") to be the best picture an Austrian has ever painted.[64]

Kraus abhorred what he considered to be the preciousness and pretension of this literary style, and he fumed at Bahr, who, like Dumba, owed his reputation to his attachment to the prestige of the Secession artists. Absent the herd mentality that made *Schubert at the Piano* so popular, Kraus was sympathetic toward Klimt only after the artist later ran afoul of official sensitivities with the rejection of his designs for the ceiling of the university's assembly hall. When *Schubert at the Piano* was subsequently displayed at Klimt's one-man show in 1903, hanging in the room with the artist's now scandalous university paintings, a punning aphorism by a more appreciative Kraus was quoted by Peter Altenberg: "In a word, he ASPIRES [KLIMMT] to the summit!"[65]

The stylistic incongruities that appear in *Schubert at the Piano* when it is compared to its historical models are replications of the sexual tensions in contemporary Viennese culture. They in turn are echoes of the artist's own personal relationships. For Klimt, Schubert's status, as apparently innocent and nostalgic as it was godlike and heavenly, permitted an artistic reverence that might mask less than Apollonian appetites. Schubertian women, with their childlike beauty and youthful figures, inspired the artist to produce works of genius. Yet contradictions lay below the surface of fin-de-siècle Viennese modernism's attitude toward women. Feminine innocence, all the more desirable to the male artist because of its purity, was emblematically attended by the image and music of Schubert. Whereas the young female body served as a metaphor for the rebirth of creative freedom, the line between artistic contemplation and physical attraction was frequently unclear; indeed, it was often deliberately erased. In fin-de-siècle Vienna, inspiration was also a kind of seduction to which the artist readily responded on both aesthetic and personal grounds, and it is indicative of its modernism that the yearning for a purer form of nature—here in the guise of an ever-younger female form—should be seen through a dreamlike and ultimately self-deluding lens.

Klimt's invocation of Schubert portrays a clash of modernist identities. It criticizes contemporary Viennese cultural aspirations by manipulating details of Schmid's painting. This was anything but a benign homage. Klimt took ostensibly familiar elements and placed them in such irrational juxtaposition that their comprehensibility was undermined. His figures inhabit a world that recalls a *gemütlich* past, but one whose imagined comfort is irreconcilable with contemporary experience. In manipulating Schubertian myths to his own advantage, in effecting a confrontation between style and subject, Klimt shook the delicate scaffolding upon which Viennese society erected its social facades. At the same time, his women served as objects of both creative inspiration and sexual desire, even as his work furnishes a paradox in which the artifice of memory both masks and reveals contemporary tensions between the sexes that responded to the demands of cultural and autobiographical impulses. Such responses are also apparent in contemporary modernist literature by the writers who came to be known as Jung-Wien.

Chapter Four

Schubert and Jung-Wien: Arthur Schnitzler and Hugo von Hofmannsthal

By the end of the nineteenth century, the Schubertian *Mädchencharakter* was a well-established tradition on both sides of the Atlantic, endemic in aesthetic and critical thought, echoed in art and literature, and burnished by the authority of philosophy and science. This was the inheritance of the culture of fin-de-siècle Vienna, but modernist writers from the generation of 1860 were quick to exploit its familiarity to achieve their own creative ends, constituting as much a critique as a reflection of the very bourgeois values that Schubert had come to symbolize. *Die Moderne* was a common enough but elusive expression in the hands of writers whose contemporaries often grouped them under the cultural umbrella of Jung-Wien, whose meaning and membership nevertheless remained elastic at the turn of the century. In 1893, Hermann Bahr, the literary Lancelot of Viennese modernism, wrote an article entitled "Das junge Österreich," in which he attempted to consecrate that particular term by differentiating it from the rootless, revolutionary naturalism of "Young Germany" as represented by the works of Gerhart Hauptmann. Bahr went so far as to reject the idea that Austrian writers had any program other than the desire to be modern. In doing so, he argued, these authors jettisoned the darkness and the hatred of the past exhibited by the youngest Germans, a distinction that, Bahr recognized, existed as much between Berlin and Vienna as between the two countries. In being modern, "Young Austria" paradoxically honored tradition, wanting not to go against it but to stand upon it: "They desire to adjust the old work of their ancestors for their own era."[1]

To be sure, appropriating tradition did not mean slavishly imitating it. Viennese modernism disavowed what one anonymous writer dubbed "epigonal classicism" in 1887 and what Hermann Broch later analyzed as the city's "muse-umness."[2] To be so indebted to older models that one failed to change either them or oneself was pointless. As Bahr observed in 1890: "We ascend into the divine or we fall, fall into night and nothingness, but staying put is meaningless."[3]

The transformation of one's cultural past as an essential component of an aesthetic plan (even in the case of modernists who claimed to reject concrete ideologies) meant that Schubert, as Vienna's greatest native musical son, was due to become a crucially important icon for manipulation by fin-de-siècle Viennese writers. As the essayist and critic Otto Stößl observed in 1901 in an article entitled "The Modernization of Myth," since composers provided particularly suitable cases for tracing contemporary myth-making, the image of Schubert, "the God of the Lied," enjoyed a unique stature by occupying "the most quiet and charming niche" in the musical pantheon.[4] Describing Schubert in this way implied locating him at the site of domestic tranquility that had marked the composer's position throughout the second half of the nineteenth century. That this placement brought with it the tradition of Schubert's *Mädchencharakter* made the composer a particularly attractive symbol for the Jung-Wien circle, since both its defenders and its critics agreed that modernism's preoccupation with the condition of women was among its most distinctive features.

In a remarkable overview of contemporary Viennese literature in 1902, Rudolf Lothar, a feuilletonist for the *Neue freie Presse*, recognized this common theme among the writers whose appropriation of Schubert will occupy the forthcoming chapters, even as he attempted to differentiate their individual approaches. For Lothar, "the feminine note" marked the entire Jung-Wien group. He recognized in Peter Altenberg a "virtuoso of receptiveness to all impressions of the external life" who "vibrated the delicate strings of the feminine, tender, inner life." Lacking "that certain power which manifests itself in more austere composition," Hugo von Hofmannsthal's feminine nature (which he shared with Bahr and Richard Beer-Hofmann) "secretly dissolves life with his dreams." Arthur Schnitzler's output exploited the female character in, "as it were, a contrary sense. Schnitzler always occupies himself with the woman. But he actually has a quiet contempt for her. For him, the woman takes care of the man to her ruin, but the man regards the woman as unimportant. And in an odd way in doing so it is nevertheless always the woman who outmatches Schnitzler's weak, irresolute men in the strength of feeling and of life."[5] For Lothar, the gendered nature of any writer's work differentiated him from his colleagues. The poetry of Julius von Ludassy, for example, displayed a masculine talent whose power was in complete contrast to the "feminine Jung-Wieners."

Although Schnitzler, Hofmannsthal, and Altenberg (whose preoccupation with the composer warrants its own chapter) responded in unique ways to the legacy that equated feminine nature with Schubert, they shared a common understanding of the tradition as one in which the composer stood for a particular type, the *femme fragile*. She was often from the *petite bourgeoisie* in cases where class was a significant component of the narrative; she was invariably young, at least to the extent that she was emotionally and physically inexperienced; and her naiveté and purity were recognizable features that authors could exploit to suit their own creative goals. The *süße Mädel* is the most familiar designation for such a woman, whom Lothar recognized as especially characteristic of Schnitzler's quintessential suburban girl or *Vorstadtmädel*: "a soft, sentimental, loving creature who is alien to any revolt against men and fate," and whose sexual submissiveness to an egotistic man, arising from a pitiably kind-hearted philosophy, is so poignant that it "actually makes one contemptuous of the woman."[6] The fact that Schnitzler used the term *süße Mädel* for a character in his play *Reigen* (1903) contributed to its association with him. The figure has a long tradition in the Austrian theater, reaching as far back as Johann Nestroy's comedy, *Das Mädl aus der Vorstadt* (1841), and we have encountered elements of her character in *Volkstücke* inspired by the biographical fragments of Schubert's relationship with Therese Grob in the first volume of this study.

As well as being exploited as a dramatic convention, the "sweet young thing" was a reality in fin-de-siècle Viennese society. In his autobiography, Schnitzler recalled his brief liaison with "blond little Anni," a prototype of the *süße Mädel*: "tainted without being sinful, innocent without being chaste, passably sincere and a little mendacious, most of the time quite good-spirited and yet sometimes riddled with fleeting traces of worry; not entirely exemplary as the good little middle-class daughter, and yet, as a sweetheart, the most selfless and respectable creature imaginable."[7] That Lothar defined such women in terms of Schnitzler's work was a tacit acknowledgment that, of all the authors associated with Jung-Wien modernism, his was the most frequently cited name. Among the individuals who attended the closing of the Café Griensteidl in 1897, he was the one writer mentioned by every newspaper that covered the event. The *Neues Wiener Tagblatt* called him the "conquering leader of the moderns" even as it enjoyed a typical Viennese joke: "Literary Jung-Wien provided a pretty strong contingent; one saw plenty of youth, young, very young youth, and older mature youth."[8]

In his plays and prose, Schnitzler created characters who do not engage one another merely for the purposes of aesthetic contemplation. As Marc Weiner has argued, their musical activity and the very works they listen to and perform represent their relationships.[9] Schnitzler used Schubert as a symbol of both gender and class because he could rely on his audience's association of the composer's works with domestic music-making. Schubert stands for a woman who is the object of desire for men above her in rank and who is naive about the sexual negotiations necessary for her to improve her standing. Lothar understood that Schnitzler's eroticism was not designed to elevate the woman whose Schubertian nature makes her more attractive even as it risks contributing to her emotional undoing. An apparently nostalgic icon, Schnitzler's composer becomes party to the author's revelation of the unequal social transactions between men and women, and is thereby absorbed into a critique of the very culture that had embraced the myth of Schubert's *Mädchencharakter*. Schnitzler the modernist recognizes the artificiality of contemporary life and, beyond this acknowledgment, exposes the hypocrisy of social relationships by exploiting the collision between innocence and sexuality, with Schubert serving as a familiar image of the former.

Among the characters created by Schnitzler that Lothar had in mind was Christine Weiring in the play *Liebelei* (1895), a young woman who certainly incarnates the sweet and innocent female who is all the more desirable to men because of these very traits. Christine is pitilessly described as just such an archetype in a conversation between her lover, the soldier Fritz, and his friend Theodor:

> Theodor: For such a sweet young thing, I'd trade ten demonic women.
> Fritz: There's no comparison.
> Theodor: We hate the same women who we love—and we love only those women who are indifferent to us.[10]

Theodor's paramour, the dressmaker Mizi, understands as he does that such liaisons are always destined to end and thus demand emotional apathy from both partners. Christine, however, wishes for a more lasting relationship; she quickly becomes infatuated with Fritz without realizing his true nature. Schnitzler could be certain of conveying the fact that Christine represented the innocent and virtuous female of contemporary Viennese society by manipulating a familiar symbol during the scene in which Fritz visits her in her rooms after their affair has begun. There, he notices a marble bust:

> Fritz (sitting): Who is that man there above the stove?
> Christine (didactically): That's Schubert, of course.
> Fritz (standing): Really.
> Christine: Because father likes him so much. Father also once wrote songs, very pretty ones.
> Fritz: No more?
> Christine: No more. (Pause.)
> Fritz (sitting): This sure is cozy![11]

It is no coincidence that when the duplicitous Fritz encounters Christine in a room containing a bust of Schubert, Schnitzler has him identify the scene as *gemütlich* because that word characterized a world that was as comforting as it was specious. The composer's likeness is only one of several furnishings that Schnitzler describes in order to convey the appearance of middle-class domestic comfort while at the same time suggesting the female protagonist's lack of awareness. As Martin Swales notes, the pictures that adorn the walls "all embody situations involving home and, by implication, there is in each picture a considerable emotional loading of the situation."[12] The objects that surround Christine represent her as respectable but also as materially and intellectually limited. She is embarrassed when Fritz notices that, along with works by Schiller and Wilhelm Hauff, she has an encyclopedia whose volumes only go through the letter G. She also possesses *Das Buch für alle*, whose contents she has not read but whose pictures she has looked at. That Christine's world is at its base one of pretense is suggested by the last object Fritz notices: a vase of dusty artificial flowers.

In critiquing his culture, Schnitzler used the familiar image of Schubert as part of a code that was easily recognizable to a contemporary audience. By revealing the real purposes behind his characters' uses of that symbol, he exposed the mendacity that underlay it. Christine's father is, for example, a hypocrite. He has his daughter's room fitted with cultural representations of chaste virtue like Schubert's bust, but he ignores the consequences of her love, preferring to consider it a mere indulgence. For her part, Christine is blind to Fritz's true nature and is unable to accept the outcomes that such a relationship in Viennese society make inevitable, outcomes that Schnitzler portrays in the two other principal female characters. Christine fails to realize the casualness and evanescence of her liaison, unlike her friend Mizi, nor does she recognize the fate of her married neighbor, Katharina Binder, who is consigned to a loveless union with a hosiery worker. When Christine finally learns that Fritz has died in a duel defending the name of another woman, she utters a despairing realization of her condition that precipitates her taking her own life:

> I was nothing more to him than an amusement—and he has died for another woman! And I—who worshiped him!—Didn't he realize this? That I gave everything to him that I could give, that I would have died for him—that he has been my master and my happiness.[13]

Christine's tragedy lies in her incapacity to confront the fraudulence of the sentimental future she has imagined, which is as nostalgic and illusory as the tradition of Schubert reception to which Schnitzler alludes. As a theatrical prop, Schnitzler's choice of a bust of the composer certainly was practical, but it was also a familiar icon, since Schubert heads were readily available and inexpensive commodities in fin-de-siècle Vienna. Members of Schnitzler's audience may have owned copies of well-known busts by either Josef Alois Dialer or Karl Kundmann, the former created in 1830 for the composer's monument in the Währing Cemetery and the latter modeled for the statue of Schubert in the Stadtpark. That same public would have recognized marble versions of the same two works standing sentinel on either side of Julius Schmid's commemorative painting of a cozy, fictitious *Schubertiade* when they entered the Schubert-Ausstellung at the Künstlerhaus commemorating the centennial of the composer's birth. Such images may have been popular, but as the Secessionist critic Ludwig Hevesi observed in 1903, they were patently inferior because they were mere stylized versions. Dialer's bust in particular was wickedly described by Hevesi as "round as a ball," putting him in mind of a "bumpkin from Himmelpfortgrund" (the suburb where Schubert was born).[14] In *Liebelei*, Schubert's head is no more a representation of artistic reality than is the romanticized life desired by its female owner. This object is destined to offer a false comfort to Christine, and her Schubertian nature will prove to be her undoing.

The very vulnerability of Schnitzler's feminine protagonist makes her the target of male desire, and the cultural safeguards available to her are soon demolished by passion.

In Schnitzler's novella *Die Nächste* (1899), Schubert again emerges as a representation of idealized femininity in the person of Therese, who has had "the simple education of a young girl of the *petite bourgeoisie*" and whose fiancé has recently died.[15] It is her beautiful voice, however, that attracts Gustav, a young man who lodges with her family and whose previous love had married someone else and left Vienna four years earlier. Within a few months they are wed. Their union is as happy as it is hermetic. Gustav withdraws from his old acquaintances, the couple conceives no children, and their occasional visitors consist only of her father or one female friend, who sometimes accompanies her hostess's singing. Aside from her voice, Therese contributes little in the way of wealth to the household, but she possesses the two great virtues of *bürgerlich* womanhood: virginity and thriftiness.

Gustav's greatest joy is to listen to Therese's solo performances, and Schnitzler chooses to have her sing Schubert's music in order to seal his protagonist's sense of *gemütlich* bliss:

> Therese frequently sang alone, however, and he loved that most of all. In her voice there resounded in him her soul, wonderfully blended from purity and fervor. Some nights he begged her to sing very softly a Schubert song. She then did so, during which she drew herself near to him, brought her lips quite close to his ear, and then the darkness of the room was all full of shivers of delight and admiration.[16]

The purity of Therese's *Mädchencharakter* is conveyed by her rendition of the composer's music, which in turn provides the symbolic terrain for ostensible domestic intimacy. Therese dies unexpectedly, however, after which Gustav meets another woman of the same name who resembles her in every way except for her voice, her most palpably Schubertian feature. The woman turns out to be a prostitute, a realization that only contributes to Gustav's inner struggle between an emotional yearning to reanimate his dead wife, whom he constantly thinks about both while awake and while asleep, and his physical desire for a woman who in appearance so strikingly resembles her. After a restless night, he calmly decides to go to the woman's apartment where he is unnerved by a sensory overload even as he tunes out her voice:

> Gustav sat there motionless and let her speak . . . How had he come to this! He, who only a few months ago had been the husband of a virtuous woman, who belonged to him alone and to none other than him . . . What did he want here? What had he to do with this? . . . Where were his desires, his wishes? . . . He stood up, as if he wanted to depart. She too got up, spread her arms around his neck and pulled him to her. He was so close to her that he could see only the light of her eyes. Again the fragrance of her

neck rose up to him, at the same time he felt her lips hot upon his . . . Truly, the kiss was none other than the one he received the previous autumn. It lodged in him with the same softness, the same warmth, the same closeness, the same pleasure . . .[17]

Gustav's logical thought patterns disintegrate as he is overwhelmed by the sight, smell, and touch of Therese's double. He blocks out the one trait that might bring him back to reality, because she does not possess the Schubertian voice of his deceased wife. Shutting out this feature from his consciousness allows Gustav to succumb to the woman's advances. After their coupling, he is desperate to confirm that the sleeping figure next to him is Therese. When she awakens, he implores her repeatedly to speak, but she only opens her arms to him again. In response, he takes the pin from her hat and fatally stabs her in the breast with it. Only then does he give voice to the situation by calling out "Murder! Murder!" from the open window and sitting back to await his fate. The final line ironically furnishes the scene with an intrusive noise: the unmusical reality of the loud ringing of the doorbell.

There is no shortage of biographical and contextual material that bears upon some of these narrative details. The significance of Therese's voice and its silencing is in part a reversal of the female protagonist's fate in Schnitzler's earlier novella, *Der Empfindsame* (1895), in which a singer regains her voice as a result of acquiring a lover. This tale and *Die Nächste* frame events in Schnitzler's own life: his liaison with a singing teacher, Marie Reinhard, resulted in a stillborn child in 1897, and this was followed two years later by the death of the mother. Schnitzler himself had a medical degree, and his most significant contribution to the field was an 1889 case study of six women suffering from aphonia or loss of voice.[18] Although Schnitzler's work frequently has an important autobiographical component, the circumstances of his fictional women did not necessarily reflect the generosity shown by the writer in promoting his own wife's singing career at the same time that the operatic version of *Liebelei*, with music by Franz Neumann, was being readied for its premiere in 1910.[19] By contrast, Christine is a powerless figure: though she is encouraged to become a singer, her principal artistic activity is copying music. She incarnates a type that was a fixture in the hierarchical structures of Viennese culture life, recalling Hans von Bülow's uncharitable apothegm that a woman could never be a creative musician but only a "re-pressed" [*sic*] copyist.[20] Christine's Schubertian muse is tragically not even heard, but remains symbolically mute and eternally frozen in the marble representation of the composer. What she conceives to be love turns out to be an exploitive sexual affair that leads to her final silencing by suicide. A similar sequence of events occurs in *Die Nächste*, only now the unwelcome realization is visited upon the male protagonist who responds with murder. Gustav's attempt to recover an idealized experience with his wife, whose purity is conveyed by her performance of Schubert's ideal music, is undone by a sordid erotic encounter. His nostalgic memory of iconic feminine domesticity clashes with the reality of physical desire. His concomitant weakness results in his killing a prostitute, an ending that would have been familiar literary terrain in an era that also produced Frank Wedekind's *Büchse der Pandora* (1895), whose heroine is brutally dispatched by Jack the Ripper.²¹

Suicide and murder are outcomes that admittedly have a sensational quality, but Schnitzler could still suffuse his protagonists' fates with tragedy even without these more lurid events. His association of Schubert with women of social or economic limitations, their innocence precipitating liaisons that bring about their calamitous end, is again manifest in his novella *Frau Berta Garlan* (1901). The title character is a small-town widow of thirty-two who, as a student, had hoped to become a concert pianist, "eine große Klavier-virtuosin" perhaps modeled upon Clara Schumann. Her ambition, however, is destroyed when her father, in a display of *bürgerlich* rectitude, refuses to allow her to continue attending the conservatory, a decision that also results in the end of her prospects for an artistic career.²² Living in a small town where she endures the tedium of giving piano lessons to indifferent children, Berta can perform only for friends and relatives. She plays Schubert with her nephew and at little Sunday dinner parties given by her brother-in-law while he and his friends play cards:

> Then her brother-in-law turned to her and regarded her with a look, by which she was to be reminded of her duty. She began to play a march of Schubert with a very strong attack. Her brother-in-law turned to her again and said: "softer."
> "That remains a specialty of this house," said Doctor Friedrich, "Tarock with musical accompaniment."²³

Berta's playing Schubert represents the obligations placed upon her by her sex and class. The association between domestic, private music-making and virtuous femininity is again revealed when Berta recalls that, at a local inn's amateur recital shortly after her marriage, she had played two four-hand marches by Schubert with another young woman from the town. Her agitation on that occasion was so great, however, that it overwhelmed her, and so she resolves never to perform in public again. She thus fails to attain her dream, not only because of the social restrictions imposed upon her by family and class, but also because her discomposure in such circumstances is a credible reaction for someone of her sex. Certainly Schnitzler, holder of a medical degree, would have been aware in 1901 of the popular idea of hysteria as a peculiarly feminine malady. The limitations that make a professional career impossible for Berta convince her that her nature is unsuitable for the public world of professional musicians such as her former schoolmate, Emil Lindbach, who has become a famous violin virtuoso. Unlike her, he was born to his career.²⁴

Schnitzler further clarifies his exposure of the hypocrisy of Viennese society with clear musical signs when Berta travels to Vienna to hear Emil play. Emil brings her to his apartment and seduces her. She is interested in marriage, but he desires only the sex, a reality that she gradually comes to comprehend. Berta is a woman of Schubertian limitations. Emil's world is symbolically denied to her when he refuses her request that he allow her to play Beethoven's *Kreutzer Sonata* with him. This paradigm of musical masculinity remains inaccessible to her. When she proposes moving to Vienna, he writes to her suggesting that she come only for one night every four to six weeks, to which she reacts with bitter and ironic self-loathing:

> Yes, right away, my dear sir, I agree to your honorable proposition with pleasure. Indeed, for myself, I desire nothing better! I will get staler here, giving lessons, going crazy in this nest. . . . You will continue to play the violin, turn women's heads, travel, be rich and famous and happy—and every four to six weeks I am allowed one night in some shabby room where you take your women of the street, in a bed where so many have lain before me.[25]

As with Therese and Christine, Berta Garlan's gender and position are defined by her identification with the music of Schubert: private, domestic, innocent, and virtuous. Schnitzler makes this connection in order to provide a modernist critique. The elaborate historical tradition that made Schubert a feminine icon was part of the artificial structure that concealed the inequality in contemporary society. Berta Garlan comes to realize "the monstrous injustice in the world" wherein desire exists for both sexes, but in her culture a woman's need is a sin requiring atonement unless it equals a longing for motherhood.[26] To be sure, Berta plays music by composers other than Schubert, including mazurkas by Chopin, Schumann's *Kreisleriana* and *Albumblatt*, and one movement from a Beethoven sonata that tellingly is neither complete nor identified. Schubert's works, however, appear most often in her repertoire, whether she plays them alone in a domestic setting for her brother-in-law and his friends, with another woman in an amateur public performance, or with her teenage nephew. The latter's subsequent attempt at an amorous advance on Berta takes place when the two practice not Schubert but Beethoven's *Die Weihe des Hauses* Overture with the intention of playing it for the birthday of the young man's father. One guesses that, given this nineteen-year-old youth's attempt at seduction, Schnitzler was enjoying the dual implication of *Weihe* as both consecration and initiation. (The metaphor of Beethoven as the sexual conqueror will be taken up in chapter 6.)

Schnitzler's treatment of the Schubertian *Mädchencharakter* reflects the nature of Viennese modernism. His works dissect the cultural fabric and expose the gap between imagined innocence and contemporary desire. Schubert furnished Schnitzler with a symbol that he could appropriate in order to observe and criticize the very culture that had created it. Yet even as Schnitzler exploited the tension between Schubertian virtue and fin-de-siècle yearning, his own life remained subject to it. The disjunction between the artifice of creativity and the lived reality was a feature of Viennese modernism which meant that its practitioners were often unwilling or unable to free themselves completely from the attractions of tradition, a trait that Bahr had already noted distinguished Austrian literary

Moderne from its German counterparts. Even as writers manipulated the image of the composer, they were not entirely free from its lure. The merging of Schubertian maiden and Jugendstil siren reflected the artist's ambivalence toward women as much as that of society. Schnitzler was merciless in exposing the fate of such women, whose innocence was that of Schubert's *Mädchencharakter*, but he nonetheless turned to the domestic comfort of the composer's music in a moment of private crisis. Although wielding Schubertian symbols with stinging irony, Schnitzler found himself equally prey to the reassuring *Gemütlichkeit* of the composer's work when he wrote in his diary on April 17, 1904, after an unnerving confrontation with his wife Olga, herself a singer:

> Nausea.—To Zank's house, darkness, not able to work, O. cries, me nervous—O. to the theater, but I'm dissuaded because of the crowds.—When she's gone, I cry and have physical cardiac pain. "I have so much to cry about."—Memory of another spring, feeling of loneliness. Distinct sensation of fading youth.—O. comes around eight, sees me turning pages in the notebook; we read the parts under "letter 96." She feels 'like I'm slipping away from her" . . . one should have parted in order not to lose one's way. Serious conversation about it, tears, discussion, during which she said beautiful things and as long ago we became conscious of our love, so that the evening ended calmly (Schubert Lieder).[27]

In Schnitzler's private world, Schubert's music supplied that comforting assurance of Biedermeier domesticity that was characteristic of contemporary Viennese culture but, when filtered through the prism of the author's fiction, belied its social interactions. A decade later, Schnitzler again suggested the solace that could be offered by Schubert's music during wartime when he wrote to Bahr on September 2, 1915—"a time for which the adjective must first be found"—requesting whether Bahr's wife, the singer Anna von Mildenburg, would perform the composer's Lieder at a war charities concert at the Vienna bookstore of Hugo Heller. Schubert, whom Mildenburg "would sing so magnificently and beautifully," was apparently more appropriate to the occasion than the operatic roles of Wagner and Richard Strauss for which she was celebrated.[28]

As Jean Leventhal has detailed, Schnitzler relished a lifelong immersion in music. He learned the piano at a young age, he performed regularly with family and friends, he enjoyed the company of performers and composers, and he often attended concerts. "I adore Schubert more and more," he wrote in his diary on December 3, 1906, after playing the Sonata in A Minor (D. 845, op. 42).[29] The repertoire with which he was familiar included every major figure of the emerging canon who would have been enjoyed by any well-educated and sympathetic individual in fin-de-siècle Vienna, although Schnitzler's fictional characters appreciated an even narrower list, from Bach to Brahms. (Wittgenstein opined that "music came to a full stop with Brahms, and even in Brahms I can begin to hear the sound of machinery.")[30] In describing Schnitzler's relationship with music as a fundamentally secure and positive one, Leventhal rejects Weiner's view that its use in his works exposes the tension between individuals and the social structures in which they exist. "The crisis of musical culture in the twentieth century lies not so much in the individual's relationship to institutions of music, as Weiner claims, but in the disappearance of the rich and lively world of amateur music-making that characterized the world of the bourgeois and upper classes in Schnitzler's lifetime."[31] One might take this view to be relatively benign, in which case it neglects the tragic fate of the people whose desire for an idealized, Schubertian world was often at the mercy of the social codes that dictated human relationships.

In her analysis of the composers that are invoked in *Frau Berta Garlan*, Leventhal emphasizes the disjunction that arises between the public and private music-making worlds of Berta and Emil as individuals. She is less interested in examining these people as representatives of larger groups, whether defined by sex or by class, and the institutions that shape their destiny. Those connections, however, are the ones that have informed a great deal of recent scholarship about Schnitzler. Katherine Arens' overview of this literature treats Schnitzler's work "as extremely political diagnoses of Vienna's gendered and class-based economic and social expectation. In this reading, Schnitzler emerges as a writer with a much broader vision of Viennese and Austrian society than he is often given credit for, writing from within a distinct class position to offer a critique of a class that suffered deeply from a disappointment of its hopes and focus."[32] In her study of *Frau Berta Garlan*, Arens ignores the subject of music, even as other details, such as the painting of a naked woman in the room where Emil seduces Berta, acquire significance worthy of mention. As a writer intimately familiar with music, Schnitzler would have been well aware of the symbolic freight carried by the names of specific composers, and he could count on his readers to understand his use of them in his literary work. However rewarding music was in the author's life, that fulfillment was denied to some of his fictional women by the societal forces that prescribed different roles according to sex.

The same forces that formed those gendered structures also erected a canonic repertoire and the cultural meanings that accrued to individual composers. Schubert certainly was an essential figure in this culture, as Schnitzler must have known. *Frau Berta Garlan* was begun two years after the composer's centennial exhibition, whose opening was likely to have been noted by the author, who attended the closing of the Café Griensteidl on the same day. To judge from Schubert's appearance in Schnitzler's works within a ten-year span at the turn of the century—precisely the time during which the composer was enjoying a much-publicized popularity—the author's private fondness did not prevent him from recognizing that the women who were delineated by Schubert's image and works were prey to a social order that resisted their entry into more public and masculine regions. Schnitzler's affection for music in his own life is without question, but his fictional women, insofar as they are attended by Schubertian symbols, are denied any fulfillment beyond that to be found in the same private and domestic world that the composer represented, and they meet a tragic end when their wish for a fuller life is exploited by the carnal play of male desire. At the same time, the denouement of *Die Nächste* demonstrates that an idealized existence may be no less impossible to attain for a man, especially when he is confronted with and overcome by the reality of consuming passion.

Schnitzler's Schubertian women are part of that larger tendency in fin-de-siècle reception wherein the composer conveyed the inherent innocence of their nature whether they performed his music or merely owned his marble likeness. Yet in every case in which the narrative articulates the *Mädchencharakter* of these women through the symbolic appearance of Schubert, their fate proves to be less a matter of possessing those traits unique to his work and by extension to their sex than of being trapped in a societal straitjacket, demanding that they behave in a manner consistent with the composer's image and leading inexorably to a tragic outcome. The male characters in *Liebelei* and *Frau Berta Garlan* recognize Schubert's music as signaling the vulnerability of its female performers whose circumstances these men are only too willing to exploit or, in the case of Gustav in *Die Nächste*, desperate to recapture. In Gustav's case, the lack of the female voice that sings the composer's Lieder triggers a disastrous outcome, and perhaps his fatal desire to attain the lost Schubertian innocence of his dead wife betrays a psychological weakness that contemporary critics of Jung-Wien literature (if not Schnitzler himself) were quick to deplore as womanly. Schnitzler nonetheless uses the cliché of Schubertian femininity in order to uncover a secret world in which inequitable social transactions take place and ultimately to expose their infamies. There is an unmistakable frisson of voyeurism in the revelation of liaisons that unfold behind closed doors, and the choice of Schubert is designed precisely to assure the authenticity of the intimate domains in which these relationships splinter and break apart.

As the climax of *Die Nächste* suggests, it is not only social interactions but also individual personalities that disintegrate under the force of desire. Once Gustav's love spins uncontrollably toward obsession, Schnitzler conveys his character's inability to comprehend reality by employing a disjointed prose that mirrors his atomized thoughts. The calamitous trajectory of this tale recurs often in Schnitzler's work, and it cast an influential shadow on contemporary literature. There are, for example, telling similarities between *Die Nächste* and Richard Schaukal's novella *Die Sängerin* (1905). In both stories, a woman's musical voice becomes a compelling fixation for an otherwise respectable man. In both cases, Schubert's music surfaces as a symbol.

As with Schnitzler, Schaukal provides a conflict between the staid rigidity of Viennese middle-class society and the erotically charged attractions of fin-de-siècle culture. The protagonist, Alexander Schreiner, is the incarnation of sedate Austrian *Bürgertum* until he encounters the singer Lucia Wendtheim-Corma. The second half of the narrative charts Schreiner's psychic unraveling as he discards the familiar icons of family and position in the vain and ultimately tragic pursuit of a woman, Lucia, whose allure proves to be irresistible even as it remains unobtainable. His hopeless quest becomes the final turn on a downward spiral of self-delusion that culminates in his decision to kill Lucia during her forth-coming recital.

As he stands expectantly in the shadow of a kiosk outside the theater, Schreiner passes into a hallucinatory state, seized by a desire so strong that he loses any sense of himself. Even as the fragmenting sentences (complete with ellipses) recall those that convey Gustav's thoughts at the conclusion of *Die Nächste*, Schubert's name appears on an old poster advertising a past recital of Lucia's:

> She just had to come. It was curtain time. Of course, she would not stay at home, this pleasure seeker, this . . . ! It would please him to hurl ugly names at her. . . . As he stood there, taking pains to give as far as possible the unselfconsciously careless appearance of a passerby, his idle gaze fell upon the kiosk in front of him. Something had attracted him, a force that subjugated him without his sensing it. . . "Lucia Corma" stood in obtrusive, thick letters, which he knew so well, printed on a yellow poster. The recent announcement. He spelled the strangely melodic name. He read on mechanically. The program. Along with Schubert's name the assistance of the accompanist came upon him. . . Hugo Wolf? Really? Had she at that time sung Hugo Wolf? Possibly, possibly, he said to himself. He had certainly not paid any attention. . . . Ticket price. . . And once again his gaze ascended to the uncannily bright letters of her name: Lucia Corma. The I-dot was as thick as the velvet balls on a Spanish bolero hat. He submerged himself in this I-dot, which began to lose its outline, spreading itself out like a blurring inkblot, spreading itself over the entire paper. . . He turned away. It was as if he had forgotten something, as if something had struck him that he would still have to test without fail.[33]

When Schreiner first heard Lucia Corma perform, he had been too preoccu-pied with looking at her to take notice of what she was singing. Now, he vainly tries to remember and, as he is doing so, the names of two composers collide in his consciousness. Schubert's name appears on the kiosk, but that of Hugo Wolf teasingly intrudes upon his memory as the possibility of a recollected perform-ance, the one that had first brought the singer to Schreiner's attention. Two musical sensibilities, one existing in the tangible present and the other emanat-ing from a dreamy past, jostle each other even as Schreiner's old existence of middle-class normality (Schaukal calls it a "slug's race") is confronted by the tan-talizing illusion represented by Lucia Corma. Schaukal captures the moment Schreiner loses his grasp of both reality and identity: the self dissolves just as the dot on the symbolic "I" (his *ich*) also melts into an inkblot. (Only in 1921 did the Swiss psychologist Hermann Rorschach publish the findings of his famous test.)

Once inside the concert hall, Schreiner undergoes a rapid change from fever-ish shakes and laughter to a disembodied calmness once the revolver finally dis-charges. The reader cannot be absolutely certain that the singer's shriek and collapse is due to her being hit or to the terror of the moment. The final sen-tence, juxtaposing Schreiner's eerie silence with the violence of many hands thrusting him toward the exit, echoes Schnitzler's denouement. Schaukal had written *Die Sängerin* in 1904, and doubtless he was aware that his fellow Viennese Wolf had died in an asylum the previous year. Equally probable is his awareness that Schubert, of all composers, could serve as the representative of a familiar and well-worn tradition from which Schreiner would become unhinged.

None of the three works by Schnitzler in which Schubert appears had yet been published at the time he had his first dramatic success, *Anatol* (1892). That circumstance made the play's assessment by Hugo von Hofmannsthal, who had just graduated from the gymnasium, all the more remarkable since he so pithily analyzed both the work's author and his modernism even as he located Schubert within its orbit. In describing Schnitzler as a specifically Viennese writer, Hofmannsthal recalled Bahr's notion that modern Austrian literature engaged in a dialogue with its cultural past:

> He [Schnitzler] is a poet, that is, a man who loves the contrived life, who yearns for everything long ago and lost, for some scattered, naive, fragrant, laughing lightness of life; he is therefore only a poet, but perhaps really a Viennese poet, because among themselves they have nothing so much in common as this mysterious nostalgia for sweet, childish bliss. This bliss has [quoting from *Anatol*] the "soft charm of a spring evening" . . . it resides somewhere outside, on the outskirts, where there still are so many gardens and where on warm nights many dizzying violins play from little twilit rooms. Perhaps it even resides in our yearning for the time when Schubert's songs were new.[34]

Schubert's Lieder signify the cultural memories of a *gemütlich* existence that was unique to Vienna, but Hofmannsthal is quick to recognize that this representation masks a less nostalgic reality in regard to human relationships. Schnitzler's conceptualization of love is not one that is viewed directly; rather, it is seen through a multihued refraction along its boundaries. For Hofmannsthal, Schnitzler is less concerned with grand events than he is with "what stands shadowy and uncanny behind them, like the sense behind the symbol, like the nightmare behind the dream image: life, mortality, being dead." Having reread *Anatol*, Hofmannsthal finds it to be "like an uncanny allegory: among the nervous, prattling little figures, the Medusa-like of life looks out from the shadows: the mindless, the mysterious, the lonely, the oblivious and dead incomprehension among those who love; the hollow knowledge, as from guilt; the twilit foreboding of lost infinity, choked, dissipated wonder."[35] (The playing of violins is the only aural image that connects Hofmannsthal's poem of 1892, "Prologue zu dem Buch *Anatol*," with his prose observations about the play, but the counterpoint between appearance and reality suffuses the imagery of its verse, including the recurring use of the word "gleiten." This sense of slipping away was an essential component in Hofmannsthal's concept of contemporary culture: for example, in 1893, he wrote: "Today two things appear to be modern: the analysis of life and the flight from life."[36] The choice is one with which Schnitzler's protagonists are constantly confronted. Coincidentally, "entgleiten" was the word Schnitzler used in his diary to describe the evaporating relationship with his wife that was subsequently ameliorated by Schubert's songs).

Hofmannsthal's description of Schnitzler's work as revealing "the sense behind the symbol" stands as an acute encapsulation of Viennese modernism, one to which Hofmannsthal himself gave poetic form when he invoked Schubert's name in a poem written within a year of his reading *Anatol*. In "Zu lebenden Bildern" (1893), the composer serves the function of an apodictic signifier of private space. The poem's central section is flanked by a prologue and epilogue, but their modest lengths belie the epic character suggested by these designations. Rather, this structural frame provides a representation of the sequestered poetic space that is itself a symbol for the imagination of a particularly sensitive individual who is amenable to the work's imagery. In the first line of the prologue, Hofmannsthal refuses to have his readers sit expectantly before a stage, with its implication of a shared, public setting, and instead, in the central section, he locates them "alone in a twilit and silent room." Echoing its form, the work's interiority is emphasized by the last lines of the prologue, in which Hofmannsthal declares: "What matters here is the diminutive art that makes no claims, but only willingly may be claimed."[37] In the epilogue, Hofmannsthal concludes that art rather than nature is the goddess who possesses noble grace, and he returns to extol "the little things, artistically shy and tender that surround us, which ennoble life."[38]

Hofmannsthal's valorization of the intimacy of art—the "kleine Kunst"—prepares the way for his introduction of Schubert, or rather for a particular appropriation of the composer, one that strategically ignores the tradition criticizing Schubert's inability to control large forms and genres. Hofmannsthal's Schubert is instead the same one who occupies the quiet niche of Stößl's received myth, or the one whose music is sung by Gustav's wife in *Die Nächste*, or, as we shall see, the one who pervades Peter Altenberg's literary vignettes and photograph collection. In the middle section, the poet enumerates sensations that affect the individual who, sealed within the formal space of the poem, the literal space of a silent room, and the figurative space of the imagination, nods off with eyes half shut, "not fully awake, nor completely asleep and dreaming." Central to the images that appear is that of Schubert:

> Then fairy tales come to mind: the fountain
> In the forest, and in the fountain Melusine . . .
> And grandmother's image: petitely old-fashioned.
> And in between there sounds softly a Schubert song,
> Gracefully old-fashioned, full of soft sadness,
> And sweet, as if the yellow summer moonlight
> Fell into languid gardens . . .
> So images come, images go, blurring,
> And all is intimate, lovely yet unfamiliar;
> Not entirely a state of wakefulness, not quite a dream.[39]

Some of this language calls upon the opaque metaphors of symbolism that were common to a great deal of fin-de-siècle literature. In the lines that precede the appearance of Schubert's song, Hofmannsthal conflates the legendary water spirit of old *Märchen* with the title character of Maurice Maeterlinck's play *Pelléas et Mélisande*, published in the preceding year. Yet it is less interesting to ask whether the poet's inspiration was a German fairy tale or a Belgian drama than to see that he placed Schubert as the mediating symbol between feminine archetypes of the seductive and the maternal. Schubert's unnamed song itself is rendered in terms that recall decades of appreciative reception. It is "altmodisch lieblich, voll von leiser Wehmut, und süß." Now, however, the composer's music is in the service of the smudging of the senses that paradoxically leads to a new consciousness.

In a contemporary essay, "Poesie und Leben" (1896), Hofmannsthal indicated that the fundamental element of the poet's art consisted of words that hover between "God and creation."[40] In Hofmannsthal's verse of the 1890s, words often serve as intercessory signs, as is the case with the spring wind in "Vorfrühling" (1892) or the ships in "Manche freilich . . ." (1896).[41] In "Zu lebenden Bildern," Schubert bridges the competing recollections of two quite disparate female emblems, Melusine and grandmother, and their attendant thematic baggage of exoticism and domesticity. At the same time, in Jung-Wien aesthetics, words are endlessly ambiguous, a condition that is replicated in "Zu lebenden Bildern," in which the sensation of the composer's music synesthetically evokes images that are paradoxically experienced as both intimate and unfamiliar. By indicating only "ein Schubertlied," Hofmannsthal plays upon the reader's recollection of something reassuringly familiar, but by leaving it unnamed, he omits the certainty of meaning that a title and its text might provide. The composer and his work are neither entirely tangible nor imaginary, and thus their use conflates awareness and memory.

In situating Schubert's music as a mediating symbol between feminine archetypes of the seductive and the maternal, Hofmannsthal creates a modernist emblem that threatens to annihilate the artificial line dividing reality and dream. Indeed, this literary maneuver recalls elements of Hofmannsthal's definition of contemporary modernism in the essay "Gabriele d'Annunzio," published in the same year as the collection of verse that includes "Zu lebenden Bildern," even as it mirrors Bahr's description in "Das junge Österreich," which also appeared in 1893. When Hofmannsthal writes "old furniture and young nervousness are modern," he offers a duality that echoes the pairing of female figures in his poem. Modernism requires the artist to engage in "the instinctive, almost somnambulistic submission to every manifestation of the beautiful, to a color-chord, to a glistening metaphor, to a wondrous allegory."[42] In this creative project, a Schubert song, hitherto so mundanely familiar, becomes transformed into the one aural sign of dreamlike revelation. This phenomenon speaks to the so-called "crisis of language," which has been identified by scholars as a condition of fin-de-siècle Viennese literature. For Hofmannsthal, the crisis reached a

creative flashpoint in 1902 with his publication of the letter by the fictive Lord
Chandos, in whom Hofmannsthal famously incarnated the writer who had come
to apprehend that poetic language was insufficient to represent experience, a
realization that finally caused Hofmannsthal to abandon poetry for drama.[43]

When Hofmannsthal's poetry first appeared under the pseudonym of Loris, it created a sensation in German and Austrian literary circles, although the androgyny
inherent in the writer's youth seems to have played a role in his reception. Thus,
Stefan George's first encounter with the sixteen-year-old in May 1891 precipitated
a series of gifts ranging from roses to a signed copy of his own collection of verse,
Hymnen, and to a transcription of Stéphane Mallarmé's *L'après-midi d'un faune* sanctioned by the poet himself, all of which suggest an "undercurrent of passionate
courtship" that unnerved the younger man.[44] When Bahr met Hofmannsthal, he
described him as "Cherubin" (suggesting the amorous young page in Mozart's *The
Marriage of Figaro*) with "a smooth, slender, pageboy body of gymnastic grace."
Bahr recalled Loris's "soft, caressing hand, the tender hand of a woman very much
in love. . . . Very young, just twenty, and utterly Viennese. . . . Merry, trusting
brown eyes, like a young girl's," which he was fond of casting in sidelong glances
of naive coquetry.[45] Two years later, when Stefan Zweig attended a reading by
Hofmannsthal, he was similarly struck by the poet's feminine characteristics: "a
slim, inconspicuous young man . . . with his soft, incipient mustache and his elastic figure, [he] appeared to be even younger than I had expected him to be. . . .
It was only in his opening sentences that I was aware of the fact that his voice was
unlovely, ofttimes close to a falsetto and near to breaking; soon his talk bore us
aloft high and free, so that we were barely aware of his voice or his face. He spoke
without a script, without notes, and possibly without careful preparation, but out
of his natural feeling for form each sentence was rounded out to perfection."[46]
Zweig observed that this and subsequent encounters made Hofmannsthal the literary model for the teenage Zweig and his schoolmates, the memory of whose
intellectual companionship could be synesthetically triggered by recalling
Schubert's music in a manner reminiscent of Hofmannsthal's own verse: " 'Thou
noble art! how oft, when sorrow thrill'd me . . .' Whenever that immortal song of
Schubert resounds, in a sort of plastic vision I see us sitting slump-shouldered on
our miserable school benches, and then on our way home, with glowing excited
faces, criticizing poems, reciting, passionately forgetting all bonds of time and
space, truly 'into a better world upborne.' "[47]

   The hagiography of the Schubert reception made the composer particularly
well suited to become an attractive icon for young writers in Vienna at the
century's end. His creative output had seemed to pour out of him without effort
during a remarkably short life span. When Zweig first heard Hofmannsthal speak
without recourse to any notes, he had been overwhelmed by the young man's
"natural feeling for form," although Zweig considered that Hofmannsthal's
greatest work had been completed by the age of twenty-four. Moreover, a
composer whose achievement had not been derailed by personal relationships

with women was likely to be embraced by members of a self-consciously "young generation" who considered that such liaisons constituted "time lost" from the pursuit of the aesthetic life.[48] The concomitant androgyny of youth, which writers saw in each other as well as themselves, found a hospitable resonance in Schubert's *Mädchencharakter*. Just as Bahr recognized these features in the young Hofmannsthal, so too did the latter observe the same characteristics in the work of Altenberg, who, like Bahr, counted Schubert as his favorite composer. Reviewing Altenberg's first novel, *Wie ich es sehe* (1896), Hofmannsthal wrote: "Thus the face of the poet, which was submerged in a hundred stories, floats to the surface. A very stylised face, with a great complicated simplicity. With feminine eyes so to speak, or what is called feminine in men."[49]

Beyond the estimation of individual writers, however, it was not unheard of for an observer at the turn of the century to opine that Austria's literature revealed an unmistakably feminine nature. Tadeusz Rittner, educated in Vienna and a regular contributor to Polish newspapers in Krakow and Lemberg, recognized that the writers of Jung-Wien represented only that aspect of youth distinguished by an unremitting indolence of such intensity that divisions no longer existed between dream and reality or illusion and truth:

> This half sad and half ironic laughter characterizes the entire local milieu, the entire emotional life, especially of the local art, the literary Jung-Wien. This womanliness, this softness, this helplessness contrary to life and its challenges, opposed to all enemies . . . alike, whether this enemy is stupidity, passion, man, or fate. This sweet *laisser aller*, this weakly smiling apathy, this indulgence even for transgressions and for the innate weaknesses of one's fellow creatures, this hideous, unhappy tolerance, which nullifies the energies, anneals the heart, cripples every attempt to set apart from this or that moral affliction, all unhealthy activities.[50]

For Rittner, writers like Schnitzler, Hofmannsthal, Altenberg, and Bahr were as disinclined to confront issues in the real world as they were to create characters willing to do so. If Schnitzler's subsequent work would prove more socially engaged than this analysis suggests, Rittner's critique was at least an accurate assessment of Hofmannsthal before the turn of the century. For the young Hofmannsthal, the problems of contemporary society were both artificial and unimportant. As he wrote to Edgar Karg von Bebenburg on June 18, 1895, what passed for social questions consisted of superficial stuff that was so remote and lifeless that it appeared not to be real at all, but rather "as though from afar one were watching through a telescope a herd of deer." That which appeared on the surface, the "outer layers," was as difficult to recognize as that which remained hidden beneath it.[51]

Bahr was remarkably prescient in observing that the young Hofmannsthal was as feminine in appearance as he was "utterly Viennese" in character, since Hofmannsthal was later to exploit these traits in his own prose. In the 1910 story "Lucidor" (which served as the basis for *Arabella*, his last operatic collaboration with Richard Strauss, even as it antedated by one year Octavian's impersonation of the chambermaid Mariandel in *Der Rosenkavalier*), there is a girl disguised as a boy "of thirteen or fourteen years," the age that, as we shall see, was of such symbolic importance for Altenberg's appreciation of Schubert. Strauss too may have noticed the aptness of recalling Schubert's music in relation to such feminine figures, given the melodic reminiscence of "Wiegenlied" (D. 498; op. 98, no. 2), sung by the three nymphs in *Ariadne auf Naxos*.[52] The tendency to equate Austria with femininity also hovers over the assessment of the country's spirit by Felix Salten, a canny chronicler of the Viennese mentality, in an article written on the eve of World War I for a popular German illustrated weekly, *Über Land und Meer*. Salten noted that the sentimental novels by Rudolf Hans Bartsch (including presumably *Schwammerl*, that most treacly of fin-de-siècle fictions inspired by Schubert's life), even when they took place in the city, "still appear somehow rustic." By comparison, the popular religious and historical novels of Enrica Handel-Mazzetti were "more masculine." Salten concluded: "We find connections and relationships in all Austrian figures, in the high-spirited, gifted chief of the general staff [Conrad von] Hötzendorf as in [the actor Alexander] Girardi, in the theatrical splendor of [the singer Anna von] Mildenburg just as in the grace of female statues carved by Edmund Hellmer. A common line passes through all of this to us, all this shines around us like the tinge of a common color."[53] One had to possess a particularly modernist sensibility to write an article, in the year in which World War I erupted, in which one equated the nation's highest military figure with a leading comic actor, with one of its most celebrated sopranos, and with the figures adorning the Kastalia fountain in the Arkadenhof of the university.

In Hofmannsthal's reception of Schubert, the features common to the otherwise disparate Viennese figures cited by Salten were considerably magnified by the outbreak of the war, during which Hofmannsthal's invocation of the composer suggests a triangulation of the Schubertian *echter Wiener* and *Mädchencharakter* with Hofmannsthal's own cultural self-identification as an Austrian in a crumbling, feminized empire. As with many of his contemporaries, the war incited in Hofmannsthal an initial patriotism that proved to be as evanescent as it was naive. Indeed, it may have been his generation's disengagement from politics and retreat into the aesthetic life that contributed to their early enthusiasm for the war effort, only to do an about-face as the reality of the carnage became known.[54] During this period, Hofmannsthal's treatment of the legacy of Austrian culture went one step further, from the feminization of the individual to the feminization of the state. His essay "Worte zum Gedächtnis des Prinzen Eugen," written in December 1914 in the immediate wake of mobilization, gave way one year later to "Wir Österreicher und Deutschland," in which he articulated a strikingly pronounced gendered paradigm: Austria and Germany as feminine and masculine. The traits of a clear mind, the strength to act, and unimpaired virility were imported from the German soul via such figures as Prince Eugene of Savoy and Beethoven.[55] Two years later, in an essay of 1917, "Wir Preusser und

Österreicher," Hofmannsthal drew up two lists that contrasted Prussia's belief in the state with his own country's love of home. Enumerating the traits that differentiated the citizenry of the two nations, Hofmannsthal compared the more efficient, manly, and severe Prussian to the Austrian's humaneness and underaged appearance.[56] Such comparisons of course had been part of the baggage of the Schubert reception (especially when juxtaposed against that of Beethoven) for more than half a century, a fact of which Hofmannsthal—who expressed admiration in 1912 for Bartsch's *Schubert-Roman*—was surely aware. These qualities also characterized modernists like Hofmannsthal himself, insofar as they are attributable to the figure of Hans Karl in Hofmannsthal's drama *The Difficult Man* (*Der Schwierige*, 1921), a character with whom the playwright apparently identified.[57]

Hofmannsthal was not the first Austrian writer to represent his country in less than masculine terms. The seeds for this image already lie in the anthropomorphic comparison offered by Grillparzer in his drama *König Ottokars Glück und Ende* (1823), in which he apostrophized the nation as an idealized realm: "Oh, good land! Oh, fatherland! In between the child Italy and the man Germany, there you lay, the rosy-cheeked youth."[58] To be sure, Grillparzer had crafted a historical tragedy that issued a warning against recent disastrous imperial designs, which, although Napoleonic in their origins, nonetheless precipitated the banning of the play in Metternich's Vienna until 1825. Three-quarters of a century later, however, the European political landscape included a unified and aggressive German state whose capital invited descriptions that were not necessarily flattering to its Habsburg counterpart, at least in terms of diplomatic stature and influence.

By the time Hofmannsthal's generation had reached literary maturity, comparisons of Berlin's arrogance and Viennese *Gemütlichkeit* were evident in everything from city planning to interior design to cooking. In a sketchbook of 1896, Bahr appreciatively quoted Ludwig Speidel's feuilleton, "Schwind und Mörike": "As Berlin is the city of men, so is Vienna the city of women, of beautiful women."[59] There is also an unmistakably gendered cast to the pianist Artur Schnabel's comparison of the two capitals in the 1890s. The nature of Vienna was one "of jesting defeatism and precious, playful morbidity [and] gradual decay. Now, Berlin seemed quite the opposite. There was the atmosphere of energy, of growing confidence, activity, alertness, and while in Vienna the character of public life was still dominated by a rather effete aristocracy, in Berlin the self-made man marked the character of his city."[60] In this milieu, Schnabel, who assumed credit for being the first pianist to play Schubert's sonatas in public with any regularity, recalled that at that time the composer's shorter keyboard pieces "were a playground for sentimental governesses, for 'Victorian' spinsters," and that even his songs were judged to be "too trivial to deserve the appreciation of the initiated."[61] When, at the end of the century, Bahr opined that Klimt's *Schubert at the Piano* was the loveliest painting by an Austrian, he did so in order to illustrate the difference from Germans: "I only know that I become angry when someone asks me if I am a German. No, I answer, I am not a German; I am an Austrian. One retorts, but that is not a nation. I say, it has been a nation, we are just different from the Germans, something for ourselves. Define it! Well, how can one 'define' it? But it is to be seen in this Schubert. This stillness, this mildness, this splendor of a *bürgerlich* diffidence—that is our Austrian nature."[62]

Hofmannsthal was also attracted to the location of the composer as an iconic representation of a lost Austria. In 1920, he wrote an introduction to a compilation of old-master drawings from the collection of his friend, the writer and art patron Benno Geiger, to which was appended one of Geiger's poems, "Deutschlands Sterbegesang." Hofmannsthal introduced the poem as a demonstration of Geiger's capacity to transcend the melancholy of the era with the melancholy of understanding. In the wake of the empire's dissolution and the realization that Schubertian Alt-Wien was even more of an unrecoverable cultural phantom than before, the poem interprets the composer's song as a kind of Austrian *Liebestod*:

> And I have time, oh so much time for everything!
> And I gladly listen to the longest Lied,
> That for me my Schubert, with velvet sound
> Composes at dawn, in deathly repose for me.[63]

Hofmannsthal was doubtless attracted to this poetic rendering of the composer, since it echoed his own feelings. In contributing to a prospectus for a series entitled *Österreischiche Bibliothek*, he included a volume edited by Felix Braun, *Schubert im Freundeskreis*: "Here is the purest site of that spiritually musical Vienna of the *Vormärz*, the purest fragrance of a time whose humanity and friendliness, whose grace and security has for us today grown almost into a fairy tale."[64] Recall that, in his poem "Zu lebendem Bildern" more than a quarter century earlier, Hofmannsthal had been reminded of fairy tales amidst whose feminine images a Schubert song had lovingly resonated. The outcome of the war certainly made the remembrance of such cultural myths more urgent, but Hofmannsthal's attitude toward Schubert and his era always had a patina of nostalgia about it. Inspired by the appearance of Bauernfeld's *Nachlass* in 1893, Hofmannsthal situated the composer's songs in a past that he symbolized as feminine by describing the central image of a woman's porcelain hand:

> Here and there one finds in our city, on a writing table, like a paperweight, a beautiful white hand, a bisque hand of a woman. It comes from the once famous old Viennese porcelain factory. It is not only beautiful, but also very characteristic. It is the hand of a quite definite kind of woman from a quite definite era. Elegant women's hands of today do not have these immature, naive fingers, not these soft and yet firm, tumescent backs of the hands; I mean, those of today have more nervousness and less childishness, they are less lovely, but more expressive. . . . I see, during a conversation, while somewhere in a nearby room someone plays Schubert songs or Lanner waltzes, the movements of this hand, as it lays itself softly and gracefully on the embroidered frame, primly

and slowly strokes a lapdog, tidily peels a pear, as with three fingers it breaks a carnation and puts it in the hair, and as it sleeps, the beautiful hand sleeps peacefully, the sleep of an honest, faithful, comfortable poodle . . .[65]

Hofmannsthal's composer may seem a more affectionate rendering than that conveyed through Schnitzler's satiric exposure of the kind of social corruption that did not easily accommodate the unexamined nobility of suffering suggested by listening to Schubert. One doubts that Hofmannsthal intended to be provocative in 1915 when, in his discussion about the prospects for an Austrian library, he juxtaposed the importance of including the composer's music among its contents with the Prussians' practice of exalting their military heroes from Moltke and Blücher even to obscure figures like Gneisenau and Yorck, along with "the least little page" by Frederick the Great.[66] For Hofmannsthal, however, Austria was less a political entity than it was a state of mind, whose strength derived from a nature that was not determined by the size of its armies. Austria's significance lay in artistic creation and aesthetic contemplation, thus raising Schubert, and not incidentally Hofmannsthal himself, to a level of importance that was formerly held by civic leaders. Hofmannsthal's composer became the symbol of a nation made feminine by its failure in world affairs even as it elevated its artistic traditions to mythic status. If Prussians were more masculine than his own countrymen, Hofmannsthal could still observe that they lacked the sense of history with which Austrians were endowed. Juxtaposed against ruthless German efficiency, the Austrian tendency toward humaneness may have evinced a greater frailty, but in 1917 it suited an author disillusioned by war and seeking an alternative in a benign past.[67]

Just as Hofmannsthal's early valuation of Schubert found a hospitable echo in his sense of Austrianness in the wake of the war, the writer's rejection of the kind of nationalism implied by the German *Volk* was not arrived at suddenly. Indeed, in his letter of 1895 to Karg von Bebenburg, Hofmannsthal expressly rejected that term in favor of *Leute*.[68] There were many different people, "even very different people among the poor, with entirely different inner worlds," although his perception of the unimportance of social issues helps to explain why he neglected to point out that what every poor person had in common was economic privation. Unlike Schnitzler during the decade following the war, Hofmannsthal evinced a yearning for the simplicity of a tradition that endorsed a patriotic allegiance to the old Habsburg dynasty. He believed that postwar European culture should turn toward Austria and not Germany. This argument played out in *Der Schwierige*, in which Hofmannsthal juxtaposed the arrogant Neuhoff against his own semiautobiographical character, nonetheless allowing the boorish Prussian to opine that people like Hans Karl (and presumably the author himself) no longer existed in the real world except as ghosts of Viennese salon society.

However sobering the realities of the war's carnage were to Austrian writers of Hofmannsthal's generation after the initial rush of patriotism, Hofmannsthal's nostalgic regret at the passing of the old order was a lament that was not universally shared. After the war and the collapse of the monarchy, he retained his belief in the superiority of the Austrian intellectual heritage, its ability to serve as Europe's model rather than the German state. However, he shifted its spiritual center from Schubert's Vienna to Mozart's Salzburg with the founding of its festival in 1920, a change that carried with it a concomitant appeal to a tradition that was more baroque than Biedermeier. In hindsight, given the course of politics during the ensuing decade, this idealized cultural project may strike one as wishful thinking. By 1927, Hofmannsthal's call for a "conservative revolution" in a speech at the University of Munich had acquired a meaning whose disquieting implications surprised him when the more politically astute Thomas Mann indicated as much to him.[69]

Chapter Five

Schubert, Modernism, and the Fin-de-Siècle Science of Sexuality

This study thus far has considered several aspects of Schubert's reception in fin-de-siècle Vienna. The prestige that the composer attained throughout Europe in the second half of the nineteenth century was particularly stirred up in the city of his birth, making him a ready object for manipulation by increasingly strident political interests. At the same time, his feminine character (the principal subject of the first volume of this study) was adopted and reimagined by Viennese modernists to suit creative agendas that included a critique of the very tradition that had determined the composer's gendered nature in the first place. These two trends had within them contradictory elements that made accommodation unlikely. Those who were engaged in crafting Schubert into a standard bearer of exclusionary Austro-German culture were not sympathetic to viewing that culture, symbolized by its favorite musical son, as feminine, if this trait were suddenly to convey an inherent weakness or enervation that could compromise national destiny.

In the nineteenth century, gendered characterizations may always have implied a certain degree of diminishment in aesthetic value—Schubert was certainly not spared this charge—but the period in which the composer reached the pinnacle of esteem in his native city was also the one in which the nature of feminine passivity acquired far more problematic connotations than ever before. At the turn of the century, the proliferation of a medical and scientific literature on sexuality had enormous repercussions on the public perception of the meanings behind being masculine and feminine. Moreover, the wholesale, indiscriminate, and often thoroughly muddled adaptation of this literature's jargon by authors wishing to provoke or titillate reflects the authority exercised by such medical studies, however specious their theories ultimately proved to be. These writings, both scientific and popular, threatened to throw into doubt and even undermine some of the most cherished notions about the established hierarchical nature of social relationships between women and men. Indeed, the opponents of modernism used its preoccupation with matters of sexuality as one of their principal pieces of evidence in order to sound an alarm against creative degeneration in contemporary arts and letters.

Given the tradition of Schubert as a *Mädchencharakter*, his exaltation by a nation which itself could be construed as feminine, and the manipulation of this image by a cadre of modernists whom their critics accused of having a deviant fascination with erotic desire, what was the relationship between the reception of the composer in fin-de-siècle Vienna and the impact of the science of sexuality on that culture? Pursuing an answer will reveal that, while medical treatises on sexuality and their widely disseminated popularizing offshoots regularly analyzed the lives of composers and other icons of culture, Schubert was rarely mentioned. Furthermore, Schubert was noticeably absent from several studies in which, because they dealt either with other musicians or with members of Schubert's circle, he would reasonably have been expected to appear. At the same time, references to Schubert in other texts, because of their reconsideration of the composer's gendered character, suggest a keen awareness of the implications of the new literature on sexuality.

Offering possible explanations for these phenomena provides a view of Schubert's reception in the fin de siècle in which old and new sensibilities collided. In the works of Schnitzler discussed in chapter 4, tragic outcomes resulted when the reality of sexual desire was played out within a skewed social order in which Schubert served as a symbol of the innocence of the female victim. Now, in the fin de siècle, the culture that had created the tradition of the composer's *Mädchencharakter* would be compelled to confront a radically reconfigured sense of sexuality in which values such as feminine passivity and intimate friendships among men could no longer be cherished and emulated without a commensurate uneasiness when contemplating their consequences. To begin to address this matter, however, requires a brief examination of the impact of the science of sexuality on the fin-de-siècle mind, an exploration that, for the moment, must set aside Schubert's reception.

The writers of Jung-Wien recognized that their preoccupation with gender was a fundamental feature of contemporary life. Although for some observers, the convergence of male and female could serve as a liberating agent for the creative imagination, for others it most definitely represented a disturbing trend. There were a variety of motivations for sounding an alarm against the feminization of culture and its concomitant influence upon Austrian national identity. One concern had to do with the fate of the Habsburg Empire's role as a European power. As early as 1877, the Viennese historian Heinrich Friedjung characterized the Austrian mentality as having a lack of energy, an abundance of sentiment, and a noble feeling for the beauty of form that contributed to its art but was counterbalanced by its political impotence. Concerned that Austria's closer ties to its Hungarian partner after the diplomatic compromise of 1867 (the *Ausgleich*) would jeopardize the unique connection between German Austrians and the citizens of the Prussian state, Friedjung argued that, without new efforts in the political sphere, the empire could offer nothing to Germany because even the greatest art arose from a masculine people. For Friedjung,

a man with deep pan-German sympathies, his nation's principal and most difficult problem was to find a way "to elevate the manly resolution of the Austrian
people."[1] This was no easy political task considering that, at the very highest
levels of power, Germany was becoming ever more dominant in central Europe.
Sensitive to the shift in dynastic superiority, Austria-Hungary's Crown Prince
Rudolf was incensed by the patronizing attitude of his German counterpart
Prince Wilhelm (later Emperor Wilhelm II). Writing to the imperial military
attaché in Berlin, Rudolf related Wilhelm's opinion of Austrians, that "we were
all pleasant people, but useless pansies and gourmands, no longer fit for life."[2]

If Friedjung was writing with fresh memories of Prussia's battlefield triumph
over the Habsburgs in 1866, in 1916 Austria's emerging status as Germany's
weak ally in war would make clear which nation possessed the manly traits that
were necessary to assure victory. For the German theologian Ernst Troeltsch, it
was the Prussian tradition that supplied "the ancient inherited masculine conviction of loyalty and trust" that was allied to its military character: "It differenti-
ates Germanness from other Germanic peoples and with its essentially Prussian
character it is also distinct from all older Germanness."[3] Writing in the same year
as Troeltsch and considering the matter from the Austrian angle, the Viennese
author Robert Müller opined that the Habsburg Empire possessed a feminine
character that in turn produced a Prussian-Austrian antithesis: "Its polarity falls
into the fundamental analogy of the masculine-feminine."[4] Müller did not conceive of the association between the empire and femininity as benign (as did, for
example, Hofmannsthal), and he certainly did not take the relationship as one
that showed off Austria to its advantage. On the contrary, the Austrian influence
on Germany at times was changing the characteristically masculine type of the
Prussian into an admixture that was "if not effeminate, then still feminine."[5] The
contrast between the two nations also had an unmistakably anti-Semitic cast to
it, whether Müller was describing mental or physical traits. For him, Viennese
modernism in particular was as Jewish as it was womanly. The misfortunes of war
were bringing about a "Schnitzler-type of Austrianness" that revealed the Jewish
consciousness of the café. Moreover, the features of the Viennese body not only
lacked "masculine athleticism," but that body's construction also betrayed traits
that, as noted in chapter 2, were often invoked in anti-Semitic contexts. "The
Viennese body is piloted by short, narrow-kneed or excessively wide-kneed legs
that are attached in a lateral, outward position to a broad, feminine pelvis."[6]
Thus, the Viennese type was neither purely masculine nor feminine, but rather
had an indeterminate nature that reminded Müller of "many Mongolian races."

Müller viewed the feminization of the state as having invidious repercussions
during a time of war, although, like so many whose enthusiastic patriotism
led them to volunteer in 1914, he experienced disillusionment after sustaining
serious injury in combat. The novelist Franz Werfel, who was Müller's colleague
at the Imperial War News Bureau (the Kriegspressequartier) designated to produce favorable propaganda, also recognized the inherently gendered nature of
nations in conflict. To the dismay of his superiors, however, Werfel decried the

consequences of male belligerence in an essay, "Fragment against the Male Sex," while he was serving on the Eastern Front:

> No, the big words say little: militarism, capitalism. The reason lies in the horrible socially underdeveloped playfulness of boys, in the horrendous fictiveness of the masculine sex. . . . Despite your great works, man, you are still the swaggering sluggard of nature. The woman is blessed when she has conceived you, she keeps you, she delivers you again.[7]

Werfel condemned the destructive futility of masculine aggression in comparison with nurturing femininity. Because it was written at the height of the war, Werfel's argument was considered sufficiently seditious by the imperial government to demand its suppression: his article was banned by the censor in June 1918 and appeared only in December, a month after hostilities ended.

Although four decades separate the writings of Friedjung and Müller, their concerns over the possible weaknesses of Austria, which they both characterized in gendered terms, arose in the context of tangible crises in the nation's political destiny. Particular diplomatic compromises or military setbacks, however, were not prerequisites for the voicing of concerns by fin-de-siècle critics about the baleful consequences of the feminization of culture. As noted in chapter 4, there was an implicit disapproval in Lothar's attribution of a womanly nature to Jung-Wien writers. At the turn of the century, there were also sterner condemnations on offer that point to the influence of something other than politics or war. For some critics, the gendered conceptualizations that appeared to suffuse contemporary literature presaged dire consequences involving abnormality. Writing in the Viennese literary journal *Neue Revue* in 1894, Julius Pap was deeply troubled by the modernist tendency to view everything through the lens of gender, which he ascribed to the contemporary preoccupation with the study of sexual pathology. He criticized authors who "would here also divulge to us the masculine and the feminine as the motivating forces behind everything. Now, their juniors therein follow suit so triumphantly, that occasionally—and in fact without mildly shivering!—they can also acknowledge in themselves the quiet, rudimentary beginnings of the Krafft-Ebing types of perversion."[8]

The contemporary fascination with the pathology of deviance was also seen as an alarming trend by the Viennese writer Ottokar Stauf von der March, whose books on folk ideals, ritual murder, and neurotic culture made him an unsurprising critic of Jung-Wien authors. Stauf von der March imaginatively censured literary modernism by interlacing its feminine character with mental illness, sexual ambiguity, drug addiction, anti-Semitism, and French influence, thus producing a cultural contagion whose antidote could only be a manly ideal: "the hectic, neuralgic poetry of hermaphrodites in whose literary organism there flows in place of blood a mixture of morphine and an *odeur de femmes*. . . . The most decadent are Semites. . . . The future will sweep the decadents from the horizon. . . . The character of the future will only conform to a strong, healthy, masculine poetry."[9] In his casual and enthusiastic appropriation of pseudoscientific language, Stauf von der March's rhetoric was typical of his age. The "bacillus of decadence" was rampant in the works of Hofmannsthal, Schnitzler, and Bahr. "The sweet play of the nerves paralyzes will power, impressions crush feeling— soon, the system of ganglia prevails everywhere and for good. The consequence is effemination, the feminization of the spirit." Moreover, this contemporary cultural malady was not a "German tumor"; the true home of the "ganglion corybants" was specifically Austria.[10] (As opposed to this warning about the dangers of nervousness, recall that for Viennese modernists like Hevesi, as I indicated in the introduction to the present volume, such agitation was instead a desirable goal of contemporary art, including Klimt's *Schubert at the Piano*.)

The particular tack taken by these Viennese diatribes against the city's modernist voices reflects the agitated response throughout fin-de-siècle Europe to the explosion of scientific studies of sexuality. Recent scholarship has recognized that "the period beginning around 1890 is a 'new,' historically specific stage in the history of sexuality."[11] Although no single factor was responsible for so characterizing the era, a significant touchstone was certainly the publication in 1886 of Richard von Krafft-Ebing's *Psychopathia Sexualis*, the first widely disseminated salvo in the production of a medical literature on sexuality that spanned the next quarter century. Between 1898 and 1908 alone, more than a thousand publications appeared on just the subject of homosexuality. At the end of that decade, with Krafft-Ebing's book in its thirteenth edition and translated into English, the American expatriate critic Edward Prime Stevenson could declare that, more than any other group, German-language writers had produced a "vast bibliography" of studies of "similisexual instincts" that were "by far the most exhaustive, intelligent, and progressive."[12]

Stevenson's observation indicates that, although medical writings on sexuality and their pseudoscientific progeny were widespread throughout Europe, the phenomenon was particularly extensive in Austria and Germany. In this context, if Vienna was not unique, it nonetheless did play host to several of the most influential figures, beginning with Krafft-Ebing, who became a professor of psychiatry at the city's university in 1889. In 1891, writing in his capacity as a physician rather than as a novelist, Schnitzler admired Krafft-Ebing's analyses of individual case studies as much for the poignancy of their ethical content as for their scientific value. Schnitzler further observed that they exposed the unsupportable position of laws that legislated sexual feelings as a sign of criminality rather than illness.[13] Following contemporary medical theory, however, Schnitzler accepted Krafft-Ebing's premise that the sexual pathologies under consideration revealed the symptoms of a sick individual, especially the "contrary sexual feeling" classified as *effeminatio*. Although at the turn of the century the novelty of the field produced a diverse terminology that as yet displayed no consensus (Krafft-Ebing, for example, constructed a taxonomy that distinguished between homosexual, urning, hermaphrodite, and effeminate), the common scientific recognition that "effeminization" constituted abnormal behavior was bound to make it a problematic trait even when considering a creative individual's artistic imagination, a subject that itself was not immune from fin-de-siècle medical studies of sexuality.

The new science of sexuality at the turn of the century required a continuous supply of subjects in order to test its hypotheses. In its ever-expanding literature, the great men of the past furnished examples that proved to be as intriguing as the anonymous case studies that filled the pages of medical tracts. Rare was the creative individual who did not surface in one context or another as a subject for speculation. Among composers, for example, Wagner's personal and professional relationship with King Ludwig II of Bavaria was a recurring topic of analysis and speculation, especially after Oskar Panizza's article "Bayreuth und die Homosexualität" (1895) appeared on the heels of Max Nordau's indictment of Wagner in his influential book on cultural degeneration, *Entartung* (1892).[14] In 1909, in the less incendiary context of music criticism, Rudolf Louis contrasted the feminine Wagner with the masculine Brahms.[15] To be sure, not every fin-de-siècle writer employed gendered language to Wagner's detriment. In a 1907 study of masculinity, Ludwig Gurlitt, the influential reformer of education in Germany, numbered Wagner among his nation's most admirable representatives: "Under manliness we understand the embodiment of all virtues that constitute the substance of a pure man, such as: veracity, fortitude, perseverance, constancy, high-mindedness. . . . Manly were [Johann] Walther, Luther, Ulrich von Hutten, Lessing, Goethe, Schiller, Bismarck, but also Richard Wagner, Beethoven, Moritz von Schwind, and the physically small [Adolf] Menzel—but each one manly in his art, none a complex of precisely abstract virtues."[16]

Given that the proliferation of medical studies about sexuality was synchronous with the public controversy over the feminization of literary modernism, one might anticipate the emergence of questionable aspects regarding Schubert, a composer who had been traditionally construed as feminine even as he was exalted as the empire's favorite musical native son. In the new scientific literature, however, Schubert was almost never mentioned, and, when he was, as often as not it was because of what Oswald Feis deemed to be the composer's abnormal addiction to alcohol.[17] Even more neglected in medical studies of the sexes, Schubert proved to be an elusive individual who was very rarely cited there. Indeed, an examination of fin-de-siècle writings on sexuality uncovers only two such appearances, and the second of these to be discussed came from someone outside the medical profession.

Consider first the case studies assembled by Krafft-Ebing, which included autobiographical sketches describing their anonymous subjects' private lives. Although the sexual habits and desires of these men and women were of paramount importance, just about any detail, including their preferences in the arts and literature, could be included if it was seen as illuminating the personal history of their sexual development and behavior. Harry Oosterhuis has found that several of Krafft-Ebing's unnamed homosexual correspondents who evinced a fondness for music referred specifically to Wagner, an unsurprising choice given that composer's reception at the turn of the century. One anonymous individual did include Schubert in company with a trio of nineteenth-century composers whose attractions he enumerated in terms that seem more in keeping with the overripe sensibilities of the decadent temperament famously incarnated in the Duc des Esseintes, the protagonist of Joris-Karl Huysmans' novel À *rebours*, than with the cloistered world of middle-class domesticity:

> Among poets and novelists, I typically prefer those who describe refined feelings, pecu-
> liar passions, and farfetched impressions; an artificial or hyperartificial style pleases me.
> Likewise, in music, it is the nervous, exciting music of a Chopin, a Schumann, a Schubert,
> or a Wagner, etc. that is in most perfect harmony with me. Everything in art that is not
> only original, but also bizarre, attracts me.[18]

Such a description, of course, accords no unique character to Schubert, although it mentions three other composers who did surface in the fin-de-siècle literature on sexuality. Indeed, the only other appearance of Schubert's name in a similar context prior to World War I occurred together with two of them, Schumann and Wagner, although its author was not from the medical profession.

Heinrich Pudor represents a characteristic phenomenon of the fin de siècle: an individual outside of the medical profession who became caught up in the whirlwind of scientific opinion about sexuality and who appropriated its terminology eagerly and indiscriminately. Pudor was a prolific writer on subjects ranging from art and poetry to politics and sociology. He had a musical background, studying at the Dresden Conservatory run by his father before completing a dissertation at Heidelberg on Schopenhauer's metaphysics of music.[19] He is known today principally as the author of some of the first books advocating nudism (books that he wrote under the pseudonym Heinrich Scham, the German for "shame"), although throughout his career he occupied himself with producing increasingly strident anti-Semitic tracts. In 1907, his article "Richard Wagners Bisexualität" appeared in *Geschlecht und Gesellschaft*, a journal begun the previous year and devoted to "historical sources on the women's movement and gender ambiguity." The brief piece appears to have been prompted in part by the previous year's reissuing of sixteen letters from Wagner to a seamstress, which detailed what readers might have construed as the composer's dubious fondness for rather too exquisite fabrics for his wardrobe. (The renewed fascination with this corner of Wagneriana may be placed in the context of the fin-de-siècle science of sexuality, for example, in the work of Krafft-Ebing, who described a particular brand of fetishism in which certain materials such as fur, velvet, and silk caused sexual arousal.)[20]

Pudor had earlier argued, in an essay of 1902, that the male artist needed to possess components that were alien to his sex. To identify such individuals, Pudor used the older terms *Urning* and *Urninde*, coined by Karl Ulrichs in the 1860s and subsequently promulgated by Krafft-Ebing and others. For Pudor, the receptive nature necessary for the artist could equally be considered feminine or homosexual: "The artist, so far as he is a masculine individual, has homosexual feelings in every representative epoch of his artistic creation: he is uranian to a certain degree in this time period."[21] Five years after this article appeared, Pudor emphasized in "Richard Wagners Bisexualität" that, of all the arts, music most clearly expressed an individual's bisexual character. Sounds took hold of the male artist in a metaphorical pregnancy; an "embodied receptivity" was necessary for a composer "because, to grasp music in itself, one must be devoted to music like a woman, much more infinitely devoted in comparison to other arts, because with music the tone enters upon you, growing in your inner being and living there inside of you."[22]

The fact that in 1907 Pudor employed the term bisexuality, which Freud had introduced in his *Three Essays on the Theory of Sexuality* in 1905, illustrates the fluidity with which medical language passed into the broader culture. The malleable nature of contemporary scientific vocabulary is underscored by Pudor's statement that "strong bisexual characteristics and in fact feminine-uranian characteristics are encountered quite often in music." To be sure, Pudor provided no detailed definition of bisexuality beyond asserting that the term presupposed the dichotomous character of male and female traits. Pudor noted that "a detailed psychology of musical heroes" would be very worthwhile from the perspective he had outlined. However, he offered no such intricate study beyond making this observation: "But naturally one assesses as bisexual one musician more than another, and one characterizes as bisexual the music of this artist more than the music of those others. So Schubert and Schumann stand in opposition to Haydn and Beethoven."[23]

Pudor's designation of the first pair of composers as more bisexual than the second pair is clarified by his statement that, regarding both strong bisexual and feminine-uranian characteristics, "one thinks of Schumann, this most wonderful blend of masculine and feminine, who was ruined by this dichotomy."[24] Apparently, an immeasurable feminine quantity had to be present for the male composer to animate his creative muse, but crossing some ill-defined boundary could consign the individual to a doomed realm of problematic sexuality. Pudor offered no similar elaboration on Schubert. His single tangential mention of the composer, however, appears to be the first statement characterizing Schubert's feminine nature in terms of the new vocabulary of sexuality that emerged from fin-de-siècle medical literature, even though Pudor was neither a physician nor a scientist. This reference tells us little beyond the fact that the tradition of the composer's *Mädchencharakter* might have made him an appealing example for a lay writer eager to appropriate medical terminology for a broader, if thoroughly foggy, purpose. Indeed, as Pudor's case illustrates, the selection of composers without discrimination or expertise could lead to haphazard and bizarre conclusions. Given that the masculine artist still needed to have some form of feminine receptivity in order to create his music, Pudor could describe both Beethoven and Tchaikovsky as uranian in their symphonic works (a peculiar pairing in hindsight, if not for the fin de siècle) and Schumann as uranian in his smaller, more lyrical utterances.[25]

The passing references to Schubert in works by Krafft-Ebing and Pudor constitute slim evidence from which to draw significant inferences about the possible interplay between the nineteenth-century legacy of the composer's *Mädchencharakter* and the emerging fin-de-siècle science of sexuality. This scarcity of citation may be observed in relation to contemporary texts where, because of their subjects, one might reasonably have expected Schubert's name to appear but where his very absence warrants attention. Two such books, both published in 1903, bear examination because, rather than being simply inadvertent, the omission of allusions to Schubert can help to shed light upon the era's consuming interest in sexuality and its accommodation of the tradition of the composer's feminine character. The matter is especially pertinent in regard to the first volume to be discussed, Otto Weininger's *Geschlecht und Charakter*, because, between the appearance of the works of Krafft-Ebing and Freud, it was Vienna's most stunning contribution to the contemporary fascination with and unease over the changing nature of sexuality.

In the decade before World War I, Otto Weininger's name turned up on almost every modernist's compendium of worthies including lists made by composers, although his treatment of music was hardly original. Writing to his wife on August 17, 1907, Alban Berg placed Weininger among "the great innovators," in the shadow of Nietzsche and Ibsen and alongside Strindberg, Wilde, Hauptmann, Wedekind, Karl Hauer, Wittels, Kraus, and Bahr. On June 23, 1910, Anton von Webern wrote to his teacher Arnold Schoenberg about those individuals who combined "a sublime intellect" with "the ardour of emotion," and he listed Weininger with Strindberg, Plato, Kant, and Kraus. Schoenberg's Jewish origins might reasonably have made him at least cautious, if not actually repelled by the anti-Semitism of *Geschlecht und Charakter*. In the preface to his *Harmonielehre* written in July 1911, however, Schoenberg likened his own exploration of thought to that of Strindberg, Maeterlinck, and Weininger.[26] (Given Strindberg's admiration for Weininger, as we shall see, it is not surprising that his name is the only other one mentioned by all three composers.)

The sensational impact of *Geschlecht und Charakter* on the denizens of Viennese high culture was not attenuated by its roiling language and often paralogical argument. Its ambitious and contradictory analysis of sexuality and race was articulated in a dense pseudoscientific prose that was at the service of proposals, which, if not always absurdly misogynistic, nonetheless articulated an anxiety over feminine nature even as they linked women's inferiority to homosexuals and Jews.[27] Following a century-old tradition traceable to German romanticism, Weininger stated that musical creativity required an imagination different from that needed for other artistic or scientific endeavors.[28] It was precisely this kind of thought that was lacking in women, hence their absolute insignificance in music history save for the most masculine of them. Music required a special type

of genius whose ideal incarnation was Beethoven: "The musician, if he is genuinely great in the language in which the direction of his special talent points
him, can truly be universal, can truly traverse the entire inner and outer world
like the poet or philosopher; such a genius was Beethoven."[29] Elsewhere,
Weininger made clear that he found nineteenth-century composers inferior to
Beethoven precisely because their work was feminine. Their condition was the
result of debilitating affairs with masculine women as in the liaisons between
Chopin and George Sand or Liszt and Marie d'Agoult (identified by her literary
pseudonym, Daniel Stern), and even in the marriage of Robert and Clara
Schumann. Relationships among men could be equally suspect: Liszt's friendship with the "not completely masculine and in any case somewhat pederastically
disposed Wagner"—a truly damning implication in contemporary discourse—
bespoke the rapturous adoration bordering on a homosexual attraction that was
shown to Wagner by Ludwig II.[30]

In an era of scientific taxonomy, Weininger was frequently given to classifying
famous creative individuals, including musical figures. In *Geschlecht und Charakter*,
he observed that Bach bore comparison with Kant whereas Weber stood next to
Eichendorff. In another text, he enumerated two other groups, priests and seekers, although Beethoven's genius warranted his placement in both: "Seekers
were Hebbel, Fichte . . . Brahms, Dürer. Priests: Shelley, Handel, Böcklin.
Seekers were Calderón, Sophocles, [and] Mozart. Beethoven is a seeker in *Fidelio*
[and] a priest in the 'Waldstein' Sonata, whose final movement is the highest
peak of Apollonian art."[31] Schubert, however, appears to be the rare major composer in the Austro-German tradition from Bach to Brahms whose name does
not surface on Weininger's aesthetic radar for either good or ill, even though
the writer displayed such a fondness for categorizing artists and thinkers. (One
wonders whether Mendelssohn's Jewish heritage removed him from Weininger's
consideration.) While this detail is interesting, it is perhaps not significant in
itself, especially given that Weininger's musical obsession was with Beethoven,
who died in the house where the writer took his own life in 1903. After all,
Weininger may not have considered Schubert's music to be sufficiently important to warrant mention, although he managed to find space to offer an opinion
on Johann Strauss's agile but narrowly limited talent.[32] If Weininger did not find
Schubert worthy of inclusion, however, his would have been a lone Viennese
voice, especially given the composer's civic and cultural anointing during the
city's celebrations of his centennial in 1897. If, however, Schubert's stature was
not a matter of doubt, the postulation of a possible reason for his absence from
Weininger's text will be aided by considering other evidence.

In the same year that saw the publication of *Geschlecht und Charakter*, there
appeared a second volume addressing the sexuality of creative individuals in
which the omission of Schubert's name was a noteworthy lacuna, but one that
seems more deliberate. The title of Hanns Fuchs's *Richard Wagner und die
Homosexualität* makes plain the centerpiece of the author's concern, although
the cases of other writers and artists receive due attention in its pages. Fuchs

began with a premise that could only have been stated in the wake of the impact made by recent medical literature: "One only knows half of a man if one does not know the nature and habit of his sexuality."[33] As a consequence, the study of an individual's life was as important as an analysis of the person's creative works. That only men could accomplish such achievements was a theme common in nineteenth-century conceptualizations of the imaginative mind. Echoing Schopenhauer, Fuchs argued that music is "the most complete manifestation of the will," and therefore neither a woman nor a "purely homosexual" man could ever become a really great composer.

The ideal man possessed a hardness that, when it yielded to softness, not only approximated a woman's nature but also resulted in the man entering into a category that Fuchs classified as "intermediate." The idea of an intermediate or "third" sex had been extant for several decades, dating back to the work of Ulrichs, although Fuchs admitted that he was not entirely satisfied with its underlying theory. The concept did, however, permit Fuchs to describe a category of individuals whose erotic behavior was heterosexual but whose creativity was suffused with a "spiritual side" of homosexuality that included such feminine traits as attentiveness, kindness, eagerness to serve, and an interest in art. Fuchs proposed to demonstrate that, whereas illustrious men like Michelangelo and Platen could have purely homosexual feelings, a richness and diversity in the sexual feelings of "truly great, all-embracing spirits" like Shakespeare, Frederick the Great, and Goethe was also possible so that "they could sensually love the woman just the same as the man."[34] The same argument held true for composers:

> Just as it is impossible that a pure homosexual can accomplish something altogether great as a composer, so it is probable that the greatest composers, the most spiritually rich among them, at one time temporarily have felt homosexual, as for example is the case with Goethe. One will not go wrong if one presumes that the life of a Bach, a Gluck, a Mozart, a Beethoven has not been free of homosexual episodes.[35]

Whether or not it was prompted by Fuchs's own musical tastes, breaking off his list of composers with the last great representative of musical classicism was an effective tactic in separating this part of his argument from his subsequent analysis of later nineteenth-century romanticism in general and the case of Wagner in particular.

At one point, Fuchs discussed the meaning of the correspondence between two of Schubert's closest friends, Franz von Schober and Moritz von Schwind, which illustrated the nature of the intense emotional attachment between creative men. Fuchs quoted at length from an 1897 biography of Schwind by Friedrich Haack, but interestingly Fuchs appropriated only selected passages. Those parts that occur in Fuchs appear below in italics while the material in brackets refers to original words by Haack that are followed by Fuchs's substitutions. The rest of the text is as it appears in Haack's biography:

[This one] *"Schwind attached himself,"* said Haack, *"to the man some eight years older, of a splendid outward appearance* (compare Schober's portrait in the catalogue of the 1897 Vienna Schubert exhibition), *with the whole* [fervent] *enthusiastic need of friendship in the way that richly soulful, talented youths tend to feel for mature men until they become touched by the affection for the opposite sex."* Such a peculiar "alliance is evidenced by the letters, papers, and notes which soon flutter to the friend; he must say everything and pour out his thoughts to him; he confides in him all his plans, he is his principal forum, his mentor and father; the first sketch of every drawing, a copy or even a description flies to him. But then to be sure, as with a young married couple still not entirely grown together, it also assumes quarreling, anger, and jealousy. Schwind himself provokes annoyance, 'uproar,' and disagreement, only soon after that to apologize most humbly for everything once again." [And as the friend was traveling to Breslau, Schwind wrote to him on December 12, 1823:]

   Haack discloses the following parts from this letter:
   "Oh you light of my soul," he enjoins in a letter of December 12, 1823: *"console me! When I say to myself a thousand times everything that I want to write to you, then everything in me disappears when I begin. I truly love the most loving on earth; I live in you. I know you are pleased with me and when I should no longer know you, dear one, I should much rather die."* [Another time he even burst out with the enraptured words:]

   In another letter he exclaimed:
   "Every moment that you spoke to me is truly more than my entire life without you. Is there anything good about me that does not come from you?—Nothing ought to separate me from the truth, to which I dedicate my life and the most sacred love. You might be my eye that sees me and that shows me to myself. The greatest thing that I know on this earth is love, beauty, and wisdom.—You yourself have classed me with you and Schubert! I rest everything on that, to be the third one among you." These letters, which are fully indebted to the extravagant manner of writing in which the eighteenth century delighted, and which plainly recall the gushing heart of the young Werther, give us a clear insight into the spiritual life of the young artist. What a difference between the tender, almost feminine tone that he strikes here, and the strong, manly, and humorous style of the exquisite letters that Schwind wrote as a more mature man.[36]

One might hypothesize that Fuchs deleted the last two sentences of this passage because Haack's explanation—that the tone of the correspondence resulted from the eighteenth century tradition of epistolary effusion—did not fit with Fuchs's psychosexual agenda. Equally intriguing, however, is the fact that Fuchs excised the two references to Schubert. To be sure, Fuchs may have simply considered them to be irrelevant to the point he wished to make. The parenthetical statement about the appearance of Schober's portrait in the Schubert centennial exhibition might reasonably fall into this category. More significant, however, Fuchs's elimination of the final sentence of Schwind's letter as quoted by Haack—a sentence in which Schwind endorsed Schober's privileged grouping of Schubert and themselves—certainly has the effect of entirely removing the composer from its heady emotional content and, as a consequence, insulating Schubert from the relationship Fuchs meant to draw between Schwind and Schober. Fuchs cited their correspondence as an example of the "spiritual homosexual," which he believed to be detectable in such "expressions of impassioned friendship."

Whatever Fuchs's motivation for editing the passage in this particular way, the outcome was that readers would not associate Schubert with a particular kind of intimacy, which older nineteenth-century studies of the composer would not have recognized or acknowledged but which, in the context of the contemporary literature about sexuality, would have suggested a certain level of deviance.

This was not the only volume that theorized on the sexuality of creative individuals who were part of Schubert's circle but failed to mention the composer. One year after the publication of the books by Fuchs and Weininger, there appeared Hans Rau's *Franz Grillparzer und sein Liebesleben*, a volume dedicated to exploring the previously unexamined nature of male desire in the life and works of the most important Viennese literary figure of Schubert's generation. As extensive as Rau's study purported to be, Schubert is conspicuous by his absence, especially given that Rau devoted half a dozen pages to Grillparzer's dealings with Beethoven. Schubert's name appears twice, but only in passing: in reference to a memoir by Toni Adamberger regarding her singing the composer's Lieder and in a footnote that mentions Schubert being in Vienna in 1821 when Grillparzer wrote about his feelings for Kathi Fröhlich. The fact that Grillparzer had penned Schubert's epitaph would have been sufficient reason alone to introduce the composer into a biography of the writer. Moreover, the presence of the two within the same artistic circle was so familiar in the public mind that it could prompt Joseph August Lux to feature Schubert extensively throughout his sentimental novel *Grillparzers Liebesroman* (1912). Although the narrative is ostensibly concerned with the amorous relationship between Grillparzer and Fröhlich, Schubert and his friends figure prominently in it. Schubert's pathetically shy inability to meet Beethoven comes to a climax when Anton Schindler brings him to see the dying composer, setting up the clichéd comparison between the prophet of the Ninth Symphony and "the humble and wistful, small little master."[37]

This type of cloying portrayal of Schubert may well have made the composer an unsuitable player in Rau's psychosexual narrative. Rau proposed that biographers of Grillparzer had not tackled the matter of male desire because they did not have confidence in dealing with the various forms of same-sex love ("gleichgeschlechtliche Liebe") that had been the exclusive domain of psychiatrists who studied sexual psychology. What Rau deemed to be false prudery, however, was not sufficient reason to keep the subject in "a narrowly limited ethical closet." The pursuit of truth trumped any other consideration, and, in any case, there was no sordid element to such an analysis: "We are also convinced that same-sex love, as it appears in Grillparzer, is absolutely noble and moral, that it does not debase him, but ennobles him. The memory of the poet will in no way be degraded through the following account."[38] The biography not only assessed Grillparzer's emotional and creative relationships with other men, but it also considered the author's literary output, which Rau argued revealed an intimate feminine understanding. Grillparzer possessed a "Frauenseele" that enabled him to look within himself in order to portray women with such truth and beauty: "Feminine feeling stands even nearer to him, the delineation of which he was able to create out of the deepest depths of his own nature, while the presentation of man, of the strong man, was based upon his observation of life."[39]

If Rau's analysis of Grillparzer's life from the standpoint of sexuality was a novelty, another assessment of the writer's work, which drew similar conclusions, was hardly unique. In *Uranisme et unisexualité: Étude sur différentes manifestations de l'instinct sexuel* (1896), Marc-André Raffalovich, a Russian émigré living in England and art patron of Aubrey Beardsley, discussed Grillparzer's journal as revealing someone who appeared to be constantly in love with an idealized woman but who was apparently more preoccupied by his friendships with men. In a nod to the terminological tradition of Ulrichs and Krafft-Ebing, Raffalovich classified Grillparzer as "the uranist with heterosexual inclinations, whose unfortunate heredity and constant sorrows repressed the unisexual instincts without destroying them or giving enough of a free development to the heterosexual instincts."[40] Like Rau, Raffalovich felt he could publish and discuss the correspondence of what he deemed "superior uranists" (a term he lifted from Magnus Hirschfeld) because they expressed themselves in a kind of heightened emotionality, the same sort that Fuchs had articulated in his discussion of Schober and Schwind and that, like Fuchs, Raffalovich considered as the particular terrain of German heterosexual friendships. Further, owing to what he saw as the connection between music and sexual inversion, Raffalovich opined that unique love for and knowledge of music among Austrians and Germans meant that one could find there "the majority of inverts, psychopaths, and sexual nonconformists with the taste, talent, or fluency in music."

Raffalovich named no names of composers, but that was unusual in the fin-de-siècle literature of sexuality. In a study of what he termed "the third sex," Otto de Joux used the expression "Doppelnatur" to describe the character of artistic uranians like Grillparzer who were "gentle and grim at the same time."[41] A human nature composed of paradoxical tendencies also happened to be frequently mentioned by Schubert's friends, beginning with obituary notices and extending to later memoirs. Bauernfeld even used exactly the same term, "Doppelnatur," to describe the contradictory impulses of gaiety and melancholy in the composer. Bauernfeld's recollection was not published until several years after De Joux's study, but anyone who had a passing familiarity with Schubert's life would have been aware that the composer's friends often recognized this feature of his character, as when Kreissle cited the poet Johann Mayrhofer's obituary, to the effect that Schubert's nature was a mixture of tenderness and roughness.[42] Nonetheless, the composer's name does not appear in De Joux's text, although the writer had no qualms about mentioning Beethoven, Berlioz, and Wagner.

For writers like De Joux, Rau, and Raffalovich, there would have been no stigma attached to associating a famous figure of the past with ambiguous sexuality—Raffalovich was himself a "uranian" poet—but such sympathetic attitudes to Grillparzer were by no means universally shared. Indeed, Grillparzer's feminine nature was construed by Leo Berg as an example of the modern, pathological poet whose characters undermined the natural order of male and female types. In *Das sexuelle Problem in Kunst und Leben* (1901), Berg was especially critical of Grillparzer's characterizations of Hero and Leander in the play *Des Meeres und der Liebe Wellen*:

> How despicable are these men! How relatively masculine, how motherly these little women! For example: this dearest teenaged Hero. How sisterly, how motherly, how nurturing is this still scarcely pubescent Hero! . . . Is the character of our new literature, at least as far it appears on the surface, not perpetually feminine, therefore unmanly? Has not the eternal cult of women enervated, emasculated man? Has he not been made even more feminine than the woman herself? Yet behold these modern men, the men of poetry: their masculinity gone all at once! They behave like hysterical old maids, like frail women who are expecting at any time! Indeed, an honorable woman does not make as much of a bother about her pregnancy.[43]

Berg was no physician. He saw Grillparzer's Hero as one of the earliest manifestations of a long line of heroines that included Zola's Nana, Ibsen's Nora, Hebbel's Judith, and Sacher-Masoch's Venus, all of them fictional incarnations of the modern woman whose breast was the central organ for all her ideas, desires, and moods.

A literary historian like Berg was not about to entertain the point of view argued by Rau, although in the scientific literature the perspective of Rau's book is apparent, for example, in Albert Moll's *Berühmte Homosexuelle* (1910), which also takes up at some length the case of Wagner. Moll, a Berlin neurologist, was one of the early pioneers of the medical study of sexuality. For him, the cult of friendship bequeathed by the late eighteenth century did not automatically reveal a homosexual nature, that this was by no means the only conclusion one might draw from examining a relationship between individuals such as Goethe and Schiller, for example. Taking an unsurprisingly clinical view, Moll felt that science could not countenance any euphemisms for what in recent times biographers had described as intense friendships, which he considered to be a delicate way of characterizing homosexual feeling.[44] At the same time, medical experts were not convinced that what Moll termed "the cult of friendship"—the often poetic expression of intense emotions toward an individual of one's own sex that had been so prevalent a hundred years earlier—was equivalent to same-sex erotic desire. Magnus Hirschfeld, the pioneering German sex researcher and indefatigable proponent of the decriminalization of homosexuality, rejected the word *Freundling* as unsuitable for describing such relationships, while his British counterpart Havelock Ellis observed that "various modern poets of high ability have given expression to emotions of exalted or passionate friendship toward individuals of the same sex, whether or not such friendship can properly be termed homosexuality."[45]

What, then, are we to make of a popular pseudoscientific literature whose authors were so easily disposed, even eager, to explore the sexualized implications of the lives of both Schubert's contemporaries and other musicians, but who managed to sidestep any consideration of Schubert himself? Although sharing an interest in assessing the relationship between sexuality and the creative mind, none of these fin-de-siècle writers—whether medical, historical, or polemical—took Schubert's life into consideration, even though members of his circle and other composers were common fodder for psychological speculation. Given that there was such a rich tradition of construing Schubert's music as feminine, and taking into account the fact that the diversity of medical opinion had classified artists and writers who understood and appropriated women's nature without necessarily concluding that they were involved in same-sex love, one might well find the composer's absence to be puzzling at the very least. Because turn-of-the-century science rejected the squeamishness of popular opinion, there were not likely to be any cultural sacred cows in the pantheon of great musicians of the past, musicians who were untouchable should their lives prove to be relevant for scrutiny. Perhaps in some instances, notably Wagner, one might hypothesize that a writer's taste might have skewed an estimation of the composer, even in tracts that considered a scientific approach to be the presumptive objective. Yet, as we have seen, individuals whose reputations were not in any doubt were still grist for the analytic mill.

One feature of Schubert's biography that appeared to be special, at least to the fin-de-siècle mind, and that might have removed him from candidacy for contemporary psychosexual examination, was the sense that the details of his personal history were so insignificant for an understanding of his inner world that an examination of them was irrelevant to an assessment of his creative life. This had been a common refrain since the publication of Kreissle's biography in 1865. Although loaded with a mass of documentary minutiae, Kreissle's study had failed to yield any event that could serve as the narrative basis for the contemporary Singspiel about the composer by Hans Max (the pseudonym of Johann Freiherr von Päumann). This lack of dramatic incident is also observable in the work of individuals like Mandyczewski, whose professional interests were grounded in comprehending the composer's music. Certainly, the prosaic details of Schubert's life did not appear to rise to the level of material that might have lured a clinical writer to introduce the composer into a collection of case studies. Whether one believed the anecdote about the encounter between Schubert and Caroline Esterházy or gave more credence to the later reminiscences by Schubert's contemporaries that elevated Therese Grob to the status of his one great love, the documentary record seemed to remove the composer from classification as an "homme à femme," to use the diplomatic expression of Otto Erich Deutsch, Schubert's most indispensable chronicler after the turn of the century.[46]

One cannot discount the possibility that the relatively pedestrian character of Schubert's career may have also rendered him an unsuitable candidate for consideration by medical experts who judged an individual's erotic life to be crucial to fathoming his nature. In the influential *Die sexuelle Frage* (1905), the Swiss psychiatrist August Forel understood superior art to consist in the formation and emanation of unusually sublime and profound but also elaborate and complex conflicts of human sexual feelings, and to communicate the deepest and innermost aspects of its creators' minds. As examples of musical geniuses, Forel listed Carl Loewe along with Mozart, Beethoven, Schumann, and Wagner.[47] One cannot imagine that by 1905, a writer (particularly one who was trained in medicine rather than music) would have naturally come up with the name Loewe rather than Schubert, especially if he was thinking of an early nineteenth-century German composer renowned for his Lieder. Given the popular image of Schubert, however, one can understand why the composer's name would not have been appropriate as an example of someone whose works conveyed the conflicts in his sexual feelings.

The apparent lack of a richness of intimacy in Schubert's life may also account for his absence from *Geschlecht und Charakter*. Weininger's so-called Law of Sexual Relations posited that the perfect union of two individuals required that the gendered character of one had to be balanced by that of the other. Masculine women were the ideal complement to men who were more feminine, even as that trait made those men inferior.[48] The modest evidence of Schubert's evanescent encounters with two feminine archetypes—the aristocratic but distant countess and the spiritually noble *Bürgerin*—in combination with the tradition of his *Mädchencharakter*, meant that the composer could hardly qualify as a useful example for Weininger's purposes. Given Weininger's certainty that genius and femininity were mutually exclusive categories, to introduce Schubert would have required that the composer be diminished in the same manner as Chopin, Liszt, and Schumann. However, since those romantics at least enjoyed relationships with masculine women, Schubert could not be placed among them, and thus he would have defied Weininger's compartmentalization as least as far as his sexual life was concerned. To describe a feminine composer who had no sustaining associations with any women would have required Weininger either to deny Schubert's genius or to locate for him an obvious partner among men, as Weininger and others did with Wagner and Ludwig II. By 1903, however, the former option would have required that one embark on the culturally impossible task of challenging the tradition of the composer's stature. At the same time, contemporary scholarship would have regarded the alternative as a notion without either logic or proof. Absent the kind of relationship, for example, between Wagner and Ludwig II, that was explicated by so many fin-de-siècle writers both in the sciences and outside them, the quite minor references to Schubert in Pudor and Krafft-Ebing were hardly going to cause a ripple.

Thus, there does not appear to be any evidence that Schubert's musical stature made him either so unimportant or by contrast so untouchably great that writers of scientific studies would deliberately avoid mentioning him. As we have observed, medical writers and lay biographers had different reasons for eschewing the establishment of connections between same-sex friendships and erotic desire, but the common result may help to explain why the usual descriptions of

Schubert and his companions in fin-de-siècle Austria and Germany never even hinted at any problematic aspects. By comparison, as detailed in chapter 5 of the first volume of this study, the few Victorian writers who criticized these social relationships did so only on the basis of the moral laxity of some of the composer's friends, which took the form of lassitude or, at worst, a fondness for alcohol. Far more common, however, was the sort of conclusion offered by Karl Storck in 1905, in which unclouded friendship rather than love for a woman occupied the great part of the composer's life: "A splendid circle of young, excellent men had assembled themselves around him and received with sympathy and understanding the gift of his overflowing talents."[49] There was likewise nothing layered about Adolph Kohut's observation in 1898 that the three relevant elements on the subject of Schubert and the opposite sex were "his carefree, cheerful, optimistic temperament; the friendship of like-minded fellow young men of the same age; and the favor of noble women."[50] A year earlier, for a member of an even older generation like the poet Paul Heyse, born in 1830, there was nothing unsettling about crafting a poetic tribute in honor of the composer's centennial that apostrophized his "eternal beauteous youth" while paraphrasing the opening lines of Goethe's "Ganymed," addressing the mythological youth and lover of Zeus: "How you glow around us in the morning light, beloved spring!"[51]

Such characterizations were by no means novel, and as such it is difficult to posit that they assumed a greater urgency at the turn of the century when the new science of sexuality may have appeared to some wardens of culture to cast a problematic shadow over the older, eighteenth-century cult of male friendship. If medical authorities were loath to draw any conclusions about this tradition, a determined effort was still made by several writers, sympathetic to intimate relationships between men, to shield their subjects from the stigma of effeminacy. Alternative expressions such as Benedikt Friedländer's "physiologische Freundschaft" and Elisarion von Kupffer's "Lieblingminne" sought to normalize the intense and even impassioned male friendship as a masculine ideal by rescuing it from the prurience of the sexual act and the consequent deviance ascribed to it in fin-de-siècle culture. In an appendix to his anthology of prose and poetry excerpts from antiquity to the present (including three letters from Ludwig II to Wagner as well as the composer's dedication of *Die Walküre* to the king), Kupffer cited Goethe's "Erlkönig" because:

> Goethe in the penultimate stanza shows thoughts and words that never could emanate from the perception of an innocent child. The poet here has only expressed the feverish fantasies of a child, in the suggestive sense of this word, especially those of a fallen one, and the poem is disingenuous and a failure or rather in "Erlkönig" the old master has in a consciously dramatic way expressed one of his perceptions, as it seems to me. "The gods love the boy who dies young." It should also be mentioned that in today's China one still dresses boys in girls' clothing, so that they might not be abducted by a deity.[52]

Kupffer thus omitted to expand upon any lascivious implications in the title character's attraction to and fatal touching of the child. Moreover, he ignored the fact that this poem served as the basis for Schubert's most famous song (D. 328, op. 1).

Of course, such an omission, like those in Fuchs and Rau, might have resulted from unrelated and immaterial reasons. Regarding the polemical goals of some of this writing, however, one final hypothesis suggesting an explanation for Schubert's absence might be worth further research. Kupffer's work was published through Adolf Brand who, along with Fuchs, founded the Gemeinschaft der Eigenen in 1903 to advocate the decriminalization of homosexuality in Germany. The effort to normalize male relationships on both moral and legal grounds may have been more amenable to enlisting famous individuals of the past who themselves were representative of what in the public mind was a masculine and hence proper nature. Under such conditions, having recourse to a figure like Schubert, whom tradition regarded as characteristically feminine, might not have best served the ends of authors who were attempting to reposition masculinity as an attribute capable of accommodating intimate relationships that society still thought of as both crimes and vices. By contrast, this attitude may help to explain why Beethoven, whom the same nineteenth-century tradition had valorized as the manliest of composers, should so often have been invoked.

For all its circumspection on the nature of emotional relationships between men, the medical literature on sexuality at the turn of the century so permeated contemporary culture that it was bound to sow doubt in the fin-de-siècle mind regarding long-established ideas about male friendships. As we have seen, a variety of motives and interests—a traditionalist defense of purity, scientific objectivism, and empathy for a new level of intimacy—influenced the reconfiguration of relationships between men, including those involving illustrious figures from the past. If one cannot always clearly measure the extent to which a particular writer was influenced by the new science of sexuality, there is no doubt that the public recognition and discussion of what was usually thought to be deviant desire could produce a sense of discomfort if not provoke the sternest condemnation.

Given the contemporary prevalence of medical theories that associated deviant pathology with effeminacy as well as a competing defense of same-sex male desire that linked intimate friendship and spiritual love, one should not be surprised to detect at times in traditional fin-de-siècle biography an uneasiness over intensely felt relationships in the past lives of great men. Such is the case, for example, with Gustav Portig's massive study on the friendship between Goethe and Schiller, published in 1894. Portig was at pains to differentiate love from friendship, a distinction that he took to be missing not only from antiquity but also from "the lower levels of our contemporary society," where "only the grosser forms of personal union are possible." In the case of the two poets, however, one could "define the relationship of love and friendship differently than was possible in earlier centuries." Given the behavior of such superior people, Schiller and Goethe's friendship "must be characterized as a spiritual marriage . . . ceaselessly working in the service of the highest poetic ideal. . . . Both considered themselves princes, as the acme of the richness of spirit, both know only the language of pure refinement, both constitute the archetype of all friendship, as even only Germans, only men can."[53] One senses here that the biographer's need to clarify the nature of male intimacy may have been spurred by his readers' awareness of the increasingly public nature of the debate over sexuality. "Grosser forms of personal union" were not admissible when contemplating the rarefied bonds between German men of the caliber of Goethe and Schiller.

In the case of Schubert, it would strain the evidence to conclude with certainty that the unproblematic characterizations of his close friendships were influenced by an anxiety over suspicions that could have been fostered by the fin-de-siècle literature of sexuality, from which the composer was largely absent. As often as not, the matter did not even arise for those writers who were convinced that the composer's career had been so uneventful as to be irrelevant. After all, if medical writings and their pseudoscientific offspring claimed that the searching analysis of their subjects' lives was necessary to produce meaningful case studies, a composer who by tradition had a thoroughly unremarkable existence apart from his music could easily be passed over. Yet, an indication that the fin-de-siècle controversies over writings on sexuality may have cast a shadow, however pale, over Schubert's reception is the occasional appearance of arguments that sought to rescue the composer from the well-worn tradition of his essentially feminine nature.

In an essay on Vienna's Schubert centennial festival in 1897, Heinrich Schenker endeavored to counter any impression that Schubert's passive relationships betrayed any dubious inborn trait. Recounting the teenage composer's recourse to working in his father's school, Schenker cited the biographical tradition suggesting that the masculine Beethoven would never have accepted such a fate against his will. Schenker rejected the notion that Schubert's decision was due to an inherently passive nature and instead averred that it was the result of economic exigency. Needing to eke out a living, "all the manliness of poor Schubert would have been to no avail."[54] Schenker's argument confronts the earlier construction of Schubert's *Mädchencharakter*, traced in chapter 2 of the first volume of this study, in which the composer's feminine nature had an almost Darwinian innate quality. Indeed, Schenker's essay could be taken as a point-by-point repudiation of Schubert's reception as encapsulated by the piano pedagogue Louis Köhler in a multipart biographical article of 1882, in which Schubert's compliant behavior was an early indication of "a characteristic of feminine passivity." Köhler stressed that this passive nature did not arise from the difficult situation in which the teenage Schubert found himself. Rather, this trait was essentially congenital: "If he suffered and submitted to wretched conditions that were themselves impairments to his great talent, then this happened because he was born a weak character, which had constructed its nature more from feeling than from industriousness." Citing Schumann as his authority, but misquoting him, Köhler described Schubert as "the feminine Beethoven": a socially timid person who had "in himself a maidenly nature."[55] For Schenker, such a comparison with Beethoven was utterly specious. As a purely practical matter, Schubert did not enjoy yearly subventions from a devoted aristocracy, as was the case with Beethoven. Instead, Schubert eventually came to rely on his young companions for lodging and money.

Schenker went further, by qualifying Schubert's friendships as innocent ("harmlos"), which could suggest a concern that a reader just might have misinterpreted the composer's intimate associations, especially as they involved an individual who was traditionally construed as less than masculine. After all, the dates of the articles by Köhler and Schenker frame a period when the science of sexuality first acquired a sensational public notoriety that could cause a hitherto innocuous trait like passivity to be placed under a psychological cloud. Schenker, of course, may not have been aware of the burgeoning literature on sexuality at this time, although his essay appeared in the same Viennese journal where three years earlier Julius Pap had worried about the familiarity of contemporary youth with the writings of Krafft-Ebing, by that time a fixture in the city's scientific community. Moreover, one suspects that Schenker's almost morbid preoccupation in the 1920s with the more perverse implications of sexuality was not a sudden addition to his critical lexicon. (In his articles in *Der Tonwille*, Schenker regularly cited as despicable those features of sexuality that threatened "the genius of Germanity." "Lecherous lusting" needed to be opposed by "total self-abnegation and ceaseless self-sacrifice." The "wondrous musical art" that was the hallmark of the Austro-German tradition was unsullied by sexuality, especially in contrast to the followers of Frenchness, which was consumed with "genital play and form." For Schenker, "a line of Goethe's poetry, a musical smile by Brahms, ha[d] more loveliness than all the bestiality of French masculinity and femininity.")[56] As someone who in 1924 described Schubert's musical notation in the manuscript of "Gretchen am Spinnrade" as "an old friend since childhood," Schenker may well have been at pains to counter the notion that the composer's apparent passivity—a term that had acquired an association with a dubious effeminate nature—could have been anything other than circumstantial.[57]

Whether or not, in Schenker's particular case, there may be a specific causal relationship between a shift in thinking about Schubert's nature and the medical discourse on sexuality, one cannot help but observe that the explosion in pseudoscientific and popular literature on the subject occurred as some writers sought to discredit nineteenth-century interpretations of the passive and feminine character of Schubert and his music. The foregoing discussion provides a context that may help to explain why the Berlin-born Walter Dahms, one of Schubert's German biographers, made the effort to break with the storied tradition of the composer's *Mädchencharakter* in 1912:

> Schubert's language is masculine in the highest degree. In his tender moods as well, in the blurring lines of many dreamy lyrics, he never turns into a feminine channel. His sensitivity was never toward sentimentality. "The Viennese element in Schubert is southernly sensual, and sentimentality is a north German sickness," apostrophized Hans von

Bülow. To the masculine element in his musical language, bursting with health, there is joined the unerotic and chaste like a refreshing breath of air. In this regard he takes after Beethoven. In the work of both there is missing the feverish, all-consuming sensual glut whose unexcelled master is Richard Wagner. Perhaps this is also justifiably due to his lack of theatrical instincts. Schubert's happiness in love keeps itself within the limits of enthusiasm [Schwärmerei]. It certainly is intensified by desire, but never by lust. A pure image always shines from it toward us. His lack of the erotic in art lies well founded in his character as an artist. He was deeply spiritual, without calculation. He was even less sensational than he was topical. Art was for him the end, not the means.[58]

Dahms's description neatly shifted the musical comparison from Beethoven and Schubert to Schubert and Wagner, a composer whose dubiously gendered sensibility had been by that time a well-rehearsed feature brought to bear against him by his critics. Much of Dahms's description echoes older biographies, but his insistence on divorcing Schubert from the traits of lust and erotic desire, while maintaining that his music exuded a robust masculinity, is particularly understandable in the wake of a quarter century of medical studies that examined the sexual yearnings between men.

The foregoing indicates that there is some evidence to suggest that during the fin de siècle a new consideration of sexuality, emerging from the medical profession but also apparent in modernist literature, may have prompted some writers, aware of the popular tradition of Schubert's *Mädchencharakter*, to avoid treating his case with any specificity or even to challenge the older gendered interpretation, which now may have connoted a more questionable type of behavior with regard to the composer's friendships. Whereas the nineteenth century had promulgated the idea of Schubert's feminine character, it had also bequeathed the notion that his life, including his personal relationships, was so mundane as to be irrelevant to an understanding of his greatness. Since the science of sexuality required such evidence, Schubert may well have escaped the level of scrutiny applied to other iconic figures of culture. Even so, one cannot easily determine whether his reception, or lack of it, was due to the fact that his case was not amenable to scientific exploration or due to wider cultural anxiety over what such a study might imply. Only in 1915 did a colleague of Freud attempt a psychoanalytical inquiry into Schubert's life, although here too the conclusions conveyed a noteworthy circumspection.

Schubert, of course, was not the only individual whose outer existence, including his erotic life, was considered by turn-of-the-century writers to be utterly subsumed by and channeled into the products of his imagination. This ability, in fact, could be regarded as a distinguishing trait of genius. Freud's 1910 essay on Leonardo da Vinci—the only lengthy discussion of a creative person that Freud produced—recognized that passion was not absent from the Renaissance master's process of transformation into an artist and scientist. Leonardo, however, directed his fervor toward creative rather than personal ends:

> He [Leonardo] had merely converted his passion into a thirst for knowledge; he then applied himself to investigation with the persistence, constancy and penetration which is derived from passion, and at the climax of intellectual labour, when knowledge had been won, he allowed the long restrained affect to break loose and to flow away freely, as a stream of water drawn from a river is allowed to flow away when its work is done.[59]

Surging water also happened to be a popular image for Schubert's output as well. Mahler had described the Symphony no. 9 in C Major (D. 944) as a work that "is like a rushing river flowing freely and indomitably, so abundant that without needing to contain it you can drink freely wherever you put your lips to the water."[60] For the fin-de-siècle mind, however, no mutual consideration of Leonardo and Schubert could easily have gone beyond this aqueous metaphor, since da Vinci's analytic genius was not part of the tradition that had characterized Schubert's unthinking lyricism.

Freud's essay had not used Leonardo's correspondence as its starting point but rather utilized a childhood recollection of the artist as the basis for a psychological study (although Freud famously mistranslated a key element in the narrative, substituting a vulture for a kite that came to the infant Leonardo's cradle and opened his mouth with its tail).[61] There was a piece of writing by Schubert, however, that did have its parallel in the composer's career: the brief document that his brother Ferdinand had entitled "Mein Traum" ("My Dream"), under which name Schumann had published it in 1839 in the *Neue Zeitschrift für Musik.* Although it was often mentioned during the nineteenth century, beginning with Kreissle, who reprinted it and left its interpretation to the reader, its meaning had baffled many fin-de-siècle writers even as they agreed on its poignant character. George Grove, Schubert's most dedicated Victorian biographer, guessed that it may have alluded to "some dispute on religious subjects," while Dahms hazarded that it was "the poetic representation of his youthful sorrows."[62] In 1908, the French musicologist Louis Bourgault-Ducoudray reiterated the view expressed more than a half century earlier by Hippolyte Barbedette, who had written a French summary of Kreissle's biography, that it was "a strange, nearly incomprehensible work," while the British critic Joseph Bennett opined in 1881 that "no clue to its meaning has ever been discovered. That it refers to himself we may well believe; but what is meant by the 'favourite garden' where in he could take no delight, and, above all, what do the dead maiden, the grave, the circle of happy youths, and the spontaneous music signify? We vainly ask the master's biographers and commentators, who have nothing to tell us."[63]

With Freud's monograph providing an early example of how a famous creative individual might be subjected to his psychoanalytic method, one of his colleagues, Eduard Hitschmann, finally took up the subject of "Mein Traum" in 1915 in the pages of the *Internationale Zeitschrift für ärztliche Psychoanalyse.* Freud had taken the lead in the founding of this journal two years earlier, and in its pages he had published several articles that expanded upon his work on the psychological interpretation of dreams. In 1913, Hitschmann had written essays elsewhere that applied Freudian techniques to famous people including Goethe, Schopenhauer, and Swedenborg, creating a body of work that prompted Freud the following year to credit his colleague with pioneering the psychoanalytic study of "philosophical systems and personalities."[64] Thus, Hitschmann was well versed in this approach by the time he arrived at his verdict on Schubert:

> In conclusion, the inner conflicts, which are postulated in our contemporary knowledge of the psychogenesis of the artist, may be perceived in their main features in *My Dream*. Love and hate, or rather love rendered unhappy by his rebellion against the powerful father, sympathetic love for the mother—the Oedipus-theme was afire in the young boy. Unable to find inward freedom from his father, he remained somewhat effeminate, passive [Weibliche, Leidende] all his life. A union of sensual and pure love remained unattainable for him.[65]

Given the professional background of both the author and his readership, Hitschmann's use of words like "effeminate" and "passive" was not likely to fall neatly within the traditional confines of the Victorian strictures against moral weakness. Although the actual German terms that Hitschmann used did not have universally agreed-upon clinical meanings, they were nonetheless becoming freighted with connotations beyond their older innocuous usage. For fin-de-siècle medical men, passivity had assumed more than a generic meaning. As Hirschfeld had remarked: "If we have perceived the essence of pure masculine spirit in activity, that of the woman in passivity [Passivität], then let us say about the uranian spirit, that it is more active than the female, but not so active as the male, further, that it appears much more passive than the male, but not as widely passive as the female psyche [weibliche Psyche]."[66]

Effeminacy, too, was a term that, following Krafft-Ebing, was acquiring significance in medical discourse beyond its customary cultural use. Iwan Bloch, another leader in the scientific study of sexuality, understood the term *Effemination* to refer to the process by which the powerful impact of habitual behaviors altered a man's psychological and physical nature. He defined it thus:

> If a male person constantly indulges himself in female pursuits, constantly squeezes himself into female dress, is constantly forced to appear in female roles, to display female characteristics, female feelings, then gradually these activities more and more have to feminize the individual in question. This feminization [Verweiblichung] then impresses itself not solely in the psyche, but also outwardly in the physical appearance.[67]

Bloch seriously doubted that such individuals necessarily had an erotic interest in members of their own sex: "There are apparently feminine men who correspond here to the ideal sketched; I would strongly be inclined to doubt, however, whether they are always *Weiblinge*, that is, uranians, homosexuals, since many men of a somewhat feminine habit feel thoroughly heterosexual, indeed are passionate friends of women and are just as passionately loved by women."[68] By the same token, individuals could still harbor same-sex desire without it ever manifesting itself in a visibly physical way.

Bloch's definition, of course, is only partly applicable to Hitschmann's Schubert, whose inner life as reflected in "My Dream," as opposed to any biographical details, remained the focus of the essay's psychoanalytic examination. Although descriptions of Schubert's face and body might have supported the conclusions Hitschmann arrived at, he was either uninterested in or unaware of the tradition that emphasized the rounded features of the composer; those tell-tale signs were among the characteristics that fin-de-siècle medical writers often cited as manifestations of a man's femininity. (Hirschfeld's survey of 100 Viennese homosexual men—a sample from which he estimated that 15,000 or 1% of the city's population were so inclined—revealed to him that most bore a clear reminder of the feminine form in the round lines of their upper arms and hips.)[69] Furthermore, elsewhere in his essay, Hitschmann enumerated a separate set of traits that were unrelated to physical appearance and that defined the poet Mayrhofer, the composer's sometime roommate, as "a homosexual type" ("ideell homosexuell"). These characteristics included Mayrhofer's "repugnance of women," his authorship of the volume *Contributions to the Education of Young Boys*, his fondness for Greek antiquity in his verse, his "moral austerity and stoical habits," and ultimately his suicide.[70] As additional evidence, Hitschmann cited Mayrhofer's poem to Schubert, the content of which displayed the same effusiveness as in the Schwind-Schober correspondence that had so interested Fuchs. Immediately following this list, however, Hitschmann provided the reader with a psychological diagnosis of the poem's recipient, whose companionable disposition, contrasted with Mayrhofer's character, was sensually less volatile. Schubert "appears to have been more capable of friendship than of love as is shown by his stronger feeling for men, a situation we usually find in cases of powerful infantile father-ties." By 1915, intense friendships may have become for some writers a problematic category with regard to same-sex relationships, but for contemporary medical men like Hitschmann it was still insufficient grounds for drawing any definitive conclusions about an individual's erotic nature.

Whatever one thinks of such psychobiography, one may understand Hitschmann's essay as a product of the scientific inquiry into sexuality that burgeoned during the fin de siècle. Because of the relatively rarefied type of journal in which it appeared, and perhaps owing to the disruptive impact of the war, the article made no discernible difference to the immediate perception of Schubert's *Mädchencharakter*. In the afterword to a little compilation of documents from and to the composer's friends that appeared a year after Hitschmann's article, Felix Braun could write about the relationship of Schubert and Schwind without any hint of a problematic cloud: "The deepest love for Schubert was felt by someone who was truly intimate with him in spirit: Mortiz von Schwind. In jest, Schubert called him his 'beloved.' "[71] (This was the same slim volume that Hofmannsthal had included in the *Österreischiche Bibliothek* series.) Even on the rare occasion when Hitschmann's essay was cited as an authority, as in the case of an article on Schubert's pathology by the music critic Ferdinand Scherber, the subject of the composer's desire warranted an explanation in which a libidinal motivation was considered to be unlikely:

> It appears—it can here only be a matter of suggestion, not a completely clarifying explanation—that Schubert was afflicted with inhibited drives, suppressed complexes, and therewith neurasthenia. What kind of complexes these were must be researched. These may not have been of an erotic nature, if Bauernfeld, who is just not that reliable, was not correct, that an intense desire for a certain woman (Countess Esterházy?) dominated Schubert and he sought to gratify this desire in another form.[72]

The coyness in this statement may be due to the timing and location of its publication, which would not have been especially conducive to expanding upon the psychological dark alleys in Hitschmann's diagnosis of an Oedipal complex. It appeared in 1928 in that most venerable of Viennese daily newspapers, the *Wiener Zeitung*, as part of an issue devoted to the commemoration of the centennial of the composer's death. Whatever Scherber may have wished to imply, neither the occasion for the article nor its audience would have been amenable to elaborating on the problematic implications of the composer's possible emotional urges.

For lay readers at the turn of the century, especially those for whom cultural modernism was a source of anxiety, medical studies on sexual pathology served principally as sources for the illustration of deviance. This connection, as we have seen, was sufficient for critics to use the feminization of fin-de-siècle literature against its exponents (and, because so many of its authors were also Jewish, at times to add an anti-Semitic patina onto the judgment.) Nor were the adherents of modernism unaware of the implications behind their enemies' appropriation of contemporary studies on sexuality. Bahr, for example, worked hard at disassociating the meaning of intimate male friendships from the taint of perversity when he extolled the poetic virtues of August von Platen, who, at the turn of the century, was the most obvious subject for a case study of an early nineteenth-century creative homosexual mind. Bahr argued that relationships between members of the same sex need not extend to the physical passion that fin-de-siècle medicine usually diagnosed as a sickness and the broader culture most often construed as both a vice and a crime. Instead, the purest rapture could be sensed through the metaphorical kiss of a beautiful mind that was motivated by virtue rather than by lust; a mere glance or turn of the head offered sufficient satisfaction. The "turbulent desire" between two men, at once free and innocent, was "aimed at a nobler occupation than the slanderers can conceive."[73] For Bahr, the attraction between such individuals achieved a spiritual connection whose devotion and tenderness evinced "the deepest morality" if only one did not view it through the lens of a Krafft-Ebing.

Schubert, however, may not have required a similar act of cultural rescue. The condemnations leveled against Jung-Wien writers and their literary forebears did not infect contemporary estimations of the composer, who could continue to be characterized as womanly without this carrying a psychological taint, notwithstanding the manipulation of the tradition of his feminine nature by the likes of Schnitzler, Hofmannsthal, and—as we will see—Peter Altenberg. To be sure, there are tantalizing hints that pursuing the interpretative path cleared by fin-de-siècle sexologists might risk entering an unsavory realm, hence the occasional contemporary effort to imbue Schubert with a masculinity that hitherto had not been a notable feature of his reception. More often, however, the old images displayed a remarkable resilience, especially if there was a nationalist agenda at stake. To take an example from the war year of 1915, the year in which Hitschmann's essay appeared, consider Konrad Huschke trotting out the hoary comparison between Schubert and Beethoven: "By contrast [with Beethoven], one could perhaps picture Schubert's muse as a wonderfully lovely maidenly bloom, whose laughing and yet wistful eyes gaze into the world, elfish and yet full of sadness, Viennese cheerfulness wondrously coalesced with deep melancholy."[74] As opposed to Beethoven's glorious confidence and reckless commitment, Schubert's greatness was hidden behind a round, soft face and an "almost pathological meekness." These attributes, however, bore no problematic connotations. As a German writer during the war, Huschke emphasized the overarching nationalistic trait that united the two composers and was revealed in Schubert's turn away from Rossini and toward Beethoven: "Thus, at one in pure German conviction, both have acted in the most beautiful sense for German art, and for her as for themselves have created a *monumentum aere perennius*."[75]

By the end of World War I, the worst criticism that might be leveled at Schubert by one of his own countrymen was not that his life might hide dubious traits but that his works carried the seeds of a rank sentimentality for which too many Austrians, even so-called modernists, had evinced an indiscriminate affection. This was not a surprising charge if one's cultural memory was nauseated by the wholesale popularity of fin-de-siècle operettas, especially if they were juxtaposed against the recent devastation wrought throughout Europe. Such was the case with Hermann Broch who, as we have earlier observed, had little sympathy for what he construed as the epigonal character of Hofmannsthal's aesthetic. In a diary entry of August 22, 1920, he noted:

After supper my brother played Schubert, to rework it into Foxtrots. He [Schubert] doesn't deserve any better: the entire world of Viennese operetta is already present in him. The problem with Schubert, as with all so-called "light" music (with few exceptions) is: it's all been said already—the construct[ion] of a relationship to all that exists [die Konstruktion des Gesamtzusammenhanges des Seienden überhaupt] as in Beethoven, for example, is no longer possible. Of course, one need not be "musical" to know this; musicality is a precarious concept anyway—music is the only art in which receptivity is seen as positive, which of course it is not.[76]

The implicit comparison to Beethoven feeds upon a tradition that was by then nearly a century old. Although it reduced Schubert to a status that made him little more than a prop for the likes of Heinrich Berté's operetta *Das Dreimäderlhaus*, it fits in with Broch's later critique of Vienna as the "metropolis of Kitsch": a place ideally suited to "the [nineteenth] century of bourgeois aestheticization and its eclecticism" but incapable of coming to terms with the postwar world.[77] That Broch should have divined in Schubert the kernel of Viennese operetta bespeaks the popularity enjoyed by compositions like *Das Dreimäderlhaus*. More than any other work of musical theater giving a wholly fictionalized account of Schubert's failed love life, it enjoyed a durability that resulted in translations into other languages as well as a sequel, and certainly became the most enduring sentimental image of the composer.[78] In one respect, Broch was prescient, since the nature of Schubert, which served as the basis for Broch's description, was one that would stubbornly endure in the popular mind throughout the ensuing decades. Broch had little use for the nostalgic masks constructed by Jung-Wien writers, some of whom nevertheless ultimately treated Schubert in this fashion. None did so with more constancy and compassion than Peter Altenberg.

Chapter Six

Peter Altenberg's Schubert

The Schubert *Mädchencharakter* bequeathed a vocabulary that the representatives of Jung-Wien employed to reflect upon the thought and art of Viennese high culture at the turn of the century. The most characteristic agent of this was Peter Altenberg. He invoked the composer's name and music more often than any contemporary, and, to that extent, he might be said to be the most Schubertian of fin-de-siècle Viennese writers. Beyond this, however, Altenberg's use of the composer exploited the tension between innocence and desire with such nuanced complexity that charting the progress of his reception of Schubert can illuminate key features of Austrian modernism at the turn of the century. Musicians know Altenberg as the literary source of a cycle of Lieder by Berg, but in the two decades before World War I, he was Vienna's shrewdest coffeehouse wit. He was greatly admired among the city's avant-garde, including Karl Kraus and Adolf Loos, and he was a formative influence on Kafka, Mann, and Rilke. We can observe Altenberg's manipulation of the Schubert *Mädchencharakter* on two interwoven fronts: first, his identification with Schubert and his work as conveying an essentially feminine character, and second, his recasting of it as a source of artistic inspiration symbolized by his interpretation of the relationship between the composer and Caroline Esterházy.

A key feature of turn-of-the-century modernism was the artist's construction of an alternative self designed to combat the dual assaults on reality of a disintegrating social order and the individual's unconscious impulses. In assuming the Bohemian life of a Viennese feuilletonist, Peter Altenberg successfully masked his old identity as Richard Engländer, son of a prosperous middle-class businessman. That name change permitted a severing of ties to bourgeois culture, which became the satiric object of his aphorisms. As a twenty-three-year-old at the Altenberg spa, he had fallen in love with the thirteen-year-old Bertha Lecher, whose nickname, Peter, completed the recasting of his identity. His assumption of her name was his first act of empathy with that feminine nature, which he argued was the center of creative inspiration and the source of redemption for a corrupt culture, an argument that accompanied his disdain for the bourgeois values that seemed to hold women in their thrall.

Contemporary photographs of Altenberg might cause one to wonder at this gender identification. Studio portraits like that of Anton Trcka did little to disguise his homeliness. With expressionist mercilessness, paintings by Oskar Kokoschka and Gustav Jagerspacher, both from 1909, exaggerated Altenberg's wild stare and agitated hands, thus drawing attention to his health, deteriorating due to alcohol. Other caricatures placed him in milieus surrounded by adoring women or cherubs, unsubtle reminders of the writer's ill-concealed fondness for prostitutes and young girls. Yet the features of the outer man were only a mask that disguised the inner spirit of the artist, as Altenberg himself emphasized in an inscription in English on Jagerspacher's painting: "Are we not all only Karikatures [sic] from the truly and ideal wishes, which God and Nature hade [sic] with our souls and our bodies?!?"[1]

The union of male body and female spirit was likewise apparent to Altenberg's contemporaries. In a brochure of 1914 entitled *Bild und Photo*, Hans Heinz Ewers described Altenberg as an androgynous figure, recalling Zweig's characterization of Hofmannsthal:

> Peter Altenberg does not know what a Danae he is himself nor that every artist must be one: masculine and feminine alike, impregnating and giving birth. The purely male man will never have a profound relationship to art, nor will the entirely female woman: Hermes and Aphrodite created the soul of the artist *together*.[2]

Ewers argued that photography required an inherently female talent because it demanded a mastery of surfaces, a position that is partly explicable by the fact that his brochure was advertising the studio of Dora Kallmus, known as Madame d'Ora, Vienna's most famous portraitist. The intersection of the surface and the feminine was precisely the point made by Hofmannsthal when he reviewed Altenberg's collection of photographs: "Thus the fact of the poet, which was submerged in a hundred stories, floats to the surface. A very stylised face, with a great complicated simplicity. With feminine eyes so to speak, of what is called feminine in men."[3] Hofmannsthal, in fact, may have been the first writer to observe this gendered nature in Altenberg's work by describing the peculiar complexity of Altenberg's first publication, *Wie ich es sehe*, in 1896. For Hofmannsthal, the book had aspects that were frivolous and childlike even as it paradoxically possessed both unscrupulousness and a self-conscious grace. Because it was completely unconcerned with everything that was important, it could not be a German book. It had to be Viennese and, as such, it operated in a feminine manner: "It therewith also flirts with its source, just as it flirts with its sentiment."[4]

That Peter should also be the second name of Altenberg's favorite composer is possibly a coincidence. Schubert, however, figured significantly in a transformative childhood memory that Altenberg commemorated in the sketch "Mama" in 1913. Altenberg recalled that, as a ten-year-old, he had suffered from a severe foot infection, which kept him bedridden for almost a year and led one doctor to advise amputation. Upon hearing from another physician that the foot would heal without recourse to this drastic measure, Altenberg's mother turned to Schubert's music to express her relief:

> My mother kneeled by my bed, but only for a moment. She then went into the next room and at the piano played and sang Schubert's "Die Forelle." The voice teacher said: "Your voice sounds fresher today, you must have had a quieter night yesterday!"— "No," she said, "but I will have one today!"[5]

The unique stature that Schubert enjoyed during Altenberg's formative years was also signaled by the inventory of names the writer created in 1919, in which he enumerated the "gods" of his youth, beginning with his own father. Whereas Wagner was among the list of poetic deities that included Hugo, Zola, Dickens, and Grillparzer, Schubert ranked as the sole "Musik-Gott" who had inspired his "impressionable young spirit."[6]

For the grown man, Schubert became precisely the fellow Viennese with whom Altenberg identified, just as the writer's career mirrored that of the composer: living a Bohemian existence unacknowledged by a frivolous bourgeois society, producing art that was inherently feminine, admired by a select few, and presenting an unassuming and even ugly appearance that masked an artist's soul. In making himself Schubert's creative offspring, Altenberg declared that an outlandish pose without artistic imagination was an insufficient means of achieving spirituality:

> Freaks are not necessarily geniuses, although geniuses were often freaks. Yet they were only just seemingly so. For behind them God and nature were enthroned, even if a little bit in all too grotesque forms. There are states of intoxication in which one composes symphonies; and there are states of intoxication in which one vomits. Both are states of intoxication, ecstasies, exaggerated conditions. But the two states are not equal; and not every staggering drunk in his solitary room writes Schubert Lieder.[7]

Altenberg's point was that he, like Schubert, was both freak and genius. As a writer who acknowledged that all his work had an element of autobiography, Altenberg found in Schubert's unprepossessing features a reflection of his own condition. Like the composer, whose appearance masked his true identity, the writer assumed the superior feminine traits of creative intuition and artistic instinct in order to achieve spiritual refinement.

A favorite Altenberg metaphor for this desired spirituality was Schubert's trout, the subject of the Lied sung by his mother. Trout fishing was an activity that provided an escape from both social obligation and physical sustenance.[8] As a modernist, Altenberg recognized that the old romantic program of art mediating between life and nature was at the mercy of the brutish, technological world of masculine culture. Thus in "Grammophonplatte" from *Märchen des Lebens* (1908), the reader becomes only gradually aware with each paragraph that the writer has constructed reality not from nature itself nor even from a performance of one of the Schubert's most popular songs, "Die Forelle" (D. 550, op. 32), but from a recording:

> In music, flowing mountain streams, murmuring crystal clear between rocks and woods. The trout, a charming predator, light gray with red spots, awaiting a victim, still, drifting, darting forth, up, down, disappearing. Mountain water; transformed into a predator. Graceful killer!
>
> The piano accompaniment is the sweet, soft, monotonous gurgling of mountain water, deep and dark green. Real life no longer exists. One senses the fairy tales of nature!
>
> I became acquainted with it in Gmunden, when a woman in the shop of a watchmaker would play the gramophone record C 2-42 531 two or three times every day in the afternoon. She sat on a stool. I stood next to the machine.
>
> We never spoke to each other.
>
> Thereafter she always held off on the concert until I appeared.
>
> One day she paid for the piece three times, then she wanted to leave. Then I paid for it a fourth time. She remained standing at the door, listening to it until the end.
>
> Gramophone record C 2-42 531, Schubert, the trout.
>
> One day she no longer came.
>
> Like a gift from her the song now stayed behind with me.
>
> Autumn came, and the esplanade was shining with sparse yellow leaves.
>
> For here as well the gramophone in the watchmaker's shop was turned off, because it didn't pay for itself any more.[9]

This dreamlike narrative articulates the desire to recreate a state of innocence that might substitute for a contemporary culture that was commercial and mundane, and hence masculine. Altenberg might evade contemporary life, but not with an old romantic strategy. The technology of the record player is what inspires the writer, not the direct experience of nature nor even the aesthetic contemplation of a musical performance. As Wendelin Schmidt-Dengler has observed, such a modernist contradiction between the "yearning for nature, pure and unalloyed" and "a way of life that is indissolubly wedded to civilization" meant the former was available to Altenberg only through the medium, at two removes, of a recording of Schubert's song, the same piece he elsewhere recalled his mother singing to assuage a boyhood illness.[10]

The desire to escape brutal reality via aesthetic experience was a popular theme in fin-de-siècle Viennese culture. For Altenberg, Schubert—with all his feminine characteristics so reminiscent of the writer himself—was the ideal incarnation of that world. Contemporary life was irreconcilable with artistic creativity, however, and the two collided in the sketch "Franz Schubert":

> When was the last time I cried bitterly?! Precisely one hour ago, three in the afternoon, 9 August 1915. What, interesting?! And why did the old fellow cry again?! He bought himself for 20 Heller the biography of his idol Franz Schubert by A. Niggli. At the passage: "Dressed in the ordinary garment of a hermit of that time, the laurel wreathed about the temple, the remains lay on the bier, 19 November 1828, in his thirty-second year of life." And why did he buy the "biography" today?!

Because on three successive days three successive gentlemen said to him: "What, don't you even know what your idol died of!?! Fish poisoning; at least you should know about that!" "S[yphilis] . . . ; at least you should know about that!" "Tuberculosis; at least you should know about that!"[11]

Altenberg once again identifies himself with the composer, moved by the romanticized death portrayed in Arnold Niggli's biography of 1889, which was a source of particular significance for Altenberg, as we shall see shortly. When Altenberg identifies himself with Schubert, however, autobiographical reality intrudes in the form of the circumstances of the composer's illnesses, which are forced upon Altenberg's idyllic daydreams. The grim litany echoes the writer's own deteriorating health, which resulted in periodic treatment at several hospitals starting in 1910 and culminating in a five-month stay at the Am Steinhof Psychiatric Hospital in early 1913. The juxtaposition of Schubert and sickness comes full circle, recalling the childhood memory in which the writer's imagination was comforted by his mother's singing "Die Forelle" while he suffered from a foot infection. Such spiritual comfort stands in direct confrontation to sordid reality, whether in the form of anonymous men inflicting upon Altenberg the knowledge of Schubert's maladies or of the doctor advising the amputation of his foot.

Altenberg's attraction to Schubert as a feminine type coincided with his belief that woman's powers of intuition and instinct, which were also the attributes of Schubert's music, could provide spiritual ennoblement and creative inspiration. As Zweig observed of Altenberg in 1901: "It is almost always the psyche of the woman that attracts him. Because for him the woman's soul is the most intimate, sensitive instrument, whose nervous oscillations he overhears with deep devotion even as he worships like an evangelist the woman's body, whose sanctity never can be blemished."[12] Altenberg's assumption of this feminine identity was the elevated core of his being that belied the facade of the itinerant Bohemian. Yet it was not only woman's spiritual refinement; physical perfection was equally necessary. For Altenberg, the more innocent and youthful the female, the purer was her essence. Indeed, the greater her unawareness of her attractiveness, the more desirable she was as a source of artistic contemplation and possibly more than that as well. Thus, in his "Wiener Ballade: Franz Schubert" of 1916, Altenberg supplies a paradoxically double perspective of Schubertian imagery. His description of the physically unattractive but creatively gifted composer stands for Altenberg himself, yet artistic inspiration is insufficient to attract the very type of *süße Mädel* whose beauty and innocence themselves constitute the essence of Schubertian femininity:

> If one is chubby,
> and if one is short-legged,
> if one is no-necked,
> and if one is asthmatic,
> if one has a thick head of curls,

and if one has short fat mitts, then not "Erlkönig,"
"Die Forelle," "Die Post," "Du bist die Ruh,"
"Der Wanderer," not even "Am Meer" will be of
any use with a sweet, sweet, sweet young thing!
One just does not like to go to sleep with fat larks!
They are for the lovely dawning day!
Poor, poor little Franz![13]

Herein lies what might be called the Altenberg problem, because whatever empathy the writer may have felt for women, even when mediated through Schubertian symbols, an unmistakable record exists of his attraction toward young girls.

Literary critics have disagreed on the extent and significance of the sexual component of Altenberg's *Frauenkult*, and it is arguably another facet of modernist paradox that the writer continually smudged the traditional line that divided *femme fatale* from *femme fragile*.[14] Such was the case with his evolving metaphor of the trout, which, by 1913 in the collection *Semmering 1912*, had become a dangerous creature that could nevertheless be caught with the right kind of lure, unlike women, who most of the time threw off the hook and consumed the bait. To what extent Altenberg may have divined an explicitly sexual symbolism in the verse of Christian Friedrich Daniel Schubart's "Die Forelle," set by Schubert, the fact that in "Grammophonplatte" he characterized the fish as both a charming predator and a graceful killer who lay in wait for a victim does invite one to hypothesize that it stood for his increasingly contradictory attitudes toward women.[15] (In this respect, contemporary art offered visual equivalents as, for example, in Klimt's *Fish Blood* and *Whitefish* from 1898–99.)

From the beginning of his career, in fact, Schubert's music served Altenberg as a symbol of the childlike female who nonetheless incited problematic feelings in men, even those whose relationship should have placed them beyond such emotions. "Friede," from *Wie ich es sehe*, follows the apparently mundane daily rituals of Christine, who is young enough to play with her potted plants as though they are little children. At the dining room table, however, her father experiences a disturbing instance of doubt: "Father drinks coffee and one notices that he loves his little daughter very much. But what sort of look does he have?! Does he desire her?! Is she like a Schubert song for him?! Does he become another man and consider himself lucky?! Perhaps a prayer of thanks sounds in his heart?! Not at all."[16] The phenomenon passes as quickly as it arrived. Yet one is left with a sense of having experienced a rather creepy moment in an otherwise uninteresting bourgeois scene in which the gulf between paternal love and male desire is bridged, however briefly, precisely because the girl's Schubertian character is both artless and alluring.

An extraordinary example of the collision between innocence and passion manifests itself in Altenberg's fascination with an event in Schubert's life whose implications of gender and sexuality he manipulated for his own expressive ends. The vignette describing this event must have held particular importance for Altenberg because, under the title "Schubert," it appeared in two different volumes of his work:

> I often read over Niggli's Schubert biography. That is to say, its intent is to convey Schubert's life, not Niggli's thoughts about it!
>
> But I've read the passage a hundred times, page 37. At the estate of Prince Esterházy in Zseliz, he was of course music teacher to the quite young countesses Marie and Caroline. But he lost his heart to Caroline. From that arose his works for piano four hands. The young countess never learned of his deep attraction. Only once, when she teased him, that he had still not dedicated any composition to her, he replied: "Why bother?! It's all for you anyhow!"
>
> It's as if so full a heart in its grief opened itself, and then closed itself for all time—. For that reason I often open to page 37 in Niggli's Schubert biography.[17]

Barely a hundred pages in length, the biography by Arnold Niggli, a Swiss writer on music, was widely disseminated at the turn of the century. It enjoyed a popular appeal in Vienna, where it was one of the sources most cited by journalists reporting on the celebrations of the composer's centennial. Niggli's reputation was sufficient for him to be invited to deliver the keynote speech for the Schubertbund's gathering in commemoration of the composer's birth at the Festsaal of the Wiedener Gemeindehaus, where he acclaimed Schubert as "the romantic par excellence, the musician who always uplifts us, in whose blood dwells no drop of pessimism, who made mankind happy with his tones."[18] Further, even if Niggli's slim volume was the only source of Schubert's life with which one was acquainted, it was still sufficient to convey to the reader a nature whose "feminine passivity" was demonstrable in the composer's acquiescence to working at his father's school.[19]

The passage in Niggli's biography to which Altenberg referred was a regurgitation of events first chronicled by Kreissle in 1865. The composer purportedly fell in love with Caroline Esterházy, the younger daughter of the Hungarian nobleman whose family he served as music teacher in 1818 and 1824, when she was eleven and seventeen respectively. In Kreissle's account:

> Schubert very often made himself merry at the expense of any friends of his who fell in love. He too was by no means proof against the tender passion, but never seriously compromised himself. Nothing is known of any lasting passion, and he never seems to have thought seriously about matrimony; but he certainly coquetted with love, and was no stranger to the deeper and truer affections [ernsterer, tieferer Neigung]. Soon after his entering into the Esterházy family, he had a flirtation with one of the servants, which soon paled before a more romantic passion, which consumed the inflammatory Schubert. This was for the Countess's younger daughter, Caroline. The flame was not extinguished before his death. Caroline esteemed him, and appreciated his genius, but did not return his love, and probably never guessed its extent and fervency. His feelings toward her must have been clear enough, by Schubert's own declaration. Once she jestingly reproached him for never having dedicated any piece of music to her; his reply was, "What would be the good of it? Everything I have ever done has been dedicated to you!"[20]

This anecdote had come to Kreissle from notes recorded by Karl von Schönstein, who was a guest of the Esterházys in 1818 and 1824 and who took part in musical performances with the family and the composer. Schönstein had originally given his reminiscence in January 1857 to Ferdinand Luib, who was collecting material for his own biography of the composer.[21] The complete details of this recollection were apparently not entirely known to Kreissle when he wrote his first biographical sketch of the composer four years earlier in 1861 (or, if he was in possession of them, he chose not to use them). There a reader learned only that "the Fantasy [in F Minor for piano duet], one of Schubert's most beautiful piano pieces, was dedicated by him to the young Countess Esterházy, his only pupil, whose talent gave him a great deal of joy and for whom he had a personal attraction."[22]

Among the reminiscences of Schubert's friends, the composer's attraction to one of the Esterházy sisters appears to have been known, although the earliest details were inconsistent and contradictory, and there is the possibility that recollections appearing after 1865 may have been influenced by the publication of Kreissle's work.[23] As the only memoirist present at Zseliz, Schönstein alone mentioned Schubert's reply to Caroline, and its presence helps to explain why the "persönliche Neigung" ("personal affection") described by Kreissle in 1861 might have been elaborated into the "ernsterer, tieferer Neigung" four years later. Moreover, we must recall that Kreissle was detailing events in the life of a composer whose creative temperament was already construed as feminine. Schubert's *Mädchencharakter* might have been acceptable on aesthetic grounds, but contemporary sensibility seems to have required that this gendered characterization not subsume the composer's personal life. Documentation might not provide a "lasting passion" for Schubert, but the encounter with Caroline proved that he "was no stranger" to such emotions.[24] The anecdote's plausibility was further confirmed by its context: this deep but brief attraction was doomed by the insensitivity of the beloved as much by the irreconcilable differences of class and wealth. The intensity of Schubert's response as recorded by Kreissle proved that, however feminine his music, his personal desires were not so compromised. Schubert's music could thus be construed as gendered without there being any doubt about his inner life. Such an accommodation helps to explain why Schubert's anguished declaration was as frequently repeated in the nineteenth century as the feminine formulation of his music.

Kreissle's account of the liaison between Schubert and Caroline Esterházy as distilled by Niggli was Altenberg's source, but for Altenberg the allure of the tale was only partly due to the romantic notion of a love thwarted by social convention. Altenberg's fascination with the story in fact necessitated his misreading of what little documentary evidence existed. Kreissle had placed Schubert in the Esterházys' employ in 1818 and again in 1824, with the encounter occurring during the latter year. In a footnote, Kreissle rejected the year 1811 as Caroline's birth year, as given in a genealogy, because he could not account for the possibility that Schubert could have had a desire for her regardless of whether she

was seven in 1818 and thirteen in 1824. Kreissle instead gave 1806 as her birth
year, citing the testimony of "a near relative" of the countess.

Niggli further complicated the matter by suggesting on his much-read page
37 that the "tieferer Neigung" had begun in 1818, a confusion that had existed
since the appearance of Kreissle's biography. On page 37, Niggli wrote:

> At that time, there appears to have already germinated in our artist a deeper affection
> for one of the "good children," as Schubert called the young countesses, namely for
> Countess Caroline. Of course, it never came to a true declaration, even as the spring-
> time of love in his heart stood in its fullest bloom. In his inner being Schubert locked
> away his blissful pain, which his darling inflicted on him and which accompanied him
> through the years, and only once did a modest hint pass from his lips, when Countess
> Caroline teased him with it, that he had still not dedicated any of his works to her, and
> Schubert's answer came: "What would be the good of it? Everything I have ever done
> has been dedicated to you!"[25]

One can readily understand Altenberg's enthusiasm for this tale. Here was the
solitary artist whose creativity as much as his pain was inflicted upon him by a
female of spiritual refinement and physical beauty. Regardless of whether a
reader might thus be left with the impression that Schubert was attracted to an
eleven-year-old child, Altenberg ignored the chronology in any case, instead
referring to Caroline as fourteen years old. This effectively reversed an earlier
generation's attitudes about the rectitude and plausibility of a relationship
between the composer and a young girl. In an article in the *Wiener allgemeine
Zeitung* in 1911, reprinted in the same year in his *Neues Altes*, Altenberg effused
over Schubert's love for a fourteen-year-old Caroline:

> So many men, one could call them Strindberg Gangs for their way of reacting physio-
> logically and psychologically, forever and ever expect from a beloved woman a com-
> pletely special something, as if she might have the duty suddenly to acquire the spirit
> of an Indian theosophist who stands a million kilometers nearer to God than all other
> only so-called men!
>
> Here I remind myself over and over again of this Franz Schubert, the poet of songs,
> to whom his fourteen-year-old pupil Countess Esterházy once said during a piano les-
> son: "But it is not at all nice, Herr Schubert, that you have never dedicated to me one
> of your songs——!"
>
> Here the divinely gifted man replied: "But all of it was always written only for
> you——."
>
> Yes, is that not the greatest thing, to have assisted a Franz Schubert with his songs,
> like the sun, dew, and rain assist with the growth of plants?!?
>
> Therefore what does she need to be to and for herself, this fourteen-year-old, under
> the bare microscope of heartless uncomprehending men?!? She helped him to his
> songs, and without her they would not have come into being——!
>
> I formulated this later in the verse:
>
> > "Oh woman, you are not what you are!
> > You are that, what we dream of you!

Our tear-soaked nights for your sake, that, you are!
Coolly you accept our homage and our pain—
Because you never know, how it came, why, whence, wherefore, to
  what end!?!"[26]

Before pursuing the matter of Altenberg's assigning Caroline the age of four-teen, a slight digression is required to explain the context for his invocation of August Strindberg.

For Altenberg's contemporaries, the plays and prose of Strindberg were required reading. Robert Musil remarked that members of his generation regarded the Swedish dramatist rather than Goethe as belonging to them, and Zweig recalled that as students he and his contemporaries subversively read Strindberg and Nietzsche under their desks.[27] Strindberg's works were at the center of a literary legacy that encouraged fin-de-siècle culture to consider women as either devouring temptresses or docile helpmates, and to value them as domestic beings for their emotional and physical subservience. His articles decrying contemporary feminism were as well known as plays such as *Miss Julie* and *The Father*. In these dramas, weak men succumbed to calculating females whose opposites were women who surrendered completely. Strindberg's disgust with contemporary feminism, itself filtered through three failed marriages, was attractive to Altenberg at those moments when his own personal life was upset by one of his numerous failed liaisons.[28] By the time Altenberg wrote his article, the "Strindberg Gangs" undoubtedly included Karl Kraus, who shared the dramatist's open contempt for women's suffrage. After 1911, Strindberg was the only author other than Kraus himself to appear in the latter's journal *Die Fackel*, in which its creator regularly railed against Vienna's women's movement.[29]

To Altenberg's gang might also be added Weininger, who held Strindberg in a reciprocal esteem that bespoke their mutual regard for Beethoven as an ideal masculine type as well as their low valuation of women. Strindberg kept a mask of Beethoven on his wall and from 1900 on he held regular soirées for the per-formance of his favorite composer's music, attended by a group of friends he called the "Beethoven boys." Specific works by Beethoven figure prominently in several of Strindberg's dramas, a fact that must have been known to Weininger, since his references to Strindberg's output indicates his approving knowledge of the playwright's treatment of women, replicating a position articulated in Strindberg's notorious article "Woman's Inferiority to Man" (1895).[30] When Weininger sent Strindberg a copy of *Geschlecht und Charakter*, the dramatist responded with "my deepest admiration and my thanks" on July 1, 1903: "Finally—to see the woman problem solved is a deliverance for me." On July 17 he wrote to Emil Schering that Weininger "quotes *Creditors*, but ought to know *The Father* and *Miss Julie*. Would you send him them? I spelled it out, but he pieced the words together. *Voilà un homme!*"[31] Upon learning of Weininger's suicide on October 4, 1903, Strindberg wrote to Kraus on October 12, agreeing to write a brief memento for *Die Fackel* and sending money for a wreath.[32] In a letter of October 19 to Strindberg, Weininger's close friend Artur Gerber wrote that Weininger had claimed: "August Strindberg is the most important man alive. He also knows woman even better than you or I." That month Strindberg returned the compliment: "According to the latest analysis, a woman's love consists of 50 per cent rut and 50 per cent hatred."[33] This mutual attitude toward women, coupled with the fact that Weininger had taken his life in the house where Beethoven died, inspired Strindberg's letter to Gerber on December 8, 1903, detailing the common nature shared by the philosopher, the playwright, and the composer:

> I also worship Beethoven, have even founded a Beethoven Club, where only Beethoven is played. But I have noticed that so-called good people cannot stand Beethoven. He is a tormented, restless spirit who cannot be called divine, yet he is most definitely other-worldly. Weininger's fate? Yes, did he betray the secrets of the Gods? Stolen fire? The air became too thick for him down here, is that why he suffocated? Was this cynical life too cynical for him? That he departed this life, means for me that he had the highest possible permission to do so. Otherwise such things do not happen. It was so written.[34]

In addition to Weininger and Strindberg, a veneration for both masculine superiority and Beethoven is apparent in the essay "Ornament and Crime" (1908) by the architect Adolf Loos, his most famous condemnation of the decorative style of Jugendstil design favored by artists such as Klimt's fellow Secessionist Joseph Maria Olbrich. Loos's argument—that ornament was a sign of sickness in contemporary life, and its removal was necessary for modern culture to evolve—was framed by two references to Beethoven. He suggested that his own program for eliminating decoration from modern art was equivalent to the composer's work, adding a backhanded jab at Wagner's purported affection for fine materials: "Lack of ornament has pushed the other arts to unimagined heights. Beethoven's symphonies would never have been written by a man who was obliged to go about in silk, velvet and lace." This conclusion, with its echo of Krafft-Ebing's description of fetishism, is paired with an earlier reference to Beethoven that suggests an equivalence between the creative and sexual acts: "The first work of art, the first artistic act, which the first artist scrawled on the wall to give his exuberance vent. A horizontal line: the woman. A vertical line: the man penetrating her. The man who created this felt the same creative urge as Beethoven, he was in the same state of exultation in which Beethoven created the Ninth."[35]

For Loos, the contemporary fondness for decorative ornament in the arts was degenerate. Writing in the *Neue freie Presse* in 1898, he criticized this development most severely in women's fashion, drawing an equivalency between it and certain primitive cultures. "The preference for ornamental and colorful effects" distinguished woman's clothing from that of men, while at the same time "the lower the culture, the more apparent the ornament." For Loos, women's nobility "knows only one desire: that she hold on to her place by the side of the big, strong man." Such desire, however, was corrupted in contemporary life by the excessive ornamentation of her clothing, which appealed "unconsciously to his sickly sensuality." It was made even more aberrant by the current fashion for the child-woman: "Whatever was womanly disappeared from woman's clothing. Woman disguised away her hips; stout forms, earlier a source of pride to her, were now embarrassing. Her head took on a childlike look because of her hairstyle and her big sleeves."[36] As we shall see, this was the very type of Schubertian woman extolled by Altenberg, and Loos was explicit in singling out Altenberg as the architect of this tendency, based solely on *Wie ich es sehe*, whose first tale includes a provocative description of nine- and eleven-year-old girls.

Altenberg, by contrast, upended the masculine image of Beethoven on several occasions. In his postcard collection, a photograph of the daughter of Crown Prince Rudolf bears the writer's caption: "<u>Beethoven-Gaze</u>! You <u>fathom</u> the <u>unfathomable</u>; but <u>only</u> with your <u>gaze</u>! Empress Elisabeth's granddaughter! Princess Windischgrätz, you are <u>spellbound</u> in worlds, which are not those of <u>yours</u>! You are the noblest, softest 'morning-extract,' sweet deep melancholy child!!"[37] Similarly, Altenberg wrote in 1911:

> Frau E... R.....
> Do you then create symphonies, feminine Beethoven visage?!?
> You are a woman, you cannot ring out!
> Cannot release yourself!
> You cannot be a mirror image of the world!
> Too great for daily action, too small for the eternal!
> So you remain woman and yet cannot be!![38]

For all its beauty, Frau E. R.'s "weibliches Beethoven-Antlitz," like the little girl's "Beethoven-Blick," bears only a surface resemblance to the Olympian posture of Max Klinger's statue, the centerpiece of the Secession's 1902 exhibition in honor of the composer. The linkage of Beethoven with the feminine owes more to Wagner's *Oper und Drama*, in which the composer had theorized about assuming the traits of both genders in order to unite masculine poetry with feminine music in the Ninth Symphony.[39] The Beethovenian desire of "Frau E. R." to express herself artistically is, however, rendered impossible by the very fact that she is a woman (just as Schnitzler's Berta Garlan cannot perform Beethoven's music with her lover). It is likewise only the child-princess's look, rather than any conscious comprehension, that merits the writer's admiration. The last line of "Frau E. R." recalls Wagner's conclusion at the end of part one of *Oper und Drama*: "To work deeds, the woman only needs *to be entirely what she is*, but in no way *to will* something; for she can will but one thing—*to be a woman!*"[40] The concept of the subjugated female was, of course, not new with Wagner, and aspirations such as those of Altenberg's "Frau E. R." were commonly criticized in a high culture dominated by men.[41] (Failed ambition, as we have seen, was precisely what plagued Schnitzler's female protagonists.) There is a further intrusion of reality, as so often occurs in Altenberg's writing. "Frau E. R." was quite probably Emma Rudolf, one of many women whose affections he was unsuccessful in winning from the competition of Vienna's intelligentsia, and to whom he wrote in 1899 about no longer being able to kiss her "beloved Beethoven-brow."[42]

For Altenberg, the answer to the fin-de-siècle crisis over the sexually dominant woman, which was emerging from the creative thought of Wagner and Strindberg and their Viennese heirs, lay in a representation of femininity in which sexual maturity and its consequent threat had not yet become a *fait accompli.* As an alternative to occupying himself with the hypermasculine image of Beethoven, Altenberg would instead harness the nineteenth-century maidenly character of Schubert to his artistic purpose. Indeed, Altenberg's novel use of the term *Kindweib* to describe his inspirational ideal—which, as we will see shortly, was to become particularly meaningful in contemporary cultural discourse in Vienna—may well have served as his aesthetic response to the ringleader of what he described as the "Strindberg Gangs." In the preface to the one-act play *Miss Julie,* which was translated into German in 1890, Strindberg had defined his title character as a modern *Halbweib* or half-woman, "a type who thrusts herself forward, who sells herself nowadays for power, decorations, honors, or diplomas as she used to for money. She signifies degeneration."[43] Unnatural and tragic, she possessed the capacity to attract equally degenerate men and thus reproduce "creatures of uncertain sex." By contrast, in *Pròdròmòs,* a collection that appeared in 1906, Altenberg cautioned the man who would be both artist and poet not to anticipate which type of female stood closer to him: the one who was still in the process of becoming a woman ("das 'werdende Weib'") or the one who already had become a woman ("das 'gewordene'"). In sentences of aphoristic brevity ending in the runic pairs of question marks and exclamation points of which he was so fond, Altenberg suggested that a creative individual should not preoccupy himself with the type of woman—that "suitably necessary 'low form' who represents this, the moaning body up against a man"— that alarmed so many of his fin-de-siècle brethren. Rather, it was the *Kindweib,* a far more Schubertian figure, who could serve as a subject much more conducive to the creative imagination. "On the contrary, in which freedom, detached from purpose, completely suspended in grace and delicacy, does the child-woman stand before you, the artist?!" That this symbol of youthful feminine inspiration should be a type that had yet to reach sexual maturity (and was all the more alluring because of that condition) is reflected in Altenberg's conclusion: "The world of 'the completed' is useful. The world of the premature is, however, beautiful."[44]

Female subjugation was doubtless the theme to which Altenberg was referring when he invoked the "Strindberg Gangs" in his sketch about Schubert and Caroline Esterházy. In contrast to a woman's surrender to men, Altenberg instead posited an idealized but by no means mutual relationship in the composer's encounter with the aristocratic fourteen-year-old, whose purity supplied

Schubert (and, at one remove, Altenberg himself) with the inspiration necessary to achieve a spiritual refinement that was in its essence feminine, but without her ever being aware of her impact upon this asymmetric transaction. This might at first recall a familiar romantic pipedream: the artist whose creative genius was motivated and sustained by his female muse even as his emotional life was tormented by her unavailability. When Altenberg's narrative incited a critical response, however, it was not because of his seemingly rhapsodic interpretation but rather because his facts were apparently wrong. An immediate correction came from Otto Erich Deutsch, early in his distinguished career as a Schubert scholar. Deutsch was moved not only to provide what he believed to be Caroline's true age, but to remove her candidacy as Schubert's great beloved and to replace her with Therese Grob, a theory to which Deutsch clung tenaciously throughout his career.[45] Aside from the documentary evidence that he offered to send to Altenberg if he could obtain the writer's address, Deutsch reasoned that, if an unhappy Schubert had been rejected, he would not have so publicly dedicated to the countess the Fantasy in F Minor for piano duet. Deutsch did not doubt Altenberg's conceit that Schubert bore an unrequited love for a woman, but he did chastise the writer for misrepresenting the true candidate for the composer's affections, if in fact they had ever been voiced. Deutsch's response made for admirable musicology but unsatisfying art. There was a modernist calculation to Altenberg's misreading of the countess's age that made fourteen an essential feature of his narrative.

Contemporary Viennese pseudoscience had promulgated a theory of adolescent female sexuality that recalls the girls who people Altenberg's sketches and photographs. On May 29, 1907, Fritz Wittels read to the Society of Psychoanalysis a lecture entitled "Die grosse Hetaere." Shortly thereafter, on July 15, it was printed under the title "Das Kindweib" in Kraus's *Die Fackel*, whose publication assured its dissemination among Austria's intellectuals. In this much-circulated article, Wittels detailed his theory of the *Kindweib*, the childwoman, whose existence he based on the Greek conception of the hetaera:

It seems as though female beauty is more attractive to man today if it renounces motherhood and decides to play the eternal child. . . . Women appear just as children, with uncovered knees, bobbed hair, soft complexion, the round inviting mouth of a baby, and big astonished eyes, which are artificially made to look larger and more astonished as though one were still interested in looking at the world like a schoolgirl. They imitate a type which is rare in nature, the childwoman, who for constitutional reasons has to remain a child for life. . . . The more or less pathological basis for the childwoman is the precocious appearance of sex appeal. When a child is attractive at an age when other children are still jumping rope, she ceases to be a child. From within, a precociously awakened sexuality arises, and from without, admiring eyes inflame her. To be desired is so absolutely the idea of this woman, that she does not continue her development. So we must add to our remark that she ceases to be a child, also the fact that she remains a child forever. This contrast within one and the same person produces her charm.[46]

The child-woman was thus both innocent and sexual; she was a combination of naiveté and narcissism that made her someone without either shame or memory.

Although her Greek ancestors' attractiveness might be idealized as a source of creative inspiration, in modern society the *Kindweib* was just as often a prostitute. As such, she was doomed to destruction even as her extraordinary charms, of which she was not entirely aware, had the capacity to consume countless numbers of men. However novel its analytical formulation may have been in Viennese psychological circles, the *Kindweib* as construed by Wittels echoed dozens of contemporary literary and artistic types, whether he had lifted the actual word from Altenberg's *Pròdrŏmŏs* of 1906 or had arrived at it independently. Constructing this type of female helped to produce a seductive theory for writers like Kraus and Altenberg, both of whom argued that prostitution was a liberating experience for its practitioners, even as they ignored its social consequences, and who themselves enjoyed indiscriminate liaisons with little regard for the fate of their partners.[47] Aside from Altenberg, Wittels' *Kindweib* is observable in Felix Salten's description of the "half-grown young things" that strolled along Vienna's Prater. Salten used the term "Frühlings-erwachen," the title of Frank Wedekind's play, to encapsulate the scene:

> There are no more children! Yet there are children, probably completely innocent children, who are not aware that their eye games are known as coquetry, that their laughter, hand waving, and chatter; their small, dainty, and affected arts of dissimulation are already the prelude to the comedy of love toward which they mature.[48]

If Wittels' theory accommodated the lure of the female adolescent and the freedom from moral guilt in any subsequent social transaction, the age of fourteen had unique significance in both Viennese medicine and jurisprudence. Sander L. Gilman has observed that Austrian medical authorities declared that girls developed into women at fourteen, which in turn was both the minimum age for registering prostitutes and the age of sexual consent, the lowest in nineteenth-century Europe. Austrian law also criminalized sex with anyone under that age, although it was a crime only if "the minor with whom the immoral act was performed had been the passive participant."[49] Viennese science provides an example that makes Altenberg's misreading of Caroline Esterházy's age appear to be characteristic of its culture: Freud's treatment of his patient, Ida Bauer. During her psychoanalysis, Dora—as she was called in Freud's case notes—revealed that as a thirteen-year-old, she had been kissed by her father's friend, whose sudden embrace she had rebuffed with a slap. Freud's now infamous analysis concluded that her behavior "was already entirely and completely hysterical."[50] What further helped to make her response seem incomprehensible to Freud was the fact that, although all the evidence indicates that he knew her true age, he described her as fourteen in his case notes.[51] However traumatic Dora's experience may have been, Freud surmised that her reaction was unnatural because she was a woman, barely one to be sure, but still a woman according to the medical establishment in fin-de-siècle Vienna. Given the laws that criminalized sexual relationships with girls younger than fourteen, Freud and his contemporaries had good reason to treat that age with such circumspection. For Krafft-Ebing, sexual behavior with a younger girl was a patent sign of the most extreme type of deviant pathology. Although the acts themselves were beyond the description of even a man of science, Krafft-Ebing characterized the perpetrators in terms that revealed them to be nothing short of depraved monsters whose crimes robbed them of their masculinity. They were typically either "young men who lack courage or have no faith in their virility" or "roués who have, to some extent, lost their power." Although the ages of these individuals varied, the perversions they engaged in were commonly "unmanly, knavish, and often silly."[52]

Apart from precedents in science and law, there were examples from both low and high culture that preceded Altenberg's rereading of the Esterházy story. The notorious pornographic novel *Josephine Mutzenbacher* (1906) ends with the title character turning fourteen, having begun her sexual history at the age of five. In a notebook of 1920, Musil made that age an essential component of his definition of "modern youth," to which he added other features that became an assemblage of physical attractiveness, superficial erudition, and sexual indifference: "girl, 14 years-of-age. Beautiful long plaits. Dresses like a Russian revolutionary. Has read [Schnitzler's] *La Ronde*, indeed has read everything. [The journalist Egon Erwin] Kisch asks her if someone is in love with her. No, she says, a man means nothing to her. She is in the fifth class of the grammar school and will be going to a children's home as a tutor."[53]

There was also no shortage of literary models for Austrian writers. Wedekind's play *Frühlings Erwachen* (1892) was staged in Vienna under the supervision of Max Reinhardt in 1907. It begins on the fourteenth birthday of Wendla Bergmann, whose combination of emotional innocence and physical maturity leads to her first sexual experience and to her subsequent abortion and death. Elsewhere in the play, another fourteen-year-old female is the subject/object in an art reproduction of Palma Vecchio's *Venus*, whose "inhuman modesty" incites the masturbatory fantasies of Hänschen Bulow. The title character of Gerhart Hauptmann's drama *Hannelles Himmelfahrt* (1893) is yet another example of the innocent and doomed fourteen-year-old girl. The type is not limited to German literature, as is apparent from Marcel Proust's story "La confession d'une jeune fille" (from the collection *Les plaisirs et les jours*, 1896), in which a fourteen-year-old allows herself to be seduced by her vicious cousin who is only a year older.[54] The budding sexuality of that age also had its male counterparts in contemporary literature. In Thomas Mann's *Death in Venice*, the beauty of Tadzio, "a long-haired boy of about fourteen," overwhelms the novella's protagonist, Gustav von Aschenbach.[55] The title character of Hofmannsthal's "Lucidor" (1910) is a girl disguised as a boy "of thirteen or fourteen years." Hofmannsthal was himself hardly more than a teenager in 1893 when he wrote an adulatory review of a diary written by a fourteen-year-old girl who exhibited "a grotesque freedom from the prejudice of reflection, that freedom and impudence of observation, which might be outrageous if it were not charming." Hers was a personality that tossed and turned between Madonna and caricature, revealing a mixture of limitless vanity and infinite grace, not above using her coquetry as a weapon to get what she wanted. [56]

The fact that such individuals might actually exist apart from the literary imagination is reflected in two cases during Altenberg's career, in which the secret lives of Viennese adolescents proved to be literary sensations. The stir caused by the publication in 1908 of extracts from the *Authentic Diary of Countess Mizzi Veith* had less to do with the fact that she had started her career as a prostitute at the age of fourteen than the revelation that she was initiated into the trade by her stepfather—an ersatz prince of dubious lineage—and, more scandalously, that she listed her encounters with the aristocrats, politicians, and businessmen whose patronage purportedly contributed to an income of some 44,000 crowns. (The lurid appeal of the inclusion of excerpts from her account book was tempered by the use of the initials of her clients on the grounds of discretion.) The salacious details of her life, however, were counterbalanced by an outcome that had a patina of moral and legal righteousness. A reader could savor without guilt this glimpse into the life of a young, lower-class prostitute since the volume concludes with her final letter before her suicide, the confession of her apprehended stepfather, and the subsequent police report on the matter.[57]

In a second example, Freud enthusiastically promoted the publication of a manuscript entitled *A Young Girl's Diary*, which had been brought to him in 1915 by Hermine von Hug-Hellmuth. Freud's introduction to the volume supplied a respectable screen for a bourgeois adolescent's observations on sexuality, by turns innocent and voyeuristic, especially when Greta, the purported diarist, surreptitiously watches a couple making love in a scene that caused the book to be censored in England, though not in Austria. The text's authenticity is uncertain, but whether it was written by a child or an adult, Greta's description of turning fourteen commingles the characteristics of emotional naiveté and physical allure that made that age such an irresistible focus of contemporary Viennese culture:

> Thank goodness this is my fourteenth!!! birthday. Olga thought that I was sixteen or at least fifteen; but I said: No thank you; to *look* like sixteen is *quite* agreeable to me, but I shouldn't like to *be* sixteen, for after all how long is one young, only two or three years at most. But as to feeling different, as Hella said she did, I really don't; I am merely delighted that no one, not even Dora, can now call me a child. I do detest the word "child," except when Mama used to say: "My darling child," but then it meant something quite different. I like Mama's ring best of all my birthday presents; I shall wear it for always and always. When I was going to cry, Papa said so sweetly: "Don't cry, Gretel, you mustn't cry on your fourteenth!! birthday; that would be a fine beginning of *grown-upness!*"[58]

As the father intimates, the age of fourteen is a societal construction, a sign of maturation that he nonetheless tenderly describes in relatively childlike terms as "grown-upness." For her part, although Greta does not feel any different emotionally, she still takes adolescent pride in the fact that her physical appearance might make her look two years older. When packaged as nonfiction first-person accounts, such narratives had the added frisson of verisimilitude. So long as the titillating details were framed by the probity of scientific or legal authorities, readers could enjoy the interplay between childhood innocence and the emerging sexuality of the fourteen-year-old female, knowing that such stories concluded with or were prefaced by cautionary explanations brimming with moral rectitude.

Given this cultural context as well as the personal interactions among Vienna's intellectuals, it is scarcely surprising that Altenberg should manipulate Caroline Esterházy's age, a gesture that was by no means unique in his literary output. Another misreading of age occurs in the 1915 story "Alma (Gustav Mahler gewidmet)" from the collection entitled *Feschsung*, in which Altenberg attempts to console Alma Mahler upon the death of her four-year-old daughter: "She sat in darker mourning dress in the Golden Hall where her dead husband's *Kindertotenlieder* in memory of their dead eleven-year-old little daughter was being performed."[59] In the case of his Schubert sketch, Altenberg's reinvention of Caroline's age was well fitted to both his aesthetic aims and his private life. The young countess was the child-woman who was unaware of her allure and whose beauty incited the composer to greatness. Such females attracted Altenberg throughout his life, populating both his stories and his photographic collection. These adolescents came in a variety of ages: in 1905, the dancer Bessie Bruce was nineteen when he wrote *Kind-Mädchen* on her photograph, and elsewhere in his quaint English he pronounced her a "Girl-Baby."[60] His choice of fourteen for Caroline Esterházy, however, is particularly significant, given its symbolic status in contemporary Viennese medical, legal, and literary circles. Two sketches from his 1909 collection *Bilderbögen des kleinen Lebens* concern fourteen-year-olds and their relationship to an unnamed older poet.[61]

The child-woman was all the more desirable because her attraction was distilled through the interpretive genius of the artist. Just as Caroline Esterházy was a type of *Kindweib*, so too did Altenberg associate Schubert with that ideal, a relationship that was not unique in fin-de-siècle Vienna. The composer's waltzes accompanied the three dancing Wiesenthal sisters' premiere of *Wiener Walzer* on January 14, 1908, at the Fledermaus Cabaret in an arrangement by Joseph Bayer. The audience, including Klimt and Hofmannsthal, were entranced. One critic effused: "Therein lay something, which men could not resist."[62] After the Klimt circle had sponsored the premiere of *The Birthday of the Infanta*, whose music the sisters had commissioned from Franz Schreker, Altenberg wrote a euphoric essay about Elsa Wiesenthal. Its subject resonated with his own life's theme: the protagonist in Schreker's piece was another aristocratic young female whose indifferent beauty destroys the dwarf who loves her. Altenberg wrote in his review: "It is all our fates!"[63] The scenario may have struck an autobiographical chord in Altenberg, who often juxtaposed his attraction to women with his own physical shortcomings—an act that was itself an echo of his characterization of Schubert's diminutive stature—and who once even described himself as a dwarf in the sketch "Konzert." At a recital of contemporary Lieder, the writer finds himself attracted to a beautiful young woman who gazes into the distance. Her contemplation of the music provides an escape from acknowledging the writer's adoration: "To you I seem like a dwarf, a worm, a stooped miserable reptile, a timid reminder of the earthly."[64]

Still another example of Altenberg's child-woman dates from 1916, when he acquired a photograph of the actress Maria Mayen, whose career was built around her roles as a *süße Mädel* type, including her portrayal of Christine in Schnitzler's *Liebelei*. Altenberg inscribed on it: "Maria Mayen, you, you, Oh you my vivacious Schubert-Lied you! And moreover, my god, moreover you still remain a great little actress at Vienna's Burg-Theater!"[65] On another photograph of the actress, from 1914, Altenberg wrote: "Miss Mayen. You, you my living Schubert-Lied you!" ("Fr[äu]l[ei]n. Mayen. Du, Du mein lebendiges Schubert-Lied Du!" See figure 6.1.)[66] Maria Mayen was twenty-two, arguably too old for *Kindweib* status, but the intimacy of the medium of photography did not prevent Altenberg from portraying his youthful child-women. Photographs of a nude fourteen-year-old Albine Ruprich convey disturbing meanings that cannot be easily explained by Altenberg's comforting aphorisms written on them. One from 1914 is captioned: "Your soul, fourteen-year-old Albine Ruprich, is as complete as your beloved body!" Another from the same year reads: "The dearest, most tender, most affectionate woman! Albine Ruprich. Fourteen years old. With gratitude."[67] The photographs were, of course, not published; Altenberg's literary imagination sought to bridge the divide separating the private desire for these adolescents and the taboo against public consumption of their images. They nevertheless unmistakably supply a link between older depictions of childhood innocence, such as Anton Romako's painting *Girl on a Swing* (ca. 1882), and the explicit work of Egon Schiele, himself a victim of the age limit written into Austrian law. Schiele, who often used girls as models, was jailed for three weeks in 1912 after a complaint was made regarding one of them, a thirteen-year-old.[68]

For Altenberg, Schubert served both autobiographical and artistic ends as old and new conceptions of the feminine merged. The story of Caroline Esterházy's charm inflaming the composer to create works of genius acquired the character of a nostalgic reminiscence. Viennese society and Altenberg's private impulses, however, permitted and even necessitated his adjusting his cultural memory to make her a modern *Kindweib*. For the writer, her attractiveness was at once more innocent and seductive, and consequently more inspirational, because of her adolescent youth. His narrative expressed both aesthetic and personal desire. Its details were idealized even as they were falsified, allowing the patina of an imagined past to accommodate, even as it masked, the more sordid reality of contemporary culture. Here is modernist paradox. The legacy of the Schubert *Mädchencharakter* supplied Altenberg with a paradigm for the feminization of the artist even as the Franz-Caroline narrative afforded him the opportunity to blur the distinction between child and siren.

The smudging of surface and symbol in Altenberg's writing extends to the glosses that he added to the many photographs and postcards that he amassed

Figure 6.1. Photograph of Maria Mayen from the collection of Peter Altenberg, signed August 12, 1915 (photograph dated 1914). © Wien Museum, Vienna.

throughout his life and in which, as observed earlier in this chapter, Schubert played a recurring role. The market in postcards was expanding in fin-de-siècle Vienna, exploiting local sites and images that might attract visitors while offering a modest income for artists of dubious talent. We have already noted that a postcard of an intimate *Schubertiade* by Fritzi Ulreich presented an ersatz copy of Klimt's *Schubert at the Piano*. When the young Adolf Hitler arrived in the city in 1908 to pursue a career in the arts, he unsuccessfully tried to eke out a meager living by supplying similar illustrations, including some related to Schubert, to be used for the postcard business.[69] Thus, it was certainly not any aesthetic subtlety that attracted Altenberg to collect such images. To the extent that they are known at all, his picture postcards are familiar only indirectly via the cycle of five orchestral songs by Alban Berg, the *Altenberg-Lieder*, whose texts, deriving from such cards, Berg found in Altenberg's *Neues Altes* (1911).

Among the actual postcards kept by Altenberg are three watercolors inspired by Schubert's songs.[70] One, "Ihr Bild" (the ninth song of *Schwanengesang*), portrays a man's candlelit encounter with a portrait of a woman hanging above a table on which sits a container of white roses in full bloom. Many other cards depict representations of idealized females like Joshua Reynolds' painting of Mrs. Sheridan as Saint Cecilia, Leonardo's portrait of Beatrice d'Este, and, in a considerable display of nude avoirdupois, François Boucher's rendering of Diana emerging from her bath. At the same time, however, there are also contemporary photographs of both girls and boys, many of which bear Altenberg's handwritten descriptions: "ideal type" or "my absolute ideal!" Taken as a whole, these photographic images suggest that Altenberg's modern prototype crossed genders as long as the male was still young enough to possess the kind of classically beautiful androgyny that recalls the fictitious Tadzio, the object of Gustav Aschenbach's fatal attraction in Thomas Mann's *Death in Venice*. The blurring of the real and the fanciful also informs postcards reproducing photographs of two buildings with Schubertian connections that became equally popular tourist attractions. Although they are not named on the backs of the cards, Altenberg's handwriting identifies them as Schubert's birthplace on the Nussdorferstrasse and the so-called Dreimäderlhaus. Another postcard is a watercolor of the birth house with Altenberg's caption, "My God," an epithet that recurs meaningfully in connection with his copy of Klimt's *Schubert at the Piano*.

Whether he assumed the guise of writer or collector, what was true of Altenberg's art was also true of his private life. To observe two frequently reproduced photographs of his apartment in a Vienna hotel is to come away with the suspicion of yet another gap between reality and invention. He made his living space a masterpiece of artifice by crowding its walls with his collection of photographs. Describing his bedroom, Altenberg again invoked Schubertian genius:

Over my bed hangs a charcoal drawing of Gustav Klimt's picture, Schubert. Schubert at the piano sings songs by candlelight with three Viennese girls. Underneath it I've written: "One of my gods! Men created gods for themselves, in order somehow to awaken to more animated existence their own hidden and yet unfulfillable ideals!"[71]

This paean to artistic genius was precisely what Schubert was meant to do for the writer. Yet when compared to Altenberg's collection of photographs, it reveals that he was as capable of misreading his own work as of manipulating the documentary record. Altenberg's copy of Klimt's painting actually appears above the washstand in one photograph. Thus, his claim that it hung over his bed provides a substitution of furniture that privileges the intimate over the utilitarian. At the same time, the image is positioned immediately above two portraits of women; one is a demure three-quarter pose showing a fully clothed sitter and the other is a complete nude. In a second photograph featuring the writer's bed, one can make out to the left of the mirror not a reproduction of Klimt's painting but a copy of Rieder's famous 1825 portrait.[72] Had Altenberg merely repositioned the portraits sometime around 1909, the year when his gloss was first published and when the photographs may have been taken?[73] It would be in character if instead his statement were yet another manipulation of reality, another contrived recasting of a Schubertian ideal. Whether this disjunction was another instance of deliberate misreading or simply a consequence of rearranging photographs cannot be ascertained. One is nevertheless left with the sense that a certain artifice governed both Altenberg's art and his private life. Its walls crowded with his collection of photographs, his apartment appears to imitate in miniature the design of historicist exhibitions like the Schubert-Ausstellung, which itself reflected the long-standing tradition of installations in galleries throughout Europe. (One thinks, for example, of Samuel F. B. Morse's painting of the Salon Carré in the Louvre from the 1830s—in which the *Mona Lisa* competes with more than three dozen other works for the viewer's attention—or, even earlier, of David Teniers the Younger's depiction of the Archduke Leopold William's gallery in Brussels from the 1650s, now in the collection of Vienna's Kunsthistorisches Museum.) In Altenberg's case, however, the public function of these large displays, in which often massive paintings compete for the viewer's attention, is replaced by the intimacy of the writer's inner world, whose objects are nonetheless products of the relatively newer, more objective technology of the photograph. With a modernist sensibility that juxtaposes privacy and transgression, the images on the apartment walls, if one were permitted access to view them, would expose a secret emotional life that is only partially revealed in Altenberg's writings.

Such calculated discontinuity between nostalgic evocation and mundane reality indeed goes to the very heart of the aphorism cited above, which has been so frequently quoted by later commentators. It is, in fact, not the actual lines that Altenberg wrote. (See figure 6.2.) The description that in truth appears underneath Altenberg's undated copy of Klimt's painting is as follows:

One of my gods: Schubert! <u>Heartfelt wish</u>. "Most beloved, I should always like it if you could listen to Schubert's songs still more transfigured than to my words——."[74]

Figure 6.2. Gustav Klimt, *Schubert am Klavier* (*Schubert at the Piano*), 1899, destroyed 1945. Undated photographic reproduction from the collection of Peter Altenberg. © Wien Museum, Vienna.

Is the transfigured beloved whom Altenberg addresses the woman on the left? One is left to wonder whether Viennese gossip had made known the connection between this decorative figure and Klimt's model, so that Altenberg was aware of it. In any case, this gloss is less interested in artistic genius than in the capacity of the artist to seduce a female listener. Here again is Altenberg's modernism: his writings mirror the composer's music in his desire to transfigure and attract the women who are his and Schubert's inspiration. The experience, however, occurs not in real life but through its visual rendering in Klimt's painting. It is as though such women were able simultaneously to occupy both actual and imagined spaces, and to serve as objects of both creative inspiration and physical desire. Altenberg accorded this role to Klimt's portraits of women, describing them elsewhere with attributes that were precisely those he gave to Schubert's childlike countess (and emphasizing features that recall Hofmannsthal's description of porcelain hands):

How the poets envision them for their tender inspirations: delicate, noble-limbed, fragile creatures, who never fade away and never find release! The hands, the expression of a gracious soul, childlike, light winged, refined and good-natured at the same time!

All find themselves beyond the burdens of this earth, even as they also might otherwise appear in the real life of this day and hour. All are princesses for better, gentler worlds.[75]

Unlike Altenberg's reception of Schubert, however, there is nothing in Klimt's manipulation of the composer that suggests the artist might have identified with Schubert's feminine nature. For a painter whose carnal appetites were not entirely secret, a self-association with Beethoven, the manly warrior-hero, was far more obvious, especially in the wake of Klimt's frieze designed for the Secession exhibit in 1902 that also featured Klinger's Rodinesque sculpture of the composer. If that show stood as a modernist response to an older ideal of Beethoven, then perhaps Altenberg's apartment in the Graben, with its fleetingly glimpsed images of Schubert—so like the quicksilver literary glosses on the composer concealed among the dozens of literary sketches in the volumes of Altenberg's prose—represented a trumping of that earlier event, whose radical conception was already passing into a tradition it had sought to challenge. How much truer to the spirit of the age could it be than to make modernism itself the self-reflective object of one's inspiration?

Chapter Seven

Arnold Schoenberg's Schubert

In a popular history of Vienna written in 1912, Richard von Kralik, an indefatigable chronicler of German Austrian culture, observed that the essence of the capital city had achieved its most perfect stylization in the music of Franz Schubert: "the most faithful mirror of an Elysian unearthly existence . . . a life that had become all flowers, fragrance, fairy tale, myth, romanticism, bliss, color, and brilliance."[1] In the history of Schubert's reception, this remark was hardly new. That it should have been made in 1912, however, was apt, since that year is notable for the extremely high sugar content of its numerous sentimental fictional concoctions on Schubert's life and works. The fin-de-siècle image of the cherubic composer of *gemütlich* songs and *Hausmusik*, whose apparently heaven-sent lyrical gifts were as unthinking as they were boundless, had been endlessly regurgitated by the time it culminated in 1912 in the unnervingly popular drivel ranging from short stories by Vicki Baum and Mathilde Weil to the novels *Schwammerl* by Rudolf Hans Bartsch, *Die Stadt der Lieder* by Martin Brussot, and *Grillparzers Liebesroman* by Joseph August Lux. The latter featured a reproduction of an icon of Schubertian nostalgia, Schmid's painting *Ein Schubertabend in einem Wiener Bürgerhause*, the most famous visual legacy of the 1897 centennial exhibition honoring Schubert's birth, a picture that in 1912 still hung in a room in the Rathaus dedicated to the composer. To this list may be added the ballet *Die Jahreszeiten der Liebe*, subtitled *Vier altwiener Tanz-Bilder*, with choreography by Heinrich Regel and Schubert's music arranged by Julius Lehnert. Its scenario—four scenes charting the seasons of life and love— was published in 1912 after its premiere in Vienna on December 2, 1911. In chapter 6, we even encountered a touch of bathos finding its way into the modernist temperament of Peter Altenberg's *Semmering 1912*. In the sketch "Mama," Altenberg recalled that the healing of a childhood foot ailment was welcomed by his mother singing "Die Forelle."[2]

The contributors to this embarrassment of hagiographic riches merely had to rely on the public's familiarity with a handful of Schubert's best-known songs to assure the success of their efforts. In the popular imagination, the subjects of the poems set by the composer served as resources for fictional episodes from his career as often as any actual documented account, even to a point where the known facts were disregarded. Brussot's novel, for example, culminates in the mawkishness of a dying Schubert's conciliatory request that the once errant love of his youth sing to him the last song of *Schwanengesang* (presumably referring to "Die Taubenpost"). The composer soulfully opines: "The two of us never really understood each other. . . . But if it is true that there is a new life in the hereafter, then we will act more wisely."[3] The wayward chambermaid who receives this touching sentiment is, however, given the unlikely name of Steffy Guschelbaur, and thus Deutsch's contemporary and repeated identification of Therese Grob as the real-life object of the composer's affection is cordially ignored.

To the extent that sentimental fiction was the fashionable engine that drove much of the composer's reception, Kralik's remark that Schubert's life had become a matter of myth and fairy tale was wholly to the point, even though he did not intend it as criticism. The same cannot be said of a far more interesting observation from 1912 regarding the connection between Schubert's music and its verse. In May of that year amid this otherwise saccharine Schubert-fest, Arnold Schoenberg's seminal essay "The Relationship to the Text" appeared in *Der blaue Reiter*. Schoenberg had taken up this topic at a moment of central importance in his creative development, as he had recently completed one song cycle, *Herzgewächse*, and was preparing to embark on the composition of another, *Pierrot lunaire*. In a statement entirely at home in a collection of expressionist manifestos and contemporary abstract art, Schoenberg concluded that "with compositions based on poetry the exactness of rendering the action is as irrelevant to its artistic value as the resemblance to the model is for a portrait."[4] Schoenberg cited his own settings of Stefan George's verse as an example: "intoxicated by the sound of the first words in the text," he had completed them "without in the least caring for the further development of the poem, without even noticing it in the ecstasy of composing."[5] Further, he observed that the process of creating his own songs was identical to his experience of listening to Schubert's vocal music:

> A few years ago I was deeply ashamed to discover that in some of Schubert's lieder, which I knew well, I had no idea what was actually happening in the poems they were based on. But when I read the poems I found that I had gained nothing in the understanding of the lieder, that they did not in the least influence my opinion of the musical statement. On the contrary, I had quite obviously grasped the content, the real content, perhaps even better than if I had clung to the surface of the actual verbal ideas. . . . I had completely understood Schubert's lieder—including the lyrics—through the music alone, Stefan George's poetry through the sound alone.[6]

Although Schoenberg did not detail the "real content" of Schubert's music, one might reasonably conclude that it was light years removed from the maudlin sentimentality of so many contemporary representations of the composer. Certainly Schoenberg's recollection contains elements far more in keeping with modernist sensibilities: the synesthetic delight in the sounds of words rather than a dependence upon their ostensible meaning, the withdrawal from the authenticity of their exterior signification, and the dreamlike delirium of creative insight whether as composer or listener.

For an essay on the relationship of text and music, Schoenberg's choice of Schubert is no surprise, given that he was fin-de-siècle Vienna's prince of song. In the 1880s, his Lieder had merited musical responses from Brahms, Mahler, and Wolf even as this genre had qualified him for greatness alongside Beethoven in contemporary histories.[7] Yet in devising such an original interpretation of Schubert songs—one that separated the essential musical content from the surface meaning of its text—Schoenberg was implicitly offering a modernist critique of the "false and trite assumptions" made by "the limited intelligence of the intellectual bourgeoisie" whom he ruthlessly characterized at the beginning of his essay.[8] It was the hostility from precisely this constituency that had prompted Schoenberg's flight from Vienna to Berlin in 1911 and incited his refusal to return the following year when he was offered a teaching position at the conservatory. The readership that seemed not to tire of cloying portrayals of Schubert was not far removed from the audience that had treated Schoenberg and his music with such contempt.

By articulating a view of Schubert contrary to popularly accepted clichés, Schoenberg was also censuring those who mindlessly embraced them, and this initiated a pattern that typified his later observations on Schubert. In a lecture at the Academy of Arts in Berlin on January 20, 1927, subsequently published under the title "Problems of Harmony," Schoenberg suggested that Schubert was the source of one of the nineteenth century's most stunning achievements:

> The conflict [between non-diatonic elements and tonality] becomes more acute in the Romantic period following the Classical. The increasing attraction exerted by foreign harmonies made them more and more a significant element of expression. I shall not adduce all the known facts, for everyone is familiar today with the road that led from Schubert through Wagner to Reger, Richard Strauss, Mahler, Debussy and others.[9]

It is perhaps no coincidence that within three weeks of making this statement, Schoenberg completed the first movement of his String Quartet no. 3, op. 30, which pays conspicuous if uneasy homage to the opening of Schubert's Quartet in A Minor. Further, in *Structural Functions of Harmony*, Schoenberg chose the harmonic richness of the A-Minor Quartet's development (*Durchführung*) as the example that "perhaps marks the actual transition to Wagnerian and post-Wagnerian composers' procedures."[10]

In his texts on composition and theory, Schoenberg subsequently made clear his Viennese predecessor's unique status, constructing a Schubert whose harmonic audacity stood at the threshold of a musical revolution. In *Fundamentals of Musical Composition*, assembled between 1937 and 1948, he tapped Schubert as a creative wellspring: "The rapid development of harmony since the beginning of the nineteenth century has been the great obstacle to the acceptance of every new composer from Schubert on."[11] In characterizing Schubert as "distinctly one of the pioneers in the field of harmony," Schoenberg was running counter to the century-old popular image of the tunefully inspired but structurally challenged miniaturist, the *Liebling der Natur* whose apparently inexhaustible melodic invention had been due more to divine intervention than to conscious thought.

Stitching together nearly four decades of Schoenberg's critical and theoretical remarks results in a vision we might deem "Schubert the Progressive," echoing Schoenberg's important "Brahms the Progressive" essay of 1947. This description of Schubert could have served as an apt title for a hitherto unpublished one-page piece written during the summer of 1928 while Schoenberg was staying at Roquebrune on the French Riviera:

> An avowal for Schubert: one might appear immodest, if one were to do it. Whoever needed to do it, desires to become important by doing so.
>
> There is still much to be said about Schubert at the next centennial celebration that has not yet been said.
>
> The following seems to me neglected up until now: the opposite certainly holds true. [Schubert had] in every detail such an inconceivably great originality next to an overwhelming figure like Beethoven. No wonder, that today one has not yet recognized it fully, even though his boldness is hardly disturbing any more. Besides, keep in mind his self-esteem: at his elbow Beethoven's overwhelming genius. Schubert does not feel a need to deny that greatness in order to be still able somehow to hold his own! What self-knowledge, what genuine aristocratic self-worth, who esteems the same thing in the great one. Schubert copied all of Beethoven's symphony scores, in order to study them and from that to find his inspiration. Might one still do that today? Scores are studied, in order to be able to copy and denigrate them. Only he who deserves respect can respect others. Respect, however, lasts through the centuries.
>
> Schubert never thought about composing for anybody in particular, for court or church, for profit or public. It was enough for him to have written for the best, and <u>so</u> it became for <u>everyone</u>. Of course one can never write for everyone, by thinking about them, but not denigrating <u>oneself</u> for them—they can do that for themselves already or have their supporters do it in their place.[12]

Schoenberg's reference to "the next centennial celebration" indicates his keen awareness of what was transpiring in Vienna that summer. His Schubert essay is in fact contemporary with the tenth Deutsche Sängerbundfest, held in the city from July 19 to 23 and dedicated to Schubert's memory. Local newspapers were full of accounts and photographs of the Sunday parade along the Ringstrasse in which an estimated 200,000 individuals participated. The procession included certainly the biggest example of Schubert kitsch: the Vienna Schubertbund's float drawn by six horses, featuring a *Kolossalfigur* of the composer flanked by forty young women in period dress (figure 7.1).[13]

This crass display may well have represented for Schoenberg a cultural defamation of Schubert. Schoenberg argued that Schubert would never have debased himself by sacrificing his creative integrity in order to achieve superficial

Figure 7.1. Schubert rendered as a Viennese parade float. The Vienna Schubertbund's *Kolossalfigur* of Schubert appearing in the parade along the Ringstrasse in celebration of the tenth festival of German singing societies. *Das interessante Blatt* 47, no. 30 (July 26, 1928): 13. Author's collection.

celebrity or financial affluence. These were the same ascendant values that appalled Schoenberg, whose career in Vienna had been marked by the indignities of economic hardship and public scandal. In constructing a Schubert who remained a unique creative spirit even as he learned from Beethoven's example, Schoenberg was holding up a mirror to his own career. In the essay "National Music" (1931), he again merged compositional independence with cultural homage: "My originality comes from this: I immediately imitated everything I saw that was good, even when I had not first seen it in someone else's work."[14] Such an elegant turn of phrase allowed Schoenberg to look back upon an artistic development that owed nothing to consciously slavish emulation, but whose rightness was confirmed by its allegiance to a tradition whose membership not coincidentally consisted only of Austrian and German composers. Further, Schoenberg placed Schubert in a unique position by separating him from other composers of the past—Bach, Mozart, Beethoven, Brahms, and Wagner—and locating him at the head of a list of his own contemporaries: "I also learned from Schubert and Mahler, Strauss and Reger too. I shut myself off from no one."[15]

Respect for the past—and concern over the absence of it—was a central preoccupation for Schoenberg in the 1920s, and his oblique reference in the 1928 essay
to those who studied in order to be able to transcribe and make a joke, and thus
to curry favor with the public, was the sort of cultural critique that had become a
regular feature of his polemic over the preceding half-dozen years and culminated
in his *Three Satires*, op. 28 (1925).[16] In the case of the untitled Roquebrune essay,
we may hypothesize about one of Schoenberg's targets by examining a newspaper
clipping that was kept by the composer. The item comes from the *Neues Wiener
Journal* of November 14, 1928, five days before the centennial of Schubert's death,
and is entitled "Jonny spielt Schubert auf," its unnamed correspondent reporting
on a lecture given by the composer Ernst Krenek. The following passage dovetails
well with the contents of Schoenberg's essay:

> For Schubert—and to have said so Krenek deserves credit in the best sense—did not
> first have to discover a new style in order for him to be who he was, rather he created
> out of existing means and with sounds, which in their limitation scarcely went beyond
> Haydn, created things which were new and even unheard of in Schubert's time. Krenek
> characterizes it as <u>more difficult</u> [Schoenberg's annotated emphasis] if someone
> should write a ländler which should be exactly in the style of all earlier ländler, and
> goes effortlessly into the ears of the people for whom this way of writing is very famil-
> iar. To discover a new dance with an individual method is the easier art. One is unre-
> strained if one has no definite form to maintain; and one must free oneself from
> restrictive rules if, through an existing form, one wants to let shine forth a unique iden-
> tity like that of Schubert.[17]

The article's title refers to Krenek's opera *Jonny spielt auf*, which had enjoyed a
sensational premiere in Leipzig on February 10, 1927, and whose success was
replicated in other cities. Prior to this stunning performance, however,
Schoenberg had already placed Krenek in his polemical crosshairs. Krenek's
article "Musik in der Gegenwart," appearing in 1926 in the yearbook *25 Jahre
neue Musik*, a product of the music publisher Universal Edition, had received a
quick response from Schoenberg in the foreword to the *Three Satires*, in which
one "droll mediocrity" ("mediokre nekisch"—note the last three letters of the
first word and the first three letters of the second) was taken to task as an example of someone who appeared to have just discovered fashionable tonics and
dominants as an easy means of achieving public popularity.[18]

At the time of the 1928 Schubert essay, Schoenberg was not necessarily aware
of Krenek's musical appropriations of Schubert. Krenek himself indicated that the
finale of Schubert's Trio in B-flat Major served as the basis for the second movement of his Piano Sonata no. 2, op. 59 (1928).[19] From a musical standpoint,
Schoenberg's *Von heute auf Morgen*, a parody of so-called *Zeitoper*, suggests that at
the end of 1928 *Jonny* was the work by Krenek that was still very much on his
mind.[20] Even if Schoenberg was unaware of Krenek's sonata, the newspaper clipping provided him with support for his own view of Schubert. For Schoenberg, it
was irrelevant whether or not that article implicated Krenek as the proponent of

the "individual method" that was the "easier art." Schoenberg underlined the
words "more difficult," and in the margin wrote archly: "He mustn't do anything
that is too difficult for him."[21] In adding that uncharitable squib, he was defending Schubert, and by extension himself, as a composer whose genius came from a
patient study that scorned obeisance to public whim. (Schoenberg tended to
launch his polemics as responses to attacks, real or perceived. Even so, he acknowledged musical ability regardless of his personal taste. He listed Krenek and Kurt
Weill along with Berg and Webern when asked by the Berlin Academy of Arts to
propose candidates for election to its membership on January 2, 1929.)[22]

Audience caprice may have seemed to Schoenberg a principal feature of the
orgy of Schubert celebrations that took place in the summer of 1928 since their
dates closely parallel the documents just described. When later in the year
Schubert's death on November 19 was commemorated in Vienna, Schoenberg
was noticeably not asked for his opinion. If reading about Krenek's lecture
annoyed him, one wonders what he might have made of Sergei Rachmaninoff's
remark, quoted ten days later in the same Neues Wiener Journal: "How do I see
Schubert? To this direct question I can only give an indirect answer: Schubert is
for me too great and too revered to explain his music with the tools of analysis."[23]
It may have been some consolation for Schoenberg to read Berg's postmortem in
a letter of December 7: "And what haven't we experienced! The Schubert week.
Naturally my faint hope that in his honor at least one chord in the dozens of concerts be played correctly was dashed. But that was nothing compared to what was
<u>spoken</u> by our dignitaries."[24] Did Berg count Krenek's lecture among the dross?
Berg was well aware of Schoenberg's polemics, having written on May 30, 1926,
congratulating him for having "finished off" Krenek with the foreword to the
Three Satires. Berg even attempted to match Schoenberg's pun: "I took a pretty
close look, with the greatest imaginable objectivity, at Krenek's Orpheus and
Euridike and was extremely doubtful whether what this Ernest [Ernst] means to say
with his music is really said in earnest [im Ernst]."[25]

That Schoenberg's polemics on Schubert in 1928 were offered in support of himself as much as in defense of the older composer is also suggested by a contemporary document dated Roquebrune, July 14, 1928, that includes a literary squib
entitled "Mit mir Kirschen essen" (see figure 7.2), a phrase that literally translates
as "Eating cherries with me" but proverbially means "Getting along with me":

> It also seems so dangerous: those who have eaten cherries with me [who have got along
> with me] still get the better of it. I overcame it once when someone dared it; I got over
> my astonishment by means of a quick symbolic justification, then I even lost interest in
> the cherries as well as in the eaters and can only live and let live. So then it is almost as
> nourishing to eat cherries with me [to get along with me], as it seems dangerous.[26]

What was the prior circumstance in which his being considered a danger was
something he overcame? By 1928, Schoenberg had had to endure more than

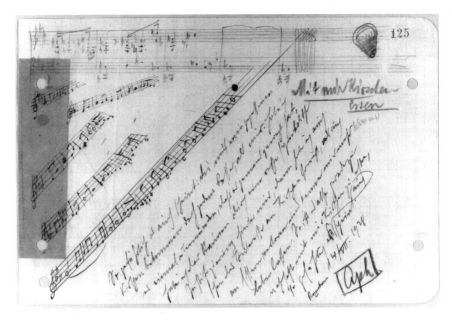

Figure 7.2. Arnold Schoenberg, "Mit mir Kirschen essen," 1928. Used by permission of Belmont Music Publishers, Los Angeles, and the Arnold Schönberg Center, Vienna (T03.17).

one round of critical attacks. The novelty of his twelve-tone method was inciting invective as contemptuous as that he endured during what he identified as the interval between his first and second periods: between the composition of the Chamber Symphony no. 1, op. 9, and the String Quartet no. 2, op. 10.

The apparently opaque "rasche symbolische Justifizierung" might refer to what appears on the page to the left of this squib in figure 7.2. Here Schoenberg jotted down five times the second theme of the first movement of Schubert's String Quintet in C Major, subjecting its intervallic content to an interesting manipulation.[27] With the exception of the pitches of lines two and three, each of the lines progressively adds more notes of the theme. The bottom four lines, with bar lines drawn at angles to suggest a three-dimensional perspective, use a key signature of three flats. The first line, however, scarcely two measures long, clearly has a key signature of two sharps.

The appearance of three flats replicates Schubert's modulation to E-flat major, which coincides with the theme's entrance at m. 60 and forms the central pillar of the three-key exposition in the trio's first movement: C major–E-flat major–G major. The modulation from C major to E-flat major is a famous Schubertian key change; it was the one example of a flatted mediant relationship cited by Schoenberg in *Structural Functions of Harmony*.[28] In 1928, its invocation might

have appealed to Schoenberg, who a year earlier had characterized Schubert as
the font of romantic harmonic experimentation rather than the embodiment of
tuneful Biedermeier *Gemütlichkeit.* Besides, this theme is undoubtedly the most
famous example from the chamber music repertoire of a tune performed by two
cellos, an attractive choice for Schoenberg, who played the cello. (There is no
direct evidence that Schoenberg performed the C-Major Quintet at this time,
although Oskar Kokoschka recalled that the composer often played *Hausmusik*
with his pupils. During the summer of 1921, Schoenberg gave his students
orchestration exercises for ensembles in which they could perform, with the
composer playing the cello. Between November 27 and December 6 of that year,
Schoenberg also arranged the scherzo of Schubert's Trio in E-flat Major, which
in 1943 he included on a list of planned piano reductions to be used as "peda-
gogic examples for practice as instrumentation assignments.")[29]

The presence of two sharps is less easily explicable. The intervallic relationship of the two versions of the melody may have had an abstract appeal, in that
the order of the major and minor seconds are rearranged while the position of
the only other interval, the minor third, remains fixed (see example 7.1). Yet it
is not clear what theoretical feature these two intervallic variants of the same
melody were intended to represent, or even if Schoenberg's purpose was analytical. The repetition of a melody whose notated position of pitches on the staff
remains unchanged, but whose intervallic content is altered by a different key
signature, is not easily accommodated by any comparable motivic or harmonic
analysis in Schoenberg's writings. It does not conform to the "juxtaposition of
motives, which are only melodically varied, but rhythmically very similar," or to
a "transformed transposition," which he illustrated with examples by Schubert
and Brahms.[30]

From an aural perspective, the two-sharp version of the melody arguably
sounds as though it is in G major rather than the D major implied by the key
signature. G major is the second key area to which a C-major movement in
sonata form would typically modulate, and indeed, in the quintet's first movement, G is the pitch tonicized immediately before the two measures (mm.
58–59) that catapult the music into E-flat major. Of course, if Schoenberg's
intention was to recall this modulation, he could more easily have written one
sharp. Moreover, the angled bar lines appear to create a visible metaphor for
the harmonic distance that is traversed by the five-fold statement of the tune.
This distinctive orthography suggests that the melody had as much a visual as
an aural significance; that is, a viewer was meant to read D major as much as
hear G major.

The only music example from Schoenberg's prose that bears comparison to
his manipulation of the quintet melody consists of two measures taken from
Schubert's "In der Ferne" from *Schwanengesang* (the same passage that had so
exercised the music historian August Wilhelm Ambros nearly a century earlier),
which appeared as part of a discussion of innovative harmonic procedures.[31]
"The juxtaposition of two unrelated triads" (B minor and B-flat major) creates a

Example 7.1. Schubert, String Quintet in C Major, D. 956, op. posth. 163, first movement, mm. 81–83, melody transcribed by Schoenberg on the same page as "Mit mir Kirschen essen" (figure 7.2). Used by permission of Belmont Music Publishers, Los Angeles, and the Arnold Schönberg Center, Vienna.

semitone relationship as a consequence of altering identical pitches by the use of different accidentals (see example 7.2). To be sure, this example is not exactly equivalent to the two versions of the quintet melody since the song's two triads are in different modes (which permits Schubert to retain the D♮ common to both triads, thus implying that the key signature of the second measure is two flats). As a symbolic illustration of romantic harmony, the example from "In der Ferne" does reinforce Schoenberg's frequent assertion that such practice was traceable to Schubert. As to the relationship of D major and E-flat major created by Schoenberg's juxtaposition of two versions of the same melody from the C-Major Quintet, which have two sharps and three flats respectively, the composer might have wished to acknowledge the structural importance of the semitone, specifically alluding to the flatted second or Neapolitan harmony that exists throughout the quintet. Yet in invoking these two particular key signatures, which in fact never occur in Schubert's composition, Schoenberg was replicating a specific relationship that he himself had often used.

Might this sudden manipulation of the quintet melody be an example of the "rasche symbolische Justifizierung" to which Schoenberg alluded in the literary squib that accompanied the tune? That Schoenberg's particular choice of a Neapolitan transformation of Schubert's melody might also refer to his own musical development is obliquely suggested by the appearance of a fragment of five incomplete measures of music that runs along the length of the page containing the five Schubert lines (see example 7.3). The location of this music starting in the top left corner suggests that it was written first, although the different orthography makes problematic any speculation as to when Schoenberg entered the other material. The fragment is nonetheless linked to the first of the Schubert phrases through the same key signature, that of two sharps.[32] The

Example 7.2. Schubert, "In der Ferne," *Schwanengesang*, D. 957, mm. 17–18. (From Schoenberg, "Brahms the Progressive"; see note 31.)

Example 7.3. Arnold Schoenberg, musical fragment from "Mit mir Kirschen essen" (figure 7.2). Used by permission of Belmont Music Publishers, Los Angeles, and the Arnold Schönberg Center, Vienna.

music is not recognizable as an actual quotation, but the principal rhythm and the melodic contour bear a resemblance to a significant motive from Schoenberg's *Verklärte Nacht*, op. 4 (1899), the string sextet that famously uses E flat and D as central pillars of its harmonic structure (see example 7.4).

In 1932, Schoenberg wrote a set of analytical notes entitled "Konstruktives in der Verklärten Nacht," whose ten music examples detailed the structural basis of the work's harmonic design. The document concludes with the composer's observation that the third of these ideas—the large-scale relationship (D minor–E-flat minor–D major–D-flat major–D major)—was the only one that he recalled as having been consciously planned.[33] To the right of this example there is a further reduction—D:E flat:D:D flat:D—and above it is a motive whose pitches are those of m. 29 in example 7.4, but with an added F♮ (presumably coming from the second note of m. 30) following the C sharp. (This motive first appears in mm. 29–31 and is subsequently varied at mm. 181–87 and 236–42.) The composer added brackets above and below three pairs of pitches (A–B flat, D–C sharp, G–F) presumably to emphasize the important part played by these

Etwas bewegter

Example 7.4. Schoenberg, *Verklärte Nacht*, op. 4, mm. 29–31 (viola). Used by permission of Belmont Music Publishers, Los Angeles.

intervals, the same ones that Schoenberg manipulated by altering the key signature of Schubert's melody. That the rhythm of this motive resembles the one in the fragment of 1928 might well be just a coincidence, even if it does come from *Verklärte Nacht*, whose use of the E flat–D dyad derives from the same Neapolitan structure that Schoenberg grafted onto the successive fragments of Schubert's melody.

In manipulating the Neapolitan pairing of E flat and D, Schoenberg was perhaps offering an echo of a work from his own past. In so doing, he emphasized a harmonic relationship that was central to his career from his earliest attempts at composition to the works that stood at the brink of atonality and even beyond. Indeed, so often does it occur in the music of his self-styled first period that we might describe it in the way Maurice J. E. Brown characterized Schubert's use of it: if it was not an addiction, it was at least something the composer relished.[34] Given Schoenberg's frequent declarations that Schubert was the originator of romantic harmonic practice as well as Schoenberg's specific association—one might say reinvention—of the Neapolitan in his transcription of the quintet melody, we may explore similar connections between the music of the two composers. To do so, we may turn back to the very beginning of Schoenberg's career in Vienna during the 1890s, the decade in which many of the city's modernists sought to reimagine Schubert's legacy.

Schoenberg's earliest essay in chamber music composition, a Presto in C Major for string quartet, is undated, although Willi Reich related an anecdote about Schoenberg, performing, in 1894, a movement from a C-major quartet for Joseph Labor, the blind organist and composer who gave music instruction to Paul Wittgenstein and Alma Schindler, and who himself had been a pupil of Simon Sechter.[35] (However coincidental, the name of Sechter invariably conjures up a picture of the theorist to whom Schubert went late in life purportedly to learn counterpoint. This biographical detail contributed mightily to the popular image of the composer as a musical naif.) The final measures of this Presto in C Major invite comparison with those of the final movement off Schubert's C-Major Quintet (see example 7.5).[36] In the last dozen measures of the quintet (mm. 418–29), one is temporarily wrenched away from the tonic by an A flat, part of an F-minor chord that appears to prepare a cadence in the parallel

Example 7.5. Schubert, Quintet in C Major, fourth movement, mm. 419–29.

minor (iv–V–i$^6_4$–V) only to resolve to C major (m. 423). This in turn is followed by a final cadence whose dominant seventh is altered by a D flat, and a final measure whose unison tonic is preceded by a unison D flat, a pitch whose Neapolitan implications were articulated throughout the composition. (These occur most notably in the formal relationships of the E-major adagio, whose central section begins in F minor, and the C-major scherzo, whose trio section is in D-flat major.)[37] This flatted second degree also governs Schoenberg's final

Example 7.6. Schoenberg, Presto in C Major, mm. 459–65. Used by permission of Belmont Music Publishers, Los Angeles.

cadence: I–iv–♭II–♭VI–iv–I (mm. 459–65, see example 7.6). To be sure, the similarities are not identical. The two examples have in common the appearance of the minor subdominant (a common initiator of the flatted second harmony) and a significant inflection on the Neapolitan, although they are used to different effect.[38] In Schoenberg's finale, the succession of triads on F minor, D flat, A flat, F minor, and C is almost appreciable as a half-cadence in F minor, reinforced by the absence of any dominant articulation in the original key.

This is not the only occasion in the presto where a striking harmony appears at a point that recalls its location in Schubert's quintet. A similar gesture occurs at the return of the opening theme at m. 257 (see example 7.7). The group of four measures, 253–56, preceding this return recalls the diminished seventh chord [F sharp–A–C–E flat] that so famously occurs in the first movement of the quintet at m. 269 (see example 7.8). In the quintet, it underlies the theme itself and as such it had already appeared earlier, at m. 3. Schoenberg's deployment of it in proximity to the recapitulation is a reminder of Schubert's chord, much as his placement of the Neapolitan in the coda serves as a harmonic echo of Schubert's use of it at a similar structural point in the quintet.

If the presence of the Neapolitan relationship in the final cadence of a chamber work in C major might invite comparison with Schubert's quintet, the connection is hardly umbilical. That the flatted second was crucial for Schoenberg's ensuing development, however, is more than suggested by his continued invocation of the Neapolitan in subsequent instrumental compositions. Thus, the first movement of the unfinished Serenade in D Major for small orchestra from the autumn of 1896 has a striking motion to E flat at m. 21.[39] The D–E flat semitone relationship is likewise noticeable in the concluding measures of the first

Example 7.7. Schoenberg, Presto in C Major, mm. 253–58. Used by permission of Belmont Music Publishers, Los Angeles.

Example 7.8. Schubert, Quintet in C Major, first movement, mm. 267–71.

Example 7.9. Schoenberg, String Quartet in D Major, first movement, mm. 263–67. Used by permission of Belmont Music Publishers, Los Angeles.

and last movements of the String Quartet in D Major, composed in the summer of 1897. At the end of its first movement, E-flat major is articulated over a span of four measures (mm. 263–66) before the final arrival of the tonic (see example 7.9). (This gesture is in turn echoed in the finale, where the return of the principal theme occurs on a unison E flat at mm. 209–19, preceding the return of the tonic. The last statement of the unison occurs in turn at m. 246 on B flat, the pitch that began the movement and that here functions as the Neapolitan of the dominant.) These relationships lead two years later to the concluding measures of *Verklärte Nacht* (mm. 411–13), where triads of E-flat major and D major are presented as climactic simultaneities, and taken together they cast their harmonic shadows over the transformative E flat–D tonalities by which Schoenberg manipulated Schubert's quintet melody (m. 411, see example 7.10).

There are also other resemblances between the first movement of the D-Major Quartet and that of Schubert's quintet. The large-scale tonal motion of the quintet articulates the second theme of the exposition in E-flat major (♭III at m. 60) and the opening of the development in A major (VI at m. 156). These two keys are the same distance, a minor third, above and below C major. Symmetrical with respect to the tonic, which behaves as a tonal axis, these minor third relationships are those employed by Schoenberg but in reverse order: a second theme in B major (VI at m. 39) and a development beginning in F major (♭III at m. 97).[40] Further, the developments of both movements strongly articulate the Neapolitan: Schoenberg at m. 109 (E flat, but in the minor mode) and Schubert beginning at m. 175 (via its dominant A flat respelled as G sharp. The motivic development

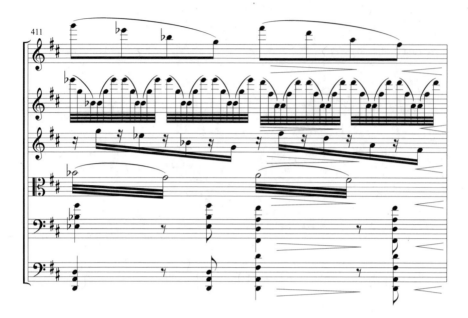

Example 7.10. Schoenberg, *Verklärte Nacht*, m. 411. Used by permission of Belmont Music Publishers, Los Angeles.

of mm. 175–97 is subsequently replicated at mm. 211–33 in B major, producing another symmetrical relationship, B and D flat, with respect to the original tonic.) Finally, both composers employ an identically functioning six-note fortissimo chord in the retransition to the recapitulation. Schubert's German sixth sonorities at mm. 259 and 261 (consisting of the pitches A flat–A flat–C–E flat–F sharp–A flat) resolve to the dominant (see example 7.11). Schoenberg initially writes the chord as A flat–F–B flat–D–F–B flat (mm. 157–65). Subsequently, at m. 166, the A flat is respelled as a G sharp, thus functioning like Schubert's chord and resolving to the tonic (see example 7.12).[41]

Are these similarities attributable to coincidence? A possible Schubertian connection is cited nowhere in the later literature on the D-Major Quartet. In the volume honoring Schoenberg's sixtieth birthday in 1934, Alexander Zemlinsky appears to have been the first to observe Brahms's shadow hovering over the work.[42] Schoenberg himself confirmed this musical influence in his essay "My Evolution" (1950), and subsequent analyses of the work's thematic contour, motivic manipulation, and contrapuntal elaboration have pointed out Brahms's importance.[43] In his 1950 essay, Schoenberg gave an equal nod to Dvořák, and in program notes to a recording of his quartets in 1936 he wrote that his youthful interest in chamber music composition had originated when "I bought secondhand, a few scores of Beethoven: the third and fourth symphonies, two

Example 7.11. Schubert, Quintet in C Major, first movement, mm. 259–60.

Example 7.12. Schoenberg, Quartet in D Major, first movement, mm. 165–67.
Used by permission of Belmont Music Publishers, Los Angeles.

Rasoumovsky [*sic*] string quartets and the *Great Fugue* for string quartet [op. 133]. From this minute, I was possessed by an urge to write string quartets."[44]

If we are to give some credence to these later pronouncements, we might also note that the harmonic richness whose evolution Schoenberg regarded as beginning with Schubert was not a stylistic trait that he listed as having inherited from either Beethoven or Brahms when, in 1931, he enumerated his musical influences. On the contrary, his early debts to Beethoven were owed to features other than harmonic practice, in particular thematic development and variation. When, in 1936, Schoenberg indicated that the first movement of Beethoven's *Eroica* Symphony had served as the model for the first movement of his own String Quartet no. 1 in D Minor, op. 7 (1905), it was in terms of "how to avoid monotony and emptiness; how to create variety out of unity; how to create new forms out of basic material; how much can be achieved by slight modifications if not by developing variation out of often rather insignificant little formulations."[45] Moreover, there exists an abandoned Quartet in D Minor from between 1901 and 1903, whose double fugue structure echoes Beethoven's *Grosse Fuge*, op. 133, but whose subject and answer have been more closely related by Walter Frisch to the String Quartet in C-sharp Minor, op. 131.[46] To be sure, one early influence does not necessarily come at the expense of another; there are several works by Beethoven in which Neapolitan gestures figure strongly, including some that may have influenced Schubert. Yet it is worth noting that those aspects of Beethoven's style that are traceable in the early works of Schoenberg and were confirmed in his later writings are related to features that traditionally were considered to be weaknesses in Schubert's output, particularly the complex working out of thematic materials. Schubert's seeking instruction in counterpoint from Sechter at a late stage in his career was a story that led a hardy existence. Likewise the "heavenly lengths" of Schubert's Ninth Symphony, as famously described by Schumann, constituted a cliché familiar to Schoenberg, and one that he did not necessarily utter with approval.[47]

The harmonic resemblances between Schubert and Schoenberg might finally be willed away if it were not for the hospitable chronology of Schoenberg composing the D-Major Quartet in Vienna during the summer of 1897, only months after the city's extravagant public commemorations of Schubert's centennial during which three different ensembles played the C-Major Quintet within the span of five days. The composer Franz Schmidt served as second cellist in performances by the Rosé Quartet on January 26 and the Hellmesberger Quartet on January 28, and the Duesburg Quartet played it on January 31 with Franz Klein.[48] The Rosé Quartet subsequently premiered three of Schoenberg's chamber works: *Verklärte Nacht* and the First and Second Quartets. Thus Schoenberg's D-Major Quartet may have served as double homage, equally inspired by the hyperbolically zealous celebrations of Schubert's centennial in January and February and by Brahms's death on April 3. The documents of 1928 illustrating Schoenberg's distinctive tribute to Schubert may thus echo a similarly honorific gesture from an earlier commemorative year.

Whether as part of a large-scale organization or as a telling detail, the Neapolitan relationship remained a central feature of Schoenberg's style into the first decade of the twentieth century. The conclusion of *Pelleas und Melisande*, op. 5 (1903) features an insistently repetitive motion from an E flat to the D-minor tonic in the bass instruments, and a similar movement animates measures 46–47 in the D-major coda of the First Quartet in D Minor, op. 7. The cadential gesture often furnished a replication of the prior musical argument. Certainly the ending of *Verklärte Nacht* (mm. 411–13) recalls an equivalent motion at mm. 222–29, in which seven measures of the harmony of E-flat minor precede the first appearance of the D-major key signature followed at mm. 236–38 by a return of the motive that first appeared in m. 29 (see example 7.4). The simultaneous utterance of E flat and D as a concluding gesture likewise provides a connection between the First Quartet and *Verklärte Nacht*, with the former completing the Neapolitan triad in the minor mode.[49] (Compare examples 7.10 and 7.13.) One cannot escape musing on the possibility that this dyadic convergence pays homage to Schubert's String Quartet in D Minor (D. 810), whose first movement culminates with yet another Neapolitan gesture (mm. 326–41), preceded by a chord in which the first violin's E-flat octave—part of a vii°/VI harmony—sounds above the cello's D–A (mm. 303 and 307, see example 7.14).

The actual stacking of two harmonies a semitone apart was later exploited to more audacious effect in the Chamber Symphony no. 1. As Frisch has pointed out, the climactic six-note quartal chord at m. 364 is framed by the dyad F–E, whose pitches anchor the harmonies of a final Neapolitan cadence in E major at mm. 582–85.[50] One might even speak of this flatted second relationship as a Schoenbergian fingerprint that remained recognizable in the String Quartet no. 2 even as he abandoned the use of key signatures. The concluding measures of the first movement in F-sharp minor have a strong bass motion from G to F sharp (mm. 217–18 and 230–31).[51] In 1909, the anonymous writer of what is probably the earliest published analysis of a work by Schoenberg noted that in the second movement's D-minor scherzo, the reprise of the theme of the trio section (first appearing in F-sharp minor) is harmonized in E-flat minor (m. 151) prior to the final allusion to the folksong "Ach, du lieber Augustin" (m. 165).[52] The analysis might have added that the motion of E flat to D is echoed in the scherzo's final measures (mm. 273–74), where downbeat E flats in the second violin and viola appear below an alternating G–C sharp in the first violin and above a D pedal in the cello. In the final movement, an explicit motion in the strings from a G-major triad to one on F-sharp major (m. 25) provides the cadential ending for the first phrase of the voice: "I feel the air of another planet" (see example 7.15).[53]

We cannot determine finally whether these points of contact between Schoenberg and Schubert were conscious strategies on Schoenberg's part. Certainly Schoenberg's fascination with the Neapolitan as (at the very least) a concluding gesture reflected his romance with the semitone and created a

Example 7.13. Schoenberg, String Quartet no. 1, op. 7, final section, mm. 45–47. Used by permission of Belmont Music Publishers, Los Angeles.

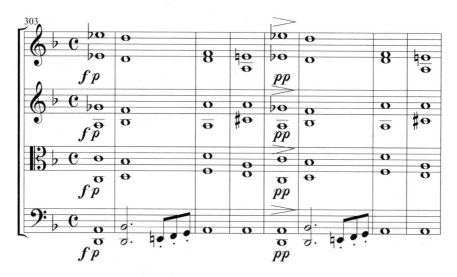

Example 7.14. Schubert, String Quartet in D Minor, D. 810, first movement, mm. 303–10.

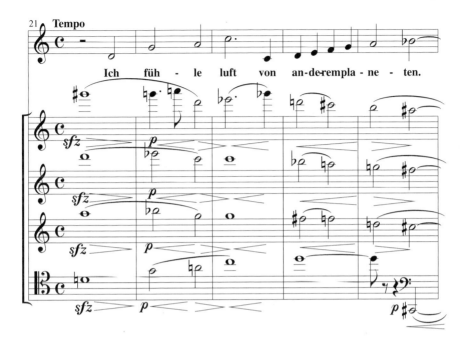

Example 7.15. Schoenberg, String Quartet no. 2, op. 10, fourth movement, mm. 21–25. Used by permission of Belmont Music Publishers, Los Angeles.

connection among his chamber works at the turn of the century.[54] Those early examples that allude to the Quintet in C Major suggest that Schubert was a part of Schoenberg's mental baggage even if by the century's end Schoenberg did not necessarily rely on the quintet as a musical parent. Conscious or not, Schoenberg's youthful allusion to the gritty cadential feature of Schubert's quintet arguably set him apart from the popular imagination in fin-de-siècle Vienna, where Schubert's beloved lyricism—a telltale sign of his *Mädchencharakter*—was a more characteristic avenue for appreciating his music. Schoenberg's separation of himself from that cliché may have been an early gesture for avoiding the *gemütlich* character of a culture that in his eyes would later at best fail to appreciate him and at worst come to regard him as a notorious aberration.

   Schoenberg's subsequent tapping of Schubert as the wellspring for the expansion of romantic harmony makes sense in this context. Even as Schoenberg's regard for Schubert as the harmonic pioneer might have found an echo in a shared fondness for the flatted second relationship in the works (especially in chamber music) leading to atonality, it was in his self-styled second period that Schoenberg later claimed he sought to move away from the more obviously flawed elements of Schubert's style. Schoenberg's compositional ideal, at least from the first Chamber Symphony onward, was set "in contrast to Schubert's love of repeating his motives and rhythms."[55] In taking a longer historical view that acknowledged Schubert's harmonic influence, Schoenberg did not avoid a tacit criticism:

> Frequent deviation from the tonic region into more or less foreign regions seemed to obstruct unity and intelligibility. However, the most advanced mind is still subject to human limitations. Thus composers of this style, instinctively feeling the danger of incoherence, counteracted the tension in one plane (the complex harmony) by simplification in another plane (the motival and rhythmic construction). This perhaps also explains the unvaried repetitions and frequent sequences of Wagner, Bruckner, Debussy, César Franck, Tchaikovsky, Sibelius and many others.[56]

That Schubert's music was marred by such flaws may have been old news, although Schoenberg elsewhere tempered the criticism by offering the statement that "constant repetition of a rhythmic figure, as in popular music, lends a popular touch to many Schubertian melodies. But their real nobility manifests itself in their rich melodic contour."[57] Further, Lona Truding, who studied under Schoenberg at the Schwarzwald School in the early 1920s, recalled that Schubert's dances were the "excellent compositions" that Schoenberg gave to his students to follow as "models for the right bass, the right harmony, and the right melody."[58]

If the language of the Second Viennese School could not comfortably accommodate the phenomenon of musical repetition implicit in Schubert's "heavenly lengths," the genius of other features of the composer's style was more than sufficient compensation. Dika Newlin recorded a similar attitude when she was Schoenberg's pupil in 1939: "How he adores Schubert! 'Many people say,' he remarked, 'that Schubert is too long. He is long—yes—but for me he is always too short!'"[59] This observation again may be attributable to the fact that Schoenberg delighted in articulating beliefs contrary to popularly accepted clichés, especially if they enhanced his stature as a solitary visionary amid the shifting trends of contemporary music. Given this viewpoint, one can imagine Schoenberg listening with approval to Mahler holding forth at a soirée on February 3, 1905, after a concert of Mahler's Lieder as recorded by Webern in his diary: "Variation is the most important factor in a musical work, he stated. A theme would have to be really especially beautiful, as some by Schubert are, in order to make its unaltered return refreshing."[60]

With such a mitigating attitude, it is not surprising that the C-Major Quintet should be the work that catapulted into Schoenberg's consciousness in 1928, the centennial of the composer's death. Manipulating the quintet melody to highlight a semitonal relationship symbolized a new harmonic language that, as Schoenberg repeatedly observed, began with Schubert and, by implication, culminated in Schoenberg's own work at the turn of the century. As an extension of that development, the evolution of Schoenberg's own style revealed no less of a continuity, as he himself often argued. On July 29, 1942, Bertolt Brecht observed as much in his diary, after a conversation at the composer's home

Example 7.16. Schoenberg, Variations for Orchestra, tonal harmonization. Used by permission of Belmont Music Publishers, Los Angeles.

following Schoenberg's University of California Los Angeles lecture on the emancipation of the dissonance: "I liked the old man a lot. He sees himself in an historical context. When somebody mentioned that so-and-so had finished schubert's [*sic*] unfinished for a competition, he said quickly, 'I could do it better, but I wouldn't dare.' "[61]

In similar fashion, Schoenberg's five-fold musical gloss on Schubert's melody is exactly contemporaneous with his completion of the Variations for Orchestra, op. 31, whose premiere on December 2, 1928, by the Berlin Philharmonic under Wilhelm Furtwängler shared the bill with Schubert's Ninth Symphony. Schoenberg later harmonized the main theme of the Variations for Orchestra in what he argued was a "quite good F major which insistently courts G-flat major, corresponding to a neapolitan sixth" (see example 7.16).[62] Written as part of a radio address in 1931, this reharmonization not only demonstrated Schoenberg's facility in tonal composition, at least the densely chromatic variety of the fin de siècle, should he have wished to continue his creative development in that vein, but also, less overtly, it harked back to a gesture that we have seen had always been a feature of his style. Perhaps it would be too much of an analytic stretch to apply Schoenberg's description to the mysterious five-measure fragment appearing on the same page as the five-fold phrase from Schubert's five-voice quintet: a "quite good" D major that courts E flat. Certainly, however, that fragment indulges in a type of voice leading that is kin to the fluid motion between two harmonies a half step apart.

Schoenberg's harmonization of the twelve-tone melody of the Variations for Orchestra may provide an additional clue to the purpose behind his curious double rendering of Schubert's quintet theme with, in turn, two sharps and three flats. The alteration of the quintet melody's pitches by the substitution of the new key signature is comprehensible simply as an application of a tonal procedure—modulation—to a diatonic melody. Now, however, the two versions result in a relationship that also suggests a tonal equivalent to the phenomenon of invariance, which was an essential factor in Schoenberg's choice of row forms (the row or series being the pre-compositional ordering of pitches from which the work is generated) during the 1920s as he developed and refined the method of composition with twelve tones.

From his earliest essays in serial procedure in the Serenade, op. 24, and the Suite for Piano, op. 25, to the large-scale instrumental works of opp. 30 and 31—two pairs of compositions framing the document of 1928—Schoenberg created row forms that possessed this invariant relationship: two or more pitch classes (pitches that sound the same regardless of their spelling, such as A flat and G sharp) remain in equivalent positions in a new row form generated by transposition or inversion of the original row. (In the row forms below, P refers to the original or prime form of the row, I indicates its inversion, and the number that follows them designates the number of half steps or semitones above the prime form, designated as P-0.)

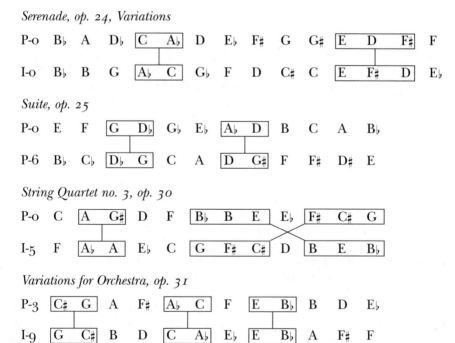

Serenade, op. 24, Variations

P-0 B♭ A D♭ C A♭ D E♭ F♯ G G♯ E D F♯ F

I-0 B♭ B G A♭ C G♭ F D C♯ C E F♯ D E♭

Suite, op. 25

P-0 E F G D♭ G♭ E♭ A♭ D B C A B♭

P-6 B♭ C♭ D♭ G C A D G♯ F F♯ D♯ E

String Quartet no. 3, op. 30

P-0 C A G♯ D F B♭ B E E♭ F♯ C♯ G

I-5 F A♭ A E♭ C G F♯ C♯ D B E B♭

Variations for Orchestra, op. 31

P-3 C♯ G A F♯ A♭ C F E B♭ B D E♭

I-9 G C♯ B D C A♭ E♭ E B♭ A F♯ F

In the relationship between each pair of row forms, the interval classes (IC, that is, the interval between pitch classes regardless of their spelling or direction) perforce remain the same, although in compositions like the String Quartet no. 3 and the *Ode to Napoleon*, Schoenberg sought to limit the number of interval classes of the original series as well.[63] With the application of two key signatures—the two sharps of D major and the three flats of E-flat major—to the notes of Schubert's melody, the pitch classes are necessarily altered, but there remains one invariant or unchanged interval class—the minor third (IC3)—in the same position. While the order of major and minor seconds change, the total number of each interval class remains the same; in both versions of the melody there are three minor seconds or semitones (IC1) and five major seconds or whole tones (IC2).

IC	1	1	2	2	2	3	2	2	1	
2 sharps	G	F♯	G	A	G	A	F♯	E	F♯	G

3 flats	G	F	G	A♭	G	A♭	F	E♭	F	G
IC		2	2	1	1	1	3	2	2	2

This treatment of Schubert's melody echoes Schoenberg's harmonization of the theme of his own Variations for Orchestra in this respect: in the former, tonal materials are manipulated to reveal a serial property whereas in the latter case, there is a demonstration of tonal features using serial components.[64] Schoenberg's transformation of Schubert's melody thus appears to pay homage to himself as much as to the older composer.

I began chapter 1 of the first volume of this study by quoting Schumann's resonant estimation of 1838, describing Schubert as a composer whose music conveyed a *Mädchencharakter* in comparison to that of Beethoven. Apart from this quality, which I argued was a positive token of romantic androgyny (and fateful because Schubert's subsequent nineteenth-century reception dispensed with the intricacies of that concept even as it invoked the authority of the term's inventor), Schumann also conferred upon Schubert the same feature that Schoenberg bestowed nine decades later. Indeed, they both chose the same word, boldness ("Kühnheit"), although that is quite likely a coincidence, despite Schoenberg's remarkable cultural memory (not excepting his familiarity with Schumann's description of Schubert's "heavenly lengths," itself a common enough piece of ⋅ critical detritus by Schoenberg's time).[65] Unlike Schumann in 1838, however, Schoenberg in 1928 was confronted with a Schubertian hagiography that had been metastasizing even before he was born in 1874. Within this panoply of myths, Schubert's feminine nature betrayed none of the subtle layers present in Schumann's creative manipulation of the term *Mädchencharakter*, a word that nonetheless proved to be endemic to the fin-de-siècle mind. As both polemicist and composer, Schoenberg, like many others of his generation, sought to rescue

Schubert from the perpetual lilac time that so dominated Schubert's reception in the public consciousness of the late nineteenth century. In doing so, Schoenberg carved for Schubert a historical niche that made the older composer an individual who possessed in equal measures a mature respect for and intimate understanding of his predecessors while having the self-awareness to forge a personal style of originality and boldness that belied the pathetically shy "little mushroom" of popular myth. These attributes were also applicable to Schoenberg's sense of his own place within the line of European music that he esteemed—a line that did not easily accommodate the implications of a feminized nature even as it took for granted that its members were exclusively Austro-German.

Schoenberg's location of Schubert as the putative begetter of romantic harmony allowed him to design a lineage with himself as its inevitable successor.[66] In doing so, he constructed a separate tradition that pointedly avoided the nineteenth-century reception that had nurtured the cliché of Schubert's feminine character with its emphasis on the composer as a fecund but unwitting tunesmith. To that extent, Schoenberg's approach was in keeping with the modernist culture in which he matured, even as it would later serve his larger historical program. However, one trait that separates Schoenberg's reception of Schubert from that of his contemporaries was that Schoenberg, as a composer and theorist, was not notably given to gendered terminology regarding either his own or Schubert's music. One element of that characterization was left to a later generation when, in 1944, Schoenberg himself was the beneficiary of a gendered compliment. On the occasion of Schoenberg's seventieth birthday the composer Roger Sessions wrote: "It is in the last analysis an act of gratitude to one who has, so much more than any other individual, been one of the masculine forces that have shaped the music of our time, even that music which seems farthest from his own."[67] As a self-identified heir, Schoenberg in his reception of Schubert echoed Schoenberg's judgment of his own compositional evolution, not as a radical departure from the past, but as a logical continuation of a language of which he was the true legatee on both musical and cultural grounds. Schoenberg's career thus became a path that was separately achieved, even as its solitariness was paradoxically mitigated by the welcoming shadows of his predecessors.

Conclusion

The two volumes of this book grew from my fascination with the ways in which Schubert's reception manifested itself in an astonishingly rich variety of cultural phenomena during the fin de siècle, even as the evidence continually exhibited the era's preoccupations with gender and nation. The fact that the contents of this study derive principally from material other than the scores of the composer's successors also satisfied my desire to write a book about Schubert's reception that would be accessible to readers who were not intimately familiar with the analysis of musical materials. In the present volume, the difficulty in comprehending the many strands of Schubert's reception in fin-de-siècle Viennese culture prompted shifts in methodological approach between individual creative responses and the grander canvas of turn-of-the-century concerns about and attitudes toward gender (the emerging theories about sexuality) and nation (the celebrations of the composer's centennial during a crucial election year). Furthermore, while these larger contexts undoubtedly contribute to a fuller understanding of the different appropriations of Schubert, it is through the works of the artistic imagination that the manipulation of this tradition is clearly manifested.

The emphasis on figures other than composers was a conscious choice, because treatments of Schubert conveyed in word and image (in the case of Schoenberg, as with Schumann in the first volume of this study, responses that were made in prose as well as music) had a greater transparency for contemporaries who, as the first volume of this study sought to demonstrate, were heirs to decades of mythologizing objects and utterances. The fact that neither artists and writers nor their audiences necessarily came armed with the complex apparatus necessary for dissecting musical composition in no way trivializes their reception of Schubert. Indeed, I have dwelled on this material so that a reader today who does not possess such analytical tools will still be able to comprehend how the composer's image was shaped by those larger cultural concerns that dominated the decades around 1900.

As a consequence, this study has remained devoted both to a historical assessment of how views of Schubert that were grounded in concepts of gender and nation developed during the late nineteenth and early twentieth centuries and to a consideration of the ways in which the composer's reception manifested itself in categories beyond the purely musical. The unique position that Schubert came to occupy during the nineteenth century provided a ready-made icon whose significance cut across both political allegiances and artistic boundaries. The particular situation in Vienna, during a period when concerns about the empire's destiny were paramount, reveals an intersection between questions of nation and gender in which the image of the composer became a contested entity. For the modernist spirits in fin-de-siècle Vienna, the lore of Schubert's life and the associative meanings of his music furnished representations that could be used to engage what in the public imagination were cherished notions about its culture, but which in the hands of its creative agents upended that seemingly secure heritage.

Although the very nature of fin-de-siècle Viennese modernism was unsuited to building a self-consciously designed uniform program, individual responses to Schubert did evince a shared disbelief in the image of the composer that had been newly minted by his nineteenth-century reception. As an "invented tradition," this view of Schubert met with continuous artistic interrogation: Klimt's refashioning of the Biedermeier idyll of a *Schubertiade*, Schnitzler's use of Schubertian objects to signify women doomed by their passivity, Hofmannsthal's coalescence of feminine symbols of composer and nation, Altenberg's blurring of Schubertian innocence and libidinal desire, and Schoenberg's positioning of Schubert as the begetter of a novel harmonic practice to which Schoenberg was the rightful heir.[1] One might even go so far as to judge the effort of rightist political entities to shape the composer into an embodiment of exclusionary Germanness as an exercise in the modernist exploitation of a particularly cynical and crass variety.

Schubertian symbology was important enough to Viennese identity at the turn of the century for it to occupy individuals who used otherwise different means of artistic expression and who desired to confront the mythic underpinnings of tradition even as the composer's image was fought over by competing political interests. The legacy of Schubert's feminine nature that had become embedded in the popular consciousness served as a reflection of fin-de-siècle preoccupations with gender whose very clichés were catechized and remade by the generation that came of artistic age in the 1890s. The challenges to the older fabrications of Schubert that were advanced by fin-de-siècle modernism followed creative rhythms designed to furnish a more complex and nuanced interpretation of the composer than the extreme sentimentality that permeated so much of the nineteenth century's construction of his *Mädchencharakter*. Turn-of-the-century modernists recognized this image of Schubert as a cultural artifice and supplied imaginative alternatives to it. The fictional protagonists who evinced an attraction to Schubert's music manifested a nature that could expose them to the vicissitudes of gendered hierarchies, especially if the individuals were women (and could problematize their temperament if they were men).

Recognizing Schubert's music as a representation of feminine nature created a tangle of relationships in fin-de-siècle Vienna beyond those reflected in works of the modernist creative imagination. Because Schubert also provided a unique symbol of Austrianness, one that was especially associated with the capital of German Austrian culture, his image provoked competing interpretations. In the nether world of frequently venomous political rhetoric, factions competed fiercely to make the composer either a model of liberal, transnational universality or a standard bearer of exclusionary, pan-German ideology. In such a turbulent environment, the idea that the composer and the country he represented were equally feminine was bound to cause controversy, especially among those who believed that the vitality of nations as well as individuals demanded a masculine forcefulness in both politics and culture.

At the same time, the emergence of a new science of sexuality brought the possibility of adding yet another layer of meaning onto an already complicated and contentious subject. In one sense, this novel field of study provided the opponents of modernism with a clarifying language. Armed with a vocabulary burnished by the apparent authority of science and medicine (many of whose most celebrated exponents were based in Vienna), critics could attack the contemporary literary preoccupation with themes of sexuality as an unmistakable indication of an author's deviance, an attribute that made turn-of-the-century modernism the enemy of the unclouded and natural division of gender roles. In this critique, it was the modernist culture represented by Jung-Wien that expressed an abnormally feminine character and made it a perversion that was inimical to the nation's health and prosperity.

This circumstance might seem to have presented a problem for fin-de-siècle writers with regard to understanding the gendered narratives that had attended Schubert's reception in the nineteenth century. In an era whose citizens were increasingly anxious in the face of emerging ideas of sexuality, might the ascription of femininity threaten to brand its recipient with a trait that was not entirely innocent and benign? The small amount of pertinent documentation from the medical literature and its offshoots that specifically cited Schubert, however, suggests that, whatever problematic inferences might have arisen from a reconsideration of the composer's *Mädchencharakter* in light of the new thinking about the sexes, the subject seemed to be best left unexamined. In the end, there may be too little evidence to construct a hypothesis as to why fin-de-siècle medical studies and their pseudoscientific progeny either failed to refer to Schubert or treated him so very gingerly on the few occasions that he was mentioned. The authors cited in chapter 5 represented too many different interests and prejudices for there to be a single encompassing supposition that satisfactorily explains Schubert's appearance in or absence from this literature.

It is curious that a composer whose music was so often regarded as feminine should not be a more visible figure in texts whose principal subject involved the sexualized characteristics and desires of men and women as well as the impact of these relationships on contemporary culture and society. This situation, however, may bear witness to the effect of the growing tendency to distinguish gender, as a socially constructed category, from the physiologically defined qualities of sexuality. This emerging separation may have permitted writers at the turn of the century to maintain Schubert's gendered status without any consideration of it finding its way into dubious theorizing about the erotic nature of either the composer's works or his life. To be sure, the contemporary literature that addressed the sexual nature of great men (and the subjects were typically men) did not invariably suggest degradation or even imply a tarnishing of these individuals: a scrutiny of their sexuality was not intended to diminish their reputations. Intentionally or not, in making conjectures about creative figures of the past—in broaching the topic of the private life and its relationship to the creative process—such studies did result in the humanization of their subjects. And whether or not we might find the description of Beethoven, for example, as a uranian type to be laughable, the connections between his career, his emotional life, and his music were so intimately intertwined in the public consciousness of the fin de siècle that no conjecture about him could inadvertently sully his stature.

Schubert's reception, however, was of a different order. Having entered the list of great composers later than most, and despite the burgeoning scholarship on his career, his was a life whose biographical details did not appear to bear meaningfully upon the essential substance of his creative output. As a consequence, gender and sexuality may have proved to be more clearly separable categories whose relevance, as they might bear upon Schubert's career and his music, were easier to parse than was the case with other composers. For many people in the fin de siècle, an existence like that of Schubert's, which was largely bereft of the kinds of occurrences that were deemed suitable for an imaginative genius (at least the type valorized in the late nineteenth century), was not only tangential to the artistic process, but it also accounted for the embarrassing number of literary fabrications of his life, whose bathetic qualities were in inverse proportion to their musical and documentary pertinence.[2] At least for a more high-minded comprehension of Schubert's works, the image of the happy-go-lucky tunesmith was as irrelevant as the depiction of a physically unattractive individual supported by a coterie of jolly friends and left largely undamaged by inconsequential and fictional romantic encounters. One could still treasure Schubert's compositions for arousing the innermost feelings of the listener and revel in the emotional intensity of such experiences. If that intimacy carried with it the baggage of the composer's gendered reception, one need not fret about any attendant suspect consequences, since the documentary record, buttressed by the authority of contemporary medical theory, had isolated the composer's feminine traits—asexual and unthreatening—within the products of his musical imagination.

Theorizing by turn-of-the-century writers about the psychology of an artist's inner life, especially given the explosion of pseudoscientific literature at the time, might have led them to represent their subject in a way that would have proved more unsuitable for Schubert than for any other composer. Whatever contemporary music scholarship may have been able to glean about Schubert's creative and personal life, the cultural mind of the fin de siècle continued to find in him a source of emotional convalescence that was unique among composers. At the same time, however, the fact that social convention also located this spiritual palliative in the domestic life of women also furnished modernists with an opportunity to offer a critique of both the artificiality of sex roles and its often ruinous consequences, and, by extension, the duplicitous machinations of the society that produced and fostered those tragic outcomes.

More than ever, Schubert needed to be rescued from the mythic accretions layered onto him by an official Viennese culture, which, in honoring him as its favorite native son, produced an icon as suspect as the *gemütlich* world it was meant to incarnate. It was precisely because this construction of Schubert was so deeply ingrained in fin-de-siècle consciousness that it demanded responses from the modernist generation, whose work amounted to a critique of the culture that had invented it. To make the composer into the font of nineteenth-century harmonic audacity, as Schoenberg did, was to question the highly popular and much beloved image of the divinely gifted but unthinking melodist incarnated in Karl Kundmann's statue, which still sits in the Stadtpark, forever "musing dreamily, as though about to put down a musical thought with his upraised pen," as Niggli so memorably described it.[3]

In this context, the fin-de-siècle reception of Schubert contains an element of paradox. As I suggested at the end of the first volume of this study, even as Viennese modernists offered interpretations of Schubert that defied the most cherished and cloying features of the composer that had resulted from the fabrications of nineteenth-century mythmaking, the generation which had come of creative age by 1900 was not completely immune to the comforting blandishments of that tradition. As Schnitzler's diary indicates, Schubert's music could provide a measure of relief from the alienation that the writer experienced in his own personal life, even as he created literary exposés in which domains of ostensible domestic concord, replete with images of Schubertian femininity, masked more sordid sexual encounters. Moreover, such relationships did not need to be limited to the realm of the artistic imagination, as Klimt's liaison with Alma Schindler illustrates. Within the creative work itself, the remade images of Schubert continually offered a challenge to disentangle the pose from the reality. One can never be entirely certain in Altenberg's stories whether even he himself could always have identified the point at which the Schubertian qualities of his idealized adolescent females crossed from dreamy evocation into the sort of libidinous attraction that can still make a reader squirm with discomfort. Perhaps there is no greater sign of the fracturing of life and art than the disorienting gulf between the fin-de-siècle manipulation of shopworn Schubertian symbols and the private impact of Schubert's music that so often seems suspiciously redolent of the very imagery against which modernism rebelled.

In the end, such ambiguity occupies the center of fin-de-siècle Viennese modernism. As the reception of Schubert demonstrates, the recasting of the composer could at once free his music from the excrescence of sentimentality even as it forged an alternative understanding. The appropriation of Schubert could be put to apparently paradoxical use, not only as the nascent musical revolutionary but as yet another pillar of the Austro-German tradition to which some-one like Schoenberg might consider himself the legitimate heir. This dual perspective placed Schubert as both source and conduit. The composer's musical style became both unprecedented and continuous, fulfilling Bahr's prescription for the unique role to be occupied by the members of his generation at the turn of the century: "They desire to adjust the old work of their ancestors for their own era."[4]

Afterword

For the study of Schubert's reception during the fin de siècle, the careers of those who remained productive in the period after 1918 pose a challenge to the maintenance of strict chronological margins. Although World War I served this study as a convenient terminus for exploring fin-de-siècle responses to the composer, the evidence often required extending the discussion beyond the years of conflict. To be sure, the alternative historical frame suggested by the twin centennials of Schubert's birth and death, in 1897 and 1928 respectively, could not be applied to every figure discussed in this volume. Klimt died in 1918 and Altenberg the following year, whereas Schoenberg's encounters with Schubert extended well into the decade after the war. Others did not necessarily retain their engagement with Schubert during the 1920s: Hofmannsthal, for example, shifted his artistic allegiance from Vienna to Salzburg.

Taking into account as obvious a reality as the lifespan of individuals underscores the degree of artificiality in assigning a clear closure to this narrative, even when its apparent endpoint is fashioned from as significant a historical event as World War I. The difficulty of preserving a tidy chronicle is not reduced by the considerable amount of evidence that results from assessing subjects as complex as gender and nationalism and analyzing them from a variety of perspectives, ranging from individual creative lives to the broader categories of culture and politics. In conjunction with the first volume, my plan was to provide and assess evidence—sometimes hitherto unexamined, sometimes seemingly familiar in different disciplinary contexts—in order to reconstruct the formation of several of the most cherished myths about the composer, to appraise them in the context of more general cultural preoccupations, and finally to recognize that, by the turn of the century, Schubertian hagiology was already so pronounced that a generation of Viennese, producing their first masterpieces at the cusp of modernism, could manipulate its characteristic elements for their own creative purposes. To the extent that some subjects in this study retained their engagement with Schubert after 1918, however, a few final remarks are in order.

Schubert's reception in postdynastic Vienna carried with it a critique that inveighed against the nineteenth-century image of the composer, not only for its rank sentimentality but also for its having been harnessed to more vulgar commercial interests. It comes as no surprise that, in 1919, Kraus would prepare a stinging indictment of what he took to be the mercenary philistinism of that most enduring bathetic fiction of the composer's life, *Das Dreimäderlhaus*, whose first performance in 1916 came at a point during the war when Austria's ability to make a meaningful contribution to its allies' military effort was in free fall. After all, in 1899 Kraus had reproached Nikolaus Dumba, one of the city's wealthiest patrons of the arts and its most passionate collector of Schubertiana, for commissioning Klimt's *Schubert at the Piano* as a mere novelty to adorn his music salon. Writing with equal acidity in his journal *Die Fackel* two decades later, Kraus mocked the opportunistic attempt to perform such an impossibly cheery operetta after the deaths of millions and the collapse of the empire. Quoted in the first volume of this study, it bears repetition:

> Is it not a symbol of this end that, under the title "a justified claim" and not as a request to the cosmos for an earthquake, it was communicated in a newspaper column that in these parts those blinded because of the war are ridiculed, and in addition it was reported on the generosity amidst the coal shortages that allowed the operetta theater to open so that the consortia for the exploitation of Schubert's immortality might not be hindered in the deal. The disgrace goes on in broad daylight and, after coffeehouse closings on every corner of the Kärntnerstrasse, forces itself upon a mindless pack of old goats who have to do nothing this side of the grave other than to make sure that, by gazing at each other, they are all there.[1]

Kraus's suggestion for relieving the despair and misery was to facilitate the mass suicide of the guilty parties.

With the eclipse of the old regime, the shriveling of national prestige appears to have been in equal proportion to the commercial exploitation of Vienna's greatest musical native son, which in turn prompted even more caustic censure. The assault on cynical entrepreneurship continued in 1924 with Schenker's condemnation of Schubert's mistreatment by the young Austrian republic:

> The state's intellectual capacity has not progressed far enough to appreciate how things stand: unscrupulously, without a qualm, it pockets Schubert's capital. To be sure, its officials know all the industries, businesses, professional craftsmen, and artists involved in marketing Schubert wares. But as to Schubert himself, who created this inexhaustible capital investment and who is more impregnable than all the industries of the world, of him they are oblivious as a co-producer of national wealth—in their current jargon, as a captain of industry. In the account books of the state, the name of Schubert is nowhere to be seen.[2]

Four years after Schenker's trenchant assault, Kraus again turned his critical lens on the disgraceful merchandising that attended the centennial of the composer's death in 1928 and its commemoration in July at the tenth Deutsche Sängerbundfest, the same event that had so exercised Schoenberg. Like his critique thirty years earlier, Kraus's new polemic was couched in social rather than artistic terms. This time, however, the target was neither the financial injustice of an industrialist purchasing his affection for Schubert nor the degraded spectacle of producing lighthearted operetta amid the ruinous debacle of war. Instead, Kraus went after the unconscionable commercialization of the composer. He remarked contemptuously: "Everyone can enjoy chocolate 'Schubert-Roulards' because they're cheaper than locks of Schubert's hair, which are still going for 350 schillings at the Dorotheum [Vienna's famed auction house]."[3]

Kraus's satiric denunciation came in a year that witnessed Schubert kitsch reaching its nadir. A cartoon entitled "The Boom in Schubert" in the newspaper *Der Morgen* on April 23, 1928, eloquently encapsulates the widespread commodification of the composer. A crowd of Viennese salesmen huddle in front of a wall of advertisements, all of which use the composer's name or image to sell everything from shoe polish and cutlery to "Schubert-trout-in-a-tin" and "Erlkönig fountain pens," to a revue called "The 3 Schubert Girls from West Virginia," a title doubtless intended as a humorous gloss on the three sisters in *Das Dreimäderlhaus*.[4] Recalling the 1897 cartoon in which a celestial Schubert muses over warring political factions, the composer, now ogled by adoring female angels, looks down from heaven and muses facetiously: "I should have taken part in *this* business when I was alive!" In addition, the syrupy tradition of idyllic female company is wickedly satirized by the earthly appearance of three bonneted crones, one who holds a fan that reads "Drei Mäderl Jubilee."

Three months later came the massive effigy of the composer that appeared in the Sängerbundfest parade, attended by forty considerably more attractive young women in Biedermeier crinolines and bonnets (see figure 7.1). In the following year, Kraus took note of another example of crass exploitation, this time at the hands of a "fanatic" who had produced a monument to the composer modeled from sugar for an exhibition on the art of gastronomy held at the Kursalon in the Stadtpark. This was a depressing signal that cooking had apparently rendered all other arts subservient in a city where "an apple strudel could be a poem, and one that causes even more of a sensation than the so-called lunatic asylum poem." (Later in the same issue of *Die Fackel*, Kraus gave as an illustration of commercial prostitution an advertisement for shaving soap featuring the operetta composer Franz Lehár.) In a typically mordant play on words, Kraus opined that, if music was to be placed at the service of innkeepers, such an ersatz monument might just qualify as a substitute for the previous year's commemoration of the composer only by way of comparison to that earlier version "made from pigs' fat [Schweineschmalz], which melted in the heat of July 1928 and was almost no longer recognizable as Schubert, but only as crap [Schweinerei]."[5]

As this brief survey suggests, the misuse of artistic values by economic opportunism in the decade after World War I was a central concern for members of the generation who came of age in fin-de-siècle Vienna, so much so that it may even have eclipsed the gendered characterizations that had been such an important component of the composer's earlier reception. Certainly the fraudulent exploitation of Schubert provoked a more heightened rhetoric of condemnation during the 1920s. The cultural corruption that had once been seen as culpable in the private tragedies of relationships between the sexes had deteriorated even further after the war into a commercial enterprise whose public vulgarity demanded an even greater vigilance.

Despite similarities in the dissection of society's ills made after 1918 by some of Vienna's better-known iconoclasts, the postwar era managed to produce strange intellectual bedfellows when it came to refashioning the image of Schubert. Those who made their living in the musical professions had a unique stake in rescuing Schubert's reputation from the downward spiral of vendible schmaltz. In this respect, and especially in the 1920s, Schoenberg had some-thing in common with more stolid, conventional minds, whose materialist and superficial tastes he contemptuously dismissed, but for whom the Austro-German creative heritage represented a civilizing bulwark in the wake of the empire's dissolution. Even absent the more offensive aspects of the exclusionary appropriation of Schubert by political rightists that had marked the composer's centennial in 1897, the desire to valorize a culture with the Austro-German musical tradition at its epicenter was no less intense after the postwar implosion of the empire, especially as the more crass and saccharine appropriations of Schubert continued unabated.

There was at times little difference between the pantheon of great Austro-German composers to which Schoenberg (and Schenker) paid homage and the list enumerated in official publications like the massive volume *Neu Österreich* (1923), written in commemoration of the new republic's creation. Although Schubert was identified as one of the stars in the musical firmament, the con-tributors to the book also revered the likes of Bartsch, whose novel was the inspiration for *Das Dreimäderlhaus* and who had done as much as anyone to estab-lish the fin-de-siècle myths of Schubert that others were so eager to dismantle. The chapter on music was the work of Max Millenkovich-Morold, a critic and former director of the Burgtheater, a lifelong champion of German Austrian culture, and the author of books on both Richard and Cosima Wagner. Millenkovich-Morold had written *Die österreichische Tonkunst* in 1918 for a series entitled "Austrian Library" and published by the "Austrian Comrades-in-Arms Union in Vienna." In this work, he tapped Schubert as the first master of that unique musical dialect combining three-quarter time and Germanic major key, but "no Slavic minor!"[6] (In 1933, he would edit *Dichterbuch*—subtitled "German Belief, German Sinews, German Feeling"—a massive "Aryan" anthology of sixty-five authors, all of them representatives of the "German race.") In *Neu Österreich*, he identified the three most distinguished contemporary orchestral works as Guido Peters' Third Symphony, Bernhard Tittel's Symphony in D Minor, and Josef Marx's *Herbst-Symphonie*. Schoenberg and his followers were conspicuous by their absence. Only in a separate chapter on Austria's cultural mission did the art historian Anton Reichel mention in passing that, along with Mahler, Schoenberg could be classified as a representative of Jewish musical creativity who evinced a German ethos.[7]

The challenge facing members of the prewar generation was to recast Schubert in a way that could free the composer's music from the dual excrescences of sentimentality and the marketplace while at the same time forging an alternative tradition to which they were rightly heir. The problem was not made any easier by the predilections of a society whose fatuousness and vapidity ran the risk of staining Schubert's reputation. The consequential ills were dire, as diagnosed by Broch, one of postwar Vienna's most scathing critics of its civilization of kitsch, who berated Schubert's "light" music because it contained within it the nucleus of every Viennese operetta. [8] Thus, maintaining one's distance from the corrupting influences of a culture symbolized by its bathetic and mercenary portrayals of Schubert, while still venerating the composer's creative legacy, warranted careful aesthetic negotiation, especially when his music could so easily be enlisted in an overt and sometimes overwrought nationalist enterprise.

When it came to rescuing Schubert from the romanticized constructions of the nineteenth century, there were too few individuals like Kraus, who, while offering no concessions in his withering condemnation of the cloying and commercial aspects of Schubert's reception, had no use for setting up in its place an alternative and exclusionary Germanic tradition. Ever the stubborn opponent of the manufactured canons of culture, Kraus had a far more jaundiced and prescient view of the brutish implications of sectarian musical Germanness. As Nietzsche had done with Bizet in the previous century, Kraus discovered a more beneficent (and feminine) archetype, not in the music of Schubert but in the works of Jacques Offenbach, which offered a corrective both to the nationalist hyperbole of Wagner and to the vacuous artifice of Lehár and Berté. [9] Not coincidentally, perhaps, and unlike Schenker and Schoenberg, both of whom also railed against misappropriations of Schubert but who embraced an exclusive Austro-German tradition, Kraus gladly admitted to being utterly uneducated in music.

What remained contested after World War I was less a matter of who among the dead had represented the authentic Schubert than who among the living merited stewardship of the composer's legacy. Ultimately, for those who came of age in the fin de siècle, the truly meaningful reception of Schubert rested not in polemics, however scintillating, but in their own creative work. That stands as a more lasting counterpoint to the trafficking in the composer's creative remains that spiraled after 1918, even if members of that prewar generation proved no more adept at finally disposing of an image of Schubert that was at once an undesirable and an alluring bequest of their ancestors.

Notes

Introduction to the Project and to Volume 1

1. Scott Messing, "The Vienna Beethoven Centennial Festival of 1870," *Beethoven Newsletter* 6, no. 3 (Winter 1991): 57–63.

2. On the distinction between sex and gender, see Joan W. Scott, "Gender: A Useful Category of Historical Analysis," *American Historical Review* 91, no. 5 (December 1986): 1053–75. An overview of the literature up to this century can be found in Merry E. Wiesner-Hanks, *Gender in History* (Malden, MA: Blackwell, 2001). More recently, Jeffrey Kallberg has used the terms sexuality and sex to distinguish between identity and behavior. See his "Sex, Sexuality, and Schubert's Piano Music," in *Historical Musicology: Sources, Methods, Interpretations,* ed. Stephen A. Crist and Roberta Montemorra Marvin (Rochester, NY: University of Rochester Press, 2004), 219–33. Much of the earlier musicological scholarship on gender comes from the 1990s, the same decade in which the topic of Schubert and sexuality produced a considerable literature. See, for example, Marcia Citron, *Gender and the Musical Canon* (Cambridge: Cambridge University Press, 1993); Suzanne G. Cusick, "Gender and the Cultural Work of a Classical Music Performance," *Repercussions* 3 (1994): 77–110; Lawrence Kramer, *Classical Music and Postmodern Knowledge* (Berkeley and Los Angeles: University of California Press, 1995); Susan McClary, *Feminine Endings: Music, Gender and Sexuality* (Minneapolis: University of Minnesota Press, 1991); and Ruth Solie, ed., *Musicology and Difference: Gender and Sexuality in Music Scholarship* (Berkeley and Los Angeles: University of California Press, 1993). By now, the category of gender has found its way into writings about all historical periods, not only into writings about periods close to Schubert's lifetime. As examples, see Scott Burnham, "A. B. Marx and the Gendering of Sonata Form," in Ian Bent, ed., *Music Theory in the Age of Romanticism* (Cambridge: Cambridge University Press, 1996), 163–86; Matthew Head, " 'Like Beauty Spots on the Face of a Man': Gender in 18th-Century North-German Discourse on Genre," *Journal of Musicology* 12 (Spring 1995): 143–67; and James Hepokoski, "Masculine-Feminine: (En)gendering Sonata Form," *Musical Times* 135 (August 1994): 494–99. For a survey of gender differences prior to the classical period, see Todd M. Borgerding, ed. *Gender, Sexuality, and Early Music* (New York: Routledge, 2002).

3. The debate received its impetus from Maynard Solomon, "Franz Schubert and the Peacocks of Benvenuto Cellini," *19th-Century Music* 12, no. 3 (Spring 1989): 193–208, although the author had broached the topic earlier in "Franz Schubert's 'My Dream,' " *American Imago* 38, no. 2 (Summer 1981): 137–54. In 1993, a special issue of *19th-Century Music* edited by Lawrence Kramer was devoted to articles dealing

with "Schubert: Music, Sexuality, Culture" by Kofi Agawu, David Gramit, Susan McClary, Kristina Muxfeldt, Maynard Solomon, Rita Steblin, James Webster, and Robert Winter. For a sampling of studies that employ gender perspectives, see Philip Brett, "Piano Four-Hands: Schubert and the Performance of Gay Male Desire," *19th-Century Music* 21, no. 2 (Fall 1997): 149–76; Lawrence Kramer, *Franz Schubert: Sexuality, Subjectivity, Song* (Cambridge: Cambridge University Press, 1998); Susan McClary, "Constructions of Subjectivity in Schubert's Music." in *Queering the Pitch: The New Gay and Lesbian Musicology,* ed. Philip Brett, Elizabeth Wood, and Gary C. Thomas (New York: Routledge, 1994), 205–33; Kristina Muxfeldt, "Schubert, Platen, and the Myth of Narcissus," *Journal of the American Musicological Society* 49, no. 3 (Fall 1996): 480–527; and David P. Schroeder, "Feminine Voices in Schubert's Early Laments," *Music Review* 55, no. 3 (August 1994): 183–201. For a reply to Muxfeldt, see Vivian S. Ramalingam, "On 'Schubert, Platen, and the Myth of Narcissus' by Kristina Muxfeldt, Fall 1996," *Journal of the American Musicological Society* 50, nos. 2–3 (Summer/Fall 1997): 530–36. For documentary studies, see Rita Steblin, "In Defense of Scholarship and Archival Research: Why Schubert's Brothers Were Allowed to Marry," *Current Musicology,* no. 62 (1998): 7–17; and "Schubert's 'Nina' and the True Peacocks," *Musical Times* 138 (March 1997): 13–20.

4. Scott Messing, *Neoclassicism in Music: From the Genesis of the Concept through the Schoenberg/Stravinsky Polemic* (Ann Arbor, MI: UMI Research Press, 1988).

5. The wave of studies about fin-de-siècle Vienna that emphasized its culture and visual arts first surged in the 1970s and 1980s. One work that actually discusses the composer, in this case in the context of Gustav Klimt's *Schubert am Klavier* (*Schubert at the Piano*), is also deservedly regarded by many, myself included, as a scholarly touchstone for the era, although I do not share all of the author's conclusions about the painting: Carl Schorske, *Fin-de-Siècle Vienna: Politics and Culture* (New York: Knopf, 1979). For a recent reconsideration of the issues emanating from Schorske's work, see the essays collected in Steven Beller, ed., *Rethinking Vienna 1900* (New York and Oxford: Berghahn Books, 2001).

6. Three works by Otto Erich Deutsch remain indispensable older documentary sources: *Schubert: Die Erinnerungen seiner Freunde* (Leipzig: Breitkopf & Härtel, 1957); *Schubert: Die Dokumente seines Lebens* (Kassel: Bärenreiter, 1964); and *Franz Schubert: Sein Leben in Bildern* (Munich and Leipzig: Georg Müller, 1913). The first two of these have appeared in English as *Schubert: Memoirs by His Friends,* trans. Rosamond Ley and John Nowell (New York: Macmillan, 1958); and *Schubert: A Documentary Biography,* trans. Eric Blom (1946; reprint, New York: Da Capo Press, 1977). More recent volumes concentrate on Schubert's lifetime and the period before the middle of the nineteenth century. See Otto Brusatti, *Schubert in Wiener Vormärz: Dokumente 1829–1848* (Graz: Akadem. Druck- u. Verlagsanst., 1978); Walburga Litschauer, *Neue Dokumente zum Schubert-Kreis aus Briefen und Tagebüchern seiner Freunde* (Vienna: Musikwissenschaftlicher Verlag Wien, 1986); and Till Gerrit Waidelich et al., *Franz Schubert: Dokumente, 1817–1830,* vol. 1 (Tutzing, Germany: Hans Schneider, 1993). In a series of articles in *Cahiers F. Schubert,* Xavier Hascher has compiled French reviews and notices through 1850. For a broader period, an interesting compilation is Ilija Dürhammer and Till Gerrit Waidelich, *Schubert 200 Jahre* (Heidelberg: Edition Braus, 1997). For bibliographies, a useful older source, although hardly exhaustive, is Willi Kahl, *Verzeichnis des Schrifttums über Franz Schubert, 1828–1928* (Regensburg, Germany: G. Bosse, 1938). For a general comprehensive work, see Ernst Hilmar, "Bausteine zu einer neuen Schubert Bibliographie—Vornehmlich der Schriften von 1929 bis 2000," *Schubert durch die Brille* 25 (2000): 98–302.

7. For examples in the scholarly literature that cite Schumann's *Mädchencharakter* comparison, see Brett, "Piano Four-Hands," 155–56; John E. Burchard, "'Prometheus' and 'Der Musensohn': The Impact of Beethoven on Schubert Reception" (PhD diss., Rutgers University, 2001), 89–90; Christopher H. Gibbs, "'Poor Schubert': Images and Legends of the Composer," in *The Cambridge Companion to Schubert*, ed. Christopher H. Gibbs (Cambridge: Cambridge University Press, 1997), 51; Kallberg, "Sex, Sexuality, and Schubert's Piano Music," 227; Kramer, *Franz Schubert: Sexuality, Subjectivity, Song*, 80–81, 97; Lawrence Kramer, *After the Lovedeath: Sexual Violence and the Making of Culture* (Berkeley and Los Angeles: University of California Press, 1997), 4–5; William S. Newman, *The Sonata Since Beethoven* (Chapel Hill: University of North Carolina Press, 1969), 193; and Sanna Pederson, "Beethoven and Masculinity," in *Beethoven and His World*, ed. Scott Burnham and Michael P. Steinberg (Princeton, NJ, and Oxford: Princeton University Press, 2000), 313.

8. The historiography of romanticism is cogently traversed by Jim Samson, "The Musical Work and Nineteenth-Century History," in *The Cambridge History of Nineteenth-Century Music*, ed. Jim Samson (Cambridge: Cambridge University Press, 2001), 17–27.

9. The literature on Schubert's influence on other composers is always expanding. On Brahms, for example, see David Brodbeck, "*Primo* Schubert, *Secondo* Schumann: Brahms's Four-Hand Waltzes, Op. 39," *Journal of Musicology* 7, no. 1 (Winter 1989): 58–80; Robert Pascall, "Brahms and Schubert," *Musical Times* 124 (May 1983): 286–91; and James Webster, "Schubert's Sonata Form and Brahms's First Maturity," *19th-Century Music* 2, no. 1 (July 1978): 18–35; 3, no. 1 (July 1979): 52–71. On Mahler, see Henry-Louis de La Grange, *Mahler*, vol. 1 (Garden City, NJ: Doubleday, 1973), 1059–65; Hermann Jung, " 'Schubert Reminiszenzen' bei Gustav Mahler," in *Franz Schubert—Werk und Rezeption: Schubert-Jahrbuch 1999: Bericht über den Internationalen Schubert-Kongreß, Duisburg 1997*, ed. Dietrich Berke, Walther Dürr, Walburga Litschauer, and Christiane Schumann (Duisburg: Deutsche Schubert-Gesellschaft e. V., 2001), 41–49; Miriam Whaples, "Mahler and Schubert's A Minor Sonata D. 784," *Music & Letters* 65, no. 3 (July 1984): 255–63; and Susan Youens, "Schubert, Mahler, and the Weight of the Past: 'Lieder eines fahrenden Gesellen' and 'Winterreise,' " *Music & Letters* 67, no. 3 (July 1986): 256–68. See also chapter 7, note 7.

10. Christopher H. Gibbs, "German Reception: Schubert's 'Journey to Immortality,' " in *The Cambridge Companion to Schubert*, ed. Christopher H. Gibbs (Cambridge: Cambridge University Press, 1997), 319. See also Christopher H. Gibbs, "The Presence of *Erlkönig*: Reception and Reworkings of a Schubert Lied," vol. 1 (PhD diss., Columbia University, 1992), 135.

11. A consideration of the division between the privacy of home and the public sphere of work among the middle classes can profitably begin with Jürgen Habermas, *The Structural Transformation of the Public Sphere: An Inquiry into a Category of Bourgeois Society*, trans. Thomas Burger and Frederick Lawrence (Cambridge, MA: MIT Press, 1989), originally *Strukturwandel der Öffentlichkeit: Untersuchungen zu einer Kategorie der bürgerlichen Gesellschaft* (Neuwied, Berlin; Luchterhand, 1962). A useful, brief historical overview is Genevieve Lloyd, *The Man of Reason: "Male" and "Female" in Western Philosophy* (Minneapolis: University of Minnesota Press, 1984). More specific citations with regard to place and time can be found throughout my text, but for a sampling of dualities, see Peter Gay, *The Cultivation of Hatred*, vol. 3 of *The Bourgeois Experience: Victoria to Freud* (New York and London: W. W. Norton &

Company, 1993), 290–93; Peter Gay, *Schnitzler's Century: The Making of Middle-Class Culture, 1815–1914* (New York: Norton, 2002), 43–48; Karin Hausen, "Family and Role-Division: The Polarisation of Sexual Stereotypes in the Nineteenth Century— An Aspect of the Dissociation of Work and Family Life," in *The German Family: Essays on the Social History of the Family in Nineteenth- and Twentieth-Century Germany*, ed. Birchard J. Evans and W. R. Lee (London: Croom Helm, 1981), 55–56; Ludmilla Jordanova, *Sexual Visions: Images of Gender in Science and Medicine between the Eighteenth and Twentieth Centuries* (Madison: University of Wisconsin Press, 1989), 18–23; Mary Poovey, *Uneven Developments: The Ideological Work of Gender in Mid-Victorian England* (Chicago: University of Chicago Press, 1988), 8–12; and John Tosh, *A Man's Place: Masculinity and the Middle-Class Home in Victorian England* (New Haven, CT: Yale University Press, 1999), 46–47. To be sure, the topic crosses disciplinary boundaries. For an anthropological perspective, see Sherry B. Ortner, *Making Gender: The Politics and Erotics of Culture* (Boston: Beacon Press, 1996), 21–42. For categorization schemes that embrace music, see Carl Dahlhaus, "Das deutsche Bildungsbürgertum und die Musik," in *Bildungsgüter und Bildungswissen*, ed. Reinhart Koselleck, vol. 2 of *Bildungsbürgertum im 19. Jahrhundert*, ed. Werner Conze and Jürgen Locka (Stuttgart: Klett-Cotta, 1990), 220–36; and Judith Tick, "Passed Away Is the Piano Girl: Changes in American Musical Life, 1870–1900," in *Women Making Music: The Western Art Tradition, 1150–1950*, ed. Jane Bowers and Judith Tick (Urbana and Chicago: University of Illinois Press), 337. The separation between public and private culture as a tool of classification is explored by Carl Dahlhaus, *Nineteenth-Century Music*, trans. J. Bradford Robinson (Berkeley and Los Angeles: University of California Press, 1989), 168–78. The paradigms of public and private music, romanticism and Biedermeier, and gender polarities in connection with Schubert have been insightfully taken up by Ruth A. Solie, *Music in Other Words: Victorian Conversations* (Berkeley and Los Angeles: University of California Press, 2004), 118–52. Like those of Dahlhaus, her principal documents come from the period before the middle of the century.

Introduction to Volume 2

1. Frederick Morton, *A Nervous Splendor* (Boston: Little, Brown, 1979), vii. A similar tactic is employed in William R. Everdell, *The First Moderns: Profiles in the Origins of Twentieth-Century Thought* (Chicago and London: University of Chicago Press, 1997), 13–29. Everdell uses 1899, the year in which Freud completed his *Interpretation of Dreams*.
2. On the pliable nature of the generational concept for Vienna ca. 1900, see John Neubauer, *The Fin-de-Siècle Culture of Adolescence* (New Haven, CT, and London: Yale University Press, 1992), 106–7; and Carl Schorske, *Thinking with History: Explorations in the Passage to Modernism* (Princeton, NJ: Princeton University Press, 1998), 154–55. See also Julián Marías, *Generations: A Historical Method*, trans. Harold C. Raley (Tuscaloosa: University of Alabama Press, 1970); and Alan B. Spitzer, "The Historical Problem of Generations," *American Historical Review* 78, no. 5 (December 1973): 1353–85.
3. I use the term nationalism as one defined by culture rather than politics, recognizing, however, that both perspectives intermingled in the nineteenth century and are equally valid categories for recent scholarship. See Ernest Gellner, *Nations and*

Nationalism (Oxford: Blackwell, 1983), 7: "Two men are of the same nation if and only if they share the same culture, where culture in turn means a system of ideas and signs and associations and ways of behaving and communicating. Two men are of the same nation if and only if they *recognize* each other as belonging to the same nation." See also Benedict Anderson, *Imagined Communities: Reflections on the Origin and Spread of Nationalism* (London: Verso, 1983), 19: "What I am proposing is that nationalism has to be understood, by aligning it not with self-consciously held political ideologies, but with the large cultural systems that preceded it, out of which—as well as against which—it came into being."

4. Dates remain significant markers in the titles of related studies. See Nicolas Powell and Adolf Opel, *The Sacred Spring: The Arts in Vienna, 1898–1918* (New York: New York Graphic Society, 1974); James Shedel, *Art and Society: The New Art Movement in Vienna, 1897–1914* (Palo Alto, CA: Society for the Promotion of Science and Scholarship, 1981); and Peter Vergo, *Art in Vienna, 1898–1918* (London: Phaidon Press, 1975). On politics, see John W. Boyer, *Political Radicalism in Late Imperial Vienna: Origins of the Christian Social Movement, 1848–1897* (Chicago: University of Chicago Press, 1981); and *Culture and Political Crisis in Vienna: Christian Socialism in Power, 1897–1918* (Chicago: University of Chicago Press, 1995). To be sure, dates that end in zero have always enjoyed a historical cachet. In the case of fin-de-siècle Vienna, the popular choices of 1890 and 1900 still serve as a frame for 1897. See Franco Borsi and Ezio Godoli, *Vienna 1900: Architecture and Design* (New York: Rizzoli, 1986); Christian Nebehay, *Vienna 1900: Architecture and Painting* (Vienna: Christian Brandstatter, 1984); Erika Nielsen, ed., *Focus on Vienna 1900: Change and Continuity in Literature, Music, Art and Intellectual History* (Munich: Wilhelm Fink, 1982); Kirk Varnedoe, *Vienna 1900: Art, Architecture and Design* (New York: Museum of Modern Art, 1986); and Robert Waissenberger, ed., *Vienna, 1890–1920* (New York: Tabard Press, 1984). One musicological study that uses 1897 as part of its design mentions the Schubert centennial only in passing. See Sandra McColl, *Music Criticism in Vienna, 1896–1897: Critically Moving Forms* (Oxford: Clarendon Press, 1996).

5. Leon Botstein, "Gustav Mahler's Vienna," in *The Mahler Companion*, ed. Donald Mitchell and Andrew Nicolson (Oxford and New York: Oxford University Press, 1999), 17. See also Leon Botstein, "Music and Its Public: Habits of Listening and the Crisis of Musical Modernism in Vienna, 1870–1914" (PhD diss., Harvard University, 1985), 1033–34.

6. Hermann Bahr, "Die Moderne" *Moderne Dichtung* 1 (January 1890): 13–15, quoted in Gotthart Wunberg, ed., *Die Wiener Moderne: Literatur, Kunst und Musik zwischen 1890 und 1910* (Stuttgart: Reclam, 1981), 189.

7. Wunberg, *Wiener Moderne*, 427.

8. Hermann Bahr, "Loris," *Freie Bühne für den Entwickelungskampf der Zeit* 3, no. 1 (1892): 94–98, quoted in Gotthart Wunberg, ed., *Das Junge Wien: Österreichische Literatur- und Kunstkritik 1887–1902*, vol. 1 (Tübingen, Germany; Max Niemeyer Verlag, 1976), 293–98. The paradoxical attitude of modernism toward the past has often been remarked upon in recent scholarship, both inside and outside musicology. See, for example, Dahlhaus, *Nineteenth-Century Music*, 334; Walter Frisch, *German Modernism: Music and the Arts* (Berkeley and Los Angeles: University of California Press, 2005), 5, 253; Jacques Le Rider, *Modernity and Crises of Identity: Culture and Society in Fin-de-Siècle Vienna*, trans. Rosemary Morris (New York: Continuum, 1990), 23; Reingard Nethersole, "Viennese Early Postmodernism: Hofmannsthal's 'Prolog zu dem Buch Anatol,'" in *Turn-of-the-Century Vienna and Its Legacy: Essays in Honor of Donald G. Daviau*, ed. Jeffrey B. Berlin, Jorun B. Johns, and

Richard H. Lawson (New York: Edition Atelier, 1993), 30; António Riberio, "Karl Kraus and Modernism: A Reassessment," in *The Turn of the Century: Le tournant de siècle* (Berlin: Walter de Gruyter, 1995), ed. Christian Berg, Frank Durieux, and Geert Lernout, 148–49; Robert Rotenberg, *Time and Order in Metropolitan Vienna: A Seizure of Schedules* (Washington, DC, and London: Smithsonian Institution Press, 1992), 38; Schorske, *Thinking with History*, 146–47; and Hinrich C. Seeba, "Hofmannsthal and *Wiener Moderne*: The Cultural Context," in *A Companion to the Works of Hugo von Hofmannsthal*, ed. Thomas A. Kovach (London: Camden House, 2002), 31. Dahlhaus in fact considered Bahr's "Die Moderne" to be as useful an exhibit in the identification of modernism as any other contemporary document.

9. Hugo von Hofmannsthal, *Gesammelte Werke in Einzelausgaben: Prosa I*, ed. Herbert Steiner (Frankfurt am Main: S. Fischer, 1956), 149. The essay "Gabriele d'Annunzio" first appeared in the *Frankfurter Zeitung*. On the self-reflective nature of modernism, see Reinhold Brinkmann, "The Lyric as Paradigm: Poetry and the Foundation of Arnold Schoenberg's New Music," in *German Literature and Music: An Aesthetic Fusion*, ed. Claus Reschke and Howard Pollack (Munich: Wilhelm Fink, 1992), 114; Michel Decaudin, "Being Modern in 1885, or, Variations on 'Modern,' 'Modernism,' 'Modernité,'" in *Modernism: Challenges and Perspectives*, ed. Monique Chefdor, Ricardo J. Quinones, and Albert Wachtel (Urbana: University of Illinois Press, 1986), 28; and Frederick R. Karl, *Modern and Modernism: The Sovereignty of the Artist, 1885–1925* (New York: Atheneum, 1985), 16.

10. Robert P. Morgan, "Secret Languages: The Root of Musical Modernism," in *Modernism: Challenges and Perspectives*, ed. Monique Chefdor, Ricardo J. Quinones, and Albert Wachtel (Urbana: University of Illinois Press, 1986), 39. See also Jürgen Habermas, "Modernity Versus Postmodernity," *New German Critique* 22 (1981): 3–14.

11. Wunberg, *Wiener Moderne*, 428.

12. Ludwig Hevesi, *Acht Jahre Sezession* (Vienna: Konegen, 1906), 148, 158.

13. Eduard Leisching [E. L.], "Acht Jahre Sezession," *Kunst und Kunsthandwerk* 9 (1906): 89. Leisching was director of the Museum für angewandte Kunst. Adorno's observation of 1960 about Vienna is apt, if also orotund in its stolid certainty that the German legacy, to which Schoenberg's stylistic development responded as a cultural duty, constituted the normative arch of musical composition: "In Vienna a consistent traditionalism protested, and not just in music, against the tradition itself and revolutionized it with the demand that it take itself seriously. Schoenberg's entire output could be discussed without doing it violence, in terms of the idea that he honoured obligations which according to the standards of Viennese Classicism a composition assumes from its very first bar." See Theodor W. Adorno, *Quasi una Fantasia: Essay on Modern Music*, trans. Rodney Livingstone (London: Verso, 1992), 204–5.

14. Hofmannsthal, *Gesammelte Werke: Prosa I*, 139; and Hermann Bahr, "Das junge Österreich," *Deutsche Zeitung* (Morgen-Ausgabe), September 20, 1893, 1–2, quoted in Wunberg, *Junge Wien*, 1:366. Bahr's mercurial shifts in identifying the artistic and literary avatars of modernism may themselves have been in keeping with its elusive character, but such fluctuations could suggest a lack of integrity, helping to make Bahr and all he touched the butt of Karl Kraus's constant and passionate condemnation.

15. Hevesi, *Acht Jahre Sezession*, 451; and Leisching, "Acht Jahre Sezession," 89.

16. Anton Kaes, "New Historicism and the Study of German Literature," *German Quarterly* 62 (1989): 215.

17. Martha M. Hyde, "Neoclassic and Anachronistic Impulses in Twentieth-Century Music," *Music Theory Spectrum* 18 (1996): 200–335; Charles Rosen, *Arnold Schoenberg*

(New York: Viking Press, 1975), 88–90; and Joseph N. Straus, *Remaking the Past: Musical Modernism and the Influence of the Tonal Tradition* (Cambridge, MA: Harvard University Press, 1990), 161–68.

Chapter One

1. Andreas Schumacher, "Nachruf. An Schubert's Grabe," *Allgemeine Theaterzeitung und Unterhaltungsblatt*, no. 153 (December 20, 1828): 1.

2. Josef Christian Baron von Zedlitz, "Nekrologische Notiz," *Wiener Zeitschrift für Kunst, Literatur, Theater und Mode*, no. 142 (November 25, 1828): 1160.

3. As examples of such titles, consider Edward Crankshaw, *The Fall of the House of Habsburg* (New York: Viking, 1963); Oscar Jászi, *The Dissolution of the Habsburg Monarchy* (Chicago: University of Chicago Press, 1929); John W. Mason, *The Dissolution of the Austro-Hungarian Empire, 1867–1918*, 2nd ed. (London and New York: Longman, 1997); Robin Okey, *The Habsburg Monarchy: From Enlightenment to Eclipse* (New York: St. Martin's Press, 2001); Alan Sked, *The Decline and Fall of the Habsburg Empire, 1815–1918* (London and New York: Longman, 1989); and George V. Strong, *Seedtime for Fascism: The Disintegration of Austrian Political Culture, 1867–1918* (Armonk, NY: M. E. Sharpe, 1998).

4. Sked, *Decline and Fall*, 188.

5. Mason, *Dissolution*, 11.

6. Kurt Mollik, Hermann Reining, and Rudolf Wurzer, *Planung und Verwirklichung der Wiener Ringstrassezone* (Wiesbaden: Franz Steiner, 1980), 299. The relationship of the Ringstrasse to political and social life is also discussed in Peter Haiko, *Vienna 1850–1930, Architecture* (New York: Rizzoli, 1992), 8–12; Péter Hanák, *The Garden and the Workshop: Essays on the Cultural History of Vienna and Budapest* (Princeton, NJ: Princeton University Press, 1998), 10–12; Donald J. Olsen, *The City as a Work of Art* (New Haven, CT: Yale University Press, 1986), 287–91; and Schorske, *Fin-de-Siècle Vienna*, 24–46.

7. Olsen, *City*, 245. A similar point is made in Robert Rotenberg, *Landscape and Power in Vienna* (Baltimore and London: Johns Hopkins University, 1995), 136–37. On liberal constituencies in the 1861 election, see Boyer, *Political Radicalism*, 187–89; and Pieter M. Judson, *Exclusive Revolutionaries: Liberal Politics, Social Experience, and National Identity in the Austrian Empire, 1848–1914* (Ann Arbor: University of Michigan Press, 1996), 82–84.

8. Reinhard Alings, *Monument und Nation: Das Bild vom Nationalstaat im Medium Denkmal—Zum Verhältnis von Nation und Staat im deutschen Kaiserreich 1871–1918* (Berlin: Walter de Gruyter, 1996), 157–58. The Prussian chancellor, Otto von Bismarck, made the new political order abundantly clear in a speech on October 26, 1867, when he declared that the monument would serve "as a reminder for everyone, who after us will be called to lead the destiny of Germany and Prussia." The German emperor, Wilhelm I, dedicated it only in 1873, thus allowing him to honor both victory in the Franco-Prussian War and the creation of the new German state. On nineteenth-century German monument culture, which boasted some eight hundred official statues by 1883, see Thomas Nipperdey, "Nationalidee und Nationaldenkmal in Deutschland," *Historische Zeitschrift* 206, no. 3 (June 1968): 529–85.

9. Selma Krasa, "Sculpture during the Biedermeier Years," in Robert Waissenberger, ed., *Vienna in the Biedermeier Era, 1815–1848* (New York: Mallard Press, 1986), 212–15. Several recent studies explore the relationship between the iconicity of

monuments and the identity of nations. For Austria, see Peter Urbanitsch, "Pluralistic Myth and Nationalist Realities: The Dynastic Myth of the Habsburg Monarchy—A Futile Exercise in the Creation of Identity?" *Austrian History Yearbook* 35 (2004): 101–41; Steven Beller, "Kraus's Firework: State Consciousness Raising in the 1908 Jubilee Parade in Vienna and the Problem of Austrian Identity"; and Nancy M. Wingfield, "Statues of Emperor Joseph II as Sites of German Identity," both in *Staging the Past: The Politics of Commemoration in Habsburg Central Europe, 1848 to the Present,* ed. Maria Bucur and Nancy M. Wingfield (West Lafayette, IN: Purdue University Press, 2001), 46–71 and 178–205. For Germany, in addition to Alings, *Monument und Nation,* see Lothar Gall, *Die Germania als Symbol nationaler Identität im 19. und 20. Jahrhundert* (Göttingen: Vandenhoeck and Ruprecht, 1993); Rudy Koshar, *From Monuments to Traces: Artifacts of German Memory, 1870–1990* (Berkeley and Los Angeles: University of California Press, 2000), 70–72; and Charlotte Tacke, *Denkmal im sozialen Raum: Nationale Symbole in Deutschland und Frankreich im 19. Jahrhundert* (Göttingen: Vandenhoeck and Ruprecht, 1995), 44–50.

10. On Kreissle's career, see Maurice J. E. Brown, *Essays on Schubert* (London: Macmillan, 1966), 170–76. Kreissle's relationship to the Verein is not mentioned, but see *Erster Jahresbericht des Männergesang-Vereines in Wien am Schluße der Vereinsjahres 1847* (Vienna: Joseph Ludwig, 1848), 3–13.

11. For a list of Verein concerts in commemoration of Schubert up to World War I, see Karl Adametz, *Franz Schubert in der Geschichte des Wiener Männgergesang-Vereines* (Vienna: Verlag des Wiener Männergesang-Vereines, 1938), 165–73.

12. Interestingly enough, neither of the two large donors who were musicians, Liszt and the Russian pianist Theodor Leschetizsky, was Viennese. See Adametz, *Franz Schubert,* 34, 39, 166.

13. Gerhardt Kapner, *Zur Geschichte der Ringstrassendenkmäler* (Wiesbaden: Franz Steiner, 1973), 102.

14. "Das Wiener Schubert-Monument und die Preiskonkurrenzen," *Beiblatt zur Zeitschrift für bildende Kunst* 1, no. 20 (September 28, 1866): 130.

15. Heinrich Kreissle von Hellborn, *Franz Schubert* (Vienna: Carl Gerold's Sohn, 1865; reprint, Hildesheim, Germany: Georg Olms, 1978), 466. Kreissle's source was *Actenmässige Darstellung der Ausgrabung und Wiederbeisetzung der irdischen Reste von Beethoven und Schubert* (Vienna: Gerold, 1863). A more clinical description was recorded on September 22, 1888, when the composer's remains, now considerably deteriorated, were exhumed and moved to the Central Cemetery. See Karl Feyerer, ed., *Jahresbericht des Wiener Männer-Gesang-Vereines über das 45. Vereinsjahr* (Vienna: Verlag des Wiener Männer-Gesang-Vereines, 1888), 78–79. A copy of the report, "Bericht über die an den Gebeinen Franz Schubert's gelegentlich der Uebertragung derselben von dem Währinger Ortsfriedhofe auf den Central-Friedhof der Stadt Wien am 22. September 1888 vorgenommene Untersuchung," by C. Toldt and A. Weisbach for the Anthropologische Gesellschaft can be found in the Wiener Stadt- und Landesbibliothek, Inv. no. E 87125.

16. Heinrich Kreissle von Hellborn, *The Life of Franz Schubert,* trans. Arthur Duke Coleridge, vol. 2 (London: Longmans, Green, and Co., 1869), 152–53; and Edward Wilberforce, *Franz Schubert: A Musical Biography* (London: Wm. H. Allen & Co., 1866), 223–24. One ought not to underestimate the implications of describing Schubert's skull in racial language. The appearance of any term other than those signifying white Europe invariably conveyed inferiority. To signal the magnitude of Austria's defeat by Prussia in 1866, Pope Pius IX, the loyal ally of the Catholic Habsburg monarchy, noted that the empire had been reduced to the position of

"a second-rate Oriental Power." See Geoffrey Wawro, *The Austro-Prussian War* (Cambridge: Cambridge University Press, 1996), 281. On Schubert's skull and racial language, see chapter 1 of the first volume of this study.

17. Eduard Kral, ed., *Jahresbericht des Männer-Gesang-Vereines über das 22. Vereinsjahr* (Vienna: Verlag des Wiener Männer-Gesang-Vereines, 1865), 36. See also Franz Hottner, "Das Schubert-Denkmal in Wien," *Zeitschrift für bildende Kunst* 7 (1872): 261–65.

18. Deutsch, *Franz Schubert: Sein Leben in Bildern*, 18. A report in the *Neue freie Presse* of April 14, 1866, reveals that the owner of Rieder's miniature would not permit it to be photographed or copied despite Dumba's entreaty. See Eva Badura-Skoda, "Eine authentische Porträt-Plastik Schuberts," *Österreichische Musikzeitschrift* 33, no. 11 (November 1978): 588. On the influence of Rieder's work on subsequent iconography, see chapter 4 of the first volume of this study.

19. "Nachrichten," *Allgemeine musikalische Zeitung* (Leipzig) 1, no. 15 (April 11, 1866): 123; and "Wiener Schubert-Monument," 130, quoted in Gustav Theodor Fechner, *Vorschule der Aesthetik*, vol. 2 (Leipzig: Breitkopf & Härtel, 1876), 129.

20. Quoted in "Wiener Schubert-Monument," 129. See also Fechner, *Vorschule der Aesthetik*, 2:129.

21. "Wiener Schubert-Monument," 130. A photograph of Kundmann's first plaster model appears in Otto Erich Deutsch, ed., "Der intime Schubert," special issue, *Moderne Welt*, December 1, 1925, 31, under the uncomplimentary one-word heading: "Erstarrung" ("stiffness"). Page 30 of this issue shows an alleged oil portrait of Schubert by Gábor Melegh, rendering the sitter with his legs crossed at the ankles. Deutsch thought that this painting did not depict the composer, but in any case it does not seem to have been reproduced during the nineteenth century and thus was probably unknown to Kundmann. Although figures in this position may not have been appropriate for the grand designs of a public monument, they were certainly suitable for interiors and middle-class residences, as evinced by the putti created by the sculptor Joseph Klieber. See Krasa, "Sculpture," 193, 214. Interestingly enough, the most provocative sculpture in fin-de-siècle Vienna, the statue of Beethoven designed by Max Klinger for the Secession exhibition of 1902, depicts one of the composer's knees crossed over the other, although the forward leaning position of the torso is far removed from the relaxed pose Kundmann gave to his model of Schubert.

22. "Wiener Schubert-Monument," 130.

23. August Littrow-Bischoff, *Aus dem persönlichen Verkehre mit Franz Grillparzer* (Vienna: L. Rosner, 1873), 175–76.

24. See, for example, Hottner, "Das Schubert-Denkmal in Wien," facing 264; and *Die österreichisch-ungarische Monarchie in Wort und Bild*, vol. 1 (Vienna: Druck und Verlag der kaiserlich-königliche Hof- und Staatsdruckerei, 1886), 131. Perhaps owing to the official nature of the latter publication, which was produced under the direction of Crown Prince Rudolf, Schubert's face bears what might be judged a far more serious, Beethovenian scowl than actually is the case in the model. Compare it to the photograph of the plaster model that appears in Deutsch, *Franz Schubert: Sein Leben in Bildern*, 70. At this time Kundmann also created a bust of the composer that passed into the hands of Nikolaus Dumba, who loaned it to the Schubert exhibition of 1897. It is clearly discernible on the left side of figure 3.1.

25. On the Beethoven monument, see Alexander Rehding, "Liszt's Musical Monuments," *19th-Century Music* 26, no. 1 (Summer 2002): 52–72. Berlioz's report

on the work's dedication and the attendant concerts is translated and annotated by Kevin Bazzana, "'Fêtes musicales de Bonn': Unveiling of the Beethoven Monument in 1845," *Beethoven Newsletter* 6, nos. 1–2 (Spring and Summer 1991): 1–11, 29–36.
26. Machold's sketch is in the collection of the Museum für angewandte Kunst, Vienna, Inv. no. 22527, whose catalogue card describes it as a study for an *Orgelfuss,* possibly for a public building. The four composers represent the topmost of three groups. The middle level depicts individuals in peasant dress, including a child throwing a ball and three men engaging in a toast. One is a soldier and another, perhaps an artisan, holds a tool. At the bottom are three men coming out of subterranean arches. The one on the left holds a knife, and the one on the right holds playing cards. Constant von Wurzbach, *Biographisches Lexikon des Kaiserthums Oesterreich,* vol. 16 (Vienna: K. K. Hof- und Staatsdruckerei, 1867), 209, lists a "drawing for a monumental goblet [Pokal] to the glorification of the wealth of German song in word and tone." A complete description of the piece, designed for an industrial exposition, appears in "Aus dem Wiener Leben," *Wiener Zeitung* (Abendblatt), March 7, 1863, 215. Machold was the pupil of Ludwig Schnorr von Carolsfeld, who also taught Schwind, and to whom Schubert in friendship dedicated two songs published as op. 37 (D. 794 and 588): "Der Pilgrim" and "Der Alpenjäger".
27. Arnold Niggli, *Schubert* (Leipzig: Philipp Reclam, 1889), 101.
28. Friedrich Nietzsche, *Human, All Too Human,* trans. R. J. Hollingdale (Cambridge: Cambridge University Press, 1986), 83. In *The Wanderer and His Shadow* (1880), the second of two additional books published with a new edition of *Human, All Too Human* in 1886, there appeared an aphorism on Schubert.
29. Statues depicting John in this manner are part of a long tradition ranging from Juan Martínez Montañés (1637) for the Convent of Santa Paula in Seville to Bertel Thorvaldsen (1824) for the Frue Kirke in Copenhagen, Hansen's hometown. The apostles also figure prominently in northern painting, most famously in Rembrandt's *The Evangelist Matthew* (1661). See Eugene Plon, *Thorvaldsen: His Life and Works,* trans. I. M. Luyster (Boston: Roberts Brothers, 1874), 242; and Howard Hibbard, *Masterpieces of Western Sculpture: From Medieval to Modern* (New York: Harper and Row, 1966), pl. 82. This image is also not unknown in depictions of composers: see, for example, Louis-François Roubillac's Handel monument in Westminster Abbey (1762) and Joseph Duplessis's portrait of Gluck (1775). For the former, see Suzanne Aspden, "Fam'd Handel Breathing, tho' Transformed to Stone": The Composer as Monument," *Journal of the American Musicological Society* 55, no. 1 (Spring 2002): 39–90.
30. Friedrich Steinebach, "Immortellenkranz gelegt auf das Grab von Franz Schubert. Als Prolog zur Schubertfeier im Vereine Hesperus am 30. Januar 1858," Wiener Stadt- und Landesbibliothek, Inv. no. E109458; reprinted in *Wiener Theaterzeitung* 52, no. 26 (February 2, 1858): 102; and *Thalia. Taschenbuch für 1859* 46 (1859): 214–16. Steinebach was editor of the latter. See also Josef Weyl, *Dem Andenken an Franz Schubert am Gedenktage des grossen Meisters Samstag den 21. März 1863 in der Künstlergesellschaft "Hesperus" gesprochen von Fräulein Auguste Baison* (Vienna: L. C. Zamarski and C. Dittmarsch, 1863), 1 (Wiener Stadt- und Landesbibliothek, Inv. no. E109423).
31. Quoted in "Kleine Zeitung," *Neue Zeitschrift für Musik* 68, no. 25 (June 14, 1872): 254–55. Given this journal's strong nationalist sentiments for specifically German music in the wake of the Franco-Prussian War, one can imagine a certain degree of editorial glee in reporting on the decidedly unheroic posture of Vienna's celebrated native son.

32. Franz Pylleman, "Die Schubert-Feier in Wien," *Allgemeine musikalische Zeitung* (Leipzig) 7, no. 26 (June 26, 1872): 417.

33. Kreissle, *Life of Franz Schubert*, 2:169.

34. "Schubertiana," *Der Floh* 4, no. 2 (May 19, 1872): 88.

35. Ferdinand Kürnberger, "Das Denkmalsetzen in der Opposition," in *Deutsche Zeitung* (late autumn) 1873, in *Literarische Herzenssachen: Reflexionen und Kritiken* (Vienna: L. Rosner, 1877), 360.

36. Fechner, *Vorschule der Aesthetik*, 2:129–30. For George Grove's excoriating criticism of the monument in a letter to the *Times* of London on October 2, 1889, see chapter 5 of the first volume of this study.

37. Robert Schumann, "Grosses Duo f. d. Pfte. zu 4 Hdn. Op. 140. und: F. Schubert's allerletzte Composition: Drei grosse Sonaten für Pianoforte," *Neue Zeitschrift für Musik* 8, no. 45 (June 5, 1838): 178; and *Schumann on Music: A Selection from the Writings*, trans. and ed. Henry Pleasants (New York: Dover, 1988), 142.

38. Ludwig Speidel, "Das Schubert-Denkmal," *Deutsche Zeitung* (1872), in *Wiener Frauen und anderes Wienerische*, vol. 2 of *Ludwig Speidels Schriften* (Berlin: Meyer & Jessen, 1910), 123. Speidel was doubtless aware of the tradition of associating Schubert with the swan, discussed in chapter 2 of the first volume of this study. Kundmann himself contributed to it when he used two swans to flank a lyre at the bottom of his monument for Schubert's grave in the Central Cemetery, designed around 1890 after the composer's remains were moved there in 1888.

39. Eduard Hanslick, *Concerte, Componisten und Virtuosen der letzten fünfzehn Jahre, 1870–1885*, 2nd ed. (1886; reprint, Westmead, NY: Gregg International Publishers Limited, 1971), 54, 57–58. Hanslick lifted much of his characterization from Franz Brendel, *Geschichte der Musik in Italien, Deutschland und Frankreich*, 2nd ed., vol. 2 (Leipzig: Matthes, 1855), 178. See also chapter 2 of the first volume of this study.

40. Eduard von Bauernfeld, "Als einer lebte noch und schafft," *Jahresbericht des Wiener Männer-Gesang-Vereines über das 29. Vereinsjahr*, ed. Karl Feyerer (Vienna: Verlag des Wiener Männer-Gesang-Vereines, 1872), 46.

41. Josef Weilen, "Sei uns gegrüßt, den endlich wir errungen!" in *Jahresbericht des Wiener Männer-Gesang-Vvereines über das 29. Vereinsjahr*, ed. Karl Feyerer (Vienna: Verlag des Wiener Männer-Gesang-Vereines, 1872), 40. For other poems commemorating the monument's dedication, see Adametz, *Franz Schubert*, 127–38.

42. The most accessible information on the Secession exhibition is in Alessandra Comini, *The Changing Image of Beethoven: A Study in Mythmaking* (New York: Rizzoli, 1987), 388–415. For an interesting comparison of the monuments of Zumbusch and Kundmann, see Marie-Agnes Dittrich, "'Jenem imponierenden Heroismus entzogen'—Franz Schubert und das Österreich-Bild nach Königgrätz," in *Franz Schubert— Werk und Rezeption: Schubert-Jahrbuch 1999: Bericht über den Internationalen Schubert-Kongreß, Duisburg 1997*, ed. Dietrich Berke, Walther Dürr, Walburga Litschauer, and Christiane Schumann (Duisburg, Germany: Deutsche Schubert-Gesellschaft e. V., 2001), 3–21. Dittrich's article is valuable in placing the images of Beethoven and Schubert in the context of the contemporary cultural dichotomy between Prussia and Austria.

43. Camillo Sitte, *The Art of Building Cities*, trans. Charles T. Stewart (New York: Reinhold Publishing Corp., 1945), 108.

44. Ibid., 66.

45. Ibid., 78. At the time Sitte was writing, the only other monument in the Stadtpark was a bust of Zelinka (1877), the city's mayor, who had been the local guiding hand in the park's construction. Of the many commemorations of Vienna's

famous dead in the Stadtpark, the best known is that of Johann Strauss Jr., for which a committee was created in 1904, but which was dedicated only in 1921 following the disruption during World War I. During the fin de siècle, artists dominated the statuary: Jakob Emil Schindler (1895), Hans Makart (1898), Friedrich von Amerling (1902), and Hans Canon (1905). Anton Bruckner rated a bust in 1899.

46. Speidel, *Wiener Frauen*, 120; Hottner, "Schubert-Denkmal," 262; and Robert Haven Schauffler, *The Unknown Brahms: His Life, Character and Works* (New York: Dodd, Mead and Company, 1933), 143. Munz was less sanguine since he considered Brahms's opinion as reflecting "a commentary on the Master's immature taste in the arts of design." Munz's recollection is not repeated in his *Österreichische Profile und Reminiszenzen* (Vienna: Deutsch-Österreichischer Verlag, 1913), 114–15, in which Munz recalled Brahms's reaction to the high number of artistically worthless monuments in Rome.

47. Otto de Joux, *Die Enterbten des Liebesglückes oder das dritte Geschlecht*, 2nd ed. (Leipzig: Max Spohr, 1897), 99.

48. Andrew Whiteside, *The Socialism of Fools: Georg Ritter von Schönerer and Austrian Pan-Germanism* (Berkeley and Los Angeles: University of California Press, 1975), 9.

49. Quoted in James J. Sheehan, *German History, 1770–1866* (Oxford: Clarendon Press, 1989), 373.

50. Johann Gottlieb Fichte, *Addresses to the German Nation*, trans. R. F. Jones and G. H. Turnbull, ed. George Armstrong Kelly (New York: Harper and Row, 1968), 126–27.

51. Johann Gabriel Seidl, "Meinem Freunde Franz Schubert! Am Vortage seines Begräbnisses: Den 20 November 1828," *Wiener Zeitschrift für Kunst, Literatur, Theater und Mode*, no. 147 (December 6, 1828): 1197–98. On Bismarck's early career, see Sheehan, *German History*, 858–59, 864–65.

52. Steinebach, "Immortellenkranz."

53. Sheehan, *German History*, 384." On the matter of nationalism and Germanness in Austria before Königgrätz, see Jászi, *Dissolution*, 258–67; Okey, *Habsburg Monarchy*, 106–13; and Whitside, *Socialism*, 9–14. The importance of culture and language in the nineteenth-century formation of German national identity has long been stressed, although recent studies have examined additional factors, including the importance of the voluntary society or *Verein*. See Abigail Green, *Fatherlands: State-Building and Nationhood in Nineteenth-Century Germany* (Cambridge: Cambridge University Press, 2001), 62–79; Bernhard Giesen, *Intellectuals and the Nation: Collective Identity in a German Axial Age*, trans. Nicholas Levis and Amos Weisz (Cambridge: Cambridge University Press, 1998), 97–111; and Brian E. Vick, *Defining Germany: The 1848 Frankfurt Parliamentarians and National Identity* (Cambridge, MA: Harvard University Press, 2002), 19–47. For an illuminating study of the role of music, see Celia Applegate, "How German Is It? Nationalism and the Idea of Serious Music in the Early Nineteenth Century," *19th-Century Music*, 21, no. 3 (Spring 1998): 274–96.

54. Eduard von Bauernfeld, "Hier war's, vor vierzig Jahren," *Jahresbericht des Wiener Männer-Gesang-Vereines über das 25. Vereinsjahr*, ed. Eduard Kral (Vienna: Verlag des Wiener Männer-Gesang-Vereines, 1868), 98.

55. R. John Rath, *The Viennese Revolution of 1848* (Austin: University of Texas Press, 1957), 43. See also John Warren, "Eduard von Bauernfeld and the Beginnings of Austrian Social Drama," in *The Biedermeier and Beyond: Selected Papers from the Symposium held at St. Peter's College, Oxford from 19–21 September 1997*, ed. Ian F. Roe and John Warren (Bern: Peter Lang, 1999), 127–45.

56. Eduard Kral, ed., *Jahresbericht des Wiener Männer-Gesang-Vereines über das 23. Vereinsjahr* (Vienna: Verlag des Wiener Männer-Gesang-Vereines, 1866), 33. The Verein's sentiments echoed those in Franz Joseph's June 17 declaration of war, a war that the emperor characterized as a conflict of "Germans against Germans." Quoted in John Breuilly, *Austria, Prussia and Germany, 1806–1871* (Edinburgh: Pearson Education, 2002), 164.

57. Kral, *Jahresbericht* (1866), 38–39.

58. "Berlin. Revue," *Neue Berliner Musikzeitung* 20, no. 27 (July 4, 1866): 212; and "Feuilleton. Die Kunst und die Politik," *Neue Berliner Musikzeitung* 20, no. 36 (September 5, 1866): 283–84. For musical works, see *Neue Berliner Musikzeitung* 20, no. 27 (July 4, 1866): 216; no. 28 (July 11, 1866): 223–24, 264. Vocal works included Franz Abt, "Mit Gott für König und Vaterland"; J. P. Cronhamm, "Soldatenlieder"; Heinrich Dorn, "Das Rheinlied: 'Vom Rhein, vom deutschen Rhein'"; Theodor Drath, "Preussenlieder für Preuss. Civil- und Militairmännerchöre"; Friedrich Kücken, "Kriegesgang: 'Die Trommel ruft, die Fahnen winken'"; and August Neithardt, "Fahnenlied 'Hoch die Fahnen.'" Piano music consisted of H. Fliege, "Blücher-Marsch"; Joseph Gungl, "Die Preussische Parade. Grosses militärisches Marsch-Potpourri"; G. Heinsdorff, "Preussischer Landwehr-Marsch"; Friedrich Lux, "Krönungs-Marsch zur Krönung Sr. Majestät Wilhelm I. König von Preussen"; H. Mendel, "Für Deutschland: Preussens Sturm-Galopp"; and Gottfried Piefke, "Herwarth-Marsch" and "Kriegerische Wiegenlieder"; as well as marches celebrating the Prussian victory over Denmark in 1864. After the battle, Piefke, the imperial music director and director of music of the third army corps, composed a march, "Der Königgrätzer," as did Oskar Bolck ("Sieges-Marsch") and Heinrich Saro ("Königgrätzer Siegesmarsch").

59. Eduard Kral, ed., *Jahresbericht des Wiener Männer-Gesang-Vereines über das 24. Vereinsjahr* (Vienna: Verlag des Wiener Männer-Gesang-Vereines, 1867), 1.

60. Anton Weiß, ed., *Fünfzig Jahre Schubertbund. Chronik des Vereines vom 1. Bis 50. Vereinsjahre* (Vienna: Verlag des Schubertbundes, 1913), 15–16.

61. *Jahresbericht des Wiener akademischen Gesangvereines über das dreizehnte Vereinsjahr. 1. October 1870 bis 30. September 1871* (Vienna: Im Selbstverlage des akademischen Gesangvereines, 1871), 4; and Adalbert Winter, *Jahres-Bericht des "Schubertbund," über das achte Vereinsjahr* (Vienna: Selbstverlag des "Schubertbund," 1871), 13.

62. "Die neuere Musik und ihre Anwendung auf die Culturaufgaben," *Neue Zeitschrift für Musik* 66, nos. 39–40 (September 23 and 30, 1870): 349–51, 357–59. German disparagement of its ally's music in the wake of war was not new. Several months after the German-Danish War of 1864, in which Prussian land forces proved the decisive victor despite the Danes' naval defeat of Austria, one German writer took note of the weak instrumentation of Austrian infantry music compared to the exquisite performance of the most difficult concert arrangements by Prussian military ensembles. See Theodor Rode, "Preussen und Oesterreich im musikalischen Bunde," *Neue Berliner Musikzeitung* 18, no. 49 (December 7, 1864): 387–88. On assuming the German throne in 1888, Wilhelm II ordered that his troops should no longer march to frivolous operetta melodies. See *Neue Berliner Zeitung* 42, no. 30 (July 26, 1888): 271.

63. Grillparzer's apothegm is quoted in Sheehan, *German History*, 911. See also Friedrich Nietzsche, *Sämtliche Werke: Kritische Studienausgabe*, ed. Giorgio Colli and Mazzino Montinari. vol. 1 (Munich: Deutscher Taschenbuch Verlag, 1980), 160.

64. For recent literature on German Austrians during this period, see Michael Hughes, *Nationalism and Society: Germany 1800–1945* (London: Edward Arnold,

1988), 164–74; Mason, *Dissolution,* 10–15; Sked, *Decline and Fall,* 218–38; and Whiteside, *Socialism of Fools,* 10–15. See also Paul W. Schroeder, "Austro-German Relations: Divergent Views of the Disjoined Partnership," *Central European History* 11, no. 3 (September 1978): 302–12.

65. Daniel Beller-McKenna, "How *deutsch* a Requiem? Absolute Music, Universality, and the Reception of Brahms's *Eine deutsches Requiem,* op. 45," *19th-Century Music* 22, no. 1 (Summer 1988): 3–19. Brahms's statement occurs in a letter to Carl Reinthaler on October 9, 1867.

66. Eduard Kral, ed., *Jahresbericht des Wiener Männer-Gesang-Vereines über das 25. Vereinsjahr* (Vienna: Verlag des Wiener Männer-Gesang-Vereines, 1868), 90–91.

67. Ibid., 95.

68. Elvira Konecny, *Die Familie Dumba und ihre Bedeutung für Wien und Österreich* (Vienna: Verband der wissenschaftlichen Gesellschaften Österreichs, 1986), 1–2, 85; originally the author's PhD dissertation from the University of Vienna. Dumba's son Konstantin Theodor, the Austrian ambassador to the United States during World War I, offered an explanation of his nation's involvement that located responsibility for the conflict in the historical aggression of Russia. See "Ambassador Dumba defends Austria," *New York Times,* section 5, January 31, 1915, 5.

69. Karl Feyerer, ed., *Jahresbericht des Wiener Männer-Gesang-Vereines über das 29. Vereinsjahr* (Vienna: Verlag des Wiener Männer-Gesang-Vereines, 1872), 37.

70. Ludwig August Frankl, "Und immer, wenn ein Volk der Fürsten Leichen," in *Jahresbericht des Wiener Männer-Gesang-Vereines über das 45. Vereinsjahr,* ed. Karl Feyerer (Vienna: Verlag des Wiener Männer-Gesang-Vereines, 1888), 84. Frankl had actually begun his career with poetic tributes to the monarchy. His early "Das Habsburglied" was a historical ballad dedicated to the Emperor Ferdinand, that most hapless of Habsburgs. Frankl's experience during the revolutionary events of March 1848, however, turned his writings toward the views of the "democratic party." See Wurzbach, *Biographisches Lexikon* (1858), 4:336.

71. Rath, *Viennese Revolution,* 100–101. See also Sigurd Paul Scheichl, "Die väterlandischen Balladen des österreichischen Biedermeier: Bausteine des Habsburgischen Mythos: Zu Ludwig August Frankls *Habsburglied*"; and Colin Walker, "Ludwig August Frankl and the Reflection of the Biedermeier," both in *The Biedermeier and Beyond: Selected Papers from the Symposium held at St. Peter's College, Oxford from 19–21 September 1997,* ed. Ian F. Roe and John Warren (Bern: Peter Lang, 1999), 45–61, 215–23.

72. Quoted in the original German by Whiteside, *Socialism of Fools,* 138.

73. Jászi, *Dissolution,* 384.

Chapter Two

1. Both concerts also featured Schubert's Lieder. Mahler served as piano accompanist for Anna von Mildenburg, Ernestine Schumann-Heink, Franz Birrenkoven, and Leopold Demuth. Strauss's wife Pauline sang "Ganymed" (D. 544; op. 19, no. 3) and "Die Allmacht" (D. 852; op. 79, no. 2) in orchestrations by her husband. See La Grange, *Mahler,* 1:901; and Paula Reber-München, "Gedenkfeier zu Franz Schubert's 100 Geburtstage," *Neue Zeitschrift für Musik* 93, no. 12 (March 24, 1897): 151.

2. "Der gereinigte Liberalismus," *Montags-Zeitung,* January 20, 1896, 1.

3. William Alexander Jenks, *The Austrian Election Reform of 1907* (New York: Octagon Books, 1974), 25. At the end of 1897, the disruptive and even violent character of

Viennese politics, which spilled over into parliamentary sittings in the months leading up to the fall of the government of Prime Minister Casimir Badeni, was memorably recorded by Mark Twain, in "Stirring Times in Austria," *Harper's New Monthly
Magazine* 96 (1898): 53–40. Twain was living in Vienna while his daughter was studying piano with Theodor Leschetizsky.

4. The leading English-language studies of the legacy of Austrian liberalism and its
relationship to fin-de-siècle political culture are Boyer, *Political Radicalism*; and
Judson, *Exclusive Revolutionaries*. On pan-German movements, see Andrew Whiteside,
Austrian National Socialism before 1918 (The Hague: M. Nijhoff, 1962). For anti-
Semitism, see the citations in note 12 below. A useful encapsulation can be found in
Okey, *Habsburg Monarchy*, 276–82, which also has a helpful general bibliography.

5. The term *Judenliberalismus* comes from Lueger's call to the Viennese public to vote
for the Christian Social Party, printed in the *Deutsches Volksblatt* on January 31, 1897,
and discussed later in this chapter. As the governing entity in the municipal council,
the Christian Social Party had the authority to select Vienna's mayor, but the appointment still required the emperor's formal approval. On Lueger, Franz Joseph, and
Vienna's elections, see Richard S. Geehr, *Karl Lueger: Mayor of Fin-de-Siècle Vienna*
(Detroit: Wayne State University Press, 1990), 91–101. The misgivings about a Lueger
mayoralty are archly symbolized in a cartoon appearing in a satirical weekly a month
before Franz Joseph finally gave his sanction. Entitled "When Dr. Lueger Becomes
Mayor," it depicts an enthroned Lueger ready to pass monarchical judgment on two
cowering Jews, whose hands are bound together, while government representatives
bow deferentially. The caption below reads: "Ave Caesar. Morituri te salutant [Hail
Caesar. Those about to die salute you.]" See *Der Floh* 29, no. 12 (March 21, 1897): 1.

6. Messing, "Vienna Beethoven Centennial Festival," 57–63, There is no study of Vienna
at the turn of the century that rivals the analyses of the interwar period in Gabriele Eder,
Wiener Musikfeste zwischen 1918 und 1938: Ein Beitrag zur Vergangenheitsbewältigung
(Vienna: Geyer Edition, 1991); and Michael P. Steinberg, *The Meaning of the Salzburg
Festival: Austria as Theater and Ideology, 1890–1938* (Ithaca, NY: Cornell University Press,
1990). For an overview, see Friedrich Karin, *Festive Culture in Germany and Europe from the
Sixteenth to the Twentieth Century* (Lewiston, NY: Edwin Mellen Press, 2000).

7. Robert Hirschfeld, "Die Schubert-Feier in Wien," *Neue musikalische Presse* 6, no. 6
(1897): 2–3.

8. Boyer, *Political Radicalism*, 72–78; and McColl, *Music Criticism in Vienna*, 116–17.

9. Robert Hirschfeld, "Die Schubert-Feier," *Wiener Abendpost (Beilage zur Wiener
Zeitung)*, February 6, 1897, 5–6. See also "Schubert-Feier im Volksbildungsverein,"
Arbeiter-Zeitung, January 22, 1897, 4; and "Schubert-Feier," *Wiener Zeitung,* January 22,
1897, 7.

10. "Die Bastille der Censur," *Wiener allgemeine Zeitung,* January 20, 1897, 1. Aside
from the newspapers themselves, useful sources for uncovering the political allegiances in Viennese journalism are McColl, *Music Criticism in Vienna*; Kurt Paupié,
Handbuch der österreichischen Pressegeschichte 1848–1959, 2 vols. (Vienna: Wilhelm
Braumüller, 1960); and Sigurd Paul Scheichl and Wolfgang Duchkowitsch, eds.,
Zeitungen im Wiener Fin-de-Siècle (Munich: R. Oldenburg, 1997). McColl analyzes liberal and antiliberal press reaction to the leading composers of the late nineteenth
century but mentions the Schubert centennial celebrations only in passing. McColl
necessarily limits herself to music critics, and the names she cites can be supple-
mented with lists published in Theodor Helm, ed., *Fromme's musikalische Welt: Notiz-
Kalender für das Jahr 1898* (Vienna: Carl Fromme, 1897), 175–76; and *Wiener Bilder*
2, no. 9 (1897): 9.

11. "Die Woche. Politische Notizen," *Die Zeit,* February 13, 1897, 108. The Jewish presence at this imperial fête coincidentally recalls the ball scene in Ferdinand von Saar's novel, *Seligmann Hirsch* (1889). See Karlheinz Rossbacher, *Literatur und Liberalismus: Zur Kultur der Ringstrasse in Wien* (Vienna: J&V, 1992), 445–46.

12. In addition to Boyer, *Political Radicalism;* Judson, *Exclusive Revolutionaries;* and Schorske, *Fin-de-Siècle Vienna;* see Steven Beller, *Vienna and the Jews, 1867–1938* (Cambridge: Cambridge University Press, 1989); Leon Botstein and Werner Hanak, eds., *Vienna: Jews and the City of Music, 1870–1938* (Annandale-on-Hudson, NY: Bard College and Wolke Verlag, 2004); Ivar Oxaal, Michael Pollack, and Gerhard Botz, eds., *Jews, Antisemitism and Culture in Vienna* (London: Routledge and Keegan Paul, 1987); Bruce F. Pauley, *From Prejudice to Persecution: A History of Austrian Anti-Semitism* (Chapel Hill: University of North Carolina Press, 1992); P. G. J. Pulzer, *The Rise of Political Anti-Semitism in Germany and Austria* (New York: John Wiley and Sons, 1964); Marsha L. Roxenblitt, *The Jews of Vienna, 1867–1914: Assimilation and Identity* (Albany: State University of New York Press, 1983); Egon Schwarz, "Germans and Jews in Viennese Culture," in *The German-Jewish Dialgoue Reconsidered,* ed. Klaus L. Berghahn (New York: Peter Lang, 1996), 99–108; and Robert S. Wistrich, *The Jews of Vienna in the Age of Franz Joseph* (Oxford: Oxford University Press, 1989). See also the biographies of Lueger and Schönerer by Geehr, *Karl Lueger;* and Whiteside, *Socialism of Fools.*

13. "Christsozialer Antisemitismus," *Ostdeutsche Rundschau,* January 18, 1897, 2; and "Die deutschnational—hie christlich-sozial," *Ostdeutsche Rundschau,* January 23, 1897, 1–2.

14. Theodor Gomperz, *Ein Gelehrtenleben im Bürgertum der Franz-Josefs-Zeit* (Vienna: Verlag der Österrichischen Akademie der Wissenschaften, 1974), 274.

15. Whiteside, *Socialism of Fools,* 148–49; and Wistrich, *Jews of Vienna,* 221. In a memoir completed in 1956, the chief editor of the *Reichspost,* Friedrich Funder (who had begun his journalistic career in 1896), was at great pains to distance his paper from Vergani's racist anti-Semitism even as he admitted the predicament of doing so. "It is certainly extremely difficult now, after half a century and after the terrible interlude of the concentration camp of Auschwitz-Maydanek, to find the right yardstick for the fundamentally different conditions in economic, political and social life which gave rise to the term 'anti-Semitism.'" Funder nonetheless explained this distance by arguing that the utterances of Christian Social politicians and journalists never precipitated "any formidable demonstration against the Jews," and "in their striving for social reform they were often concerned with certain unsound facts which undoubtedly called for open criticism. Such censure was often interpreted, both falsely and superficially, as an expression of anti-Semitism, with the conscious or unconscious intention of casting a slur upon the Christian-Social attitude." Cloaked in this rationalization, Funder could still complain that the "ruthless drive for monetary gain pursued out of all proportion by a certain section of the Jewish population threatened to destroy many fundamental values, both moral and material." See Friedrich Funder, *From Empire to Republic,* trans. Barbara Waldstein (New York: Unger, 1963), 37–40.

16. Beller, *Vienna and the Jews,* 38–39; and Wistrich, *Jews of Vienna,* 170–72.

17. Karl Lueger, *"I Decide Who Is a Jew!" The Papers of Dr. Karl Lueger,* trans. and ed. Richard S. Geehr (Washington, DC: University Press of America, 1982), 325.

18. See, for example, David B. Dennis, *Beethoven in German Politics, 1870–1989* (New Haven, CT: Yale University Press, 1996); and McColl, *Music Criticism.* Jill E. Mayer has observed that in 1887, four years ahead of the event, there was already a political

character to the *Salzburger Zeitung*'s consideration of the centennial of Mozart's death. She errs, however, in suggesting that such celebrations were analogous to the modern escapist treatment of movie stars. Jill E. Mayer, "'By Drip and by Drop': The Discourse of German Nationalism in the Press of Habsburg Austria—Salzburg, Styria, Vienna: 1877–1897" (PhD diss., University of Manitoba, 1993), 92.

19. Eduard Hanslick, "Feuilleton. Zum Schubert-Jubiläum. I. Die Austellung," *Neue freie Presse* (Morgenblatt), January 21, 1897, 2.

20. Mayer, "By Drip and by Drop," 315. For views on the Schorskian model of generational change, see Beller, *Rethinking Vienna 1900*, 1–24; and Neubauer, *The Fin-de-Siècle Culture*, 104–9.

21. McColl, *Music Criticism*, 107.

22. Hanslick, "Feuilleton," 3.

23. Josef Scheu, "Feuilleton. Franz Schubert," *Arbeiter-Zeitung*, January 31, 1897, 6–7. Scheu is best known as the composer of the workers' song "Lied der Arbeit" (1868). See William J. McGrath, *Dionysian Art and Populist Politics in Austria* (New Haven, CT, and London: Yale University Press, 1974), 214.

24. Julius Pap, "Feuilleton. Künstlerhaus," *Arbeiter-Zeitung*, February 5, 1897, 6.

25. "sch" [Ludwig Basch], "Die Schubert-Ausstellung," *Illustrirtes Wiener Extrablatt*, January 20, 1897, 4–5.

26. *Illustrirtes Wiener Extrablatt*, January 20, 1897, 1.

27. Karl Storck, "Der Schubert Franzl," *Illustrirtes Wiener Extrablatt*, January 20, 1897, 13. For a similar treatment that includes favoring the murder as the front page story, see "Zu Franz Schubert's 100. Geburtstage," *Neuigkeits Welt-Blatt*, January 31, 1897, 17–19. See also Karl Storck, *Geschichte der Musik*, 6th ed., vol. 2 (Stuttgart: Metzler, 1926), 99–103.

28. "Die Huldigung der Sänger," *Illustrirtes Wiener Extrablatt* (Abend-Ausgabe), February 3, 1897, 1. Mayer ("By Drip and by Drop," 101) concludes that the paper's format and contents "could have been aimed at the consumer with lighter tastes or a lighter pocketbook."

29. "A. S." [Alfred Schnerich], "Schubert als religiöser Componist," *Das Vaterland* (Morgenblatt), January 31, 1897, 2. An author of some dozen works about Viennese church music, Schnerich's opinion of Schubert's sacred compositions can be found in *Der Messen-Typus von Haydn bis Schubert* (Vienna: Im Selbstverlage des Verfassers, 1892).

30. Carl Staubach, "Ein deutsche Liederfürst," *Deutsches Volksblatt* (Morgen-Ausgabe), January 31, 1897, 5. The prevalence in Vienna of Catholic men's singing societies was evidence of the intertwining of religion and music. On December 8, 1896, only weeks after its establishment, the group "Dreizehnlinden" made its first public appearance "with God and for God" by participating with all the Catholic men's singing societies in a performance of Schubert's *Deutsche Trauermesse* (D. 621) at the Universitätskirche "Zu Mariä Himmelfahrt." See Friedrich Strobl, *Jahres-Bericht des Sängerbundes "Dreizehnlinden" in Wien über das I. Vereinsjahr 1896–1897* (Vienna: Verlag des Sängerbundes "Dreizehnlinden," 1897), 4.

31. "M.," "Jüdisches von der Schubert-Ausstellung," *Die Neuzeit: Wochenschrift für politische, religiöse und Cultur-Interessen*, no. 7 (February 12, 1897): 66. See also Eduard Birnbaum, "Schubert als Synagogenkomponist," *Allgemeine Zeitung Judenthum* (Berlin) 61 (1897): 52, 65, 81.

32. "Concerte," *Neue musikalische Presse* 6, no. 5 (1897): 15. The reviewer is only identified as "–i–." The year 1897 proved to be critical in the struggle for women's rights in Vienna. In February, the Allgemeiner österreichischer Frauenverein (General

Austrian Women's Association) held a meeting to protest the government's rejection of its petition denouncing the introduction of brothels into the city. The year 1896 saw the appearance of texts by three leaders of the emancipation movement: Auguste Fickert, Marianne Hainisch, and Rosa Mayreder. See Harriet Anderson, *Utopian Feminism: Women's Movements in "fin-de-siècle" Vienna* (New Haven, CT, and London: Yale University Press, 1992), 72–74.

33. Richard von Kralik, "Musik," *Das Vaterland* (Morgenblatt), January 24, 1897, 11; and "M.," "Concerte," *Die vornehme Welt: Illustrirte Wochenschrift für die Gesellschaft, Kunst, Wissenschaft, Litteratur, Mystik, Sport, Mode, Reisewesen, Fremdenverkehr, Volkswirthschaft etc.* 1, no. 6 (February 11, 1897): 104. The poet and critic Richard von Kralik was one of the leading literary proponents of closer ties between Catholicism and Austrian Germanness.

34. Richard Heuberger, "Konzerte," *Wiener Tagblatt*, February 23, 1897, 2. In the winter of 1897, the University of Vienna began to allow women to pursue degrees. In 1878, the Vienna Conservatory had adopted the recommendation of its director Josef Hellmesberger that it should not admit women as cello students but that it should accept female violinists who were not beginners. See Botstein, "Music and Its Public," 64. The violist of the Soldat-Röger Quartet was Natalie Bauer-Lechner (known today as Mahler's adoring memoirist), who did study at the conservatory.

35. "Der hunderste Geburtstag Schuberts," *Deutsche Zeitung*, February 1, 1897, 1. The owner, Rudolph Wittmann, sold the house to the city in 1908.

36. "Franz Schubert und die—Polizei," *Wiener neueste Nachrichten*, January 25, 1897, 4.

37. "Die Huldigung der Sänger," *Illustrirtes Wiener Extrablatt*, February 3, 1897, 1.

38. Lueger, *Papers*, 315.

39. "Der hunderste Geburtstag Schubert's," *Wiener Tagblatt*, February 1, 1897, 3; and "Die Schubert-Feier in Wien," *Neues Wiener Tagblatt*, February 1, 1897, 1.

40. Robert Hirschfeld, "Die Schubert-Feier," *Wiener Abendpost (Beilage zur Wiener Zeitung)*, February 6, 1897, 5–6.

41. Robert Hirschfeld, "Scharfe Ecke: Meteorologische Schubert-Feier," *Neue musikalische Presse* 6, no. 5 (1897): 17. The translation attempts to retain some of the poetic end rhyme. For another, partial translation and a commentary on Hirschfeld's responses to the Schubert festival in this particular journal, see Botstein, "Music and Its Public," 1033–36.

42. "G" [Gustav Schönaich?], "Concerte," *Neue musikalische Presse* 6, no. 6 (1897): 7.

43. "Die Schubert-Feier," *Illustrirtes Wiener Extrablatt*, February 1, 1897, 2.

44. "Der hunderste Geburtstag Schubert's," *Deutsches Volksblatt* (Abend-Ausgabe), February 1, 1897, 5.

45. "–ch–," "Das 'Volkskonzert' im Rathhause," *Ostdeutsche Rundschau*, February 1, 1897, 3.

46. "Kunst und Wissenschaft," *Arbeiter-Zeitung*, February 7, 1897, 8. Only in 1908 did the creation of the Vienna Tonkünstler Orchestra finally provide support for low-priced concerts. See Botstein, "Music and Its Public," 83.

47. Wiener Stadt- und Landesbibliothek, Inv. no. C117029. From May to June 1896, the appeal was published outside of Vienna in the *Allgemeine Zeitung* (Munich), *Badischer General-Anzeiger* (Baden), *Berliner Börsen-Courier, Bohemia* (Prague), *Bürger-Zeitung* (Düsseldorf), *Deutsche Rundschau* (Berlin), *Frankfurter Journal, Frankfurter Zeitung, Fränkische Kurier* (Nuremberg), *General Anzeiger* (Nuremberg), *Harmonie* (Hannover), *Le Journal des Arts* (Paris), *Klagenfurter Zeitung, Kölnische Volkszeitung* (Cologne), *Moderne Tonkunst* (Berlin), *Mainzer Journal, Münsterischer Anzeiger,*

National-Zeitung (Basel), *Neue Berliner Musikzeitung, Neuer Tagblatt* (Stuttgart), *Oesterreichisch-Ungarische Musiker-Zeitung, Prager Tagblatt, Die Sängerhalle* (Leipzig), *Salzburger Zeitung, Schwäbischer Merkur* (Stuttgart), *Signale für die musikalische Welt* (Leipzig), *Tagblatt der Stadt Zürich, Tagesbote* (Brünn), and *Weimarische Zeitung.*

48. "Die Eröffnung der Schubert-Ausstellung," *Neue freie Presse* (Abendblatt), January 20, 1897, 2.

49. Wiener Stadt- und Landesbibliothek Inv. no. A33718.

50. "Die Eröffnung der Schubert-Ausstellung," *Oesterreichische Volks-Zeitung* 43, no. 21 (January 21, 1897): 4; and "Franz Schubert," *Oesterreichische Volks-Zeitung* 43, no. 28 (January 28, 1897): 2.

51. "Franz Schubert," *Wiener allgemeine Zeitung,* January 31, 1897, 3.

52. "h. w." [J. G. von Wörz], "Schubert-Feier," *Wiener Sonn- und Montags-Zeitung* 35, no. 6 (February 8, 1897): 3.

53. "Franz Schubert," *Neues Wiener Journal,* January 21, 1897, 1.

54. "Franz Schubert," *Wiener Tagblatt,* January 21, 1897, 1.

55. Ibid., 1.

56. Judson, *Exclusive Revolutionaries,* 1–10. For the expression *deutscher Genius,* see note 59 below.

57. Guido List, "Zu Franz Schubert's hundertstem Geburtstag," *Ostdeutsche Rundschau,* January 31, 1897, 5. The poem was a *Festprolog* written for Schubert celebrations given by the Troppau Männergesangverein on January 31, by the Wiedener Sängerbund on January 30, and in Vienna by the Frauen- und Mädchenbund "Freya" on January 31, where it was spoken by Anna Wittek, an actress who married List in 1899. The poem also appeared in the *Volksblatt für Stadt und Land* 28, no. 5 (February 4, 1897): 2.

58. Brigitte Hamann, *Hitler's Vienna: A Dictator's Apprenticeship,* trans. Thomas Thornton (Oxford: Oxford University Press, 1999), 206–14, 262; and Nicholas Goodrick-Clarke, *The Cult Roots of Nazism: Secret Aryan Cults and Their Influence on Nazi Ideology* (New York: New York University Press, 1992), 36–40.

59. Wilhelm Schriefer, "Zu Schubert's hundertjährigem Geburtstag," *Deutsches Volksblatt* (Morgen-Ausgabe), January 30, 1897, 21.

60. Staubach, "Ein deutsche Liederfürst," 5. On Vergani's career, see Helmut Andics, *Luegerzeit: Das schwarze Wien bis 1918* (Vienna: Jugend und Volk, 1984), 145–47; and Boyer, *Political Radicalism,* 78, 225–26.

61. Albert Weltner, "Drei Freunde," *Deutsche Zeitung* (Morgen-Ausgabe), January 30, 1897, 1.

62. Theodor Helm, "Franz Schuberts künstlerische Bedeutung," *Deutsche Zeitung* (Morgen-Ausgabe), January 31, 1897, 1–3.

63. Otto Keller, "Prolog zur Schubert-Feier des Wiener Männergesangvereines 'Arion' am Samstag, den 6. Februar 1897," *Deutsche Kunst- und Musik-Zeitung* 24, no. 4 (February 15, 1897): 42.

64. O[scar] Merz, "Prolog zur Schubertfeier des Wiener Sängerbund," *Deutsche Kunst- und Musik-Zeitung* 24, no. 4 (February 15, 1897): 43.

65. "Franz Schubert," *Neue Musik-Zeitung* 18, no. 2 (1897): 22.

66. "Die Eröffnung der Schubert-Ausstellung," *Reichspost,* January 21, 1897, 5.

67. "Das Café Griensteidl," *Wiener neueste Nachrichten,* January 25, 1897, 4.

68. "Von unseren Literaturhebräern," *Deutsches Volksblatt,* Feburary 7, 1897, 8.

69. Gomperz, *Gelehrtenleben,* 153–54.

70. For studies in the traditions of anti-Semitic treatments of the Jewish mind, body, and voice in nineteenth-century Austro-German culture, see Sander L. Gilman, *Difference and*

Pathology: Stereotypes of Sexuality, Race, and Madness (Ithaca, NY, and London: Cornell University Press, 1985), 150–62; Sander L. Gilman, "Chicken Soup, or the Penalties for Sounding Too Jewish," in *Insiders and Outsiders: Jewish and Gentile Culture in Germany and Austria*, ed. Dagmar C. G. Lorenz and Gabriele Weinberger (Detroit: Wayne State University Press, 1994), 15–29; George L. Mosse, *Germans and Jews* (New York: Howard Fertig, 1970), 61–76; and Ritchie Robertson, *The "Jewish Question" in German Literature, 1749–1939* (Oxford: Oxford University Press, 1999), 151–232. For the musical counterpart in Strauss and Wagner, see Sander L. Gilman, *Disease and Representation: Images of Illness from Madness to AIDS* (Ithaca, NY, and London: Cornell University Press, 1988), 155–81; and Marc A. Weiner, *Richard Wagner and the Anti-Semitic Imagination* (Lincoln and London: University of Nebraska Press, 1995), 103–43, 261–306. From a musical standpoint, Wagner's essay "Judaism in Music" (1850) is doubtless the cultural touchstone for the stereotype of the Jewish voice. See *Richard Wagner's Prose Works*, trans. William Ashton Ellis, vol. 3 (1893; reprint, St. Clair Shores, MI: Scholarly Press, 1972), 84–85.

71. George E. Berkley, *Vienna and Its Jews: The Tragedy of Success* (Cambridge, MA: Abt Books, 1988), 129–130. See also Pauley, *From Prejudice*, 27–44; and Pulzer, *Rise of Political Anti-Semitism*, 127–88.

72. "An das christliche Volk in Oesterreich!" *Deutsches Volksblatt* (Morgen-Ausgabe), January 31, 1897, 1–2. Under the same title, the proclamation also appeared in *Freiheit!* February 5, 1897, 1–2, only there it shared the page with an article entitled "Judäo-socialistische Geschichtsbelehrung" and was followed on the next page by a poem by Vincenz Totzauer, "Für Freiheit und Recht," which begins: "Whether you are German or Slav, yet you remain Christian above all."

73. "Ein Gedenktag," *Deutsches Volksblatt*, January 31, 1897, 2.

74. Ibid., 2. Compare this to an excerpt from the 1912 speech by Lueger's successor, Josef Neumayer: "For the love of music is not the business of individual ethnic groups; the cultivation of music is not an objective of individual parties, it is much more a matter of heart for the entire Viennese population." Quoted in Botstein, "Music and Its Public," 81. There is more than a hint of irony in this, however, since within a month of his speech, Neumayer's party ousted him from the mayoralty because he was such an inept and factional obstructionist. See Boyer, *Culture and Political Crisis*, 267, 279.

75. Anton August Naaff, "Zur Schubert-Jahrhunderfeier," *Die Lyra* 20, no. 7 (January 1, 1897): 76. Whoever Naaff may have had in mind when he mentioned younger artists is not clear. In accordance with its conservative viewpoint, the journal had little use for modernists who "sought other models and domains, attaching themselves more to painting and the plastic-realistic." See Anton August Naaff, "Franz Schubert und seine Liederdichter," *Die Lyra* 20, no. 10 (February 15, 1897): 111. Regarding Naaff, see also his "Franz Schubert und seine Liederdichter," *Deutsches Volksblatt* (Morgen-Ausgabe), January 30, 1897, 1–3, in which he argued that only poets of German origin guided the composer's "correct path to creativity." Elsewhere, Naaff could not even bring himself to mention Schubert's Austrian homeland, instead identifying it as the "Donaulande der deutschen Ostmark." See Anton August Naaff, "Der Meister des deutschen Liedes und der Wiener Music," *Die Lyra* 20, no. 8 (January 15, 1897): 87.

76. "Die Judenfrage im niederösterreichischen Landtage," *Deutsches Volksblatt* (Morgen-Ausgabe), January 24, 1897, 2–4; and "Aussperrung und jüdischer Streik," *Reichspost*, January 23, 1897, 1–2.

77. Sandra McColl, "A Model German," *Musical Times* 138 (March 1997): 7–12; and Margaret Notley, "Brahms as Liberal: Genre, Style, and Politics in late 19th-Century Vienna," *19th-Century Music* 17, no. 2 (Fall 1993): 107–23.

78. Max Kalbeck, "Epilog zur Schubert-Feier," *Neues Wiener Tagblatt,* February 9, 1897, 1–2.

79. "Aus dem Schandtag," *Der Floh* 29, no. 4 (1897): 3. Tapping into the Viennese craze for cycling, the front page of the next issue of *Der Floh* depicted Lueger working a bicycle pump to inflate a balloon-like Strobach. "Fat Strobach" comes from a satiric poem in the same publication. See note 88 below. A particularly biting contemporary critique is "Der blechende Bürgermeister," *Wiener allgemeine Zeitung,* January 26, 1897, 1. Strobach was also ridiculed as "the straw man." See Andics, *Luegerzeit,* 229.

80. "Niederösterreichischer Landtag," *Neues Wiener Tagblatt,* January 21, 1897, 4. The proposal under consideration was called the "Christianization of the stenographic bureau."

81. "Die Eröffnung der Schubert-Ausstellung," *Neues Wiener Journal,* January 21, 1897, 4.

82. Robert Musil, "*Anschluss* with Germany," in *Precision and Soul: Essays and Addresses,* trans. and ed. Burton Pike and David S. Luft (Chicago: University of Chicago Press, 1990), 94.

83. Daniel Louis Unowsky, "The Pomp and Politics of Patriotism: Imperial Celebrations in Habsburg Austria, 1848–1916" (PhD diss., Columbia University, 2000), 335.

84. "Die Woche: Politische Notizen," *Die Zeit,* February 13, 1897, 108; and "Auf dem Balle der Stadt Wien," *Wiener Sonn- und Montags-Zeitung* 35, no. 7 (February 15, 1897): 1–2; and "Der Ball der Stadt Wien," *Arbeiter-Zeitung,* February 9, 1897, 6. The latter predictably described the event as "the alliance between anti-Semitism and feudalism."

85. "Wie die Juden mit Geld bombardirt werden," *Deutsches Volksblatt* (Abend-Ausgabe), February 10, 1897, 2; and "Ehrung für den geheimen Rath Dumba," *Neues Wiener Journal,* January 22, 1897, 7. By contrast, Dumba's act of largesse was treated sympathetically in the liberal press. See "Jüdisches von der Schubert-Ausstellung," *Die Neuzeit,* no. 7 (February 12, 1897): 66.

86. "Einige Schubert-Lieder mit modernisirten Texten (Der Gemeinderathsmajorität gewidmet.)," *Wiener Caricaturen,* no. 5 (January 31, 1897): 2.

87. "Eine Schubert-Phantasie," *Der Floh* 29, no. 6 (1897): 5. That year, hovering cherubs also made their appearance in *Schubert im Himmel,* a frequently reprinted silhouette by Otto Böhler, which he presented to the Vienna Schubertbund. An entire orchestra of putti cavorts around Schubert, who is welcomed by a queue of composers in an intriguing pecking order: Mozart, Beethoven, Mendelssohn, Haydn, Handel, Bach, Wagner, Weber, Liszt, Schumann, and finally Bruckner, who died in 1896. That year, in another silhouette by Böhler, Schubert had already joined the ranks of the composers greeting the deceased Bruckner, managing to get third in line behind Liszt and Wagner. Schubert was also on hand to greet the recently deceased Brahms in Böhler's silhouette of 1897. See Max Hayek, *Dr. Otto Böhler's Schattenbilder* (Vienna: R. Lechner, 1914), 9, 19–20; and Anton Weiß, *Fünfzig Jahre Schubertbund,* 189–90.

88. "Das 'Ständchen' im Künstlerhause," *Der Floh* 29, no. 4 (1897): 3.

Chapter Three

1. "Die Eröffnung der Schubert-Ausstellung," *Neue freie Presse* (Abendblatt), January 20, 1897, 2.

2. "Der Kaiser in der Schubert-Ausstellung," *Neues Wiener Tagblatt,* January 21, 1897, 7. More than one story circulated regarding the surprise with which the conservative

emperor greeted any novelty. He registered disbelief on seeing the electric lighting
when he visited the resort at Gastein, and he might equally have found its presence
at the exhibition to be a surprise, since as late as 1900 fewer than three per cent of
Viennese households were equipped with electricity. See Roman Sandgruber, trans.
Richard Hockaday, "The Electrical Century: The Beginnings of Electricity Supply in
Austria," in *Fin de Siècle and Its Legacy*, ed. Mikulás Teich and Roy Porter (Cambridge:
Cambridge University Press, 1990), 44–45.

3. *Schubert-Ausstellung der k. k. Reichshaupt- und Residenzstadt Wien. Aufruf*, Wiener
Stadt- und Landesbibliothek, Inv. no. C117029; and Anton August Naaff, "Die
Schubert-Jahrhundertfeier in Wien," *Die Lyra* 20, no. 11 (March 1, 1897): 122–23.

4. Ludwig Hevesi ["L. H.-i"], "Feuilleton: Aus der Schubert-Ausstellung," *Fremden-Blatt*
(Morgen-Blatt), January 24, 1897, 13–14; and Max Kalbeck, *Johannes Brahms*, vol. 4, part
2 (Berlin: Deutsches Brahms-Gesellschaft m. b. H., 1914), 495. For other reports of
the exhibition, see "Schubert-Ausstellung," *Deutsche Zeitung* (Morgen-Ausgabe),
February 9, 1897, 6; "Theater, Kunst und Literatur," *Neues Wiener Tagblatt*, January
24, 1897, 8; and "Schubert-Ausstellung," *Wiener Tagblatt*, February 28, 1897, 4.
Brahms's urging came on January 22, although it is not clear whether the composer
was too sick to go himself and instead wished to receive a report, which Kalbeck duti-
fully gave the following day. At a soirée on New Year's Eve, the composer's pallor
already betrayed unmistakable signs of liver disease. See Albert Gutmann, *Aus dem
Wiener Musikleben: Künstler-Erinnerungen, 1873–1908*, vol. 1 (Vienna: Verlag der k. u.
k. Hofmusikalienhandlung Albert J. Gutmann, 1914), 36. Earlier that week, the ail-
ing Brahms sat through Edvard Grieg's December concert, "a thing he never does in
these later years." See David Monrad-Johansen, *Edvard Grieg*, trans. Madge Robertson
(Princeton, NJ: Princeton University Press, 1938), 364. Both Brahms and Kalbeck
had loaned manuscripts to the exhibition.

5. Robert Hirschfeld, "Die Schubert-Feier," *Wiener Abendpost (Beilage zur Wiener Zeitung)*,
February 6, 1897, 5–6. See also "Schubert-Feier," *Wiener Zeitung*, January 22, 1897, 7.
For the German readership of the Stuttgart weekly magazine *Über Land und Meer*,
Hirschfeld ascribed the relative success of the exhibition to the Viennese love for
visual display while taking a swipe at the festival performances: "The Schubert exhibi-
tion in the Künstlerhaus was thoroughly silent and pleasurable, the glittering focus
of the noisy, but not equally brilliant Schubert festival in Vienna. There we saw
Schubert in the light of his contemporaries; in the Schubert concerts we heard
Schubert in the twilight of a century, which in the end did not once have a single
young powerful Schubert singer more to spare." See Robert Hirschfeld, "Die Franz
Schubert-Ausstellung in Wien," *Über Land und Meer* 39 (1897): 407.

6. "Schubert-Feier im Volksbildungsverein," *Arbeiter-Zeitung*, January 22, 1897, 4.

7. Heinrich Schenker, "Ein Epilog zur Schubertfeier," *Neue Revue* 8, no. 1 (February,
1897): 211; reprinted in *Heinrich Schenker als Essayist und Kritiker: Gesammelte Aufsatze,
Rezensionen und kleiner Berichte aus den Jahren 1891–1901*, ed. Hellmut Federhofer
(Hildesheim, Germany: Georg Olms, 1990), 209. In addition to writing for the *Neue
Revue*, Schenker was a regular contributor to *Die Zeit*, where Hermann Bahr served as
editor and chief theater critic.

8. "Vorträge des Wiener Volksbildungsvereins," *Oesterreichische Volks-Zeitung*, January
30, 1897, 9. Schenker illustrated the composer's creative periods with examples
from songs and piano works. See W. F., "Schubertfeier," *Neue Zeitschrift für Musik* 93,
no. 13 (1897): 152.

9. Friedrich von Boetticher, *Malerwerke des neunzehnten Jahrhunderts*, vol. 1, pt. 1
(1891; reprint, Leipzig: H. Schmidt & C. Günther, 1948), 387.

10. Historisches Museum der Stadt Wien, Inv. no. 13919. See the report in "Die Schubert-Ausstellung," *Illustrirtes Wiener Extrablatt,* January 13, 1897, 4. On Geiger, see Erwin Fröhlich, "Der Historienmaler Karl Josef Geiger," unpublished manuscript, Handschriftsammlung, Österreichische Nationalbibliothek, Vienna, 1965; Werner Kitlitschka, *Die Malerei der Wiener Ringstrasse* (Wiesbaden: Franz Steiner Verlag, 1981), 24-31; and Hermann Julius Meyer, *Meyers Konversations-Lexikon,* 4th ed., vol. 7 (Leipzig: Bibliographisches Institut, 1888), 22.

11. Richard Batka, "Allerlei von Franz Schubert," *Kunstwart* 11, no. 24 (September 1898): 366. For contemporary reproductions, see Richard Heuberger, *Franz Schubert* (Berlin: "Harmonie," Verlagsgesellschaft für Literatur und Kunst, 1902); Joseph August Lux, *Grillparzers Liebesroman: Die Schwestern Fröhlich: Roman aus Wiens klassischer Zeit* (Berlin: R. Bong, 1912); and *Musica,* no. 45 (1897): 89. For a color reproduction, see Ernst Hilmar, *Schubert* (Graz: Akademische Druck- u. Verlaganstalt., 1989), 193. Deutsch, *Franz Schubert: Sein Leben in Bildern,* 114, shows it hung in a room dedicated to Schubert in the Rathaus from March 20, 1902, to early 1912. Another version of the painting came into the possession of the Wiener Männergesang-Verein as a gift from Dumba's widow. According to Heinrich Fuchs, *Die österreichischen Maler des 19. Jahrhunderts,* vol. 4 (Vienna: Dr. Heinrich Fuchs Selbstverlag, 1974), 22, Schmid's painting was awarded a gold medal in Berlin in 1894. This may be a misprint, as none of the newspaper reports of 1897 suggest that it was painted earlier, and the *Österreichisches Biographisches Lexikon, 1815-1950,* vol. 10 (Vienna: Verlag der österreichsichen Akademie der Wissenschaften, 1994), 279, gives 1897 as the date of completion. On Schmid, see Werner Kitlitschka, *Die Malerei der Wiener Ringstrasse* (Wiesbaden: Franz Steiner Verlag, 1981), 189.

12. Hirschfeld, "Die Franz Schubert-Ausstellung in Wien," 407. Hirschfeld also observed the relationship between the works of Schwind and Schmid in "Quer durch die Schubert-Ausstellung," *Neue musikalische Presse* 6, no. 5 (1897): 2-5. The setting for Schmid's painting was his own home, where Johann Strauss Jr. lived when he wrote *Die Fledermaus* (1874), according to a letter from Armgard von Bardeleben, "Schubert Sonatas," *New York Times,* section 2, January 8, 1995, 4. Bardeleben cited the testimony of Schmid's daughter. If this detail is true, it is a further suggestion that Schmid may have been aware of Bayros's painting, whose interior depicts Strauss's palatial residence at no. 4 Igelgasse. For a reproduction, see *Traum und Wirklichkeit: Wien 1870-1930* (Vienna: Eigenverlag der Museen der Stadt Wien, 1985), 79. One fin-de-siècle report identified the locale of Schmid's painting as Franz von Bruchmann's house at no. 21 Weihburggasse, where several *Schubertiaden* took place. See Richard Heuberger, "Schubert-Ausstellung," *Wiener Tagblatt,* January 22, 1897, 1-2. For a recent comparison of the works of Schwind and Schmid, see Christopher H. Gibbs, *The Life of Schubert* (Cambridge: Cambridge University Press, 2000), 17-20.

13. Hevesi, "Feuilleton," 13. For typical responses from the press, in addition to Heuberger, see Otto von Kapff, "Die Schubert-Ausstellung," *Deutsche Kunst- und Musik-Zeitung* 24, no. 4 (February 15, 1897): 44-45; Carl Schreder, "Die Schubert-Ausstellung in Künstlerhause," *Deutsches Volksblatt* (Morgen-Ausgabe), January 31, 1897, 24; "sch" [Ludwig Basch], "Die Schubert-Ausstellung," *Illustrirtes Wiener Extrablatt* January 20, 1897, 4-5; "Die Schubert-Ausstellung," *Neue freie Presse* (Morgenblatt), January 20, 1897, 35; "Franz Schubert und seine Zeit im Bilde," *Neues Wiener Journal,* January 20, 1897, 3-4; and "Freidank," "Die Schubert-Ausstellung," *Die vornehme Welt* 1, no. 4 (January 28, 1897): 69-70.

14. A complete inventory of the exhibition was published as the catalogue, *Schubert-Ausstellung der Stadt Wien* (Vienna: Künstlerhaus, 1897).

15. Vicenz Chiavacci, "Der Schwan von Wien," *Wiener Bilder* 2, no. 5 (January 31, 1897): 2. A more extensive description of the residence is given by Ludwig Hevesi, "Das Heim eines Wiener Kunstfreundes (Nikolaus Dumba)," *Kunst und Kunsthandwerk* 2 (1899): 341–65. On Dumba's career as a collector of Schubertiana, see Brown, *Essays on Schubert*, 184–87.

16. Hevesi, "Das Heim," 345, provides a photograph of the music room in a view that only shows Klimt's *Music II* over one door. For literature on the work's exhibitions and sketches, and a black-and-white reproduction showing the frame, see Fritz Novotny and Johannes Dobai, *Gustav Klimt*, trans. Karen Olga Philippson (Boston: New York Graphic Society, 1975), 310. Although the painting was destroyed in 1945 during a fire at the Schloss Immendorf, quality color processing permitted its wide distribution. Color reproductions can be found in Gottfried Fliedl, *Gustav Klimt, 1862–1918: The World in Female Form*, trans. Hugh Beyer (Cologne: Benedikt Taschen, 1991), 47; Werner Hofmann, *Gustav Klimt*, trans. Inge Goodwin (Greenwich, CT: New York Graphic Society, 1971), plate 2; and Christian M. Nebehay, *Gustav Klimt: From Drawing to Painting*, trans. Renée Nebehay-King (New York: Harry N. Abrams, 1994), 47. For a description of the reproduction process employed by the Munich firm of Hanfstaengl, see Günter Metken, "Schubert am Klavier (Gustav Klimt pinx.)," *Merkur* 41, no. 4 (1987): 349–54.

17. Three letters from Klimt to Dumba are reprinted in Christian M. Nebehay, *Gustav Klimt Dokumentation* (Vienna: Nebehay, 1969), 177–78. The original correspondence is in the Handschriftsammlung of the Wiener Stadt- und Landesbibliothek, Inv. no. 54768. For descriptions of the music room, see Hevesi, "Das Heim," 350–52; and Nebehay, *Gustav Klimt: From Drawing to Painting*, 45–46. According to one recent source, Klimt took part in a competition to produce a painting for the centennial exhibition. There are no references to this, however, either in reports at that time or in the scholarship on Klimt. See Dürhammer and Waidelich, *Schubert 200 Jahre*, 206.

18. "Die Schubert-Feier," *Wiener Sonn- und Montags-Zeitung* 35, no. 4 (February 1, 1897): 5. At this time, Klimt's studio was located on the Josefstädterstrasse. The obvious way to reach Dumba's residence would have been to travel along the southern portion of the Ring, one block north of the Künstlerhaus. If, however, Klimt's journey took him to the Secession building, he might as easily have found himself passing along the Friedrichstrasse in front of the entrance to the Künstlerhaus.

19. Nebehay, *Dokumentation*, 177–78.

20. Bertha Zuckerkandl, *My Life and History*, trans. John Sommerfield (New York: Knopf, 1939), 180–81.

21. Ibid., 178.

22. Hermann Bahr, *Secession*, 2nd ed. (Vienna: Wiener Verlag, 1900), 76–77. Bahr's comparison originally appeared under the title "Klimt, Engelhart, Moll" in 1899.

23. Ludwig Boltzmann, "A German Professor's Trip to El Dorado," *Physics Today*, January 1992, 44–51.

24. *Wittgenstein Familienbriefe*, ed. Brian McGuinness, Maria Concetta Ascher, and Otto Pfersmann (Vienna: Verlag Hölder-Pichler-Tempsky, 1996), 44.

25. Ludwig Wittgenstein, *Philosophical Investigations*, 3rd ed., trans. G. E. M. Anscombe (New York: Macmillan, 1958), 215. See also Gary Hagberg, *Art as Language: Wittgenstein, Meaning, and Aesthetic Theory* (Ithaca, NY: Cornell University Press, 1995), 67–70; and Garth Hallett, *A Companion to Wittgenstein's "Philosophical Investigations"* (Ithaca, NY: Cornell University Press, 1977), 705. On Wittgenstein's affection for Schubert's music, see William M. Johnston, *The Austrian Mind: An*

Intellectual and Social History, 1848–1938 (Berkeley and Los Angeles: University of California Press, 1972), 20; P. B. Lewis, "Wittgenstein on Words and Music," *British Journal of Aesthetics* 17, no. 2 (Spring 1973): 111–21; Brian McGuinness, *Wittgenstein: A Life* (Berkeley and Los Angeles: University of California Press, 1988), 18, 123–24, 142, 181, 198; and Rush Rhees, ed. *Recollections of Wittgenstein* (Oxford: Oxford University Press, 1984), 48, 112.

26. See "Der Ball der Stadt Wien," *Deutsche Zeitung* (Morgen-Ausgabe) February 9, 1897, 4. See also "Ball der Stadt Wien," *Das Vaterland* (Morgenblatt), February 9, 1897, 5. Of the contributors, Alfred Roller (*Morgengruss*) is the only artist who attained a stature equal to that of Klimt. The others were Eduard Veith (*Der Wanderer*), Hugo Charlemont (*Frühlingsglaube*), Eduard Zetsche (*Wohin?* and *Die Post*), Heinrich Lefler (*Heidenröslein*), Hugo Darnaut (*Der Lindenbaum*), Angelo Trentin (*Gretchen am Spinnrade*), Karl Maria Schuster (*Der Fischer*), and Carl Friedrich Gsur (*Ständchen*). Moser's work is reproduced in Waissenberger, *Vienna, 1890–1920*, 124. At some point in his long career, Schuster (1871–1953) apparently created a work in which "a young woman devoutly plays music by Schubert on the parlor piano; in the background hangs a portrait of the composer." See *Ausstellungskatalog: Franz Schubert* (Vienna: Heimatmuseum Alsergrund) 38, no. 146 (March 1997): 11.

27. "Gustav Klimt," *Ver Sacrum* 1, no. 3 (March 1898): 1.

28. Novotny and Dobai, *Gustav Klimt*, plate 6. On the dating of the sketch, see note 32.

29. For a more benign interpretation, see Schorske, *Fin-de-Siècle Vienna*, 221, who calls it "a lovely dream . . . of an innocent, comforting art that served a comfortable society . . . a Biedermeier Paradise Lost." See also David Greene, *Mahler, Consciousness and Temporality* (New York: Gordon and Breach, 1984), 125–26. Greene finds it to be a "scene suffused with a nostalgia that presumably could not have characterized the time depicted." In contrast to Schorske, Novotny rates the painting as more important than the companion *Music II*. His stylistic analysis emphasizes the work's "juxtaposition of naturalism and stylization." Novotny and Dobai, *Gustav Klimt*, 11–16. See also Fritz Novotny, "Zu Gustav Klimts 'Schubert am Klavier,'" *Mitteilungen der Österreichische Galerie* 7, no. 51 (1963): 90–101.

30. Its title is given as *Scharade der Schubertfreunde in Atzenbrugg, "Vertreibung aus dem Paradies"* in Rupert Feuchtmüller, *Leopold Kupelwieser und die Kunst der Österreichischen Spätromantik* (Vienna: Osterr. Bundesverl., 1970), 174. See also Deutsch, *Franz Schubert: Sein Leben in Bildern*, 3–4. Novotny, "Zu Gustav Klimts 'Schubert am Klavier,'" 101, indicates that it hung in Dumba's music salon along with Klimt's painting, although the photograph in Hevesi's article of 1899 does not show it.

31. Ludwig Hevesi, *Oesterreichische Kunst im 19. Jahrhundert* (Leipzig: E. A. Seemann, 1903), 58. Kupelwieser's detail of Schubert, cropped at the chest, appeared in "Franz Schubert," *Deutsche Kunst- und Musik-Zeitung* 24, no. 3 (February 1, 1897): 29. Alois Trost, "Franz Schubert's Bildnisse," *Berichte und Mittheilungen des Alterthums-Vereines zu Wien* 33, no. 2 (1898): 85–95, reproduces both works, along with a key to the identities of Schwind's figures. This key is also given in the *Neue musikalische Presse* 6, no. 5 (1897): 3; and in Deutsch, *Franz Schubert: Sein Leben in Bildern*, 38. Schwind began an oil painting based on the drawing, but it remained unfinished. For its history, see Brown, *Essays on Schubert*, 155–69. This incomplete version appeared in the Schubert-Ausstellung catalogue of 1897. Trost concluded that Schwind was unaware of Kupelwieser's work, since Schwind's letter to the Männergesang-Verein of October 23, 1865, in connection with the planned monument, makes no mention of it.

32. For reproductions of the sketches, see Novotny and Dobai, *Gustav Klimt*, 310; Emil Pirchan, *Gustav Klimt* (Vienna: Bergland, 1956), ill. 44; and Alice Strobl, *Gustav Klimt: Die Zeichnungen, 1878–1903* (Salzburg: Verlag Galerie Welz, 1980), 101–9. Strobl has theorized that the earliest sketches may date from ca. 1894, and she cites a document of December 21, 1893, in which Klimt stated: "At present I am working . . . on the decoration of a music salon." The dating of the oil sketch, sometimes called the first version of *Schubert at the Piano*, is very difficult to determine. Strobl suggested a date as early as 1896 based on the stylistic similarities between the figures in the sketch and those in two other Klimt paintings of 1895: *Music I* and *Love*. This theory is in contrast to the idea that the fairly advanced stage of composition in the oil sketch would place it closer to 1898, as indicated in Novotny and Dobai, *Gustav Klimt*, 309. On the sketches, see also Toni Stooss and Christoph Doswald, eds., *Gustav Klimt* (Stuttgart: G. Hatje, 1992), 110; and Colin B. Bailey, ed., *Gustav Klimt: Modernism in the Making* (New York: Harry Abrams, 2001), 168–69. On February 6, 2001, and February 21, 2002, Sotheby's auctioned sketches of a man seated at a piano and a woman singing.

33. For other sketches of Schubert and Vogl, see Deutsch, *Franz Schubert: Sein Leben in Bildern*, 37, 247. A pencil drawing of Vogl by Kupelwieser from about 1821 vaguely resembles the man in Klimt's painting, but it is doubtful that Klimt knew it, since it was in the possession of the artist's family.

34. Hevesi, *Acht Jahre Sezession*, 147–48; and Arthur Roessler, *In Memoriam Gustav Klimt* (Vienna: Officina Vindobonensis, 1926), 9–10. See also Nebehay, *Dokumentation*, 178, 203.

35. Nebehay, *Gustav Klimt: From Drawing to Painting*, 264; Christian M. Nebehay, "Gustav Klimt schreibt an eine Liebe," *Mitteilungen der Österreichischen Galerie* 22/23, nos. 66/67 (1978/79): 102–18; and Susanna Partsch, *Gustav Klimt: Painter of Women*, trans. Michael Robertson (Munich and New York: Prestel, 1994), 58.

36. Klimt never denied his offspring. In a letter to Mizzi, he appended congratulations to his son: "Now you are already one year old so that you can now be called a little man who can be expected to walk by himself, who is able or learns to say Mama and Papa." Nebehay, "Gustav Klimt schreibt an eine Liebe," 106. Another model, Maria Ucicky, also had a son by Klimt at this time. An oil sketch of an unnamed woman dating from 1898/99, and similar to the left-hand figure in the painting, was in the possession of Ucicky's son Gustav, who became a well-known film director. The year of his birth is variously given as 1898 and 1899. See Wolfgang G. Fischer, *Gustav Klimt and Emilie Flöge: An Artist and His Muse*, trans. Michael Robinson (Woodstock, NY: Overlook Press, 1992), 112; and Partsch, *Gustav Klimt*, 58.

37. Kreissle, *Franz Schubert* (1865): 135.

38. "Erläuterung zu [Catalogue] Nr. 1," in *Schubert-Ausstellung*, fig. 11. Schmid's sketches for four of the figures (Franz von Bruchmann, Johann Mayrhofer, Moritz von Schwind, and Johann Michael Vogl) are reproduced in Erich Wolfgang Partsch and Oskar Pausch, eds., *Der vergessene Schubert: Franz Schubert auf der Bühne* (Vienna: Böhlau Verlag, 1997), 167. Schmid appears to have used a single model, placing him in different positions, before giving each figure its own unique features. When the sketches are compared to the painting, it is obvious that the head of Bruchmann was changed to that of Schubert. Another sketch of two figures is reproduced in Dürhammer and Waidelich, *Schubert 200 Jahre*, 209. Here, Schmid has clarified Schubert's likeness by adding spectacles.

39. For reproductions of the three works, see Nebehay, *Gustav Klimt: From Drawing to Painting*, 27; Partsch, *Gustav Klimt*, 33; and Leon Botstein and Linda Weintraub, eds.,

Pre-modern Art of Vienna: 1848–1898 (Annandale-on-Hudson, NY: Edith C. Blum Art Institute, 1987), 136. Both Nebehay and Partsch date the first portrait from 1891, and the former gives her age as eighteen. Emilie Flöge was born in 1874. Klimt's most famous painting of her, done in 1902, is in the Wien Museum, Karlsplatz. The classical association of oleander with fertility may have relevance to these works.

40. Fischer, *Gustav Klimt and Emilie Flöge*, 128; and Nebehay, *Gustav Klimt: From Drawing to Painting*, 241.

41. To my knowledge the only writer to suggest a kinship between the Flöge sisters and the figures in Klimt's painting was Novotny, "Zu Gustav Klimts 'Schubert am Klavier,'" 101. Novotny noted that the right-hand figure might have been a portrayal of Emilie in the tradition of Klimt's drawings and the oil painting of her from 1902: "However an explicit likeness was surely not intended; the faces of the girls rather recall mutually analogous 'pictorial types' perhaps alluding to the Flöge sisters."

42. The key passage is variously translated in Fischer, *Gustav Klimt and Emilie Flöge*, 127; Nebehay, *Gustav Klimt: From Drawing to Painting*, 247; and Partsch, *Gustav Klimt*, 14. For the original, see Hans Tietze, "Gustav Klimts Persönlichkeit: Nach Mitteilung seiner Freunde," *Die bildenden Künste* 2 (1919): 1–14. This was also apparently the first suggestion that the relationship remained platonic.

43. Alma Mahler-Werfel, *Diaries 1898–1902*, trans. Anthony Beaumont (Ithaca, NY: Cornell University Press, 1999), 5.

44. Ibid., 21–22.

45. Gustav Nottebohm, *Briefe an Robert Volkmann*, ed. Hans Clauss (Lüdenscheid, Germany: Rudolf Beucker, 1967), 27.

46. Kreissle, *Life of Franz Schubert*, 2:143.

47. Mahler-Werfel, *Diaries*, 95.

48. Ibid., 104.

49. Ibid., 105.

50. Ibid., 143. After hearing *Winterreise* the previous year, Alma wrote in her diary that she preferred Schumann. As to Alma's appreciation and understanding of art, she admitted that she did not comprehend Klimt's sketch for *Music II*, the companion work to *Schubert at the Piano*, when it was reproduced in the third volume of the journal *Ver Sacrum*. See Mahler-Werfel, *Diaries*, 12, 14.

51. Ibid., 125.

52. Kreissle, *Life of Franz Schubert*, 2:143.

53. Susanne Keegan, *The Bride of the Wind: The Life and Times of Alma Mahler-Werfel* (New York: Viking, 1992), 49. The letter surfaced at an auction in 1981. For excerpts and a facsimile of the first page, see Christian M. Nebehay, *Gustav Klimt: Das Skizzenbuch aus dem Besitz von Sonja Krips* (Vienna: Tusch, 1987), 30–31. For an alternative translation, see Henry-Louis de La Grange, *Gustav Mahler*, vol. 2 (Oxford and New York: Oxford University Press, 1995), 695–97.

54. Ibid., 2:696.

55. Mahler-Werfel, *Diaries*, 136. Alma's version of events more than half a century later was considerably more sympathetic. See Alma Mahler, *And the Bridge Is Love* (New York: Harcourt, Brace, 1958), 13.

56. Social position may not have been the only determining factor in Klimt's liaisons. Salomon Grimberg, "Adele," *Art and Antiques*, Summer, 1986, 70–75, describes an affair between Klimt and Adele Bloch-Bauer, whose husband commissioned two portraits of her from the artist. In the absence of any other references, this suggestion is difficult to assess. On April 1, 1913, Robert Musil recorded in his diary that a model named Jella told his wife that Klimt was one of her "two official

lovers," the other being a lieutenant who got her pregnant. Nonetheless, Klimt paid for the subsequent abortion. See Robert Musil, *Diaries, 1889–1942*, trans. Philip Payne, ed. Adolf Frisé and Mark Mirsky (New York: Basic Books, 1998), 148.

57. For reproductions of the two works, see Fliedl, *Gustav Klimt*, 216; and Erwin Mitsch, *The Art of Egon Schiele* (New York: Hudson Hills Press, 1988), 167. Portraits of Arnold Schoenberg and Anton von Webern aside, music played no role in Schiele's art, even though his wife was an accomplished pianist and his guardian Leopold Czihaczek had a deep love of music. There does not appear to be any relationship between Schiele's great *Tod und das Mädchen* and Schubert's work of that title, since Schiele himself called it by three different names in his correspondence. Manfred Wagner has asserted that Schiele's "self certainly also afforded a kind of protection to an artist who, if his own statements are to be believed, saw himself as the spiritual successor to Franz Schubert." Wagner does not give any documentary evidence, however, and no published source indicates that Schiele ever mentioned Schubert. See Manfred Wagner, "Egon Schiele as Representative of an Alternative Aestheticism," in *Egon Schiele: Art, Sexuality, and Viennese Modernism*, ed. Patrick Werkner (Palo Alto, CA: Society for the Promotion of Science and Scholarship, 1994), 86.

58. For the dating of the sketch, see Otto Breicha, ed., *Gustav Klimt: Die Goldene Pforte* (Salzburg: Verlag Galerie Welz, 1978), 38.

59. Anton Lindner, "Schubert im Bilde," *Bühne und Welt* 9, no. 18 (June 1907): 235.

60. Karl Kraus, "Die Kenner.—Tina Blau.—Herr Klimt und das revolutionierte Kunstempfinden des Herrn von Dumba," *Die Fackel*, no. 1 (April 1899): 28. Khnopff's work was displayed prominently at the first Secession exhibition in March 1898. *Ver Sacrum* devoted its December issue to the artist. Kraus's readers would surely have recalled that the high point of Makart's fame came in 1879 with his designs for the public procession commemorating the silver anniversary of the imperial couple.

61. Bahr, *Secession*, 122.

62. Ibid., 124.

63. An elite Jesuit boarding school founded in 1856 was located in the municipality of Kalksburg, south of the Vienna Woods. At the turn of the century, its most famous pupil would have been the boy who became Karl I, the last emperor of Austria-Hungary.

64. Kraus, "Die Kenner," 28. Kraus's lifelong enmity toward Bahr is detailed in Donald Daviau, *Understanding Hermann Bahr* (St. Ingbert, Germany: Röhrig Universitätsverlag, 2002), 315–39. See also Edward Timms, *Karl Kraus, Apocalyptic Satirist: The Post-war Crisis and the Rise of the Swastika* (New Haven, CT, and London: Yale University Press, 2005), 38, 276–77. Bahr's advocacy of Secession artists like Klimt was well known and thus they made a tempting target for Kraus, who was contemptuous of all of Bahr's work. Bahr would later claim that he had a study for *Schubert at the Piano* hanging on his wall. See Hermann Bahr, *Gustav Klimt, 50 Handzeichnungen* (Leipzig: Thyrsos-Verlag, 1922), preface; and Nebehay, *Gustav Klimt: From Drawing to Painting*, 92.

65. Peter Altenberg, "Gustav Klimt," *Kunst: Monatsschrift für Kunst und alles andere*, no. 3 (December 1903): 7.

Chapter Four

1. Wunberg, *Junge Wien*, 1:366. Four years later, Bahr rejected the application of the expression "deutsch-österreichisch" to literature, suggesting instead that Austrian writers had the capacity for an egalitarian approach to outside influence, whether it

came from France or Germany. See Hermann Bahr, "Oesterreichisch," *Die Zeit* 12 (July 24, 1897): 59–60, quoted in Wunberg, *Junge Wien*, 2:762. Bahr's significance in articulating a uniquely Austrian form of modernity is advocated by Daviau, *Understanding Hermann Bahr*, 469–83. As much as any contemporary critic, Karl Kraus was responsible for making Jung-Wien a familiar term when, with withering contempt for his subject, he wrote "Die demolirte Literatur" for the *Wiener Rundschau*. "Die demolirte Literatur" was the title of a multipart article inspired by the tearing down of the Café Griensteidl, at which many writers congregated. See Karl Kraus, "Die Einakter," *Die Fackel*, no. 1 (April 1899): 24–27. Bahr's "Die Moderne" appeared in *Moderne Dichtung* 1 (January 1890): 13–15.

2. Anonymous, "Thesen zur literarischen Moderne aus der *Allgemeinen Deutschen Universitätszeitung*," quoted in Gotthart Wunberg, ed., *Die literarische Moderne: Dokumente zum Selbstverständnis der Literatur um die Jahrhundertwende* (Frankfurt am Main: Athenäum, 1971), 1–2; and Hermann Broch, *Hugo von Hofmannsthal and His Time*, trans. and ed. Michael P. Steinberg (Chicago: University of Chicago Press, 1984), 61.

3. Bahr, "Die Moderne" (1890), quoted in Wunberg, *Wiener Moderne*, 189.

4. Otto Stößl, "Die Erneuerung des Mythos," *Die Wage* 4, no. 34 (August 19, 1901): 541, quoted in Wunberg, *Junge Wien*, 2:1163.

5. Rudolf Lothar, "Wien," *Das litterarische Echo* 4, no. 8 (January 1902): 513–15, quoted in Wunberg, *Junge Wien*, 2:1175–77.

6. Rudolf Lothar, "Vom Burgtheater," *Die Wage* 1, no. 49 (December 1898): 814, quoted in Wunberg, *Junge Wien*, 2:919.

7. Quoted in *The German Mind of the Nineteenth Century: A Literary and Historical Anthology*, trans. David Jacobson, ed. Hermann Glaser (New York: Continuum, 1981), 45. The most blatant expression of this type of relationship known to this author is that of a certain Viennese "Dr. Kr. L." as reported by Robert Musil: "You know what I mean, one may well get along very well if one meets for a f . . . once or twice a week. But when one is together day and night things may be different." See Musil, *Diaries*, 152.

8. "Cafe Griensteidl," *Neues Wiener Tagblatt*, January 21, 1897, 7. See also "Die letzte Nacht im Café Griensteidl," *Illustrirtes Wiener Extrablatt* 26, no. 25 (January 25, 1897): 1.

9. Marc A. Weiner, *Arthur Schnitzler and the Crisis of Musical Culture* (Heidelberg: C. Winter, 1986), 50–54, 58–60.

10. Arthur Schnitzler, *Die dramatischen Werke*, vol. 1 (Frankfurt am Main: S. Fischer, 1962), 226–27.

11. Ibid., 1:250.

12. Martin Swales, *Arthur Schnitzler: A Critical Study* (Oxford: Clarendon Press, 1971), 192.

13. Schnitzler, *Die dramatischen Werke*, 1:262.

14. Hevesi, *Oesterreichische Kunst*, 58. Following Kreissle, Hevesi thought Dialer's bust had been begun by a certain Arnold based upon a drawing of Franz von Schober and assisted by the architect Ludwig Förster. Consequently, it was an instance of "too many cooks." For an accurate account, see Badura-Skoda, "Authentische Porträt-Plastik," 578–95. One cannot help but observe a similarity in Hofmannsthal's description of Empress Maria Theresa: "Here is the most complete roundness and no contour at all." Hugo von Hofmannsthal, *Gesammelte Werke in Einzelausgaben: Prosa III*, ed. Herbert Steiner (Frankfurt am Main: S. Fischer, 1952), 388.

15. Arthur Schnitzler, *Die erzählenden Schriften*, vol. 1 (Frankfurt am Main: S. Fischer, 1961), 320.

16. Ibid., 1:321.

17. Ibid., 1:334–35. The ellipses are Schnitzler's own.

18. On Schnitzler's knowledge of medicine and its relationship to his writings, see Hillary Hope Herzog, " 'Medezin ist eine Weltanschauung': On Schnitzler's Medical Writings," in *A Companion to the Works of Arthur Schnitzler*, ed. Dagmar C. G. Lorenz (Rochester, NY: Camden House, 2003), 227–41; and Bernd Urban, "Schnitzler and Freud as Doubles: Poetic Intuition and Early Research on Hysteria," trans. John Menzies and Peter Nutting, *Psychoanalytic Review* 65, no. 1 (Spring 1978): 131–65. On Schnitzler's relationship with his mistresses, see Gay, *Schnitzler's Century*, 69–75. In the literature on Schnitzler, *Die Nächste* has received little commentary. See Achim Aurnhammer, "Schnitzlers 'Die Nächste [1899]': Intertexualität und Psychologisierung des Erzählens im Jungen Wien," *Germanisch-romanische Monatsschrift* 44, no. 1 (1994): 37–51; and Richard H. Lawson, "Thematic Reflections of the 'Song of Love and Play of Death' in Schnitzler's Fiction," in *Arthur Schnitzler and His Age: Intellectual and Artistic Currents*, ed. Petrus W. Tax and Richard H. Lawson (Bonn: Bouvier, 1984), 70–89.

19. Weiner, *Arthur Schnitzler*, 18, 32. Interestingly, however, Schnitzler's support appears to have waned after World War I as his wife attempted to extend her public performances. Her failure to do so coincidentally echoes the fate of Schnitzler's women a decade earlier. See Jean H. Leventhal, *Echoes in the Text: Musical Citation in German Narratives from Theodor Fontane to Martin Walser* (New York: Peter Lang, 1995), 68–69.

20. "Hans von Bülow über Tonkünstler und Tonwerke," *Neue Musik-Zeitung* 18, no. 3 (1897): 35. The citation is from the second volume of Bülow's *Briefe und Schriften*, which coincidentally appeared in the same year as Schnitzler's *Liebelei*.

21. The sexual violence of Wedekind's play delayed its appearance until, with the aid of Karl Kraus, it was given a private performance in Vienna on May 29, 1905, at which Wedekind acted the role of Jack. In the audience was Alban Berg who later used it as the basis for his opera *Lulu*. On prostitution in Vienna, see Anderson, *Utopian Feminism*, 70–71; and Gilman, *Difference and Pathology*, 42–44. The so-called *Lustmord* has been examined as a phenomenon in Weimar Germany because of its appearance in the art of George Grosz and Otto Dix as well as Wedekind. See Beth Irwin Lewis, " 'Lustmord': Inside the Windows of the Metropolis," in *Women in the Metropolis: Gender and Modernity in Weimar Culture*, ed. Katharina von Ankum (Berkeley and Los Angeles: University of California Press, 1997), 202–32; and Maria Tatar, *Lustmord: Sexual Murder in Weimar Germany* (Princeton, NJ: Princeton University Press, 1995). Similar events were sensationalized in the Viennese press. One such example shared the headlines with newspaper reports of Schubert's centennial on January 31, 1897.

22. Schnitzler, *Die erzählenden Schriften*, 1:392. The tale first appeared in the *Neue deutsche Rundschau* (January–March 1901).

23. Schnitzler, *Die erzählenden Schriften*, 1:402. Tarock was and remains a popular card game in Austria. A fin-de-siècle silhouette by Otto Böhler depicts it being played by Brahms, Johann Strauss Jr., and Hans Richter. See William Murdoch, *Brahms* (New York: Sears Publishing Co., n.d.), facing 198.

24. Schnitzler, *Die erzählenden Schriften*, 1:399–400.

25. Ibid., 1:507–8.

26. Ibid., 1:513.

27. Arthur Schnitzler, *Tagebuch*, vol. 6 (Vienna: Verlag der Österreichischen Akademie der Wissenschaften, 1991), 68. In 1903, Schnitzler had married Olga Gussman, after she had had his child in the previous year.

28. Arthur Schnitzler, *The Letters of Arthur Schnitzler to Hermann Bahr*, ed. Donald D. Daviau (Chapel Hill: University of North Carolina Press, 1978), 114.

29. Schnitzler, *Tagebuch*, 6:236.

30. Rhees, *Recollections of Wittgenstein*, 112. See also Leventhal, *Echoes in the Text*, 62–70.

31. Leventhal, *Echoes in the Text*, 69.

32. Katherine Arens, "Schnitzler and the Discourse of Gender in *Fin-de-Siècle* Vienna," in *A Companion to the Works of Arthur Schnitzler*, ed. Dagmar C. G. Lorenz (Rochester, NY: Camden House, 2003), 243–44. For another analysis of Schnitzler's novel that discusses Berta Garlan's innocence in relation to contemporary culture, see Nancy C. Michael, *Elektra and Her Sisters: Three Female Characters in Schnitzler, Freud, and Hofmannsthal* (New York: Peter Lang, 2001), 11–34.

33. Richard Schaukal, *Mimi Lynx. Die Sängerin: Novellen (Eine Tragigroteske)*, ed. Ingo Warnke and Andreas Wicke (Siegen, Germany: Carl Böschen Verlag, 1999), 93–94.

34. Rudolf Hirsch, *Beiträge zum Verständnis Hugo von Hofmannsthals: Nachträge und Register* (Frankfurt am Main: S. Fischer, 1998), 558.

35. Ibid., 559.

36. Hugo von Hofmannsthal, *Gesammelte Werke in Einzelausgaben: Gedichte und lyrische Dramen*, ed. Herbert Steiner (Frankfurt am Main: S. Fischer, 1952), 43–44, 149. On December 23, 1892, Hofmannsthal wrote to Schnitzler about the emotional effort of reading *Anatol*: "The near overwhelming fatigue which it cost me, startled me." Hirsch, *Beiträge*, 557.

37. Hofmannsthal, *Gesammelte Werke: Gedichte*, 96.

38. Ibid., 99.

39. Ibid., 97.

40. Hofmannsthal, *Gesammelte Werke: Prosa I*, 266.

41. Carsten Strathausen, *The Look of Things: Poetry and Vision around 1900* (Chapel Hill and London: University of North Carolina Press, 2003), 163; and Andreas Thomasberger, "Hofmannsthal's Poems and Lyric Dramas," in *A Companion to the Works of Hugo von Hofmannsthal*, ed. Thomas A. Kovach (London: Camden House, 2002), 53–54.

42. Hofmannsthal, *Gesammelte Werke: Prosa I*, 149. The essay "Gabriele d'Annunzio" first appeared in the *Frankfurter Zeitung*.

43. Hofmannsthal's "Ein Brief" is probably his most discussed early work. For a range of interpretations over the last four decades, see Donald G. Daviau, "Hugo von Hofmannsthal and the Chandos Letter," *Modern Austrian Literature* 4, no. 2 (1971): 28–44, II. A. Hammelmann, *Hugo von Hofmannsthal* (New Haven, CT: Yale University Press, 1957), 16–22; Thomas A. Kovach, "Hofmannsthal's 'Ein Brief': Chandos and His Crisis," in *A Companion to the Works of Hugo von Hofmannsthal*, ed. Thomas A. Kovach (London: Camden House, 2002), 49–56; and Klaus Weissenberg, "Hofmannsthals Entwicklung des Essays zur inneren Zwangsläfigkeit von Typologie und Form," in *Wir sind aus solchem Zeug wie das zu Träumen: Kritische Beiträge zum Werk Hugo von Hofmannsthals*, ed. Joseph P. Strelka (Bern: Peter Lang, 1992), 81–108. On the Viennese context, see Broch, *Hofmannsthal*, 121–25; Allan Janik and Stephen Toulmin, *Wittgenstein's Vienna* (New York: Touchstone, 1973), 112–17; and Le Rider, *Modernity*, 48–51. For the larger phenomenon of the crisis of language, see Hans-Joachim Hahn, "From Individual to Ideology: The Crisis of Identity at the Turn of the Century," *New German Studies* 17, no. 1 (1992/93): 1–27; and Richard Sheppard, "The Crises of Language," in *Modernism 1890–1930*, ed. Malcolm Bradbury and James McFarlane (Harmondsworth, UK: Penguin, 1976), 328.

44. Hugo von Hofmannsthal, *Selected Writings*, trans. and ed. Michael Hamburger (New York: Pantheon, 1963), xx–xxi.

45. Hermann Bahr, "Loris," *Freie Bühne für den Entwickelungskampf der Zeit* 3, no. 1 (January 1892): 94–98, quoted in Wunberg, *Junge Wien*, 1:293–98; and Le Rider, *Modernity*, 108. Although Bahr placed Hofmannsthal's age at twenty, he was actually born in 1874. Bahr also likened Hofmannsthal to the actor Josef Kainz, famous for his portrayals of young lovers like Shakespeare's Romeo. When Kainz died in 1910, Hofmannsthal wrote a poem in his memory: "How slim he stood, just like a boy!" See Hofmannsthal, *Gesammelte Werke: Gedichte*, 52.

46. Stefan Zweig, *The World of Yesterday* (Lincoln and London: University of Nebraska Press, 1964), 49–50.

47. Ibid., 57.

48. Ibid., 49, 57.

49. Quoted in Leo A. Lensing, "Peter Altenberg's Fabricated Photographs: Literature and Photography in Fin-de-Siècle Vienna," *Vienna 1900: From Altenberg to Wittgenstein*, ed. Edward Timms and Ritchie Robertson (Edinburgh: Edinburgh University Press, 1990), 53.

50. Tadeusz Rittner, *Czas*, August 9, 1902, quoted in Anna Milanowski, "Der Zeitzeuge Tadeusz Rittner und seine polnischen Feuilletons," in *Wien 1897: Kulturgeschichtliches Profil eines Epochenjahres*, ed. Christian Glanz (Frankfurt am Main: Peter Lang, 1999), 144.

51. Hugo von Hofmannsthal and Edgar Karg von Bebenburg, *Briefwechsel*, ed. Mary E. Gilbert (Frankfurt am Main: S. Fischer, 1966), 80. On the creative struggle of Hofmannsthal and Schnitzler over the social disengagement of Viennese modernism in the 1890s, see Schorske, *Fin-de-Siècle Vienna*, 8–22. In the 1899 essay, "Modern," Max Burckhard, director of the Burgtheater, injected a rare element of civic responsibility by characterizing the modern man as a revolutionary regardless of whether his field was politics, social issues, or art. See Wunberg, *Wiener Moderne*, 275.

52. For opinions about this musical allusion, see Norman Del Mar, *Richard Strauss: A Critical Commentary on His Life and Works*, vol. 2 (Ithaca, NY: Cornell University Press, 1986), 48; Karen Forsyth, *Ariadne auf Naxos by Hugo von Hofmannsthal and Richard Strauss: Its Genesis and Meaning* (Oxford: Oxford University Press, 1982), 170–71; and Bryan Gilliam, *The Life of Richard Strauss* (Cambridge: Cambridge University Press, 1999), 99.

53. Felix Salten, "Geistiges Leben in Österreich," *Über Land und Meer* 56 (1914): 232–33.

54. Richard R. Laurence, "Viennese Literary Intellectuals and the Problem of War and Peace, 1889–1914," in *Focus on Vienna 1900: Change and Continuity in Literature, Music, Art and Intellectual History*, ed. Erika Nielsen (Munich: Wilhelm Fink, 1982), 12–22. Berg's letters to Schoenberg trace his conversion from enthusiast to pessimist. See Alban Berg and Arnold Schoenberg, *The Berg-Schoenberg Correspondence*, ed. Juliane Brand, Christopher Hailey, and Donald Harris (New York: W. W. Norton & Company, 1987), 213–20. For recent studies that have considered Austrian culture and propaganda during the war years, see Steven Beller, "The Tragic Carnival: Austrian Culture in the First World War," in *European Culture in the Great War: The Arts, Entertainment, and Propaganda, 1914–1918*, ed. Aviel Roshwald and Richard Stites (Cambridge: Cambridge University Press, 1999), 127–61; Mark Cornwall, *The Undermining of Austria-Hungary: The Battle for Hearts and Minds* (London: Macmillan, 2000); and Maureen Healy, *Vienna and the Fall of the Habsburg Empire: Total War and Everyday Life in World War I* (Cambridge: Cambridge University Press, 2004).

55. Hugo von Hofmannsthal, "Wir Österreicher und Deutschland," *Reden und Aufsätze II, 1914–1924* (Frankfurt am Main: Fischer Taschenbuch Verlag, 1979), 395–96.

56. Ibid., 449.

57. Hugo von Hofmannsthal and Max Mell, *Briefwechsel* (Heidelberg: Verlag Lambert Schneider, 1982), 88; Hofmannsthal, *Selected Writings*, lxx–lxxi; and W. E. Yates, "Hofmannsthal's Comedies," in *A Companion to the Works of Hugo von Hofmannsthal*, ed. Thomas A. Kovach (London: Camden House, 2002), 151–52. In a letter to Strauss on December 22, 1927, Hofmannsthal mentioned "that magnificent *Dreimädlerhaus*," referring to the operetta that used *Schwammerl* as its literary inspiration. See Richard Strauss and Hugo von Hofmannsthal, *A Working Friendship: The Correspondence between Richard Strauss and Hugo von Hofmannsthal*, trans. Hanns Hammelmann and Ewald Osers (New York: Vienna House, 1974), 463.

58. Franz Grillparzer, *Grillparzers Werke in acht Bänden*, vol. 4 (Stuttgart: J. G. Cotta, n.d.), 87.

59. Hermann Bahr, *Tagebücher, Skizzenbücher, Notizhefte*, vol. 2, ed. Moritz Csáky, Helene Zand, Lukas Mayerhofer, and Lottelis Moser (Vienna: Böhlau Verlag, 1996), 194. Bahr followed the quotation with one from another Speidel feuilleton, "Franz Schubert in der Höldrichsmühle," which imagined the composer writing *Die schöne Müllerin* in an idealized, bucolic setting. See also Philipp Frey, "Zum Thema 'Wien-Berlin,' " *Österreichische Rundschau* 17 (October–December 1908): 305–7.

60. Artur Schnabel, *My Life and Music* (New York: St. Martin's Press, 1963), 46.

61. Artur Schnabel, "Schubert Sonatas," *New York Times*, January 4, 1942, section 9, 7. At the time, Schnabel was embarked on performing a cycle of Schubert's piano music in New York, and his comment may reflect his desire to maintain his position as the discoverer of and enduring authority on that repertoire. Adolph Lippe, "From the Mail Pouch," *New York Times*, February 1, 1942, section 9, 8, challenged Schnabel's recollection: "I spent a considerable part of my life in Schubert's home town, Vienna. I still remember the galaxy of great piano teachers at the Vienna Conservatory of that time—Anton Door [professor, 1869–1901], Julius Epstein [professor, 1867–1901], Dacks [Joseph Dachs, professor from 1861], [Hans] Schmitt [studied with Dachs, later professor],—who laid special stress on the study of Schubert's piano sonatas. Indeed, they were cultivated in every musical family and were considered as belonging to the highest in music."

62. Hermann Bahr, "Die vierte Ausstellung: Klimt, Engelhart, Andri, Fräulein Ries (März 1899)," in Bahr, *Secession*, 123. See also Daviau, *Understanding Hermann Bahr*, 155, describing the painting as "the triumph of the fourth exhibit."

63. Hofmannsthal, *Gesammelte Werke: Prosa III*, 484. Geiger's poetry had appeared in a private printing under the title *Das Fenster in der Mitternacht* (Vienna: Amalthea-Verlag, 1919).

64. Hofmannsthal, *Gesammelte Werke: Prosa III*, 512. Braun's little book is a chronological compilation of letters, recollections, and diary entries of Schubert's friends. In a brief postscript, Braun wrote that the composer's friendships constituted his one joy and that they sustained him in poverty and difficult times, a sentiment that surely resonated with Hofmannsthal during the war years. See Felix Braun, *Schubert im Freundeskreis* (Leipzig: Insel-Verlag, 1916), 86.

65. Hofmannsthal, *Gesammelte Werke: Prosa I*, 159–60.

66. Hofmannsthal, *Gesammelte Werke: Prosa III*, 283–84.

67. Hofmannsthal, *Reden und Aufsätze*, 449. Hofmannsthal was by no means unique in this regard. In the same year that his comparison of Prussians and Austrians

appeared, the Viennese cultural geographer Erwin Hanslick wrote: "The patriotism of the Austrian is rooted in his feeling for humanity." See Erwin Hanslick, *Österreich: Erde und Geist* (Vienna: Verlag Institut für Kulturforschung, 1917), 67. Of course, a non-Austrian might look at the comparison less charitably. In 1915, the writer Hans Natonek extolled the purposeful and decisive thought of Germans at the expense of the Austrians' aimless musing. He argued that Berliners "have no time to be reflective because they are thinking. . . . Reflectiveness is an Austrian sickness." See Wunberg, *Wiener Moderne*, 681.

68. Hofmannsthal and Bebenburg, *Briefwechsel*, 80.

69. C. E. Williams, *The Broken Eagle: The Politics of Austrian Literature from Empire to Anschluss* (London: Paul Elek, 1974), 1–19, 239; and Egon Schwarz, "Hugo von Hofmannsthal as Critic," in *On Four Modernists*, ed. Arthur R. Evans, Jr. (Princeton, NJ: Princeton University Press, 1970), 31–48. On the political aspects of Hofmannsthal's work, see Judith Beniston, "Hofmannsthal and the Salzburg Festival"; Katherine Arens, "Hofmannsthal's Essays: Conservation as Revolution"; and Nina Berman, "Hugo von Hofmannsthal's Political Vision"; all in *A Companion to the Works of Hugo von Hofmannsthal*, ed. Thomas A. Kovach (London: Camden House, 2002), 159–225. While the contributors to this anthology agree on the consistency of Hofmannsthal's views before and after the war, they do not all ascribe entirely benign reasons to it. Beniston, "Hofmannsthal and the Salzburg Festival," 164, suggests that the author's removal from the urban modernism of Vienna was partially motivated by an anti-Semitic attitude. For a comparison of Schnitzler and Hofmannsthal, see Schorske, *Fin-de-Siècle Vienna*, 19–22. After the war, Hofmannsthal was not alone in turning toward the Baroque era for a new model of civilization. See Daviau, *Understanding Hermann Bahr*, 353–74.

Chapter Five

1. Heinrich Friedjung, *Der Ausgleich mit Ungarn: Politische Studie über das Verhältnis Österreichs zu Ungarn und Deutschland*, 3rd ed. (Leipzig: Wigand, 1878), 30, 98–99.

2. Quoted in John C. G. Röhl, "The Emperor's New Clothes: A Character Sketch of Kaiser Wilhelm II," in *Kaiser Wilhelm II: New Interpretations*, ed. John C. G. Röhl and Nicolaus Sombart (Cambridge: Cambridge University Press, 1982), 44. When Wilhelm sent word to the Habsburgs in 1888 that he had inherited the throne, he apparently ignored Rudolf. "From the first Wilhelm had made it clear that he considered Rudolf an intellectualizing sissy who would never be able to make Austria strong." See Morton, *Nervous Splendor*, 107.

3. Ernst Troeltsch, "Der Geist der deutschen Kultur," in *Deutschland und der Weltkrieg*, ed. Otto Hintze et al. (Leipzig: B. G. Teubner, 1916), 74–77, quoted in Roderick Stackelberg and Sally A. Winkle, *The Nazi Germany Sourcebook: An Anthology of Texts* (London: Routledge, 2002), 40–41. In a similar vein in the following year, a German military newspaper carried a squib entitled "Masculine and Feminine Nations," attributed to the late Bismarck. The iron chancellor declared that, as fantastic as it might at first appear, nations exhibited the male and female traits found in nature. The Germanic peoples were composed of men whose idiosyncrasies made them ungovernable until they were united. "But if they are brought together, then they are like a torrent that irresistibly brings everything down before it." Not surprisingly, the Slavs and the Celts, the ancestors of Germany's enemies in World War I, were feminine

and passive. See "Männliche und weibliche Völker," *Im Unterstand:* 2. *Beilage zum Champagne-Kamerad Feldzeitung der 3. Armee 3* (December 9, 1917): 9. On the propagandistic use of gender at this time, see Robert L. Nelson, "German Comrades— Slavic Whores: Gender Images in the German Soldier Newspapers of the First World War," in *Home/Front: The Military, War and Gender in Twentieth-Century Germany,* ed. Karen Hagemann and Stefanie Schüler-Springorum (Oxford: Berg, 2002), 69–86.

4. Robert Müller, *Österreich und der Mensch: Eine Mystik des Donau-Alpenmenschen* (Berlin: Fischer, 1916), 33.

5. Ibid., 34. Although defeat and failure need not have attended such descriptions of the national character, one can nonetheless also locate historical assessments of Austria's feminine nature at the end of World War II: "The Austrian man is distinguished by an unheard of adaptability, the gift of resignation, and a softness that otherwise is inherent only in children and women." See Friedrich Heer, "Österreich?" *Die Furche* 26 (October 1946): 1, quoted in Siegfried Mattl, "Geschlecht und Volkscharakter," *Österreichische Zeitschrift für Geschichtswissenschaften* 7, no. 4 (1996): 499–515.

6. Müller, *Österreich und der Mensch,* 31, 62–63.

7. Franz Werfel, *Zwischen Oben und Unten: Prosa. Tagebücher. Aphorismen. Literarische Nachträge* (Munich: Langen-Müller, 1975), 208, 210; originally "Fragment gegen das Männergeschlecht," *Der Friede* 2 (December 1918): 530–32. On Werfel's antimilitarism, see Scott Spector, "Marginalizations: Politics and Culture beyond *Fin-de-Siècle Vienna,*" in *Rethinking Vienna 1900,* ed. Steven Beller (New York: Berghahn Books, 2001), 140–41. Although he does not discuss gender, Beller shrewdly observes: "There was a distinct tendency in leading Austrian circles to rely on art as compensation for a lack of political or military power." Such a recourse was itself an invitation to view the culture as feminine. See Beller, "Tragic Carnival," 131.

8. Julius Pap, "Unsere Jugend," *Neue Revue* 5, no. 10 (February 1894): 309, quoted in Wunberg, *Junge Wien,* 1:439.

9. Quoted in Franz Koch, *Geschichte deutscher Dichtung* (Hamburg: Hanseatische Verlagsanstalt, 1942), 529, 533; and Seeba, "Hofmannsthal and *Wiener Moderne,*" 38. Ottokar Stauf von der March (the pseudonym of Ottokar F. Chalupka) was the author of *Der Ritualmord, Die Neurotischen,* and *Völker-Ideale: Beiträge zur Völkerpsychologie.*

10. Wunberg, *Wiener Moderne,* 241–44; originally appearing as Ottokar Stauf von der March, "Die Neurotischen," *Die Gesellschaft* 10 (April 1894): 526–33.

11. John C. Fout, "Sexual Politics in Wilhemine Germany: The Male Gender Crisis, Moral Purity, and Homophobia," *Journal of the History of Sexuality* 2 (January 1992): 391. The classic statement on the significance of the late nineteenth-century scientific literature of sexuality is Michel Foucault, *The History of Sexuality,* trans. Robert Hurley, vol. 1 (New York: Pantheon Books, 1978), 53–73. See also Carolyn J. Dean, *Sexuality and Modern Western Culture* (New York: Twayne Publishers, 1996), 18–31; George L. Mosse, *Nationalism and Sexuality: Respectability and Abnormal Sexuality in Modern Europe* (New York: Howard Fertig, 1985), 37–47; and Jeffrey Weeks, *Sexuality and Its Discontents: Meanings, Myths, and Modern Sexualities* (London: Routledge, 1985), 64–79.

12. Edward Prime Stevenson [Xavier Mayne, pseud.], *The Intersexes: A History of Similisexualism as a Problem in Social Life* (1908; reprint, New York: Arno Press, 1975), 324. For the statistical data, see Magnus Hirschfeld, *Sexual Anomalies* (New York: Emerson Books, 1948), 226, quoted in Weeks, *Sexuality and Its Discontents,* 67. For useful studies on the development of the fin-de-siècle science of sexuality, see Vern L. Bullough, *Science in the Bedroom: A History of Sex Research* (New York: Basic Books, 1994), 34–91; David F. Greenberg, *The Construction of Homosexuality* (Chicago and London: University of Chicago Press, 1988), 397–433; and Vernon A. Rosario, ed.,

Science and Homosexualities (New York and London: Routledge, 1997), which includes essays on Hirschfeld and Karl Ulrichs. Graham Robb, *Strangers: Homosexual Love in the Nineteenth Century* (New York: Norton, 2003), makes up in liveliness what it lacks in bibliographic rigor. On Krafft-Ebing, see Harry Oosterhuis, *Stepchildren of Nature: Krafft-Ebing, Psychiatry, and the Making of Sexual Identity* (Chicago and London: University of Chicago Press, 2000).

13. Arthur Schnitzler, *Medizinische Schriften*, ed. Horst Thomé (Vienna: Paul Zsolnay, 1988), 241. On the fight against the criminalization of male same-sex desire at this time, see James Steakley, *The Homosexual Emancipation Movement in Germany* (New York: Arno Press, 1975).

14. Oskar Panizza, "Bayreuth und die Homosexualität," *Die Gesellschaft: Monatsschrift für Literatur, Kunst und Socialpolitik* 11 (1895): 88–92; and Max Nordau, *Degeneration* (New York: D. Appleton, 1895), 171–72. A particularly memorable reference to Wagner in the fin-de-siècle literature on sexuality occurs in Stevenson's "categoric personal analysis," designed to answer the question: "Am I at all an Uranian?" With regard to musical influence, the respondent is asked: "Are you particularly fond of Wagner?" See Stevenson, *Intersexes*, 633.

15. Rudolf Louis, *Die deutsche Musik der Gegenwart*, 2nd ed. (Munich: G. Müller, 1912), 159–60.

16. Ludwig Gurlitt, *Erziehung zur Mannhaftigkeit* (Berlin: Concordia deutsche Verlags-Anstalt, Hermann Ehbock, 1907), 6–7. Although the painter Schwind, Schubert's close friend, was Viennese by birth, he spent most of his career in Munich.

17. Oswald Feis, *Studien über die Genealogie und Psychologie der Musiker* (Wiesbaden: J. F. Bergmann, 1910), 49–50. Schubert's consumption of spirits had been a thorny topic of debate ever since Spaun hotly challenged Kreissle's description of the composer's love of wine. See Kreissle, *Franz Schubert* (1865): 477–79; and Deutsch, *Memoirs*, 360–61.

18. Oosterhuis, *Stepchildren of Nature*, 267. This particular case history apparently appeared in the 1891 edition of *Psychopathia Sexualis*.

19. Thomas Adam, "Heinrich Pudor—Lebensreformer, Antisemit und Verleger," in *Das bewegte Buch: Buchwesen und soziale, nationale und kulturelle Bewgungen um 1900*, ed. Mark Lehmstedt and Andreas Herzog (Wiesbaden: Harrassowitz, 1999), 183–96.

20. Richard von Krafft-Ebing, *Psychopathia Sexualis*, trans. Harry E. Wedeck (New York: G. P. Putnam's Sons, 1965), 293. The letters appeared as *Briefe Richard Wagners an eine Putzmacherin* (Vienna, 1906), and later as *Richard Wagner and the Seamstress*, trans. Sophie Prombaum, ed. Leonard Liebling (New York: F. Unger, 1941). The Viennese feuilletonist Daniel Spitzer first brought the letters to light in the *Neue freie Presse* on June 16–17, 1877, under the title "Sechzehn Briefe Richard Wagners aus den Jahren 1864–1868 sonderbaren Inhalts." A contemporary cartoon entitled "Frou-Frou Wagner" appeared in the Viennese satiric journal *Der Floh*, depicting the composer draped in velvet and silk and stabbed in the back by Spitzer with a quill pen.

21. Heinrich Pudor, "Männliches und weibliches Empfinden in der Kunst," *Politisch-anthropologische Revue* 1, no. 8 (November 1902): 641.

22. Heinrich Pudor, "Richard Wagners Bisexualität," *Geschlecht und Gesellschaft* 2, no. 3 (1907): 141.

23. Ibid., 142.

24. Ibid., 141.

25. Pudor, "Männliches und weibliches Empfinden," 647. For a similar pairing of Beethoven and Tchaikovsky, see Stevenson, *Intersexes*, 396–97. Stevenson's allusion to the debate concerning Tchaikovsky's possible suicide over a homosexual scandal is not surprising. Beethoven's "idealized homosexualism" is also in keeping with many writers, who, sympathetic to the legal and moral emancipation of homosexuality at the turn of the century, sought to enlist great men of the past in order to support the normalcy of intimate male relationships. Stevenson's argument, however, is certainly unusual: "In Beethoven's sad latest days can be traced a real passion for that unworthy nephew Carl: who, it is said, once sought to extort money from Beethoven, on threats to disclose an homosexual relationship! Beethoven's beautiful sonata, Opus 111, is often called among German and Austrian Uranians, 'The Uranian Sonata,' from some legendary 'in-reading' of the work." However, see also De Joux, *Die Enterbten*, 85: "There are two sonatas by Beethoven, of which the uranians say that they speak to them from the soul, which emits in tones their cycles, their entire, deep human misery."

26. Alban Berg, *Letters to His Wife*, trans. and ed. Bernard Grun (New York: St. Martin's Press, 1971), 27; Hans Moldenhauer and Rosaleen Moldenhauer, *Anton von Webern: A Chronicle of His Life and Work* (New York: Alfred A. Knopf, 1979), 113; and Arnold Schoenberg, *Harmonielehre*, 3rd ed. (Vienna: Universal Edition, 1922), vi.

27. Without ignoring Weininger's more baleful aspects, several studies have sought to treat his work as more than an embarrassing and one-dimensional racist and sexist harangue. See Nancy A. Harrowitz and Barbara Hyams, eds., *Jews and Gender: Responses to Otto Weininger* (Philadelphia: Temple University Press, 1995); Andrew Hewitt, *Political Inversions: Homosexuality, Fascism, and the Modernist Imaginary* (Stanford, CA: Stanford University Press, 1996); Allan Janik, *Essays on Wittgenstein and Weininger* (Amsterdam: Rodopi, 1985); David S. Luft, *Eros and Inwardness in Vienna: Weininger, Musil, Doderer* (Chicago and London: University of Chicago Press, 2003); and Chandak Sengoopta, *Otto Weininger: Sex, Science, and Self in Imperial Vienna* (Chicago: University of Chicago Press, 2000). At the same time, Weininger's attitude toward music has only rarely been touched upon in the literature. See Luft, *Eros and Inwardness*, 57.

28. Otto Weininger, *Geschlecht und Charakter*, 26th ed. (Vienna and Leipzig: Wilhelm Braumüller, 1925), 146–47.

29. Ibid., 137. On Weininger and genius, see Luft, *Eros and Inwardness*, 69–70.

30. Weininger, *Geschlecht und Charakter*, 79–80. Pederasty was thought to be so loathsome that one advocate for the sympathetic tolerance of loving male relationships even sought to sunder any link between the obscenity of physical contact and the spirituality of intimate friendship. See Benedikt Friedlaender, *Renaissance des Eros Uranios: Die physiologische Freundschaft, ein normaler Gruntrieb des Menschen und eine Frage der männlichen Gesellschaftsfreiheit* (Schmargendorf-Berlin: Verlag "Renaissance,"1904; reprint, New York: Arno Press, 1975), 12, 196.

31. Ibid., 138; and Otto Weininger, *Genie und Verbrechen*, ed. Walther Schneider (Graz and Vienna: Stiasny Verlag, 1962), 75–76.

32. Weininger, *Geschlecht und Charakter*, 137.

33. Hanns Fuchs, *Richard Wagner und die Homosexualität* (Berlin: H. Barsdorf, 1903), 2.

34. Ibid., 62.

35. Ibid., 56.

36. Ibid., 67–68. See also Friedrich Haack, *M. v. Schwind*, 4th ed. (Bielefeld and Leipzig: Velhagen and Klasing, 1913), 16–18. Schwind's letters are taken from Hyacinth Holland, *Moritz von Schwind* (Stuttgart: Neff, 1873).

37. Lux, *Grillparzers Liebesroman*, 261. In 1926, Lux published a novel about Beethoven's "Immortal Beloved," and two years later, upon the centenary of Schubert's death, there appeared his *Franz Schuberts Lebenslied, ein Roman der Freundschaft.*
38. Hans Rau, *Franz Grillparzer und sein Liebesleben* (Berlin: H. Barsdorf, 1904), 136–37.
39. Ibid., 211.
40. Marc-André Raffalovich *Uranisme et unisexualité: Étude sur différentes manifestations de l'instinct sexuel* (Lyons: Storck, 1896), 329–30. On Raffalovich, see Vernon A. Rosario, *The Erotic Imagination: French Histories of Perversity* (New York: Oxford University Press, 1997), 97–106.
41. De Joux, *Die Enterbten*, 132.
42. Kreissle, *Franz Schubert* (1865): 471. For Mayrhofer's obituary of Schubert, see Deutsch, *Memoirs*, 14. Bauernfeld's recollection comes from an 1857 letter in reply to Luib's request for information about the composer. It was first published in Heuberger, *Franz Schubert*, 111. For this and similar descriptions of Schubert's dual nature, see Deutsch, *Memoirs*, 45, 82, 86, 234. The intersection of a "double nature" with a "third sex" may go back as far as Plato's *Symposium.*
43. Leo Berg, *Das sexuelle Probem in Kunst und Leben*, 5th ed. (Berlin: Hermann Walther, 1901), 23–24.
44. Albert Moll, *Berühmte Homosexuelle* (Wiesbaden: J. F. Bermann, 1910), 10–11.
45. Magnus Hirschfeld, *Der urnische Mensch* (Leipzig: Max Spohr, 1903), 5; and Havelock Ellis, *Studies in the Psychology of Sex*, vol. 1, pt. 4 (New York: Random House, 1942), 339. Hirschfeld posited that many male uranians, intensely attracted to heterosexual men, subsumed their desire in relationships that the latter unwittingly accepted as devout friendship. Even Raffalovich acknowledged that uranists expressed themselves in much the same way as German heterosexuals, so much so that "the vivid and striking expression of a friendship . . . I would like to call German." Raffalovich, *Uranisme*, 157. Nonscientific studies might or might not suggest a connection between male friendship and same-sex desire. One that did was Edward Carpenter's *Ioläus: An Anthology of Friendship* (1902), which discussed both Platen and Wagner.
46. Otto Erich Deutsch, "Neue Mitteilungen über Franz Schubert," *Österreichische Rundschau* 23 (April–June 1910): 320. Deutsch published the reminiscences of Schubert's friends Anselm Hüttenbrenner and Anton Holzapfel in the *Jahrbuch der Grillparzer-Gesellschaft.* See Deutsch, *Memoirs*, 59, 70, 182. On Deutsch's importance to Schubert studies at this time, see chapter 6, note 43.
47. August Forel, *Die sexuelle Frage* (Munich: Ernst Reinhardt, 1920), 260.
48. Sengoopta, *Otto Weininger*, 82–83, 86–87.
49. Storck, *Geschichte der Musik*, 2:103.
50. Adolph Kohut, "Franz Schubert und die Frauen," in *Das Ewig-Weibliche in der Welt-Kultur und Litteraturgeschichte* (Leipzig: Neupert, 1898), 71.
51. Paul Heyse, "Zu Franz Schubert's hundertjährigem Geburtstage," in *Neue Gedichte und Jugendlieder*, 2nd ed. (Berlin: Hertz, 1897), 333. Heyse wrote lyrical tributes in commemoration of Germany's political leaders that were to be read prior to musical performances of works by the nation's great composers. A poem in honor of Bismarck's eightieth birthday appeared prior to a performance of Beethoven's Ninth Symphony in 1895, and a poem for the centennial festival of Wilhelm I preceded Weber's *Jubel* Overture in 1897.
52. Elisarion von Kupffer, *Lieblingminne und Freundesliebe in der Weltliteratur* (Berlin-Neurahnsdorf: Adolf Brand's Verlag, 1900; reprint, Berlin: Verlag rosa Winkel,

1995), 206. See also Benedikt Friedlaender, "Die physiologische Freundschaft als normaler Grundtrieb des Menschen und als Grundlage der Sozialität," *Jahrbuch für sexuelle Zwischenstufen* 6 (1904): 181–213; in *Die Liebe Platon im Lichte der modernen Biologie* (Treptow bei Berlin: Bernhard Zack's Verlag, 1909), 13–40. An extended version of Friedlaender's article appeared as "Biologische Deutung der gleichgeschlechtlichen Liebe: Die physiologische Freundschaft als normaler Grundtrieb des Menschen und als Grundlage der Sozialität: Ihre Wichtigkeit für den Einzelnen und für die Völker: Ihre Function im Leben der Menschheit," part 5 of *Renaissance des Eros Uranios,* 211–52. On Friedlaender, see Hewitt, *Political Inversions,* 98–105. Outside of German-speaking Europe, Raffalovich and Carpenter mounted similar defenses.

53. Gustav Portig, *Schiller in seinem Verhältnis zur Freundschaft und Liebe sowie in seinem inneren Verhältnis zu Goethe* (Hamburg and Leipzig: Leopold Voss, 1894), 13–14, 21, 263–64. On the changing relationship between friendship and male desire, see Oosterhuis, *Stepchildren of Nature,* 245–47; Mosse, *Nationalism and Sexuality,* 66–89; and Hans Dietrich, *Die Freundesliebe in der deutschen Literatur* (Leipzig: Woldemar Hellbach, 1931), 25–45.

54. *Schenker als Essayist,* 212–13.

55. Louis Köhler, "Franz Schubert's Leben und Schaffen," *Musikalisches Centralblatt* 2, no. 12 (March 23, 1882): 124; no. 15 (April 13, 1882): 152.

56. Heinrich Schenker, *Der Tonwille: Pamphlets in Witness of the Immutable Laws of Music, Offered to a New Generation of Youth,* trans. Ian Bent et al., ed. William Drabkin, vol. 1 (Oxford: Oxford University Press, 2004), 4, 6, 17. This anti-French bias was extant among more conservative writers well before World War I. In 1894, Ottokar Stauf von der March pointed out that "decadence" was a word that Germans characteristically had to borrow from France. See Wunberg, *Wiener Moderne,* 239.

57. Heinrich Schenker, *Der Tonwille: Pamphlets/Quarterly Publication in Witness of the Immutable Laws of Music, Offered to a New Generation of Youth,* trans. Ian Bent et al., ed. William Drabkin, vol. 2 (Oxford: Oxford University Press, 2005), 3.

58. Walter Dahms, *Schubert,* 10th–14th ed. (Berlin and Leipzig: Schuster & Loeffler, 1918), 274. The passage also appeared in Walter Dahms, "Schlusskapitel der neuen Schubert-Biographie," *Die Musik: Schubert-Heft* 11, no. 23 (September 1, 1912): 259–79.

59. Sigmund Freud, "Leonardo da Vinci and a Memory of His Childhood," trans. Alan Tyson, in *The Standard Edition of the Complete Psychological Works of Sigmund Freud,* trans. James Strachey et al. (London: Hogarth Press, 1962), 75.

60. La Grange, *Gustav Mahler,* 2:240, quoting Natalie Bauer-Lechner, *Gustav Mahler in den Erinnerungen von Natalie Bauer-Lechner,* ed. Herbert Killian and Knud Martner (Hamburg: Wagner, 1984), 153. The metaphor was an old one. After hearing Schubert's Ninth Symphony played in Cologne in 1862, Ludwig Bischoff wrote that it was "so immediate, so flowing in a single gush, so spontaneously and easily welling forth, that it left him [Schubert] no time for any sort of reflection." See Robert Lee Curtis, *Ludwig Bischoff: A Mid-Nineteenth-Century Music Critic* (Cologne: Arno Volk, 1979), 191.

61. For analyses of Freud's study from historical and psychological viewpoints respectively, see Meyer Schapiro, "Leonardo and Freud: An Art-Historical Study," *Journal of the History of Ideas* 17, no. 2 (April 1956): 147–78; and R. Richard Wohl and Harry Trosman, "A Retrospect of Freud's Leonardo, an Assessment of a Psychoanalytic Classic," *Psychiatry* 18 (1955): 27–39. Elsewhere in Freud's writings, Schubert was not the composer who leapt to his mind: "When we declare, for instance Goethe, Leonardo da Vinci, and Beethoven to be great men, then something else must move us to do so beyond the admiration of their grandiose

creations." See Sigmund Freud, *Moses and Monotheism,* trans. Katherine Jones (New York: Vintage, 1955), 138.

62. Kreissle, *Franz Schubert* (1865): 333; George Grove, *Beethoven, Schubert, Mendelssohn* (London: Macmillan & Co., 1951), 166; and Dahms, *Schubert,* 137.

63. Louis Bourgault-Ducoudray, *Schubert* (Paris: H. Laurens, 1908), 26; and Joseph Bennett, "The Great Composers, Sketched by Themselves," *Musical Times* 22 (February 1, 1881): 68. "My Dream" may have served as a literary inspiration for Theodor Storm's novel *Ein stiller Musikant,* discussed in chapter 3 of the first volume of this study, in which the protagonist's father, a music teacher, strikes his misfit son and precipitates his flight from home. The fact that the boy is subsequently reminded of a song from *Die schöne Müllerin* suggests that the similarities between the novel and "My Dream" are not entirely coincidental.

64. Freud, *Standard Edition,* 5:38. Freud's groundbreaking *The Interpretation of Dreams* (1900) occasionally cites the dreams of famous people, but they are invariably accompanied by the analyses of other writers. In the years between the publication of this book and the appearance of the Leonardo monograph, Isidor Sadger published psychoanalytic studies of Kleist, Lenau, Meyer, and Platen.

65. Edward Hitschmann, "Franz Schubert's Grief and Love," trans. Edna Spector, *American Imago* 7, no. 1 (March 1950): 74; originally published as "Franz Schuberts Schmerz und Liebe," *Internationale Zeitschrift für ärztliche Psychoanalyse* 3 (1915): 287–92. Hitschmann's interpretation was taken up in Solomon, "Franz Schubert's 'My Dream,'" 137–54. The possible contribution of "My Dream" to an understanding of the composer's life and works continues to be a source of scholarly interest. See Ilija Dürhammer, "Zu Schuberts Literaturästhetik," *Schubert durch die Brille* 14 (1995): 5–99; Charles Fisk, *Returning Cycles: Contexts for the Interpretation of Schubert's Impromptus and Last Sonatas* (Berkeley and Los Angeles: University of California Press, 2001), 8–11, 133–35, 270–71; Gernot Gruber, "Franz Schuberts *Mein Traum*— Und unsere Träume, ihn zu verstehen," in *"Dialekt ohne Erde . . ." Franz Schubert und das 20. Jahrhundert,* ed. Otto Kolleritsch (Vienna: Universal Edition, 1998), 139–49; Andreas Mayer, "Der Psychoanalytisches Schubert," *Schubert durch die Brille* 9 (1992): 7–31; and Elizabeth Norman McKay, *Franz Schubert: A Biography* (Oxford: Clarendon Press, 1996), 127–29. McKay, who posits that the document may have been "the result of an opium reverie," concludes: "It is rather unlikely that 'Mein Traum' can explain or point to anything of appreciable significance about the composer's psychology."

66. Hirschfeld, *Der urnische Mensch,* 71.

67. Iwan Bloch, *Beiträge zur Aetiologie der Psychopathia sexualis,* vol. 1 (Dresden: H. R. Dohrn, 1902), 234. See also Krafft-Ebing, *Psychopathia Sexualis,* 402–4; and Oosterhuis, *Stepchildren of Nature,* 243–44.

68. Bloch, *Beiträge zur Aetiologie,* 230.

69. Magnus Hirschfeld, "Die Homosexualität in Wien," *Wiener klinische Rundschau,* no. 42 (1901), quoted in Numa Praetorius [Eugen Daniel Wilhelm], "Die Bibliographie die Homosexualität für das Jahr 1901 mit Ausschluss der Belletristik," in *Jahrbuch für sexuelle Zwischenstufen mit besonderer Berücksichtigung der Homosexualität,* vol. 4 (Leipzig: Max Spohr, 1902), 797. It was just as well that Hitschmann limited himself to a purely psychoanalytic method, given the pliant terminology of fin-de-siècle sexual science. Havelock Ellis wrote about the Marquis de Sade's "small and well-formed" skull and cited an unnamed phrenologist who thought its shape could be taken for the head of a woman. He concluded that there was an evidentiary relationship between sadism and "a somewhat feminine organization," a phrase that

eerily echoes the often-cited description of Schubert's skull as having a "zarte, fast weibliche Organisation" (a "delicate, almost womanly structure"). See Ellis, *Psychology of Sex*, 1:2:109; and Kreissle, *Franz Schubert* (1865): 466.

70. Hitschmann, "Schubert's Grief and Love," 71. On the debatable matter of Mayrhofer's sexuality, see Rita Steblin, "Schubert's Problematic Relationship with Johann Mayrhofer: New Documentary Evidence," in *Essays on Music and Culture in Honor of Herbert Kellman*, ed. Barbara Haggh (Paris: Minerve, 2001), 465–95.

71. Braun, *Schubert im Freundeskreis*, 87.

72. Ferdinand Scherber, "Schubert-Pathologie," *Wiener Zeitung*, November 18, 1928, 3.

73. Hermann Bahr, "Platens Memoiren," *Die Zeit* 9, no. 117 (December 26, 1896): 208–9, quoted in Wunberg, *Junge Wien*, 1:667–68. Bahr was probably aware that Platen's diaries had appeared in 1896. In *Jokes and Their Relation to the Unconscious* (1905), Freud described "a regular wasp's nest of the most stinging allusions," referring to the satiric dismemberment of Platen's homosexuality at the hands of Heinrich Heine in *Die Bäder von Lucca*, See Freud, *Standard Edition*, 8:78. By that time, several studies on the poet's sexuality had been published. See Ludwig Frey, "Aus dem Seelenleben des Grafen Platen," *Jahrbuch für sexuelle Zwischenstufen* 1 (1899): 159–214; and 6 (1904): 357–447; Max Kaufmann, "Heinrich Heine contra Graf August von Platen und die Homo-Erotik," in *Heines Charakter und die moderne Seele* (Zurich: Müller, 1902); and Isidor Sadger, "August von Platen, eine pathologische Studie," *Nord und Süd* 115 (1905): 103–223. Beyond Vienna, one can find a residual relationship of symbols between Thomas Mann's *Death in Venice* (1911) and Platen's *Sonette aus Venedig*. For musicological perspectives on Schubert's settings of Platen, see Kramer, *Franz Schubert*, 105–19; and Muxfeldt, "Schubert, Platen," 480–527.

74. Konrad Huschke, "Gemeinsame Züge der 'Antipoden' Beethoven und Schubert," *Neue Musik-Zeitung* 36, no. 21 (1915): 253.

75. Ibid., 257. In the wake of the war's end, writing about gender, even in a historical context, required greater rhetorical finesse in order to avoid any problematic implications about the sexuality of one's subject, especially if the author was a citizen of one of the defeated nations. In a lengthy and detailed analysis of androgyny in German romantic literature, the psychologist Fritz Giese emphasized repeatedly that, however much the German romantics based their aesthetics on Hellenic models, there was not a scintilla of evidence that either their theories or their personal friendships betrayed any hint of Platonic boy love. Giese argued that pederasty remained a concept utterly alien to German literature around 1800, precisely because it was "southern, Greek, un-German." See Fritz Giese, *Die Entwicklung des Androgynenproblems in der Frühromantik* (Langensalza, Germany: Wendt and Kaluwell, 1919), 268, 272–74. An indication of the spiraling public anxiety over sexuality can be gleaned from comparing Giese's explicit unease to a discussion of literary androgyny two decades earlier. In 1899, when Ricarda Huch referred to "Mannweib" as a century-old term that had once represented "the most beautiful and complete form in which man can present himself," she only noted obliquely that in her own era the meaning of the word had sunk so low that it had taken on an unnamed debased tone. See her *Blütezeit der Romantik*, vol. 1 of *Die Romantik*, 13th and 14th ed. (Leipzig: H. Haeffel, 1924), 203.

76. John A. Hargraves, *Music in the Works of Broch, Mann, and Kafka* (Rochester, NY: Camden House, 2002), 3–4; and Hermann Broch, *Das Teesdorfer Tagebuch für Ea von Allesch*, ed. Paul Michael Lützeler (Frankfurt am Main: Suhrkamp Verlag, 1995), 16–17.

77. Broch, *Hofmannsthal*, 55, 171.

78. *Das Dreimäderlhaus*, the product of Alfred Willner and Heinz Reichert, with Schubert's music arranged by Berté, was based upon Rudolf Hans Bartsch's popular 1912 novel *Schwammerl*. It enjoyed widespread fame in other countries: *Chanson d'amour* with a French libretto by Hugues Delorme and Leon Abric premiered in Paris on May 7, 1921; *Blossom Time* with a new text by Dorothy Donnelly and music arranged by Sigmund Romberg premiered in New York on September 29, 1921; and *Lilac Time* with English lyrics by Adrian Ross and music arranged by George Howard Clutsam premiered in London on December 22, 1922. Willner and Reichert crafted a three-act sequel, *Hannerl*, with Schubert's music arranged by Carl Lafite, premiering at the Raimund-Theater on February 8, 1918. For other works for the stage that exploit Schubertian hagiography, see the first volume of the present study. For useful evaluations of *Schwammerl* and *Das Dreimäderlhaus*, which nonetheless do not analyze the treatment of their female characters, see Alexander Stillmark, " 'Es war alles gut und erfüllt.' Rudolf Hans Bartsch's *Schwammerl* and the Making of the Schubert Myth," in *The Biedermeier and Beyond: Selected Papers from the Symposium held at St. Peter's College, Oxford from 19–21 September 1997*, ed. Ian F. Roe and John Warren (Bern: Peter Lang, 1999), 225–34; and Sabine Giesbrecht-Schutte, " 'Klagen eines Troubadours.' Zur Popularisierung Schuberts im Dreimäderlhaus," in *Martin Geck: Festschrift zum 65. Geburtstag*, ed. Ares Rolf und Ulrich Tadday (Dortmund: Klangfarben, 2001), 109–33.

Chapter Six

1. Robert Waissenberger, ed., *Wien, 1870–1930: Traum und Wirklichkeit* (Salzburg and Vienna: Residenz, 1984), 293. For contemporary photographs of Altenberg and an analysis comparing them to Kokoschka's portrait, see Leo A. Lensing, "Scribbling Squids and the Giant Octopus: Oskar Kokoschka's Unpublished Portrait of Peter Altenberg," in *Turn-of-the-Century Vienna and Its Legacy: Essays in Honor of Donald G. Daviau*, ed. Jeffrey B. Berlin, Jorun B. Johns, and Richard H. Lawson (New York: Edition Atelier, 1993), 193–220.

2. Quoted in Lensing, "Peter Altenberg's Fabricated Photographs," 54.

3. Ibid., 51.

4. Hugo von Hofmannsthal, "Ein neues Wiener Buch," *Die Zukunft* 4 (September 5, 1896): 452–57; also in Hofmannsthal, *Gesammelte Werke: Prosa I*, 272.

5. Peter Altenberg, "Mama," in *Semmering 1912* (Berlin: S. Fischer, 1913), 42. One of the physicians was, coincidentally, Theodore Billroth, a passionate lover of music and close friend of Brahms.

6. Peter Altenberg, "Die 'Götter' meiner holden Jugendzeit," in *Mein Lebensabend*, 9th–12th ed. (Berlin: S. Fischer, 1919), 90.

7. Peter Altenberg, "Entwicklung," in *Neues Altes*, 4th–5th ed. (Berlin: S. Fischer, 1919), 22.

8. Altenberg, "Forellenfang," in *Semmering*, 33–34. Altenberg also used trout imagery in "Diese ist sein," which appeared in the *Wiener Rundschau* on July 1, 1898, and later in *Was der Tag mir zuträgt*, 7th–8th ed. (Berlin: S. Fischer, 1919), 92–96.

9. Peter Altenberg, "Grammophonplatte," in *Märchen des Lebens* (Berlin: S. Fischer, 1908), 21. An earlier version minus the last four sentences appeared in the short-lived *Kunst: Monatsschrift für Kunst und alles andere*, no. 6 (March 1904): 15. The

specific recording to which Altenberg referred was by the Hofoper baritone Leopold Demuth. It was listed in an advertisement for "Grammophone-Platten Nadeln und Zuberhörteile der Deutschen Grammophon-Aktiengesellschaft H. Weiss & Co., Wien" in that issue of *Kunst*. In 1947, Wittgenstein had a different but equally remarkable encounter with a gramophone recording of Schubert's Ninth Symphony, as recalled by F. R. Leavis: "A moment after the music began to sound he lifted the tone arm, altered the speed, and lowered the needle on to the record again. He did this several times, until he was satisfied." See Rhees, *Recollections of Wittgenstein*, 58.

10. Wendelin Schmidt-Dengler, "Literature and Theatre," in *Vienna 1890–1920*, ed. Robert Waissenberger (New York: Tabard Press, 1984), 250. The aestheticization of nature is also apparent in Hofmannsthal's story "Das Dorf im Gebirge" from 1896, in which the net of a tennis court set in a meadow appears from a distance to resemble a spider's web. Standing in the court, however, one sees the countryside through the net, as though it were a lattice of fine, continuous cracks on the enamel of Japanese jars. See Hofmannsthal, *Gesammelte Werke: Prosa I*, 279.

11. Peter Altenberg, "Franz Schubert," in *Nachfechsung*, 4th–5th ed. (Berlin: S. Fischer 1919), 156–57. The quotation can be found in Arnold Niggli, *Schubert*, rev. ed. (Leipzig: Philipp Reclam, 1925), 114, although Altenberg added the last phrase, "19. November 1828 im 32. Lebensjahre."

12. Stefan Zweig, "Peter Altenberg," *Stimmen der Gegenwart: Monatsschrift für moderne Litteratur und Kritik* 1, no. 2 (February 1901): 26, quoted in Wunberg, *Junge Wien*, 2:1156.

13. Altenberg, "Wiener Ballade: Franz Schubert," in *Nachfechsung*, 102–3. A facsimile of an earlier version in manuscript that is not identical to the published version appears in Andrew Barker and Leo A. Lensing, *Peter Altenberg: Rezept die Welt zu sehen* (Vienna: Braumüller, 1995), 193.

14. The most extensive study of Altenberg is Andrew Barker, *Telegrams from the Soul: Peter Altenberg and the Culture of Fin-de-Siècle Vienna* (Columbia, SC: Camden House, 1996). From the same author, see "'Die weiseste Ökonomie bei tiefester Fülle'—Peter Altenberg's *Wie ich es sehe*," in *Studies in Nineteenth-Century Austrian Literature*, ed. B. O. Murdoch and M. G. Ward (Glasgow: Scottish Papers in Germanic Studies, 1983), 82–97; "The Persona of Peter Altenberg: 'Frauenkult,' Misogyny and Jewish Self-Hatred," in *Studies in German and Scandinavian Literature after 1500: A Festschrift for George C. Schoolfield*, ed. James A. Parente, Jr. and Richard Erich Schade (Columbia, SC: Camden House, 1993), 129–39; and "Peter Altenberg's Literary Catalysis," in *From Vormärz to Fin de Siècle: Essays in Nineteenth Century Austrian Literature*, ed. Mark G. Ward (Blairgowrie, UK: Lochee Publications, 1986), 91–106. For a further range of opinion, see Pamela S. Saur, "Peter Altenberg: The 'Radical Bachelor,'" in *Joinings and Disjoinings: The Significance of Marital Status in Literature*, ed. JoAnna Stephens Mink and Janet Doubler Ward (Bowling Green, OH: Bowling Green University Popular Press, 1991), 120–31; Barbara Z. Schoenberg, "'Woman-Defender' and 'Woman-Offender,' Peter Altenberg and Otto Weininger: Two Literary Stances vis-à-vis Bourgeois Culture in the Viennese 'Belle Epoque,'" *Modern Austrian Literature* 20, no. 2 (1987): 51–69; Josephine M. N. Simpson, *Peter Altenberg: A Neglected Writer of the Viennese Jahrhundertwende* (Frankfurt am Main: Peter Lang, 1987), 66–85, 114–15; Ariane Thomalla, *Die "femme fragile": Ein literarischer Frauentypus der Jahrhundertwende* (Düsseldorf: Bertelsmann, 1972), 60–75; and Edward Timms, "Peter Altenberg—Authenticity or Pose?" in *Fin de Siècle Vienna*, ed. G. J. Carr and Eda Sagarra (Dublin: Trinity College, 1985), 126–42. The least sympathetic interpretation is Gilman, *Difference and Pathology*, 43–45; first appearing as

"Freud and the Prostitute: Male Stereotypes of Female Sexuality in *fin-de-siècle* Vienna," *Journal of the American Academy of Psychoanalysis* 9, no. 3 (1981): 337–60.

15. Altenberg, "Noch nicht einmal Splitter von Gedanken," in *Semmering*, 211. Over his career, Altenberg's attitude toward women deteriorated considerably, taking on more blatant misogynist overtones. This, too, may have resulted from personal experience. In 1911, his companion Helga Malmberg left him for good while he was recuperating at the Fries sanatorium in Inzersdorf. On Altenberg's relationships with specific women, see Harold B. Segel, *The Vienna Coffeehouse Wits: 1890–1938* (West Lafayette, IN: Purdue University Press, 1993), 117–19. For an examination of the sexual nature of Schubart's poem "Die Forelle" and Schubert's setting, see Kramer, *Franz Schubert*, 75–92. Among the works depicted in the popular postcard market after World War I is one entitled "Schubert, Die Forelle," by Erich Schütz, a popular illustrator of Viennese books, in which a Jugendstil mermaid cavorts among a school of trout. The *femme fatale* qualities of such *art nouveau* creatures, however, has a pre-war pedigree, as is observable in the drawing by Fritz Hass depicting the song in *Schubert-Lieder: 10 Zeichnungen* (Berlin: Fischer, 1902).

16. Peter Altenberg, *Wie ich es sehe*, 5th ed. (Berlin: S. Fischer, 1910), 277.

17. Peter Altenberg, "Schubert," in *Bilderbögen des kleinen Lebens* (Berlin: S. Fischer, 1909), 73. See also his *Nachfechsung*, 107–8.

18. Zur Schubert-Feier," *Neues Wiener Tagblatt*, January 30, 1897, 5. See also "Theater und Kunst," *Fremden-Blatt* (Morgen-Blatt), January 30, 1897, 8; "Zu Franz Schubert's 100. Geburtstage," *Neuigkeits Welt-Blatt*, January 31, 1897, 17–19; Theodor Helm, "Franz Schuberts künstlerische Bedeutung," *Deutsche Zeitung*, January 31, 1897, 1–4; and Carl Staubach, "Ein deutsche Liederfürst," *Deutsches Volksblatt*, January 31, 1897, 1–5.

19. Niggli, *Schubert* (1925), 13. Niggli's source for the expression "feminine passivity" was an article by the piano pedagogue Louis Köhler, "Franz Schubert's Leben und Schaffen," *Musikalisches Centrablatt* 2, no. 12 (March 23, 1882): 124. Köhler also wrote: "Where Schubert acquiesced so submissively, a Beethoven would have been defiant and would have manfully stood firm against the distressing circumstances." 1897 happens to be the year when Niggli's daughter Julia first met the eighteen-year-old Albert Einstein, and the two of them "played Schubert Lieder together, she on the piano and he on the violin." See John Stachel, ed., *The Collected Papers of Albert Einstein*, vol. 1 (Princeton, NJ: Princeton University Press, 1987), 219.

20. Kreissle, *Life of Franz Schubert*, 2:142–43. See also Kreissle, *Franz Schubert* (1865), 139–40.

21. Deutsch, *Memoirs*, 100.

22. Heinrich Kreissle von Hellborn, *Franz Schubert, eine biografische Skizze* (Vienna: Druck und Verlag der typographisch-literarisch-artistischen Anstalt, 1861), 23.

23. An early subject of confusion entailed exactly which Esterházy sister was the object of Schubert's love. Spaun's "Notes on My Association with Franz Schubert" (1858), used by Kreissle, indicated the elder sister Marie. Schober, with whom Kreissle corresponded, did not supply a first name. In response to a question from Ferdinand Luib, Josef Hüttenbrunner declined to say which daughter Schubert loved. For these and other reminiscences, see Deutsch, *Memoirs*, 73, 134, 233–34, 265, 362, 371.

24. Leopold von Sonnleithner's notes to Luib in 1857 appear to have been Kreissle's source for characterizing the nature of Schubert's attraction to women. "As regards his relationship with the opposite sex, I know little; he was certainly not indifferent; but with him this tendency was not nearly so much in evidence as it usually is in men

of lively imagination. On an estate in Hungary he is said to have languished greatly for a lady of superior social position." Deutsch, *Memoirs*, 114. For the gradual public dissemination and reception of Schubert's encounter with Caroline Esterházy, see also chapter 2 of the first volume of this study.

25. Niggli, *Schubert* (1889), 37. See also Niggli, *Schubert* (1925), 40.

26. Altenberg, "Nichts Neues," in *Neues Altes*, 185–86. The original, which is slightly different from the version that appeared in Altenberg's *Neues Altes*, was published in the *Wiener allgemeine Zeitung*, September 11, 1911, 3.

27. Hannah Hickman, *Robert Musil and the Culture of Vienna* (La Salle, IL: Open Court Publishing Company, 1984), 51; and Zweig, *The World of Yesterday*, 39.

28. In a letter to Emil Franzos on October 17, 1917, Altenberg railed against Paula Schneider for luring him to and abandoning him in Innsbruck "for *appallingly-Strindbergian* reasons in order to '*demonstrate her power.*'" See Barker, *Telegrams*, 209. That same month he dedicated *Vita Ipsa* to her, "in unforgettableness!" One sketch from that collection concludes: "A woman has the holy mission to serve, to help gravely struggling man in the 'labyrinth of this life!' Everything else about her is demonic and obstructive! The world is conceived 'according to God's most ingenious plans,' and not according to 'woman's devilishly backward plans!' August Strindberg was overcome, not Peter Altenberg!" Peter Altenberg, "De Femina," in *Vita Ipsa*, 5th–7th ed. (Berlin: S. Fischer, 1918), 26–27.

29. Janik and Toulmin, *Wittgenstein's Vienna*, 68. On Kraus and the women's movement, see Anderson, *Utopian Feminism*, 3–4, 55. On Strindberg's misogyny, see Walter Johnson, *August Strindberg* (Boston: Twayne Publishers, 1976), 24–27; and John Ward, *The Social and Religious Plays of Strindberg* (London: Althone Press, 1980), 18–25. A favorable review of Strindberg's *Der Vater* by Kraus appeared in the *Breslauer Zeitung* on May 16, 1897. See Karl Kraus, *Frühe Schriften: 1892–1900*, ed. Johannes J. Braakenburg, vol. 2 (Munich: Kosel, 1979), 61.

30. Weininger, *Geschlecht und Charakter*, 154, 557. Beethoven's music figures prominently in Strindberg's *Crime and Crimes* and *The Ghost Sonata*. In his idyll *The Journey to the City*, an autobiographically inspired sexton, after exchanging a grand piano for his old upright, plays the *Appassionata* Sonata. See Olof Lagercrantz, *August Strindberg*, trans. Anselm Hollo (New York: Farrar, Straus, Giroux, 1984), 315, 326, 333.

31. August Strindberg, *Strindberg's Letters*, trans. and ed. Michael Robinson, vol. 2 (Chicago: University of Chicago Press, 1992), 700.

32. Ibid., 2:703.

33. Ibid., 2:703; and Lagercrantz, *August Strindberg*, 316.

34. *Strindberg's Letters*, 2:706. On Strindberg's identification with Beethoven, see Richard Vowles, "Strindberg and Beethoven," in *Växelverkan Mellan Skönlitteraturen Och Andra Konstarter* (*Sixth International Study Conference on Scandinavian Literature*) (Uppsala, Sweden: International Association for Scandinavian Studies, 1967), 163–81.

35. Ludwig Münz and Gustav Künstler, *Adolf Loos: Pioneer of Modern Architecture*, trans. Harold Meek (New York: Praeger, 1966), 226, 231. On Beethoven and masculinity, see Peri Elizabeth Shamsai, "The Case of Beethoven: Aesthetic Ideology and Cultural Politics in Fin-de-Siècle Viennese Modernism" (PhD diss., Columbia University, 1997).

36. Adolf Loos, *Spoken into the Void: Collected Essays 1897–1900*, trans. Jane O. Newman and John H. Smith (Cambridge, MA: MIT Press, 1982), 100, 102, 103. The article "Ladies' Fashion" first appeared on August 21, 1898, in the *Neue freie Presse* and was reprinted in *Dokumente der Frau*, March 1, 1902.

37. *Traum und Wirklichkeit* (1985), 322–23. Altenberg's elaborate calligraphy surrounding the child's face is as much a part of the work as the portrait itself.

38. Altenberg, "Text auf Ansichtskarten," in *Neues Altes*, 60. It precedes the texts that Berg adapted for his *Altenberg-Lieder*. For an illuminating discussion of the connections between poet and composer, see David P. Schroeder, "Alban Berg and Peter Altenberg: Intimate Art and the Aesthetics of Life," *Journal of the American Musicological Society* 46, no. 2 (Summer 1993): 261–94. Schroeder draws interesting though different connections between the "weibliches Beethoven-Antlitz" and Klimt's Beethoven frieze.

39. *Richard Wagner's Prose Works*, 2:107.

40. Ibid., 2:115.

41. Anderson, *Utopian Feminism*, 213–15.

42. See Barker, *Telegrams*, 80. Altenberg's unsuccessful overtures to Emma Rudolf were made during the summer of 1899, well before the Secession's Beethoven exhibition of 1902. Common in fin-de-siècle Vienna were liaisons in which young women, often of the lower class, almost appeared to be divided up among the city's intellectuals. Thus, in addition to losing Emma Rudolf to Alfred Polgar, Altenberg lost Lina Obertimpfler to Adolf Loos and Annie Kalmar to Karl Kraus. Coincidentally the life of another "Frau E. R.," Elisabeth Reitler, ended disastrously when her unsuccessful attempts to compete with her sister for the affections of Kraus contributed to her suicide on November 7, 1917. See Edward Timms, "The 'Child-Woman': Kraus, Freud, Wittels, and Irma Karczewska," in *Vienna 1900: From Altenberg to Wittgenstein*, ed. Edward Timms and Ritchie Robertson, 87–107 (Edinburgh: Edinburgh University Press, 1990), 92–93.

43. August Strindberg, *Pre-Inferno Plays*, trans. Walter Johnson (Seattle: University of Washington Press, 1970), 78.

44. Peter Altenberg, *Pròdrŏmŏs* (Berlin: S. Fischer, 1906), 53–53. See also Thomalla, *Femme fragile*, 71. With regard to the two female types, Altenberg disdained the sexually tumescent women found in the drawings of Hugo Höppener (known as Fidus) in favor of the more spiritual relationship between Dante and Beatrice. One of Fidus's more famous works depicts a gargantuan, scowling head of Beethoven, which dwarfs a naked woman who, on tiptoe and seen from behind, reaches up to touch the tightly closed lips of the composer.

45. Otto Erich Deutsch, "Etwas Neues," *Wiener allgemeine Zeitung*, September 13, 1911, 2. See also Otto Erich Deutsch, "Anselm Hüttenbrenners Erinnerungen an Schubert," *Jahrbuch der Grillparzer-Gesellschaft* 16 (1906): 99–163; "Schuberts Herzeleid," *Bühne und Welt* 9, no. 18 (June 1907): 227–31; "Neue Mitteilungen über Franz Schubert," 319–22; and "Schubert und die Frauen," *Jahres-Bericht des Schubertbundes in Wien über das siebenundvierzigste Vereinsjahr vom 1. Oktober 1909 bis 30. September 1910*, ed. Anton Weiß (Vienna: Verlag des Schubertbundes, 1912), 81–89. Rita Steblin has plausibly challenged elements of Deutsch's position. See her "Neue Forschungsaspekte zu Caroline Esterhazy," *Schubert durch die Brille* 11 (1993): 21–33. Kreissle (*Franz Schubert* [1865], 141) cited the word of "a near relative," who gave Caroline's birth year as 1806. This date was confirmed in Max Friedlaender, *Beiträge zur Biographie Franz Schubert's* (Berlin: A. Haack, 1887), but see also Ignaz Weinmann, "Franz Schuberts Beziehungen zu Zseliz," typescript (Vienna, 1975), 18, in the Musiksammlung, Österreichische Nationalbibliothek, 1.277.024.

46. Fritz Wittels, *Critique of Love* (New York: The Macaulay Company, 1929), 285, 294.

47. On Kraus and Wittels, see Timms, "Child-Woman," 91–92. Regarding the hetaera, Timms notes that Wedekind's *Büchse der Pandora* was identified by Kraus in the

October 1903 edition of *Die Fackel* as the "tragedy of a hetaera" and that the Greek text by Lucian to which Wittels referred was reprinted in German in 1907 with images by Klimt. For a relevant essay that considers the theme of adolescent female sexuality among Viennese artists while also discussing many of these same individuals, see Alessandra Comini, "Toys in Freud's Attic: Torment and Taboo in the Child and Adolescent Themes of Vienna's Image-Makers," in *Picturing Children: Constructions of Childhood between Rousseau and Freud*, ed. Marilyn R. Brown (Aldershot, UK: Ashgate, 2002), 167–88. The cultural distance between the *Kindweib*, as a representative symbol of the fin de siècle, and her Victorian forebears is suggested by comparing Wittels' formulation to the description of "the little woman-child" offered by Sarah Tyler in 1887 in the first issue of the journal *The Mother's Companion:* "the born queen, and, at the same time, the servant of home." Quoted in Deborah Gorham, *The Victorian Girl and the Feminine Ideal* (Bloomington: Indiana University Press, 1982), 5.

48. Felix Salten, "Junge Liebe," *Wurstelprater* (Vienna: Rosenbaum, 1911; reprint, Vienna: Molden, 1973), 111–15. Four photographs by Emil Mayer illustrate the narrative.

49. Gilman, "Freud and the Prostitute," 343–44. These legal details were probably familiar in Viennese intellectuals' circles, to judge from Loos's specific reference to them in his article on ladies' fashion in the *Neue freie Presse: "The sentences meted out according to paragraphs 125 through 133 of our Penal Act are the most reliable fashion journal."* See Loos, *Spoken into the Void*, 100. Another law mandated compulsory education to the age of fourteen. See J. Robert Wegs, *Growing Up Working Class: Continuity and Change among Viennese Youth, 1890–1938* (University Park: Pennsylvania State University Press, 1989), 80–82.

50. Quoted in Hannah S. Decker, *Freud, Dora, and Vienna 1900* (New York: Free Press, 1991), 124. See Erik H. Erikson's description of the case as "one of the great psychotherapeutic disasters," in Patrick Mahony, *Freud's Dora: A Psychoanalytic, Historical, and Textual Study* (New Haven, CT: Yale University Press, 1995), 148–49.

51. Decker, *Freud*, 118. After the publication of the analysis in 1905, Freud did not write about women for another fifteen years. See Teresa Brennan, *The Interpretation of the Flesh: Freud and Femininity* (London and New York: Routledge, 1992), 25–26.

52. Krafft-Ebing, *Psychopathia Sexualis*, 569. For the relevant statutes, see Leo Geller, ed., *Allgemeines Strafgesetz*, 4th ed. (Vienna: Moritz Perles, 1894), 124–26. The legal definition of minors as girls not yet fourteen had existed since 1824. See Leo Geller, ed., *Allgemeines bürgerliches Gesetzbuch*, 6th ed. (Vienna: Moritz Perles, 1900), 28, 1311.

53. Musil, *Diaries*, 213.

54. An earlier literary example of the fourteen-year-old girl's allure is Pauline, "cette charmante créature," in Balzac's novel *La peau de chagrin* (1831). A combination of "les grâces de la femme et l'ingénuité de l'enfance," she at first impresses the narrator Raphaël, a boarder in her mother's home, as a sister before he finds himself wondering whether she might also be able to provide him with nights of love. Honoré de Balzac, *La peau de chagrin* (Paris: Garnier-Flammarion, 1971), 148–51. See also Honoré de Balzac, *Works* (New York: The Review of Reviews Co., n.d.), 91. Regarding boundaries to acceptable relationships between the sexes, at least in literature, the transgressive limit demarcated by the age of fourteen is suggested by a list of forty-eight fictional females from 1847 to 1933 that includes no one that young. See Stephen Kern, *The Culture of Love: Victorian to Moderns* (Cambridge, MA, and London:

Harvard University Press, 1992), 407–8. The most significant visual rendering of a fourteen-year-old in the nineteenth century is Edgar Degas' seminal sculpture, *Petite danseuse de quatorze ans*. At its exhibition in 1881, critics recognized that the figure held an intimate allure that belied her youth. Huysmans observed that she was old before her time, at once refined and barbaric. Degas may have inscribed her age into the title in order to emphasize his intention to overcome the contemporary belief that the adolescent female form posed insoluble sculptural difficulties. See Charles W. Millard, *The Sculpture of Edgar Degas* (Princeton, NJ: Princeton University Press, 1976), 98–99, 119–26.

55. Aschenbach 's undoing occurs in part because of his self-delusion in believing that he can contemplate Tadzio's beauty through the aesthetic filter of the mythic forms of classical antiquity. Altenberg echoes such a posture in his 1917 caption for a photograph of Evelyn Landing: "modern Greece: dreaming of you naked, stark naked! Evelyn Landing, my ideal from head to toe! Your boyish figure enchants me! For me no one is more beautiful than you! To imagine you naked, to be allowed to worship you!" See *Traum und Wirklichkeit* (1985), 326. Of course, the nineteenth century is overstocked with "official" art—the French *art pompier* of William Bouguereau comes to mind—in which paintings of nude females could pass muster because of their exotic locales. During the fin de siècle, however, the limits on both age and sex become increasingly elastic. A famous example is Vaslav Nijinsky's final gesture in his choreography for the *Ballets russes* production of Debussy's *Prelude to "The Afternoon of a Faun."* Even more striking are the photographs of nude boys and young men by Wilhelm von Gloeden. Without the recourse to obvious Mediterranean locales and allusions to classical art, they might easily have been accused of being flagrantly salacious. The conflation of age and sexual ambiguities has a rich history, with the character of Mignon from Goethe's *Wilhelm Meister* serving as a particularly important touchstone. See Reinhard Kuhn, *Corruption in Paradise: The Child in Western Literature* (Hanover, NH: University Press of New England, 1982), 186–88.

56. Hofmannsthal, "Das Tagebuch eines jungen Mädchen: Journal de Marie Bashkirtseff," in Hofmannsthal, *Gesammelte Werke: Prosa I*, 107.

57. *Authentisches Tagebuch der Komtesse Mizzi Veith* (Budapest: G. Grimm, 1908), 105–6.

58. *A Young Girl's Diary*, ed. Daniel Gunn and Patrick Guyomard (New York: Doubleday, 1990), 151.

59. See Barker and Lensing, *Peter Altenberg*, 199–200.

60. *Traum und Wirklichkeit* (1985), 324–26. Exactly contemporary to Altenberg's "Nichts Neues," the soubrette Mirzl Kirchner's review *Süsses Mädel* was enjoying a long run at the Salonkapelle Landauer on the Kärntnerstrasse beginning on August 24, 1911, and was still playing at the year's end.

61. Peter Altenberg, "Maske der Vierzehnjährigen," and "Die Vierzehnjährige," in *Bilderbögen*, 66–67, 90. Fourteen-year-olds also appear in "Die Vierzehnjährige," in *Vita Ipsa*, 202–3; "Dolomiten" and "Erster Schnee," in *Semmering*, 39–40, 140; "Götzendämmerung," in *Was der Tag mir zuträgt*, 83–86; and *Pródromŏs*, 108. Equally, there is no shortage of sketches extolling the ideal virtues of thirteen- and fifteen-year-old girls.

62. Rudolf Huber-Wiesenthal, *Das Schwestern Wiesenthal: Ein Buch eigenen Erlebens* (Vienna: Saturn-Verlag, 1934), 128. See also Otto Stoessl, "Die Schwestern Wiesenthal," *Österreichische Rundschau* 14 (January–March 1908): 231–32.

63. Altenberg, "Gartentheater in der 'Kunstschau,'" in *Bilderbögen*, 123. Franz Schreker wrote several scores for the Wiesenthal sisters. *Pantänze* and *Der Wind*, the latter with a scenario by Grete, were premiered on March 2, 1910.

64. Altenberg, "Konzert," in *Neues Altes*, 25. The composer of "the sounds of your new music world" is not specified, but George, Richard Dehmel, and Jens Peter Jacobsen are mentioned as poets; all of them were literary sources for Schoenberg. Perhaps Altenberg's turn of phrase echoes the opening line of George's "Entrückung"—"I feel the air of another planet"—which Schoenberg set as the final movement of his String Quartet no. 2, op. 10. This quartet was premiered in Vienna on December 21, 1908. Altenberg seems to have had little interest in contemporary music, however, and his attitude toward it is encapsulated in his pithy remark: "There are two sorts of modern music: the respected who continue the music of Richard Wagner and the disrespected who are original!" See Altenberg, *Semmering*, 204. For another beauty/beast metaphor, see his description of a trained ape not coincidentally named Peter. Altenberg, "Der Affe Peter," in *Neues Altes*, 73–74.

65. The photograph and text are reproduced in Hans Bisanz, *Peter Altenberg: Mein äusserstes Ideal* (Vienna: C. Brandstätter, 1987), 100–101.

66. Historisches Museum der Stadt Wien, Inv. no. 94924. Altenberg dated the aphorism July 12, 1915. The portrait is dated 1914 by the photographer Letzer. Maria Mayen arrived in Vienna in 1913. Her Burgtheater career often cast her in roles portraying innocent young females, such as Ophelia in *Hamlet* and Cordelia in *King Lear*.

67. Bisanz, *Peter Altenberg*, 95; and *Traum und Wirklichkeit* (1985), 327.

68. For Romako's painting, see the front cover of Botstein and Weintraub, *Pre-modern Art of Vienna*. For relevant examples by Schiele, see Jane Kallir, *Egon Schiele: The Complete Works* (New York: Harry N. Abrams, 1990), 133. The details of Schiele's trial and incarceration are given by Alessandra Comini, *Schiele in Prison* (Greenwich, CT: New York Graphic Society, 1973). In a telling coincidence that blurs the distinction between fin-de-siècle imagination and reality, Romako's young girl wears around her waist a blue ribbon, similar to the one that adorns a lock of Bertha Lecher's hair, which Altenberg kept with her photograph. See Bisanz, *Peter Altenberg*, 39.

69. A friend at that time, Reinhold Hanisch, recalled that Hitler had produced a postcard of a "Schubert evening concert." See Hanisch, "I Was Hitler's Buddy," *The New Republic*, April 19, 1939, 297–98. Three drawings of the courtyard of Schubert's birthplace ascribed to Hitler appear in Billy F. Price, *Adolf Hitler, The Unknown Artist* (Houston, TX: Billy F. Price Publishing Co., 1984), 111. After Hitler's death, another friend from Hitler's youth, August Kubizek, wrote an affectionate memoir in which he used as his literary template the idyllic relationship between Schwind and Schubert in Bartsch's *Schwammerl*. Compare August Kubizek, *The Young Hitler I Knew*, trans. E. V. Anderson (Boston: Houghton Mifflin, 1955), 222; and Rudolf Hans Bartsch, *Schwammerl: Ein Schubert-Roman* (Leipzig: L. Staackmann, 1912), 111. More recently, Lothar Mathan put forward the hotly disputed hypothesis that there was a sensually charged relationship between Hitler and Kubizek, which he also ascribed to Bartsch's novel. See his *The Hidden Hitler*, trans. John Brownjohn (New York: Basic Books, 2001), 35–36.

70. The albums are now in the Wiener Stadt- und Landesbibliothek, Zuwachs Protokoll (Accession Record) 917. Other postcards include reproductions of watercolors inspired by "Lied der Mignon" (D. 877, op. 62) and "Die Post" (D. 911, no. 13; op. 89). On the rise of the postcard industry in Vienna, see Jill Steward, "'Gruss aus Wien': Urban Tourism in Austria-Hungary before the First World War," in *The City in Central Europe: Culture and Society from 1800 to the Present*, ed. Malcolm Gee, Tim

Kirk and Jill Steward (Aldershot, UK: Ashgate, 1999), 129–30. The trafficking in postcards with Schubertian themes really flourished after World War I and culminated in 1928 with the centennial of the composer's death. With characteristic mordancy, Karl Kraus observed that, with the increase in postwar tourism, "the intellectual level has dropped beneath point zero." See Karl Kraus, *In These Great Times: A Karl Kraus Reader*, trans. and ed. Harry Zohn (Montreal: Engendra Press, 1976), 97. For the names of artists who contributed to the postcard market, see Janet Wasserman, "A Schubert Iconography: Painters, Sculptors, Lithographers, Illustrators, Silhouettists, Engravers, and Others Known or Said to Have Produced a Likeness of Franz Schubert," *Music in Art* 28, nos. 1–2 (2003): 199–241. Some two hundred postcards relating to the composer appeared in an exhibition at the Alsergrund district museum in Vienna. See Helga Maria Wolf, ed. *Franz Schubert in Kunst und Kitsch* (Vienna: Bezirksmuseum, Galerie Alsergrund, 1978).

71. Altenberg, "Schubert," in *Bilderbögen*, 73; and *Nachfechsung*, 107. Following the paragraph is the material about Niggli's biography.

72. For reproductions of the photographs, see *Traum und Wirklichkeit* (1985), 313; Bisanz, *Peter Altenberg*, 36–37; and Nebehay, *Gustav Klimt: From Drawing to Painting*, 124. Rieder's watercolor, dated May 1825, was one of the most frequently reproduced portraits of Schubert and, as detailed in chapter 4 of the first volume of this study, served as the basis for many subsequent images of the composer. See Walter Koschatzky, *Viennese Watercolors of the Nineteenth Century* (New York: Harry N. Abrams, 1988), 79. In 1897, it was in the possession of Dumba, who loaned it to the centennial exhibition. Altenberg ("Zimmereinrichtung," in *Vita Ipsa*, 60–61) gives a list of photographs on his walls, including separate references to "Franz Schubert" and "Gustav Klimt's 'Schubert-Idyll.'" A copy of Rieder's portrait is also clearly visible in a 1924 photograph of Reginald Fessenden, who is renowned for transmitting the first wireless broadcast of music in 1906. See Robert Andreas, ed., *100 Events that Shook Our World: A History in Pictures of the Last 100 Years* (New York: Life Books, 2005), 15.

73. The sources for the two photographs listed in note 72 above identify the location as the Graben Hotel, where Altenberg lived from 1913 until his death, and date the photographs around 1914. A more recent source, however, indicates that these photographs show Altenberg's apartment in the Hotel London, dating them around 1909, the year in which Altenberg indicated that his copy of Klimt's painting hung over his bed. See Heinz Lunzer and Victoria Lunzer-Talos, *Peter Altenberg, Extracte des Lebens* (Salzburg: Residenz Verlag, 2003), 164–67. This source also reproduces a photograph of Altenberg's bed in his Graben apartment, dating it 1917 or 1919, in which a portrait of Wagner is clearly visible.

74. Historisches Museum der Stadt Wien, Inv. no. 95020.

75. Altenberg, "Kunstschau 1908 in Wien," *Bilderbögen*, 115. To accompany the publication of two photographs of Rosa Horn's left hand, Altenberg wrote a gloss that began: "Hand. Hand, most precious, most delicate of all shapes, you artwork of God, when does one behold you?!?" See Peter Altenberg, "Die Hand des Frau E. H.," *Kunst: Halbmonatsschrift für Kunst und alles andere*, no. 1 (October 1903): 8–9.

Chapter Seven

1. Richard von Kralik and Hanns Schlitter, *Wien: Geschichte der Kaiserstadt und ihrer Kultur* (Vienna: A. Holzhausen, 1912), 607.
2. Peter Altenberg, "Mama," in *Semmering*, 260.

3. Martin Brussot, *Die Stadt der Lieder* (Leipzig, 1912; 3rd–10th ed., Munich: Renaissance Bücherei, 1923), 366. *Schwanengesang* originally appeared in two books. The text of "In der Ferne," the final song from the second book, conveys sentiments that perhaps are more in keeping with denouement of Brussot's novel.

4. Arnold Schoenberg, "The Relationship to the Text," in Wassily Kandinsky and Franz Marc, eds., *The "Blaue Reiter" Almanac*, trans. Henning Falkenstein, Manug Terzian, and Gertrude Hinderlie, ed. Klaus Lankheit (New York: Viking, 1974), 102. Schoenberg expressed a similar sentiment in 1931 in answer to a questionnaire by Julius Bahle about composing songs: "Once one has reached the stage of real composition, which is already a technical matter, one has overcome any dependence on the subject-matter, its content, artistic value, etc." See Willi Reich, *Schoenberg: A Critical Biography*, trans. Leo Black (New York: Praeger, 1971), 239.

5. Schoenberg, "Relationship to the Text," 95.

6. Ibid., 94–95.

7. In 1885, Mahler completed the *Lieder eines fahrenden Gesellen*, whose first song, "Wenn mein Schatz Hochzeit macht," alludes to the drone bass and melodic figure of "Der Leiermann," the last song of *Winterreise*, even as it skews its repetitive rhythmic pattern. More than one scholar has observed that Hugo Wolf's "Ganymed"—one of three Goethe settings at the end of Wolf's 1889 collection of songs—has a conclusion that reinterprets the same pitches used in Schubert's setting. See Lawrence Kramer, *Music as Cultural Practice, 1800–1900* (Berkeley and Los Angeles: University of California Press, 1990), 171; Eric Sams, *The Songs of Hugo Wolf* (London: Eulenburg, 1983), 243; and Frank Walker, *Hugo Wolf: A Biography* (New York: Knopf, 1952), 251. That same year, Brahms produced a contrapuntal manipulation of "Der Leiermann" as the thirteenth of his Thirteen Canons for six women's voices, op. 113, even as he deleted the quotation from Schubert's "Am Meer" from his revision of the Trio in B Major, op. 8. See also chapter 4 of the first volume of this study. See, however, note 57 below for less sanguine opinions about Schubert's unsophisticated approach to poetic texts.

8. Schoenberg, "Relationship to the Text," 90. Schoenberg was not above appropriating Schubert's music for financial reasons. He arranged *Rosamunde* for piano duet for Universal in 1903, and he orchestrated three songs for Julia Culp in 1912: two settings of "Suleika" (D. 717 and D. 720) and "Ständchen" (D. 889). See Hans Heinz Stuckenschmidt, *Schönberg: Leben, Umwelt, Werk* (Zürich and Freiburg: Atlantis-Verlag, 1974), 72–73; and Joseph Rufer, *The Works of Arnold Schoenberg*, trans. Dika Newlin (New York: Free Press of Glencoe, 1962), 196. In a letter to Berg on October 3, 1912, Schoenberg mentioned that he had orchestrated four songs, but one remains unidentified. See Berg and Schoenberg, *Berg-Schoenberg Correspondence*, 115.

9. Arnold Schoenberg, *Style and Idea*, trans. Leo Black, ed. Leonard Stein (Berkeley and Los Angeles: University of California Press, 1975), 277. The article appeared in the journal *Modern Music* in 1934.

10. Arnold Schoenberg, *Structural Functions of Harmony*, rev. and ed. Leonard Stein (London: Faber, 1969), 156. Schoenberg's copy of the Peters quarto edition of Schubert's A-Minor Quartet includes his chord analysis of the development. For analyses comparing the two works, see Hyde, "Neoclassic and Anachronistic Impulses," 200–235; and Straus, *Remaking the Past*, 161–68. Rudolf Kolisch, whose ensemble premiered the Third Quartet on September 19, 1927, recalled that Schoenberg "was open to ideas—Mozart, Schubert, Brahms." The composer also coached the Kolisch Quartet in its preparation of older works including those of Schubert. See Joan Allen Smith, *Schoenberg and His Circle* (New York: Schirmer Books, 1986), 58, 103.

11. Arnold Schoenberg, *Fundamentals of Musical Composition*, ed. Gerald Strang and Leonard Stein (New York: St. Martin's Press, 1967), 31, 61.

12. The essay is listed in Rufer, *Works of Arnold Schoenberg*, 168, and assigned to 1928, although no date appears on the page. The handwritten location "Roquebrune" appears in the margin. Two-thirds of the text is typed, and the last paragraph is hand-written. I am grateful to the Arnold Schoenberg Institute for providing a copy of the essay as well as a transcription by Anita M. Luginbühl of the handwritten portion.

13. For photographs and descriptions, see *Das interessante Blatt* 47, no. 30 (July 26, 1928): 13; and *Offizielles Erinnerungsalbum an das 10. Deutsches Sängerbundesfest Wien 1928* (Vienna: Lechner, 1928), 184.

14. Schoenberg, *Style and Idea*, 174.

15. Ibid., 174.

16. In the 1926 foreword to the *Three Satires*, Schoenberg's attack upon those who desire "a return to . . ." had to have been leveled at least in part at Stravinsky, the "kleine Modernsky" of the second movement, "Vielseitigkeit," who wore a wig like "Papa Bach." See Messing, *Neoclassicism in Music*, 146–49. Schoenberg's concern with respect inevitably invites comparison with Stravinsky's famous aphorism: "You respect, but I love." See Igor Stravinsky and Robert Craft, *Expositions and Developments* (Garden City, NY: Doubleday, 1962), 129. Stravinsky's neoclassic initiatives were a ripe target for Schoenberg's polemics during the 1920s, although Schoenberg was surely unaware that Stravinsky had lifted the bon mot from contemporary reviews of *Pulcinella*, including a conversation between Serge Diaghilev and Reynaldo Hahn reported by the latter in "Les théâtres—Les premières," *Excelsior*, May 17, 1920, 4.

17. Schoenberg's copy of the clipping was graciously provided by the Arnold Schoenberg Institute. The copy is lacking the newspaper's title, but the clipping is from the *Neues Wiener Journal*, November 14, 1928, 5. The article notes that the talk was given "in the impressive rooms of the Lechner bookshop." Krenek delivered the lecture "Franz Schubert und wir" at the Vienna Schubert Congress in the same month. Aside from secondhand reports, however, Schoenberg could not have known the specifics of Krenek's writings on Schubert until the following year. See Ernst Krenek, "Das Schubert-Jahr ist zu Ende," *Musikblätter des Anbruch* 11 (1929): 11–15. See also John L. Stewart, *Ernst Krenek: The Man and His Music* (Berkeley and Los Angeles: University of California Press, 1991), 96, 99.

18. Schoenberg also shot off an unpublished riposte on February 26, 1926. See Joseph Auner, *A Schoenberg Reader: Documents of a Life* (New Haven, CT, and London: Yale University Press, 2003), 194–96. Krenek's article derived from a talk at the Congress for Music Aesthetics in Karlsruhe on October 19, 1925, which included "some satirical remarks on the twelve-tone system." See Stewart, *Ernst Krenek*, 96. Schoenberg had contributed the essay "Gesinnung oder Erkenntnis?" to the same Universal Edition compilation.

19. Bálint András Varga, "Three Questions on Music: Extracts from a Book of Interviews in the Making," *New Hungarian Quarterly* 25, no. 93 (Spring 1984): 198. "I tried to apply the same trick that Schubert used in the last movement of his B-flat major Trio by transforming the $\frac{2}{4}$ of the main theme into the $\frac{3}{2}$ of the second without changing the tempo of the quarternotes. I did the same thing by using the tempo of the quarternotes of the march ($\frac{4}{4}$) in the $\frac{3}{2}$ section of the second idea. Incidentally, he did the same thing in one of the late Three Piano Pieces, which I don't have handy. Obviously, the whole cycle of the *Reisebuch aus den österreichischen Alpen* [op. 62 (1929)] is influenced by Schubert, as well as various details of period construction in several works of the period 1925 to 1930." See also Garrett H. Bowles, *Ernst Krenek:*

A Bio-Bibliography (New York: Greenwood, 1989), 374. Krenek had previously studied "innumerable Schubert songs" with the composer and pianist Eduard Erdmann in Berlin. See Stewart, *Ernst Krenek*, 98. Krenek was also good friends with Artur Schnabel, who at that time was a rarity among contemporary pianists in regularly performing Schubert's sonatas in his recitals.

20. Schoenberg, in Berlin since January 1926, could hardly have failed to take note of the *Jonny* premiere in that city on October 8, 1927, and its subsequent premiere in Vienna on December 31. As he and Krenek shared the same publisher, Universal Edition, Schoenberg may have been aware of the publicity generated on the opera's behalf, including the sale of the film rights to Metro-Goldwyn-Mayer for $10,000. *Von heute auf Morgen* was begun on October 25, 1928. In a letter of October 4, 1929, to William Steinberg, who was to conduct the Frankfurt premiere, Schoenberg urged that the performers avoid any suggestion of musical or gestural exaggeration: "Better colourless than crude—better no humor than this disgusting slapstick which is rampant in Berlin." See Rufer, *Works of Arnold Schoenberg*, 55. Schoenberg may well have had more than *Jonny* in mind. Kurt Weill's one-act comic opera *Der Zar lässt sich photographieren* had its Berlin premiere on October 14, 1928, and *Die Dreigroschenoper* was first performed there on August 31 of the same year. On Schoenberg and Weill, see Kim Kowalke, *Kurt Weill in Europe* (Ann Arbor, MI: UMI Research Press, 1979), 156–57. On Schoenberg and *Jonny spielt auf*, see Susan C. Cook, *Opera for a New Republic: The "Zeitopern" of Krenek, Weill, and Hindemith* (Ann Arbor, MI: UMI Research Press, 1988), 85.

21. My appreciation goes to Camille Crittenden, formerly of the Archive of the Arnold Schoenberg Institute, for assistance in deciphering the composer's handwriting.

22. See Han Heinz Stuckenschmidt, *Arnold Schoenberg: His Life, World and Work*, trans. Humphrey Searle (New York: Schirmer Books, 1977), 325–26. In 1985, Krenek recalled a conversation with Schoenberg around 1923 that included discussion of the relative merits of Beethoven and Schubert. See Ernst Hilmar, "Schubert und die Zweite Wiener Schule," in *Schubert durch die Brille: The Oxford Bicentenary Symposium*, ed. Elizabeth Norman McKay and Nicholas Rast (Tutzing, Germany: Hans Schneider, 1998), 78. Krenek's affection for Schubert dates at least to 1921, when Universal Edition published his completion of the Sonata in C Major (D. 279).

23. "Schubert-Huldigungen des Auslandes," *Neues Wiener Journal*, November 24, 1928, 4. An amusing if oblique reference to Schoenberg's style occurs in a report on the opening event of Vienna's official Schubert festival. One of the two boys performing the solos in the Gloria of the Mass in A-flat Major (D. 678) miscued, so that "for fifteen measures Schubert became atonal." See "Oesterreichs Schubert-Huldigung: Die offizielle Feier der Regierung," *Neues Wiener Journal*, November 19, 1928, 2.

24. Berg and Schoenberg, *Berg-Schoenberg Correspondence*, 380.

25. Ibid., 345. In comparison with Webern, Berg's fondness for Schubert's music is barely documented, although Felix Galimir recalled an instance around 1930 when the composer interrupted a quartet rehearsal. "'Oh no, don't stop,' he said. 'What were you playing?' It was the *Quartett-Satz* [D. 703]. So we started playing again, and the man—I swear this is not an exaggeration—the man was sitting there crying like a child." See Joseph Horowitz, "Felix Galimir Recalls Berg and Webern in Vienna," *New York Times*, Section 2, January 11, 1981, 19.

26. I am grateful to the Arnold Schoenberg Institute for providing me with a transcription of this passage by Anita M. Luginbühl and a translation by Susan Sloan. My translation is based upon this translation, but is not exactly the same in all respects.

27. Jean and Jesper Christensen, *From Arnold Schoenberg's Literary Legacy: A Catalog of Neglected Items* (Warren, MI: Harmonie Park, 1988), 70–71. Schoenberg's library includes two copies (without annotations) of the C-Major Quintet—a Philharmonia pocket score and a larger Universal Edition score—each bound by the composer with other chamber works of Schubert. The Arnold Schoenberg Institute graciously provided a list of these works.

28. Schoenberg, *Structural Functions*, 57.

29. Oskar Kokoschka, *Mein Leben* (Munich: Bruchmann, 1971), 282; and Rufer, *Works of Arnold Schoenberg*, 44, 138. Schoenberg also orchestrated Schubert's "Ständchen" (D. 889) for an ensemble that, as Ernst Hilmar has noted, closely resembles the scoring for the Serenade, op. 24, whose first movement was begun later that year. See Hilmar, "Schubert und die Zweite Wiener Schule," 79–80; and Rufer, *Works of Arnold Schoenberg*, 124, 197. A facsimile of Schoenberg's arrangement for clarinet, bassoon, mandolin, guitar, two violins, viola, and cello appears in *The London Sinfonietta: The Complete Instrumental and Chamber Music of Arnold Schoenberg and Roberto Gerhard* (London: Sinfonietta Productions Limited, 1973), 70–71.

30. The examples from the scherzo of Schubert's Piano Sonata in D Major (D. 850, op. 53) and the first movement of Brahms's String Quartet in C Minor, op. 51, no. 1, appear respectively in "Criteria for the Evaluation of Music" (1941) and "Brahms the Progressive" (1947). See Schoenberg, *Style and Idea*, 128, 403.

31. From "Brahms the Progressive," in Schoenberg, *Style and Idea*, 403. See also August Wilhelm Ambros, *Zur Lehre vom Quinten-Verbote* (Leipzig: Heinrich Matthes, 1859), 21, discussed in chapter 2 of the first volume of this study.

32. The most problematic feature of the transcription is whether or not a low bass note should appear in the first measure. Given the octaves on the downbeats of the other four measures, a low E sharp is implied. Below the staff, one might discern an accidental and, underneath this, possibly two ledger lines. These markings do not determine clearly what pitch, if any, was intended.

33. For a facsimile and analysis of "Konstruktives in der Verklärten Nacht" see Walter Bailey, *Programmatic Elements in the Works of Schoenberg* (Ann Arbor, MI: UMI Research Press, 1984), 32–37; and Walter Frisch, *The Early Works of Arnold Schoenberg: 1893–1908* (Berkeley and Los Angeles: University of California Press, 1993), 123–27. Frisch notes Dika Newlin's observation that this "important detail of harmonic structure . . . , while it must always have been latent in Schoenberg's mind, did not come to him as a consciously formulated concept until years after the composition of *Verklärte Nacht.*" See Dika Newlin, *Bruckner, Mahler, Schoenberg* (New York: Norton, 1978), 214. However, Schoenberg himself claimed in a letter to the conductor Bruno Walter on December 23, 1943: "I was always conscious while composing that the D♭ major is a counterbalance against the E♭ major, but I had not known that the basis for this apparently lies in the principal motive." See Auner, *Schoenberg Reader*, 297. For a harmonic analysis of the work, including its Neapolitan gestures, see Richard Swift, "1-XII-99: Tonal Relations in Schoenberg's *Verklärte Nacht*," *19th-Century Music* 1, no. 1 (July 1977): 3–14.

34. Brown, *Essays on Schubert*, 91, 94.

35. Reich, *Schoenberg*, 5. The movement is dated ca. 1895 in Arnold Schoenberg, *Sämtliche Werke*, ed. Christian Martin Schmidt, Abt. VI, Reihe B, Bd. 20 (Mainz: Schott, 1986), 218. Rufer (*Works of Arnold Schoenberg*, 100) indicates the possibility that it was intended for string orchestra. Labor's name appears often in Alma's diary. He was a favorite of the Wittgenstein family, which arranged a concert for him at the Musikverein. See McGuinness, *Wittgenstein: A Life*, 125.

36. For discussions of the significance of the quintet's Neapolitan harmony in relationship to Schubert's compositions from the 1820s, see Donald Francis Tovey, *The Main Stream of Music and Other Essays* (New York: Oxford University Press, 1949), 147–51; originally appearing as "Tonality," *Music & Letters* 9, no. 4 (October 1928): 341–63. Tovey's analytical context was that "major and minor keys on the same tonic are identical," an apt comment with regard to Schubert. Thus the Neapolitan harmony figures as prominently in the Impromptu in A-flat Major (D. 935, no. 2; op. posth. 142) as it does in the contemporary Fantasy in F Minor (D. 940, op. 103). The harmony's presence in the fifth and sixth *Moments musicaux*, in F Minor and A-flat Major (D. 780, op. 94), suggests an attempt on Schubert's part to pair the two works. C-sharp minor plays an important structural role in two C-major works: the *Wanderer* Fantasy (D. 760, op. 15) and the *Grand Duo* (D. 812, op. posth. 140). See also the first movement of the Ninth Symphony, whose move to D-flat minor in the recapitulation mirrors an expository turn to ♭vi. Similarly, in the outer movements of the Trio in E-flat Major (D. 929, op. 100), modulations to the minor Neapolitan (written as E minor) occur as structural parallels to earlier modulations to ♭vi. The second theme of the same work's scherzo moves to the major Neapolitan via a characteristically Schubertian pivot note: A flat respelled as G sharp, which becomes part of an E-major (F-flat major) triad.
37. Schubert's fondness for the Neapolitan relationship in 1828 is apparent in the Fantasy in F Minor. A work whose four continuous sections are reminiscent of the four movements of a larger instrumental work, its central largo and scherzo are both in F-sharp minor. G-flat major reappears in turn in the final twelve measures. The fugal finale pays obvious homage to similar constructions by Beethoven. (Karl Holz claimed that he participated in a performance of Beethoven's Quartet in C-sharp Minor, op. 131, for Schubert one month before his death.) Less obvious is the opening theme's allusion to Haydn's keyboard Variations in F Minor, not only in the rhythmic and harmonic character of its principal theme, but in the striking articulation of the Neapolitan harmony prior to a turn to the parallel major mode. The Fantasy in F Minor was the work that Schubert insisted on dedicating to Caroline Esterházy in a letter to Schott on February 21, 1828. See Deutsch, *Documentary Biography*, 739. More recently, Rita Steblin has argued that Schubert's choice of key was a coded reference to the relationship between Schubert and Caroline Esterházy. See Steblin, "Neue Forschungsaspekte," 21–33.
38. For Schoenberg the theorist, the Neapolitan was necessarily obtained through the minor subdominant regardless of the mode of the tonic. See Arnold Schoenberg, *Theory of Harmony*, trans. Roy E. Carter (Berkeley and Los Angeles: University of California Press, 1978), 234. This origin was not universally accepted in fin-de-siècle Vienna. Schenker, for example, saw this harmony as a derivative of the Phrygian mode. See Heinrich Schenker, *Harmony*, trans. Elisabeth Mann Borgese, ed. Oswald Jonas (Chicago and London: University of Chicago Press, 1954), 109–10.
39. See the facsimile reproduced in Ulrich Thieme, *Studien zum Jugendwerk Arnold Schönbergs: Einflüsse und Wandlungen* (Regensburg, Germany: G. Bosse, 1979), 100.
40. "Tonal axis" is the term used by Rey M. Longyear, "Beethoven and Romantic Irony," *The Creative World of Beethoven*, ed. Paul Henry Lang (New York: Norton, 1970), 145–62, to describe large-scale harmonic planning such as is found in the rondo finale of Beethoven's Violin Sonata in G Major, op. 30, no. 3. There, however, the two surrounding harmonies, B major and E-flat major, are at the distance of a major third. Beethoven replicated this relationship in the sonata form first movement of the String Quartet in B-flat Major, op. 130, where the subsidiary theme appears in G-flat major and the development begins in D major. Schubert himself employed a similar strategy

in the first movement of the Ninth Symphony, with its subsidiary theme in E minor and development starting in A-flat major. This unfolding of key relationships was echoed in turn by Brahms in the first movement of the Symphony no. 3 in F Major, using A major and C-sharp minor. This movement is also relevant to the present discussion since its opening harmonic gesture so strikingly resembles the beginning of Schubert's quintet. As Michael Musgrave has shown, Schoenberg's interest in mediant areas that are equally distant from the tonic governs the keys of the four movements of his D-Major String Quartet, whose inner movements are in F major and B-flat minor respectively. This method of organization does not appear to have an "obvious parallel in the tradition on which Schoenberg drew," although Musgrave relates it most directly to Brahms's works. See Michael Musgrave, "Schoenberg and Brahms: A Study of Schoenberg's Response to Brahms's Music as Revealed in His Didactic Writings and Selected Early Compositions" (PhD diss., London University, 1979), 284–86.

41. For an analysis of Schoenberg's first movement, see Frisch, *Early Works*, 33–39. Frisch astutely observes its indebtedness to Brahms for its motivic creation and manipulation. Such a relationship, however, does not negate the possibility that the quintet might also have loomed large in its influence on the young Schoenberg's harmonic language. Noting the first appearance of the German sixth chord at mm. 55 and 57 of Schoenberg's movement, Frisch, *Early Works*, 37, continues: "Our ears cannot, I think, fail to make the association [of its appearance at m. 157 and after] with the earlier occurrence." In Schubert's movement, there is also an earlier occurrence of an augmented sixth (m. 38) at a pitch level (B flat–D–G sharp) that reinforces the D-minor harmony (by way of its A-major dominant) and that had earlier undergirded a repetition of the first theme (mm. 11–16). Schoenberg later used these opening measures of the quintet's first movement to illustrate a "Dorian" transposed sequence. See Schoenberg, *Structural Functions*, 126–27. Interestingly, Schoenberg analyzed the sonority F sharp–A–C–E flat (mm. 3–4) and its Dorian relative (G sharp–B–D–F at mm. 13–14) as altered second chords. Whether or not the diminished sonority of m. 3 subsequently metamorphoses into the German sixth is an analytical issue beyond the scope of this inquiry. Certainly, the latter was an intriguing sonority for Schubert since it begins "Am Meer," written in the same year as the quintet and in the same key.

42. Zemlinsky apparently advised Schoenberg on the quartet's composition. See Frisch, *Early Works*, 32–33. The two had met around 1894 or 1895 when Zemlinsky was writing two movements, in D minor (October–November 1894) and D major (January 1896), of a string quintet with the traditional second viola. The D-minor movement was performed in Vienna on March 5, 1896. See Lawrence A. Oncley, "The Works of Alexander Zemlinsky: A Chronological List," *Notes* 34, no. 2 (December 1977): 291–302.

43. Schoenberg, *Style and Idea*, 80; Frisch, *Early Works*, 37–39; Rufer, *Works of Arnold Schoenberg*, 101; and Stuckenschmidt, *Arnold Schoenberg*, 33. In 1936, Schoenberg expressed the notion of early influences in an archly offhand manner, recalling that "in my youth I composed songs à la Brahms, and before that à la Schubert, and even further back, when I knew only violin music, I composed à la Viotti, and Bériot, and . . . Singele!" See Reich, *Arnold Schoenberg*, 248. One wonders whether Schoenberg appreciated the echo of Schubert's quintet in Brahms's lengthy peroration on the D flat–C dyad in mm. 176–93 of the scherzo of the Piano Quintet in F Minor, op. 34. This allusion was noted in Donald Francis Tovey, *The Forms of Music* (London: Oxford University Press, 1957), 127. Greg Vitercik, *The Early Works of Felix Mendelssohn* (Philadelphia: Gordon and Breach, 1992), 308, has suggested that the C-minor andante of Mendelssohn's Octet (1825, pub. 1833) was as likely a model for Brahms.

44. Nuria Schoenberg Nono, ed., *Arnold Schoenberg Self-Portrait* (Pacific Palisades, CA: Belmont, 1988), 71. See also Frisch, *Early Works*, 184–87.

45. Schoenberg Nono, *Arnold Schoenberg Self-Portrait*, 72.

46. Frisch, *Early Works*, 185–87. Inasmuch as Frisch notes that the first sketches for the "kräftig" section of Schoenberg's String Quartet no. 1 carry the designation "Neues Leben fühlend," one suspects an echo of Beethoven's "Neue Kraft fühlend" marking in the andante section of the third movement of the Quartet in A Minor, op. 132. At this time, Beethoven was much on the minds of the Viennese avant-garde. From April 15 through June 15, 1902, the Secession had dedicated their fourteenth exhibition to Max Klinger's Beethoven statue. This show depicted a striking amalgam of styles. The physical design, which included Klimt's famous frieze, was an arresting example of *Die Moderne* and, one suspects, a representation that was calculated to be unlike the traditionally art historical commemoration of Schubert at the Künstlerhaus in 1897. Yet Klinger's statue was a palpable confirmation of the Jovian Beethoven whose very presence, in another treasured and hoary legend, could deter the pathetically shy Schubert from visiting the great man.

47. Schoenberg, *Style and Idea*, 131. On the musical relationship between Beethoven and Schubert, see Edward T. Cone, "Schubert's Beethoven," *Musical Quarterly* 56, no. 4 (October 1970): 779–93. Beethoven's *Appassionata* Sonata in F Minor, op. 57, has been observed as an influence on both Schubert's Fantasy (D. 48) and "Die junge Nonne" (D. 828; op. 43, no. 1). See Nigel Nettheim, "How the Young Schubert Borrowed from Beethoven," *Musical Times* 132 (July 1991): 330–31; and Brian Newbould, *Schubert: The Music and the Man* (Berkeley and Los Angeles: University of California Press, 1997), 297. "Die junge Nonne" is one of several songs that link the Neapolitan with images of the storm, as in "Erlkönig," mm. 117–23 and 143–48; "Einsamkeit," mm. 28–34; and "Der Lindenbaum," mm. 45–51. (These last two are nos. 5 and 12 of *Die Winterreise*, D. 911, op. 89.) Chamber works of Beethoven that feature striking Neapolitan gestures early on include the second movement of the Quartet in F Major, op. 59, no. 1; the first movement of the Quartet in E Minor, op. 59, no. 2; and the first movement of the Quartet in F Minor, op. 95. The first two might well be the pair of *Rasumovsky* Quartets to which Schoenberg referred. In "Brahms the Progressive," Schoenberg gave the latter two works as examples of Neapolitan triads. See Schoenberg, *Style and Idea*, 404. Given the theoretical derivation of the Neapolitan, it is hardly surprising that all of these compositions should be in minor keys, unlike Schubert's Quintet and Trio in E-flat Major, although the opening of the *Quartett-Satz* in C Minor falls into the same category. Beethoven's *Hammerklavier* Sonata in B-flat Major, op. 106, however, is a pungent representative of the appearance of the Neapolitan in every movement.

48. On January 29, Hellmesberger again played the work at a private soirée given by Erich Graf von Kielmansegg, the governor of Lower Austria. The C-Major Quintet was a popular work in the Vienna of the 1890s. Other performances include those given by the Bohemian Quartet on February 4, 1896, the Rosé Quartet on 10 March 10, 1896, the Hellmesberger Quartet on January 16, 1895, and the Winkler Quartet on December 13, 1894.

49. In the essay "How One Becomes Lonely" (1937), Schoenberg invited a comparison of the two works when he cited the ending of his First Quartet as an example where "as in *Verklärte Nacht*, parts of understandable smoothness could not calm down the public or reassure them." Schoenberg, *Style and Idea*, 44. Regarding the First Quartet, David Lewin has pointed out that the principal theme in the opening section of its first movement articulates respectively D–E flat–C sharp–D, but he plays down the

Neapolitan effect of the passage. This observation does not negate a relationship to the E flat–D of the coda. See David Lewin, "Inversional Balance as an Organizing Force in Schoenberg's Music and Thought," *Perspectives of New Music* 6, no. 2 (Spring–Summer, 1968): 4. Also, the D–E flat–C sharp–D sequence unmistakably recalls the D:E flat:D:D flat:D that in 1932 Schoenberg indicated was the organizing principle for *Verklärte Nacht*. That Lewin's "inversional balance" is comparable to Schoenberg's treatment of mediant areas around a tonal axis as described earlier in this chapter is a possibility broached by Musgrave, "Schoenberg and Brahms," 292–93.

50. Frisch, *Early Works*, 244–45.

51. The first violin's D–B flat resolution to A (mm. 216–17) emphasizes the Neapolitan pedigree of the harmony. The leading tone function of the viola's F♮ is undercut by its failure to resolve to the tonic in m. 218. The cadence at mm. 230–31, in which both C sharp and E sharp are present in the upper parts, has been analyzed as a dominant with an altered fifth by Catherine Dale, *Tonality and Structure in Schoenberg's Second String Quartet, Op. 10* (New York and London: Garland, 1993), 121–22.

52. "Arnold Schoenbergs Fis-Moll-Quartett," *Erdgeist* 4, no. 7 (February 20, 1909): 225–34, reprinted in the *Journal of the Arnold Schoenberg Institute* 16, nos. 1/2 (June/November 1993): 295–304.

53. Similar motion from G to F sharp appears, although less strongly articulated, toward the end of the finale (mm. 145–46). The 1909 analysis gives three measures in the finale (mm. 110–12) "in which the actual main motive of the movement resounds with greatest force" on the word "heiligen." The D–E flat motion of the first two measures coupled with the arpeggiations in the second viola recall the final measures of *Verklärte Nacht*. See Dale, *Tonality and Structure*, 229. Myles Jordan has observed a relationship between the rhythm of the first violin melody in measure one of the first movement of Schoenberg's String Quartet no. 2 and the first phrase in the voice of Schubert's "Der Doppelgänger" (no. 13 of *Schwanengesang*). He made the connection in part because of textual similarities between Heine's poem and George's "Litanei," which Schoenberg used in the third movement. See Myles Jordan, "Autobiographical Aspects of Schoenberg's Second String Quartet" (master's thesis, Temple University, 1999), 76–83. As it happens, the intervallic contour of Schoenberg's measure is reminiscent of the second phrase of Schubert's song, which ends on an open fifth of F sharp–C sharp and thus recalls the key of Schoenberg's movement.

54. The Neapolitan relationship was by no means limited to Schoenberg's instrumental works. For discussion of its appearance in *Gurrelieder*, "Traumleben" (op. 6, no. 1), and "Natur" (op. 8, no. 1), see Frisch, *Early Works*, 149–50, 238. Schubert, of course, used Neapolitan harmonies in many of his songs, frequently in association with images of despair and death.

55. Newlin, *Bruckner, Mahler, Schoenberg*, 132.

56. Schoenberg, *Fundamentals*, 31.

57. Ibid., 27. Composers of Schoenberg's generation at times chided Schubert for his limited understanding in setting poetry compared to their own superior comprehension. Max Reger allowed that Schubert, in his Goethe songs, displayed brilliant inspiration, which nonetheless was due to his being "a musical child of nature." As such, Schubert's approach was "naive" in relation to Reger's own critical faculty, owing to Reger's status as a "modern man." See Grete Wehmeyer, *Max Reger als Liederkomponist* (Regensburg, Germany: Gustav Bosse, 1955), 261, quoting Adalbert Lindner, *Max Reger* (Stuttgart: Engelhorn, 1923), 281. Hugo Wolf considered

Schubert's "Ganymed" and "Prometheus" to be unsatisfactory; "a truly Goethean spirit" could only be fulfilled by "the post-Wagnerian era." See Hugo Wolf, *Briefe an Emil Kauffmann* (Berlin: S. Fischer, 1903), 25, quoted in Susan Youens, *Hugo Wolf: The Vocal Music* (Princeton, NJ: Princeton University Press, 1992), 335. For Wolf, the symphonic works of Schubert, "the amiable islander," fared even worse compared to those of Beethoven, "a god annihilating with a mere glance whomever he encountered." See Hugo Wolf, *The Music Criticism of Hugo Wolf*, trans. and ed. Henry Pleasants (New York: Holmes & Meier, 1978), 38.

58. Smith, *Schoenberg and His Circle*, 169. The pedagogical value of studying Schubert's music also appears in a reminiscence of Richard Strauss, who recalled that Brahms advised him to "take a close look at Schubert's dances and practice inventing simple eight-bar melodies." Quoted in Gilliam, *Life of Richard Strauss*, 33. The teenaged Erich Wolfgang Korngold orchestrated Schubert's "Kindermarsch" (D. 928), but one did not need to be at the beginning of a career to pursue such an endeavor, as illustrated by Webern's orchestration of Schubert's *German Dances* (D. 820) upon their discovery in 1931.

59. Dika Newlin, *Schoenberg Remembered* (New York: Pendragon, 1980), 132. That Schoenberg, at least in old age, was aware of the historical tradition of this Schubert cliché is suggested by a remark in his essay "Criteria for the Evaluation of Music" (1948): "Much depends upon the viewpoint whether criteria are judged as merits or as shortcomings. When Schumann speaks of the 'heavenly length' of Schubert's music, one might be led to consider length, heavenly or earthly, a merit." See Schoenberg, *Style and Idea*, 131. When, in December 1943, Bruno Walter asked to make a cut in *Verklärte Nacht*, Schoenberg's refusal reflected a less than generous attitude toward Schubert's length: "I also find the piece [*Verklärte Nacht*] too long in many sections. But I believe: if its other qualities are not capable of compensating for that, then it is just as bad as most of Schubert—who is always much too long—without wanting to compare myself with him further, or at most in this respect." See Auner, *Schoenberg Reader*, 298.

60. Moldenhauer and Moldenhauer, *Anton von Webern*, 75. Webern's affection for Schubert may have been encouraged by his attendance at Guido Adler's music history lectures. See Webern's letter to Ernst Diez on November 5, 1902, in Ernst Hilmar, ed., *Anton Webern, 1883–1983: Eine Festschrift zum hundertsten Geburtstag* (Vienna: Universal Edition, 1983), 60. By 1903, Webern had made five arrangements of Schubert songs for voice and orchestra as well as four instrumental arrangements of parts of piano sonatas. See Hans Moldenhauer, "A Webern Archive in America," in *Anton von Webern Perspectives*, ed. Demar Irvine (Seattle: University of Washington Press, 1966), 133–34. These were apparently undertaken as school assignments in orchestration. During the 1903–1904 Philharmonic season, Webern heard Schubert's Ninth Symphony and gushed in his diary: "It shone in fullest warmth and most sublime radiance. Such splendour of melodious invention, such healthy sensuousness; now a sweet dreaminess, then again the brightest, most joyful jubilation. So genuinely 'wienerisch.'" See Moldenhauer and Moldenhauer, *Anton von Webern*, 58. This affection was long-standing. In 1916, Anton Anderluh recalled Webern's "special love for Schubert" manifesting itself in his playing cello in performances of the A-Minor and D-Minor Quartets (D. 804 and 810), and the *Trout* Quintet (D. 667, op. posth. 114). On November 5, 1933, Webern invited Josef Humplik to a concert at which he conducted his orchestration of the *German Dances* along with music from *Rosamunde* (D. 797) and Brahms's Serenade in D Major; "all dear, friendly music." See Anton Webern, *Letters to Hildegard Jone and Josef Humplik*,

ed. Josef Polnauer (Bryn Mawr, PA: Theodore Presser, 1967); Moldenhauer and Moldenhauer, *Anton von Webern,* 218; and Moldenhauer, "Webern Archive," 140.

61. Bertolt Brecht, *Journals, 1934–1955,* trans. Hugh Rorrison, ed. John Willett (New York: Routledge, 1993), 251. In 1928, the year of the centennial of Schubert's death, the International Columbia Companies sponsored the Schubert Centenary Prize. Some of the submissions constituted "attempts to 'complete' the 'Unfinished' Symphonies [*sic*], other works [were] supposedly written in the spirit of Schubert." The grand prizewinner was Kurt Atterberg's Symphony no. 6, and the French zone winner was René Guillemoteau's "Hommage à Schubert." See R. D. Darrell, *The Gramophone Shop Encyclopedia of Recorded Music* (New York: The Gramophone Shop, 1936), 425.

62. Quoted in Glenn Watkins, *Soundings: Music in the Twentieth Century* (New York: Schirmer, 1988), 334–35. I am grateful to Professor Watkins for drawing this to my attention. Schoenberg's lecture was printed in *The Score,* July 1960, 33.

63. In the String Quartet no. 3, each hexachord uses interval classes 3, 5, and 6: the minor third, perfect fourth, and tritone. The *Ode to Napoleon* uses six minor seconds, each separated by a major third within the hexachord. See Ethan Haimo, *Schoenberg's Serial Odyssey* (Oxford: Clarendon Press, 1990), 26–28, 79–80, 155; Lewin, "Inversional Balance," 10; David Lewin, "A Theory of Segmental Association in Twelve-Tone Music," *Perspectives of New Music* 1, no. 1 (Fall 1962): 93–94; and Josef Rufer, *Composition with Twelve Tones,* trans. Humphrey Searle (London: Barrie and Rockliff, 1961), 90–91.

64. Set-class invariance has recently been used as a means of analyzing Schubert's "Der Doppelgänger." See Janna K. Saslaw and James P. Walsh, "Musical Invariance as a Cognitive Structure: 'Multiple Meaning' in the Early Nineteenth Century," in *Music Theory in the Age of Romanticism,* ed. Ian Bent (Cambridge: Cambridge University Press, 1996), 211–37.

65. Schoenberg, *Style and Idea,* 131. In 1936, Béla Bartók described "Schubertian 'heavenly length'" as something "which we forgive without hesitation for the sake of the youthfully exuberant and astonishingly beautiful ideas." See his *Essays,* ed. Benjamin Suchoff (Lincoln and London: University of Nebraska Press, 1976), 503. For a less charitable gloss that associates "heavenly" with the argot of teenage girls, see Anton Halm, *Die Symphonie Anton Bruckners* (Munich: Georg Müller, 1923), 100.

66. Although it would likely not have pleased Schoenberg's sensibilities, there were other fin-de-siècle claimants to Schubertian harmonic innovations who lay outside of the Austro-German tradition. In 1906, upon hearing a performance of Schubert's Ninth Symphony arranged for piano duet, Nikolai Rimsky-Korsakov pointed out over and over those aspects of the work "that subsequently had an influence on Glinka and Borodin. 'You know,' he said, 'Schubert was the first composer in whom one can meet such bold and unexpected modulations. Before Schubert there was no such thing.'" The performers were Rimsky's wife and her husband's pupil, Igor Stravinsky, who in old age would claim that his teacher had given him Schubert marches to orchestrate, thus mirroring Schoenberg's pedagogical practice. If true, was that experience still in Stravinsky's compositional memory when he interjected a raucous version of Schubert's *Marche militaire* (D. 733; op. 51, no. 1) into the final measures of *Circus Polka?* See Richard Taruskin, *Stravinsky and the Russian Traditions,* vol. 1 (Berkeley and Los Angeles: University of California Press, 1996), 255; and Igor Stravinsky and Robert Craft, *Conversations with Igor Stravinsky* (1958; reprint, Berkeley and Los Angeles: University of California Press, 1980), 39.

67. Roger Sessions, "Schoenberg in the United States," *Tempo,* no. 103 (1972): 15.

Conclusion

1. The classic locution comes from Eric Hobsbawm, "Introduction: Inventing Traditions," in *The Invention of Tradition*, ed. Eric Hobsbawm and Terence Ranger (Cambridge: Cambridge University Press, 1983), 1–14.

2. The rehabilitation of Schubert's career continued apace in the 1920s, lest doubts still linger about his sensibilities. A particularly pointed offering came from Frederick H. Martens, who found that earlier discussions of the composer's relationships with women made him into "a species of disembodied spirit." Martens countered: "This is unfair to Schubert, who was no plaster saint, but a single man in the barracks of Vienna's 'joie de vivre.' It robs him of the sane, natural virility which was his in every sense, and it makes him a biologic impossibility." Nonetheless, Martens concluded that Schubert's encounters with women remained incidental to his music. See Frederick H. Martens, "Schubert and the Eternal Feminine," *Musical Quarterly* 14, no. 4 (October 1928): 539–52. A contemporary but quite different rationale for asserting Schubert's manliness came in Richard Eichenauer's notoriously anti-Semitic *Musik und Rasse* (1932), in which this amateur music historian and SS member deliberately avoided citing Schubert's Viennese lineage and instead made him "alpine-nordic." The alpine heritage discernible in the "relaxed softness" of the composer's harmony was, however, never mawkish, because Schubert "always keeps unseen limits beyond which feminine warmth would turn into effeminacy." See Richard Eichenauer, *Music und Rasse*, 2nd ed. (Munich: J. F. Lehmann, 1937), 235.

3. Niggli, *Schubert* (1925), 116.

4. Quoted in Wunberg, *Junge Wien*, 1:366.

Afterword

1. Karl Kraus, "Nachruf," *Die Fackel*, nos. 501–7 (January 1919): 41. Kraus was also no fan of the author of *Schwammerl*. See his "Die Dankbarkeit des Rudolf Hans Bartsch," *Die Fackel*, nos. 381–83 (September 1913): 26–32; and Timms, *Karl Kraus*, 38. The critique of the operetta's commercialism continued in 1932 with Theodor W. Adorno: "*Das Dreimäderlhaus*, with its abuse of Schubert's music, is a necessary component of the economic substructure of hit song fabrication, both as an advertisement and ideology." See Theodor W. Adorno, *Essays on Music*, trans. Susan H. Gillespie, ed. Richard Leppert (Berkeley and Los Angeles: University of California Press, 2002), 429. This essay was entitled "On the Social Situation of Music" and was originally translated by Wes Blomster. In his provocative essay from the centennial year of 1928, however, Adorno displayed a more nuanced consideration of kitsch, and he did not unilaterally dismiss the meaning that the operetta's potpourri assemblage might hold for a consideration of Schubert's music. See Esteban Buch, "Adorno's 'Schubert': From the Critique of the Garden Gnome to the Defense of Atonalism," *19th-Century Music* 29, no. 1 (Summer 2005): 25–30.

2. Schenker, *Der Tonwille*, 2:36.

3. Karl Kraus, "Schober im Liede," *Die Fackel*, nos. 781–86 (June 1928): 105. On the political ramifications of the Sängerbundfest, see Timms, *Karl Kraus*, 449–50.

4. *Ausstellungskatalog: Franz Schubert*, 13. The Schubert centenary of 1928 is amply discussed in Gabriele Eder, *Wiener Musikfeste zwischen 1918 und 1938: Ein Beitrag zur Vergangenheitsbewältigung* (Vienna: Geyer Edition, 1991), 200–242. See also Ilija

Dürhammer, "Der Wandel des Schubert-Bildes im 20. Jahrhundert," in *"Dialekt ohne Erde . . . " Franz Schubert und das 20. Jahrhundert*, ed. Otto Kolleritsch (Vienna: Universal-Edition, 1998), 238–58.

5. Karl Kraus, "Im dreißigsten Kriegsjahr. Gesprochen in der 300. Wiener Vorlesung am 30. November," *Die Fackel*, nos. 800–805 (February 1929): 12–13. The cooking exhibition had come to Kraus's attention through an article in the *Neue freie Presse*, a newspaper that Kraus disliked intensely. Kraus elsewhere indicted the inescapable intrusion of posters and their slogans on modern Viennese life, although by contrast Bruno Bettelheim recalled that in his childhood the billboards for the city's water and Anker bread created a "most convincing association: like my mother, like my home, this larger home in which we all lived, the city, nurtured me well." See Kraus, *In These Great Times*, 44–45; and Bruno Bettelhim, *Freud's Vienna and Other Essays* (New York: Knopf, 1990), 135.

6. Max Millenkovich-Morold, *Die österreichische Tonkunst* (Vienna: Carl Fromme, 1918), 47–48.

7. *Neu Österreich: Seine Kultur, Bodenschätze, Wirtschaftsleben und Landschaftsbilder*, ed. Eduard Stepan (Amsterdam and Vienna: S. L. van Looy, 1923), 159–60, 172–73, 285. In the chapter on literature by Karl Wache, Bartsch was recognized as one of Austria's most read authors. The chapter on Vienna as a cultural center was authored by Joseph August Lux, whose *Grillparzers Liebesroman* (published in 1912, the same year as Bartsch's *Schwammerl*) exploits the legend of Schubert's timidity in meeting Beethoven. See also Max Millenkovich-Morold, *Dichterbuch: Deutscher Glaube, deutsches Sehnen und deutsches Fühlen in Österreich, mit Beiträgen hervorragender österreichischer Dichter, ergänzt durch Biographien und Bildnisse* (Vienna: Adolf Luser, 1933).

8. Broch, *Teesdorfer*, 16–17.

9. On Kraus's postwar critique of Viennese operetta and his elevation of Offenbach, see Timms, *Karl Kraus*, 413–21, 433–40. Vienna's mayor Karl Seitz summed up the political implications of the 1928 celebrations: "a great demonstration of our resolute will to establish in the middle of Europe a single Germany." See "Der Besuch der deutschen Oberbürgermeister," *Wiener Zeitung*, November 17, 1928, 5–6.

Journals and Newspapers Cited

Allgemeine musikalische Zeitung (Leipzig)
Allgemeine Theaterzeitung und Unterhaltungsblatt
Allgemeine Zeitung Judenthum
Arbeiter-Zeitung
Beiblatt zur Zeitschrift für bildende Kunst
Die bildenden Künste
Blätter für Musik, Theater und Kunst
Bühne und Welt
Czas
Deutsche Kunst- und Musik-Zeitung
Deutsches Volksblatt
Deutsche Zeitung
Erdgeist
Der Floh
Freiheit!
Fremden-Blatt
Fromme's musikalische Welt
Geschlecht und Gesellschaft
Die Gesellschaft: Monatsschrift für Literatur, Kunst und Socialpolitik
Illustrirtes Wiener Extrablatt
Internationale Zeitschrift für ärztliche Psychoanalyse
Jahrbuch der Grillparzer-Gesellschaft
Jahrbuch für sexuelle Zwischenstufen
Jahres-Bericht des "Schubertbund"
Jahresbericht des Wiener akademischen Gesangvereines
Jahresbericht des Wiener Männer-Gesang-Vereines
Kunst: Monatsschrift für Kunst und Alles andere
Kunst und Kunsthandwerk
Die Lyra
Musica
Musical Times
Die Musik
Musikalisches Centralblatt

Neue Berliner Musikzeitung
Neue deutsche Rundschau
Neue freie Presse
Neue musikalische Presse
Neue Musik-Zeitung
Neue Revue
Neue Zeitschrift für Musik
Neues Wiener Journal
Neues Wiener Tagblatt
Neuigkeits Welt-Blatt
Die Neuzeit
New York Times
Nord und Süd
Oesterreichische Volks-Zeitung
Ostdeutsche Rundschau
Reichspost
Über Land und Meer
Das Vaterland
Ver Sacrum
Volksblatt für Stadt und Land
Die vornehme Welt
Die Wage
Wiener Abendpost
Wiener allgemeine Zeitung
Wiener Bilder
Wiener Caricaturen
Wiener neueste Nachrichten
Wiener Rundschau
Wiener Sonn- und Montags-Zeitung
Wiener Tagblatt
Wiener Theaterzeitung
Wiener Zeitschrift für Kunst, Literatur, Theater und Mode
Wiener Zeitung
Die Zeit
Zeitschrift für bildende Kunst
Die Zukunft

Selected Bibliography

Abrams, M. H. *The Mirror and the Lamp: Romantic Theory and the Critical Tradition.*
Oxford: Oxford University Press, 1953.
Adam, Thomas. "Heinrich Pudor—Lebensreformer, Antisemit und Verleger." In *Das
bewegte Buch: Buchwesen und soziale, nationale und kulturelle Bewgungen um 1900,*
edited by Mark Lehmstedt and Andreas Herzog, 183–96. Wiesbaden:
Harrassowitz, 1999.
Adametz, Karl. *Franz Schubert in der Geschichte des Wiener Männgergesang-Vereines.*
Vienna: Verlag des Wiener Männergesang-Vereines, 1938.
Adorno, Theodor W. *Essays on Music.* Translated by Susan H. Gillespie and edited by
Richard Leppert. Berkeley and Los Angeles: University of California Press, 2002.
———. *Quasi una Fantasia: Essays on Modern Music.* Translated by Rodney
Livingstone. New York: Verso, 1992.
Ahrens, Christian. "Franz Schuberts Kammermusik in der Musikkritik des 19.
Jahrhunderts." In *Festschrift Rudolf Elvers zum 60. Geburtstag,* edited by Ernst
Herttrich and Hans Schneider, 9–27. Tutzing, Germany: H. Schneider, 1985.
Alings, Reinhard. *Monument und Nation: Das Bild vom Nationalstaat im Medium
Denkmal—Zum Verhältnis von Nation und Staat im deutschen Kaiserreich 1871–1918.*
Berlin: Walter de Gruyter, 1996.
Altenberg, Peter. *Bilderbögen des kleinen Lebens.* Berlin: S. Fischer, 1909.
———. "Gustav Klimt." *Kunst: Monatsschrift für Kunst und Alles andere,* no. 3
(December 1903): 7.
———. "Die Hand des Frau E. H." *Kunst: Halbmonatsschrift für Kunst und alles andere,*
no. 1 (October 1903): 8–9.
———. *Märchen des Lebens.* Berlin: S. Fischer, 1908.
———. *Mein Lebensabend.* 9th–12th ed. Berlin: S. Fischer, 1919.
———. *Nachfechsung.* 4th–5th ed. Berlin: S. Fischer 1919.
———. *Neues Altes.* 4th–5th ed. Berlin: S. Fischer, 1919.
———. *Pròdròmös.* Berlin: S. Fischer, 1906.
———. *Semmering 1912.* 2nd ed. Berlin: S. Fischer, 1913.
———. *Vita Ipsa.* 5th–7th ed. Berlin: S. Fischer, 1918.
———. *Was der Tag mir zuträgt.* 7th–8th ed. Berlin: S. Fischer, 1919.
———. *Wie ich es sehe.* 5th ed. Berlin: S. Fischer, 1910.
Anderson, Benedict. *Imagined Communities: Reflections on the Origin and Spread of
Nationalism.* London: Verso, 1983.
Anderson, Eugene N., and Pauline R. Anderson. *Political Institutions and Social Change
in Continental Europe in the Nineteenth Century.* Berkeley and Los Angeles: University
of California Press, 1967.

Anderson, Harriet. *Utopian Feminism: Women's Movements in "fin-de-siècle" Vienna.* New Haven, CT, and London: Yale University Press, 1992.

Andics, Helmut. *Luegerzeit: Das schwarze Wien bis 1918.* Vienna: Jugend und Volk, 1984.

Applegate, Celia. "How German Is It? Nationalism and the Idea of Serious Music in the Early Nineteenth Century." *19th-Century Music* 21, no. 3 (Spring 1998): 274–96.

Arens, Katherine. "Hofmannsthal's Essays: Conservation as Revolution." In *A Companion to the Works of Hugo von Hofmannsthal,* edited by Thomas A. Kovach, 181–202. Rochester, NY: Camden House, 2002.

———. "Schnitzler and the Discourse of Gender in *Fin-de-Siècle* Vienna." In *A Companion to the Works of Arthur Schnitzler,* edited by Dagmar C. G. Lorenz, 243–64. Rochester, NY: Camden House, 2003.

Ariès, Philippe, and Georges Duby, eds. *A History of Private Life.* 5 vols. Cambridge, MA: Harvard University Press, Belknap Press, 1990.

"Arnold Schoenbergs Fis-Moll-Quartett." *Journal of the Arnold Schoenberg Institute* 16, nos. 1/2 (June/November, 1993): 295–304.

Aronson, Alex. *Music and the Novel.* Totowa, NJ: Rowman and Littlefield, 1980.

Auner, Joseph. *A Schoenberg Reader: Documents of a Life.* New Haven, CT, and London: Yale University Press, 2003.

Aurnhammer, Achim. "Schnitzlers 'Die Nächste [1899]': Intertexualität und Psychologisierung des Erzählens im Jungen Wien." *Germanisch-romanische Monatsschrift* 44, no. 1 (1994): 37–51.

Ausstellungskatalog: Franz Schubert. Vienna: Heimatmuseum Alsergrund, 38, no. 146 (March 1997).

Austin, George Lowell. *The Life of Franz Schubert.* Boston: Shepard and Gill, 1873. Reprint, New York: AMS Press, 1979.

Badura-Skoda, Eva. "Eine authentische Porträt-Plastik Schuberts." *Österreichische Musikzeitschrift* 33, no. 11 (November 1978): 578–95.

Bahr, Hermann. *Gustav Klimt, 50 Handzeichnungen.* Leipzig: Thyrsos-Verlag, 1922.

———. "Die Moderne." *Moderne Dichtung* 1 (January 1890): 13–15.

———. *Secession.* 2nd ed. Vienna: Wiener Verlag, 1900.

———. *Tagebücher, Skizzenbücher, Notizhefte.* Vol. 2. Edited by Moritz Csáky, Helene Zand, Lukas Mayerhofer, and Lottelis Moser. Vienna: Böhlau Verlag, 1996.

Bailey, Colin B., ed. *Gustav Klimt: Modernism in the Making.* New York: Harry Abrams, 2001.

Bailey, Walter. *Programmatic Elements in the Works of Schoenberg.* Ann Arbor, MI: UMI Research Press, 1984.

Banister, Henry C. *Musical Art and Study, Papers for Musicians.* London: George Bell & Sons, 1887.

Barker, Andrew. "The Persona of Peter Altenberg: 'Frauenkult,' Misogyny and Jewish Self-Hatred." In *Studies in German and Scandinavian Literature after 1500: A Festschrift for George C. Schoolfield,* edited by James A. Parente, Jr. and Richard Erich Schade, 129–39. Columbia, SC: Camden House, 1993.

———. "Peter Altenberg's Literary Catalysis." In *From Vormärz to Fin de Siècle: Essays in Nineteenth Century Austrian Literature,* edited by Mark G. Ward, 91–106. Blairgowrie, UK: Lochee Publications, 1986.

———. *Telegrams from the Soul: Peter Altenberg and the Culture of Fin-de-Siècle Vienna.* Columbia, SC: Camden House, 1996.

Barker, Andrew, and Leo A. Lensing. *Peter Altenberg: Rezept die Welt zu sehen.* Vienna: Braumüller, 1995.

Bartók, Béla. *Essays.* Edited by Benjamin Suchoff. Lincoln and London: University of Nebraska Press, 1976.

Bartsch, Rudolf Hans. *Schwammerl: Ein Schubert-Roman.* Leipzig: L. Staackmann, 1912.

Bauer-Lechner, Natalie. *Gustav Mahler in den Erinnerungen von Natalie Bauer-Lechner.* Edited by Herbert Killian and Knud Martner. Hamburg: Wagner, 1984.

Bauernfeld, Eduard von. "Als Einer lebte noch und schafft." In *Jahresbericht des Wiener Männer-Gesang-Vereines über das 29. Vereinsjahr,* edited by Karl Feyerer, 45–47. Vienna: Verlag des Wiener Männer-Gesang-Vereines, 1872.

———— [Rusticocampius, pseud.]. *Ein Buch von uns Wienern.* Leipzig: Verlag von C. L. Hirschfeld, 1858.

————. "Hier war's, vor vierzig Jahren." In *Jahresbericht des Wiener Männer-Gesang-Vereines über das 25. Vereinsjahr,* edited by Eduard Kral, 97–98. Vienna: Verlag des Wiener Männer-Gesang-Vereines, 1868.

————. *Schubert-Feier: Am 28. Februar 1851.* Vienna: Gerold, 1851.

Behler, Ernst. *German Romantic Literary Theory.* Cambridge: Cambridge University Press, 1993.

Beller, Steven. "Kraus's Firework: State Consciousness Raising in the 1908 Jubilee Parade in Vienna and the Problem of Austrian Identity." In *Staging the Past: The Politics of Commemoration in Habsburg Central Europe, 1848 to the Present,* edited by Maria Bucur and Nancy M. Wingfield, 46–71. West Lafayette, IN: Purdue University Press, 2001.

————. "The Tragic Carnival: Austrian Culture in the First World War." In *European Culture in the Great War: The Arts, Entertainment, and Propaganda, 1914–1918,* edited by Aviel Roshwald and Richard Stites, 127–61. Cambridge: Cambridge University Press, 1999.

————. *Vienna and the Jews, 1867–1938.* Cambridge: Cambridge University Press, 1989.

————, ed. *Rethinking Vienna 1900.* New York and Oxford: Berghahn Books, 2001.

Beniston, Judith. "Hofmannsthal and the Salzburg Festival." In *A Companion to the Works of Hugo von Hofmannsthal,* edited by Thomas A. Kovach, 159–80. Rochester, NY: Camden House, 2002.

Berg, Alban. *Letters to His Wife.* Translated and edited by Bernard Grun. New York: St. Martin's Press, 1971.

Berg, Alban, and Arnold Schoenberg. *The Berg-Schoenberg Correspondence.* Edited by Juliane Brand, Christopher Hailey, and Donald Harris. New York: W. W. Norton & Company, 1987.

Berg, Leo. *Das sexuelle Problem in Kunst und Leben,* 5th ed. Berlin: Hermann Walther, 1901.

Berkley, George E. *Vienna and Its Jews: The Tragedy of Success.* Cambridge, MA: Abt Books, 1988.

Berman, Nina. "Hugo von Hofmannsthal's Political Vision." In *A Companion to the Works of Hugo von Hofmannsthal,* edited by Thomas A. Kovach, 205–25. Rochester, NY: Camden House, 2002.

Bettelhim, Bruno. *Freud's Vienna and Other Essays.* New York: Knopf, 1990.

Biba, Otto. *Johannes Brahms und Franz Schubert.* Vienna: Archiv der Gesellschaft der Musikfreunde in Wien, 1997.

Bisanz, Hans. *Peter Altenberg: Mein äusserstes Ideal.* Vienna: C. Brandstätter, 1987.

Bloch, Iwan. *Beiträge zur Aetiologie der Psychopathia sexualis.* 2 vols. Dresden: H. R. Dohrn, 1902.

Boetticher, Friedrich von. *Malerwerke des neunzehnten Jahrhunderts.* 2 vols. 1901. Reprint, Leipzig: H. Schmidt & C. Günther, 1944–48.

Boltzmann, Ludwig. "A German Professor's Trip to El Dorado." *Physics Today,* January 1992, 44–51.

Borsi, Franco, and Ezio Godoli. *Vienna 1900: Architecture and Design.* New York: Rizzoli, 1986.

Botstein, Leon. "Gustav Mahler's Vienna." In *The Mahler Companion,* edited by Donald Mitchell and Andrew Nicolson, 6–38. Oxford and New York: Oxford University Press, 1999.

———. "History, Rhetoric, and the Self: Robert Schumann and Music Making in German-Speaking Europe, 1800–1860." In *Schumann and His World,* edited by R. Larry Todd, 3–46. Princeton, NJ: Princeton University Press, 1994.

———. "Listening through Reading: Musical Literacy and the Concert Audience." *19th-Century Music* 16, no. 2 (Fall 1992): 129–60.

———. "Music and Its Public: Habits of Listening and the Crisis of Musical Modernism in Vienna, 1870–1914." PhD diss., Harvard University, 1985.

Botstein, Leon, and Werner Hanak, eds. *Vienna: Jews and the City of Music, 1870–1938.* Annandale-on-Hudson, NY: Bard College and Wolke Verlag, 2004.

Botstein, Leon, and Linda Weintraub, eds. *Pre-modern Art of Vienna: 1848–1898.* Annandale-on-Hudson, NY: Edith C. Blum Art Institute, 1987.

Bourgault-Ducoudray, Louis. *Schubert.* Paris: H. Laurens, 1908.

Bovenschen, Silvia. *Die imaginierte Weiblichkeit: Exemplarische Untersuchungen zu kulturgeschichtlichen und literarischen Präsentationsformen des Weiblichen.* Frankfurt am Main: Suhrkamp, 1979.

Bowles, Garrett H. *Ernst Krenek: A Bio-Bibliography.* New York: Greenwood, 1989.

Boyer, John W. *Culture and Political Crisis in Vienna: Christian Socialism in Power, 1897–1918.* Chicago: University of Chicago Press, 1995.

———. *Political Radicalism in Late Imperial Vienna: Origins of the Christian Social Movement, 1848–1897.* Chicago: University of Chicago Press, 1981.

Braun, Felix. *Schubert im Freundeskreis.* Leipzig: Insel-Verlag, 1916.

Brecht, Bertolt. *Journals, 1934–1955.* Translated by Hugh Rorrison and edited by John Willett. New York: Routledge, 1993.

Breicha, Otto, ed., *Gustav Klimt: Die Goldene Pforte.* Salzburg: Verlag Galerie Welz, 1978.

Brendel, Franz. *Geschichte der Musik in Italien, Deutschland und Frankreich.* 2nd ed. 2 vols. Leipzig: Matthes, 1855.

Brennan, Teresa. *The Interpretation of the Flesh: Freud and Femininity.* London and New York: Routledge, 1992.

Brett, Philip. "Piano Four-Hands: Schubert and the Performance of Gay Male Desire." *19th-Century Music* 21, no. 2 (Fall 1997): 149–76.

Breuilly, John. *Austria, Prussia and Germany, 1806–1871.* Edinburgh: Pearson Education, 2002.

Brinkmann, Reinhold. "The Lyric as Paradigm: Poetry and the Foundation of Arnold Schoenberg's New Music." In *German Literature and Music: An Aesthetic Fusion,* edited by Claus Reschke and Howard Pollack, 95–129. Munich: Wilhelm Fink, 1992.

Broch, Hermann. *Hugo von Hofmannsthal and His Time.* Translated and edited by Michael P. Steinberg. Chicago: University of Chicago Press, 1984.

———. *Das Teesdorfer Tagebuch für Ea von Allesch.* Edited by Paul Michael Lützeler. Frankfurt am Main: Suhrkamp Verlag, 1995.

Brodbeck, David. "*Primo* Schubert, *Secondo* Schumann: Brahms's Four-Hand Waltzes, Op. 39." *Journal of Musicology* 7, no. 1 (Winter 1989): 58–80.

Brower, Edith. "Is the Musical Idea Masculine?" *Atlantic Monthly* 73 (March 1894): 332–39.

Brown, Maurice J. E. *Essays on Schubert.* London: Macmillan, 1966.

———. *Schubert: A Critical Biography.* New York: Da Capo Press, 1988.

Brusatti, Otto. *Schubert in Wiener Vormärz: Dokumente 1829–1848.* Graz: Akadem. Druck- u. Verlagsanst., 1978.

Brussot, Martin. *Die Stadt der Lieder.* 3rd–10th ed. Munich: Renaissance Bücherei, 1923.

Buch, Esteban. "Adorno's 'Schubert': From the Critique of the Garden Gnome to the Defense of Atonalism." *19th-Century Music* 29, no. 1 (Summer 2005): 25–30.

Bullough, Vern L. *Science in the Bedroom: A History of Sex Research.* New York: BasicBooks, 1994.

Bülow, Hans von. *Briefe und Schriften.* Edited by Marie von Bülow. 8 vols. Leipzig: Breitkopf & Härtel, 1899–1936.

———. *Hans von Bülows Leben: Dargestellt aus seinen Briefen.* Edited by Marie von Bülow. 2nd ed. Leipzig: Breitkopf & Härtel, 1921.

Christensen, Jean, and Jesper Christensen. *From Arnold Schoenberg's Literary Legacy: A Catalog of Neglected Items.* Warren, MI: Harmonie Park Press, 1988.

Citron, Marcia. *Gender and the Musical Canon.* Cambridge: Cambridge University Press, 1993.

Clive, Peter. *Schubert and His World: A Biographical Dictionary.* Oxford: Clarendon Press, 1997.

Cocalis, Susan L., and Kay Goodman, eds. *Beyond the Eternal Feminine: Critical Essays on Women and German Literature.* Stuttgart: Akademischer Verlag Hans-Dieter Heinz, 1982.

Comini, Alessandra. *The Changing Image of Beethoven: A Study in Mythmaking.* New York: Rizzoli, 1987.

———. "From Biedermeier to Secession: The Golden Age of Franz Joseph, 1848–1898." In *Pre-Modern Art of Vienna: 1848–1898,* edited by Leon Botstein and Linda Weintraub, 66–79. Annandale-on-Hudson, NY: Edith C. Blum Art Institute, 1987.

———. *Schiele in Prison.* Greenwich, CT: New York Graphic Society, 1973.

———. "Toys in Freud's Attic: Torment and Taboo in the Child and Adolescent Themes of Vienna's Image-Makers." In *Picturing Children: Constructions of Childhood between Rousseau and Freud,* edited by Marilyn R. Brown, 167–88. Aldershot, UK: Ashgate, 2002.

Cone, Edward T. "Schubert's Beethoven." *Musical Quarterly* 56, no. 4 (October 1970): 779–93.

Conze, Werner, and Jürgen Kocka, eds. *Bildungsbürgertum im 19. Jahrhundert.* 4 vols. Stuttgart: Klett-Cotta, 1985–92.

Cook, Susan C. *Opera for a New Republic: The "Zeitopern" of Krenek, Weill, and Hindemith.* Ann Arbor, MI: UMI Research Press, 1988.

Cooke, Michael G. *Acts of Inclusion: Studies Bearing on an Elementary Theory of Romanticism.* New Haven, CT, and London: Yale University Press, 1979.

Cornelius, Peter. *Literarische Werke.* Edited by Carl Maria Cornelius, Edgar Istel, and Adolf Stern. 4 vols. Leipzig: Breitkopf & Härtel, 1904–5.

Cornwall, Mark. *The Undermining of Austria-Hungary: The Battle for Hearts and Minds.* London: Macmillan, 2000.

Costa, Carl. *Franz Schubert.* Vienna: Im Selbstverlage des Verfassers, 1904.

Crankshaw, Edward. *The Fall of the House of Habsburg.* New York: Viking, 1963.

Crowest, Frederick James. *A Catechism of Musical History and Biography.* London: William Reeves, 1883.

————. *The Great Tone-Poets: Being Short Memoirs of the Greater Musical Composers.* London: Richard Bentley and Son, 1874.

Curtis, Robert Lee. *Ludwig Bischoff: A Mid-Nineteenth-Century Music Critic.* Cologne: Arno Volk, 1979.

Cusick, Suzanne G. "Gender and the Cultural Work of a Classical Music Performance." *Repercussions* 3 (1994): 77–110.

Dahlhaus, Carl. *Nineteenth-Century Music.* Translated by J. Bradford Robinson. Berkeley and Los Angeles: University of California Press, 1989.

Dahms, Walter. "Schlusskapitel der neuen Schubert-Biographie." *Die Musik: Schubert-Heft* 11, no. 23 (September 1, 1912): 259–79.

————. *Schubert.* 10th–14th ed. Berlin and Leipzig: Schuster & Loeffler, 1918.

Dale, Kathleen. *Tonality and Structure in Schoenberg's Second String Quartet, Op. 10.* New York and London: Garland, 1993.

Daviau, Donald G. "Hugo von Hofmannsthal and the Chandos Letter." *Modern Austrian Literature* 4, no. 2 (1971): 28–44.

————. *Understanding Hermann Bahr.* St. Ingbert, Germany: Röhrig Universitätsverlag, 2002.

Dean, Carolyn J. *Sexuality and Modern Western Culture.* New York: Twayne Publishers, 1996.

Decaudin, Michel. "Being Modern in 1885, or, Variations on 'Modern,' 'Modernism,' 'Modernité.'" In *Modernism: Challenges and Perspectives,* edited by Monique Chefdor, Ricardo J. Quinones, and Albert Wachtel, 25–32. Urbana: University of Illinois Press, 1986.

Decker, Hannah S. *Freud, Dora, and Vienna 1900.* New York: Free Press, 1991.

De Joux, Otto. *Die Enterbten des Liebesglückes oder das dritte Geschlecht.* 2nd ed. Leipzig: Max Spohr, 1897.

Del Mar, Norman. *Richard Strauss: A Critical Commentary on His Life and Works.* 3 vols. Ithaca, NY: Cornell University Press, 1986.

Dennis, David B. *Beethoven in German Politics, 1870–1989.* New Haven, CT: Yale University Press, 1996.

Deutsch, Otto Erich. "Anselm Hüttenbrenners Erinnerungen an Schubert." *Jahrbuch der Grillparzer-Gesellschaft* 16 (1906): 99–163.

————. "Der falsche Schubert." *Wiener Magazin* 2, no. 7 (July 1928): 51–55.

————. *Franz Schubert: Sein Leben in Bildern.* Munich and Leipzig: Georg Müller, 1913.

————. "Neue Mitteilungen über Franz Schubert." *Österreichische Rundschau* 23 (April–June 1910): 319–22.

————. *Schubert: A Documentary Biography.* Translated by Eric Blom. 1946. Reprint, New York: Da Capo Press, 1977.

————. *Schubert: Die Dokumente seines Lebens.* Kassel: Bärenreiter, 1964.

————. *Schubert: Die Erinnerungen seiner Freunde.* Leipzig: Breitkopf & Härtel, 1957.

————. *Schubert: Memoirs by His Friends.* Translated by Rosamond Ley and John Nowell. New York: Macmillan, 1958.

————. "Schubert und die Frauen." In *Jahres-Bericht des Schubertbundes in Wien über das siebenundvierzigste Vereinsjahr vom 1. Oktober 1909 bis 30. September 1910,* edited by Anton Weiß, 81–89. Vienna: Verlag des Schubertbundes, 1912.

Deutsch, Otto Erich. "Schuberts Herzeleid." *Bühne und Welt: Zeitschrift für Theaterwesen, Litteratur und Musik* 9, no. 18 (June 1907): 227–31.

———, ed. "Der intime Schubert": Special issue, *Moderne Welt*, December 1, 1925.

Dietrich, Hans. *Die Freundesliebe in der deutschen Literatur.* Leipzig: Woldemar Hellbach, 1931.

Dittrich, Marie-Agnes. "'Jenem imponierenden Heroismus entzogen'—Franz Schubert und das Österreich-Bild nach Königgrätz." In *Franz Schubert—Werk und Rezeption: Schubert-Jahrbuch 1999: Bericht über den Internationalen Schubert-Kongreß, Duisburg 1997,* edited by Dietrich Berke, Walther Dürr, Walburga Litschauer, and Christiane Schumann, 3–21. Duisburg, Germany: Deutsche Schubert-Gesellschaft e. V., 2001.

Duncan, Edmondstoune. *Schubert.* London: J. M. Dent, 1905.

Dürhammer, Ilija. "Der Wandel des Schubert-Bildes im 20. Jahrhundert." In *"Dialekt ohne Erde . . . " Franz Schubert und das 20. Jahrhundert,* edited by Otto Kolleritsch, 238–58. Vienna: Universal-Edition, 1998.

———. "Zu Schuberts Literaturästhetik." *Schubert durch die Brille* 14 (1995): 5–99.

Dürhammer, Ilija, and Till Gerrit Waidelich. *Schubert 200 Jahre.* Heidelberg: Edition Braus, 1997.

Eder, Franz X. *Sexualized Subjects: Medical Discourses on Sexuality in German-speaking Countries in the Late Eighteenth and Nineteenth Centuries.* Minneapolis, MN: Center for Austrian Studies, 1995.

———. "Von 'Sodomiten' und 'Konträrsexualen': Die Konstruktion des 'homosexuellen' Subjekts im deutschsprachigen Wissenschaftsdiskurs des 18. und 19. Jahrhunderts." In *Que(e)rdenken: Weibliche/männliche Homosexualität und Wissenschaft,* edited by Barbara Hey, Ronald Pallier, and Roswith Roth, 15–39. Innsbruck: Studien Verlag, 1997.

Eder, Gabriele. "Schubert und Caroline Esterházy." *Schubert durch die Brille* 11 (1993): 6–20.

———. *Wiener Musikfeste zwischen 1918 und 1938: Ein Beitrag zur Vergangenheitsbewältigung.* Vienna: Geyer Edition, 1991.

Eichenauer, Richard. *Music und Rasse.* 2nd ed. Munich: J. F. Lehmann, 1937.

Einstein, Alfred. *Schubert: A Musical Portrait.* New York: Oxford University Press, 1951.

Ellis, Havelock. *Studies in the Psychology of Sex.* 2 vols. New York: Random House, 1942.

Elshtain, Jean. *Public Man, Private Woman: Women in Social and Political Thought.* Princeton, NJ: Princeton University Press, 1981.

Everdell, William R. *The First Moderns: Profiles in the Origins of Twentieth-Century Thought.* Chicago and London: University of Chicago Press, 1997.

Farnsworth, Paul R., J. C. Trembley, and C. E. Dutton. "Masculinity and Femininity of Musical Phenomenon." *Journal of Aesthetics and Art Criticism* 9, no. 3 (March 1951): 257–62.

Fechner, Gustav Theodor. *Vorschule der Aesthetik.* 2 vols. Leipzig: Breitkopf & Härtel, 1876.

Feis, Oswald. *Studien über die Genealogie und Psychologie der Musiker.* Wiesbaden: J. F. Bergmann, 1910.

Felski, Rita. *The Gender of Modernity.* Cambridge, MA: Harvard University Press, 1995.

Feyerer, Karl, ed. *Jahresbericht des Wiener Männer-Gesang-Vereines über das 29. Vereinsjahr.* Vienna: Verlag des Wiener Männer-Gesang-Vereines, 1872.

———. *Jahresbericht des Wiener Männer-Gesang-Vereines über das 45. Vereinsjahr.* Vienna: Verlag des Wiener Männer-Gesang-Vereines, 1888.

Fischer, Wolfgang G. *Gustav Klimt and Emilie Flöge: An Artist and His Muse.* Translated by Michael Robinson. Woodstock, NY: Overlook Press, 1992.

Fisk, Charles. *Returning Cycles: Contexts for the Interpretation of Schubert's Impromptus and Last Sonatas.* Berkeley and Los Angeles: University of California Press, 2001.

Fliedl, Gottfried. *Gustav Klimt, 1862–1918: The World in Female Form.* Translated by Hugh Beyer. Cologne: Benedikt Taschen, 1991.

Forel, August. *Die sexuelle Frage.* Munich: Ernst Reinhardt, 1920.

Forsyth, Karen. *Ariadne auf Naxos by Hugo von Hofmannsthal and Richard Strauss: Its Genesis and Meaning.* Oxford: Oxford University Press, 1982.

Fout, John C., ed. *German Women in the Nineteenth Century: A Social History.* New York: Holmes & Meier, 1984.

——. "Sexual Politics in Wilhemine Germany: The Male Gender Crisis, Moral Purity, and Homophobia." *Journal of the History of Sexuality* 2 (January 1992): 388–421.

Freud, Sigmund. *Moses and Monotheism.* Translated by Katherine Jones. New York: Vintage, 1955.

——. *The Standard Edition of the Complete Psychological Works of Sigmund Freud.* Translated by James Strachey et al. 24 vols. London: Hogarth Press, 1962.

Frey, Philipp. "Zum Thema 'Wien-Berlin.' " *Österreichische Rundschau* 17 (October–December 1908): 305–7.

Friedjung, Heinrich. *Der Ausgleich mit Ungarn: Politische Studie über das Verhältnis Österreichs zu Ungarn und Deutschland.* 3rd ed. Leipzig: Wigand, 1878.

Friedlaender, Benedikt. *Die Liebe Platon im Lichte der modernen Biologie.* Treptow bei Berlin: Bernhard Zack's Verlag, 1909.

——. *Renaissance des Eros Uranios: Die physiologische Freundschaft, ein normaler Gruntrieb des Menschen und eine Frage der männlichen Gesellungsfreiheit.* Schmargendorf-Berlin: Verlag "Renaissance," 1904. Reprint, New York: Arno Press, 1975.

Friedlaender, Max. *Beiträge zur Biographie Franz Schubert's.* Berlin: A. Haack, 1887.

Frisch, Walter. *The Early Works of Arnold Schoenberg: 1893–1908.* Berkeley and Los Angeles: University of California Press, 1993.

——. *German Modernism: Music and the Arts.* Berkeley and Los Angeles: University of California Press, 2005.

Fröhlich, Erwin. "Der Historienmaler Karl Josef Geiger." Unpublished manuscript. Handschriftsammlung, Österreichische Nationalbibliothek, Vienna, 1965.

Frost, Henry Frederic. *Schubert.* London: S. Low, Marston and Co., 1885.

Fuchs, Hanns. *Richard Wagner und die Homosexualität.* Berlin: H. Barsdorf, 1903.

Fuchs, Heinrich. *Die österreichischen Maler des 19. Jahrhunderts.* 4 vols. Vienna: Dr. Heinrich Fuchs Selbstverlag, 1972–74.

Funder, Friedrich. *From Empire to Republic.* Translated by Barbara Waldstein. New York: Unger, 1963.

Gall, Lothar. *Die Germania als Symbol nationaler Identität im 19. und 20. Jahrhundert.* Göttingen: Vandenhoeck and Ruprecht, 1993.

Gay, Peter. *The Cultivation of Hatred.* Vol. 3 of *The Bourgeois Experience: Victoria to Freud.* New York and London: W. W. Norton & Company, 1993.

——. *The Education of the Senses.* Vol. 1 of *The Bourgeois Experience: Victoria to Freud.* New York: Oxford University Press, 1984.

——. *Schnitzler's Century: The Making of Middle-Class Culture, 1815–1914.* New York: Norton, 2002.

——. *The Tender Passion.* Vol. 2 of *The Bourgeois Experience: Victoria to Freud.* New York: Oxford University Press, 1986.

Geehr, Richard S. *Karl Lueger: Mayor of Fin de Siècle Vienna.* Detroit: Wayne State University Press, 1990.

Geiger, Benno. *Das Fenster in der Mitternacht.* Vienna: Amalthea-Verlag, 1919.

Gellner, Ernst. *Nations and Nationalism.* Oxford: Blackwell, 1983.

Gerhard, L[eo]. "Franz Schuberts Charakter." *Neue Zeitschrift für Musik* 95, no. 13 (March 29, 1899): 141–42.

The German Mind of the Nineteenth Century: A Literary and Historical Anthology, Translated by David Jacobson and edited by Hermann Glaser. New York: Continuum, 1981.

Gibbs, Christopher H. "German Reception: Schubert's 'Journey to Immortality.'" In *The Cambridge Companion to Schubert,* edited by Christopher H. Gibbs, 241–53. Cambridge: Cambridge University Press, 1997.

———. *The Life of Schubert.* Cambridge: Cambridge University Press, 2000.

———. "'Poor Schubert': Images and Legends of the Composer." In *The Cambridge Companion to Schubert,* edited by Christopher H. Gibbs, 36–55. Cambridge: Cambridge University Press, 1997.

———. "The Presence of *Erlkönig*: Reception and Reworkings of a Schubert Lied." 2 vols. PhD diss., Columbia University, 1992.

———. "Schubert in deutschsprachigen Lexika nach 1830." *Schubert durch die Brille* 13 (1994): 70–78.

Giesbrecht-Schutte, Sabine. "'Klagen eines Troubadours.' Zur Popularisierung Schuberts im Dreimäderlhaus." In *Martin Geck, Festschrift zum 65. Geburtstag,* edited by Ares Rolf und Ulrich Tadday, 109–33. Dortmund: Klangfarben, 2001.

Giese, Fritz. *Die Entwicklung des Androgynenproblems in der Frühromantik.* Langensalza, Germany: Wendt and Kaluwell, 1919.

Gilliam, Bryan. *The Life of Richard Strauss.* Cambridge: Cambridge University Press, 1999.

Gilman, Sander L. "Chicken Soup, or the Penalties for Sounding Too Jewish." In *Insiders and Outsiders: Jewish and Gentile Culture in Germany and Austria.* Edited by Dagmar C. G. Lorenz and Gabriele Weinberger, 15–29. Detroit: Wayne State University Press, 1994.

———. *Difference and Pathology: Stereotypes of Sexuality, Race, and Madness.* Ithaca, NY, and London: Cornell University Press, 1985.

———. *Disease and Representation: Images of Illness from Madness to AIDS.* Ithaca, NY, and London: Cornell University Press, 1988.

———. "Freud and the Prostitute: Male Stereotypes of Female Sexuality in *fin-de-siècle* Vienna." *Journal of the American Academy of Psychoanalysis* 9, no. 3 (1981): 337–60.

———. "Sexology, Psychoanalysis, and Degeneration: From a Theory of Race to a Race to Theory." In *Degeneration: The Dark Side of Progress,* edited by J. Edward Chamberlin and Sander L. Gilman, 72–96. New York: Columbia University Press, 1985.

Gomperz, Theodor. *Ein Gelehrtenleben im Bürgertum der Franz-Josefs-Zeit.* Vienna: Verlag der Österreichischen Akademie der Wissenschaften, 1974.

Goodman, Kay. "Motherhood and Work: The Concept of the Misuse of Women's Energy, 1895–1905." In *German Women in the Eighteenth and Nineteenth Centuries: A Social and Literary History,* edited by Ruth-Ellen B. Joeres and Mary Jo Maynes, 110–27. Bloomington: Indiana University Press, 1986.

Goodrick-Clarke, Nicholas. *The Cult Roots of Nazism: Secret Aryan Cults and Their Influence on Nazi Ideology.* New York: New York University Press, 1992.

Greenberg, David F. *The Construction of Homosexuality.* Chicago and London: University of Chicago Press, 1988.

Greene, David. *Mahler, Consciousness and Temporality.* New York: Gordon and Breach, 1984.

Greenfield, Liah. *Nationalism: Five Roads to Modernity.* Cambridge, MA: Harvard University Dept. of Sociology, 1992.

Grillparzer, Franz. *Grillparzers Werke in acht Bänden.* 8 vols. Stuttgart: J. G. Cotta, n.d.

Grimberg, Salomon. "Adele." *Art and Antiques,* Summer 1986, 70–75.

Grove, George. *Beethoven, Schubert, Mendelssohn.* London: Macmillan & Co., 1951.

Gruber, Gernot. "Franz Schuberts *Mein Traum*—Und unsere Träume, ihn zu verstehen." In *"Dialekt ohne Erde . . ." Franz Schubert und das 20. Jahrhundert,* edited by Otto Kolleritsch, 139–49. Vienna: Universal Edition, 1998.

Gurlitt, Ludwig. *Erziehung zur Mannhaftigkeit.* Berlin: Concordia deutsche Verlags-Anstalt, Hermann Ehbock, 1907.

Gutmann, Albert. *Aus dem Wiener Musikleben: Künstler-Erinnerungen, 1873–1908.* Vol. 1. Vienna: Verlag der k. u. k. Hofmusikalienhandlung Albert J. Gutmann, 1914.

Haack, Friedrich. *M. v. Schwind.* 4th ed. Bielefeld and Leipzig: Velhagen and Klasing, 1913.

Habermas, Jürgen. "Modernity Versus Postmodernity." *New German Critique* 22 (1981): 3–14.

———. *Strukturwandel der Öffentlichkeit: Untersuchungen zu einer Kategorie der bürgerlichen Gesellschaft.* Neuwied, Berlin: Luchterhand, 1962.

Hagberg, Gary. *Art as Language: Wittgenstein, Meaning, and Aesthetic Theory.* Ithaca, NY, Cornell University Press, 1995.

Hahn, Hans-Joachim. "From Individual to Ideology: The Crisis of Identity at the Turn of the Century." *New German Studies* 17, no. 1 (1992/93): 1–27.

Haiko, Peter. *Vienna 1850–1930, Architecture.* New York: Rizzoli, 1992.

Haimo, Ethan. *Schoenberg's Serial Odyssey.* Oxford: Clarendon Press, 1990.

Hallett, Garth. *A Companion to Wittgenstein's "Philosophical Investigations."* Ithaca, NY: Cornell University Press, 1977.

Halm, Anton. *Die Symphonie Anton Bruckners.* Munich: Georg Müller, 1923.

Hamann, Brigitte. "Die Habsburger und die deutsche Frage im 19. Jahrhundert." In *Österreich und die deutsche Frage im 19. und 20. Jahrhundert,* edited by Heinrich Lutz and Helmut Rumpler, 212–30. Munich: R. Oldenbourg, 1982.

———. *Hitler's Vienna: A Dictator's Apprenticeship.* Translated by Thomas Thornton. Oxford: Oxford University Press, 1999.

Hanák, Péter. *The Garden and the Workshop: Essays on the Cultural History of Vienna and Budapest.* Princeton, NJ: Princeton University Press, 1998.

Hanslick, Eduard. *Concerte, Componisten und Virtuosen der letzten fünfzehn Jahre, 1870–1885.* 2nd ed. 1886. Reprint, Westmead, UK: Gregg International Publishers Limited, 1971.

———. *Vienna's Golden Years of Music, 1850–1900.* Translated and edited by Henry Pleasants. New York: Simon and Schuster, 1950.

Hanslick, Erwin. *Österreich: Erde und Geist.* Vienna: Verlag Institut für Kulturforschung, 1917.

Hargraves, John A. *Music in the Works of Broch, Mann, and Kafka.* Rochester, NY: Camden House, 2002.

Harrowitz Nancy A. and Barbara Hyams, eds. *Jews and Gender: Responses to Otto Weininger.* Philadelphia: Temple University Press, 1995.

Hausen, Karin. "Family and Role-Division: The Polarisation of Sexual Stereotypes in the Nineteenth Century—An Aspect of the Dissociation of Work and Family Life." In *The German Family: Essays on the Social History of the Family in Nineteenth- and Twentieth-Century Germany,* edited by Birchard J. Evans and W. R. Lee, 51–83. London: Croom Helm, 1981.

Hayek, Max. *Dr. Otto Böhler's Schattenbilder.* Vienna: R. Lechner, 1914.

Healy, Maureen. *Vienna and the Fall of the Habsburg Empire: Total War and Everyday Life in World War I.* Cambridge: Cambridge University Press, 2004.

Helm, Theodor. *Fünfzig Jahre Wiener Musikleben, 1866–1916: Erinnerungen eines Musikkritikers.* Vienna: Im Verlages des Herausgebers, 1977.

Hepokoski, James. "Masculine-Feminine: (En)gendering Sonata Form." *Musical Times* 135 (August 1994): 494–99.

Herzer, Manfred. *Bibliographie zur Homosexualität: Verzeichnis des deutschsprachigen nicht-belletristischen Schrifttums zur weiblichen und männlichen Homosexualität aus den Jahren 1466 bis 1975 in chronologischer Reihenfolge.* Berlin: Winkel, 1982.

Herzog, Hillary Hope. " 'Medezin ist eine Weltanschauung': On Schnitzler's Medical Writings." In *A Companion to the Works of Arthur Schnitzler,* edited by Dagmar C. G. Lorenz, 227–41. Rochester, NY: Camden House, 2003.

Heuberger, Richard. *Franz Schubert.* Berlin: "Harmonie," Verlagsgesellschaft für Literatur und Kunst, 1902.

Hevesi, Ludwig. *Acht Jahre Sezession.* Vienna: Konegen, 1906.

———. "Das Heim eines Wiener Kunstfreundes (Nikolaus Dumba)." *Kunst und Kunsthandwerk* 2 (1899): 341–65.

———. *Oesterreichische Kunst im 19. Jahrhundert.* Leipzig: E. A. Seemann, 1903.

Hewitt, Andrew. *Political Inversions: Homosexuality, Fascism, and the Modernist Imaginary.* Stanford, CA: Stanford University Press, 1996.

Heyse, Paul. *Neue Gedichte und Jugendlieder.* 2nd ed. Berlin: Hertz, 1897.

Hickman, Hannah. *Robert Musil and the Culture of Vienna.* La Salle, IL: Open Court Publishing Company, 1984.

Hilmar, Ernst. "Bausteine zu einer neuen Schubert Bibliographie—Vornehmlich der Schriften von 1929 bis 2000." *Schubert durch die Brille* 25 (2000): 98–302.

———. *Schubert.* Graz: Akademische Druck- u. Verlagsanstalt, 1989.

———. "Schubert und die Zweite Wiener Schule." In *Schubert durch die Brille: The Oxford Bicentenary Symposium,* edited by Elizabeth Norman McKay and Nicholas Rast, 77–88. Tutzing, Germany: Hans Schneider, 1998.

———. "Das Schubert-Bild bei Liszt." *Schubert durch die Brille* 18 (1997): 59–68.

Hilmar, Ernst, and Margret Jestremski, eds. *Schubert-Lexikon.* Graz: Akademische Druck- u. Verlagsanstalt, 1997.

Hinrichsen, Hans-Joachim. *Untersuchungen zur Entwicklung der Sonatenform in der Instrumentalmusik Franz Schuberts.* Tutzing, Germany: Hans Schneider, 1994.

Hirsch, Rudolf. *Beiträge zum Verständnis Hugo von Hofmannsthals: Nachträge und Register.* Frankfurt am Main: S. Fischer, 1998.

Hirschfeld, Magnus. *Sexual Anomalies.* New York: Emerson Books, 1948.

———. *Der urnische Mensch.* Leipzig: Max Spohr, 1903.

Hirschfeld, Robert. "Die Franz Schubert-Ausstellung in Wien." *Über Land und Meer* 39 (1897): 407.

———. "Quer durch die Schubert-Ausstellung." *Neue musikalische Presse* 6, no. 5 (1897): 2–5.

———. "Die Schubert-Feier in Wien." *Neue musikalische Presse* 6, no. 6 (1897): 2–3.

Hitschmann, Edward. "Franz Schubert's Grief and Love." Translated by Edna Spector. *American Imago* 7, no. 1 (March 1950): 67–75.

———. "Franz Schuberts Schmerz und Liebe." *Internationale Zeitschrift für ärztliche Psychoanalyse* 3 (1915): 287–92.

Hobsbawm, Eric. "Introduction: Inventing Traditions." In *The Invention of Tradition*, edited by Eric Hobsbawm and Terence Ranger, 1–14. Cambridge: Cambridge University Press, 1983.

Hoeveler, Diane Long. *Romantic Androgyny: The Women Within*. University Park and London: Pennsylvania State University Press, 1990.

Hofmann, Werner. *Gustav Klimt*. Translated by Inge Goodwin. Greenwich, CT: New York Graphic Society, 1971.

Hofmannsthal, Hugo von. *Gesammelte Werke in Einzelausgaben*. Edited by Herbert Steiner. 15 vols. Frankfurt am Main: S. Fischer, 1946–59.

———. Preface to *Drawings of Old Masters from the Collection of Dr. Benno Geiger*. Zurich: Amalthea, 1925.

———. *Reden und Aufsätze II, 1914–1924*. Frankfurt am Main: Fischer Taschenbuch Verlag, 1979.

———. *Selected Writings*. Translated and edited by Michael Hamburger. New York: Pantheon, 1963.

Hofmannsthal, Hugo von, and Edgar Karg von Bebenburg. *Briefwechsel*. Edited by Mary E. Gilbert. Frankfurt am Main: S. Fischer, 1966.

Hofmannsthal, Hugo von, and Max Mell. *Briefwechsel*. Heidelberg: Verlag Lambert Schneider, 1982.

Holland, Hyacinth. *Moritz von Schwind*. Stuttgart: Neff, 1873.

Honegger, Claudia. *Die Ordnung der Geschlechter: Die Wissenschaften vom Menschen und das Weib, 1750–1850*. Frankfurt am Main: Campus Verlag, 1991.

Hornstein, Robert von. *Memoiren*. Edited by Ferdinand von Hornstein. Munich: Süddeutsche Monatshefte G. m. b. H., 1908.

Hottner, Franz. "Das Schubert-Denkmal in Wien." *Zeitschrift für bildende Kunst* 7 (1872): 261–65.

Huber-Wiesenthal, Rudolf. *Das Schwestern Wiesenthal: Ein Buch eigenen Erlebens*. Vienna: Saturn-Verlag, 1934.

Huch, Ricarda. *Blütezeit der Romantik*. Vol. 1 of *Die Romantik*. 13th and 14th ed. Leipzig: H. Haeffel, 1924.

Hughes, Michael. *Nationalism and Society: Germany 1800–1945*. London: Edward Arnold, 1988.

Huschke, Konrad. "Gemeinsame Züge der 'Antipoden' Beethoven und Schubert." *Neue Musik-Zeitung* 36, no. 21 (1915): 253–57.

Huyssen, Andreas. *After the Great Divide: Modernism, Mass Culture, Postmodernism*. Bloomington and Indianapolis: Indiana University Press, 1986.

Hyde, Martha M. "Neoclassic and Anachronistic Impulses in Twentieth-Century Music." *Music Theory Spectrum* 18 (1996): 200–235.

Izenberg, Gerald N. *Modernism and Masculinity: Mann, Wedekind, Kandinsky through World War I*. Chicago and London: University of Chicago Press, 2000.

Janecka-Jary, Friederike. "Franz Schubert in der deutschsprachigen Bühnenliteratur 1828–1928." PhD diss., University of Vienna, 1996.

Janik, Allan. *Essays on Wittgenstein and Weininger*. Amsterdam: Rodopi, 1985.

Janik, Allan, and Stephen Toulmin. *Wittgenstein's Vienna*. New York: Touchstone, 1973.

Jászi, Oscar. *The Dissolution of the Habsburg Empire*. Chicago: University of Chicago Press, 1929.

Jenks, William Alexander. *The Austrian Election Reform of 1907*. New York: Octagon Books, 1974.

Jensen, Robert. *Marketing Modernism in Fin-de-Siècle Europe*. Princeton, NJ: Princeton University Press, 1994.

Joachim, Joseph. *Letters from and to Joseph Joachim.* Translated by Nora Bickley. 1914. Reprint, New York: Vienna House, 1972.

John, Michael. "'We Do Not Even Possess Our Selves': On Identity and Ethnicity in Austria, 1880–1937." *Austrian History Yearbook* 30 (1999): 17–64.

Johnston, William M. *The Austrian Mind: An Intellectual and Social History, 1848–1938.* Berkeley and Los Angeles: University of California Press, 1972.

Jordan, Myles. "Autobiographical Aspects of Schoenberg's Second String Quartet." Master's thesis, Temple University, 1999.

Jordanova, Ludmilla. *Sexual Visions: Images of Gender in Science and Medicine between the Eighteenth and Twentieth Centuries.* Madison: University of Wisconsin Press, 1989.

Judson, Pieter M. *Exclusive Revolutionaries: Liberal Politics, Social Experience, and National Identity in the Austrian Empire, 1848–1914.* Ann Arbor: University of Michigan Press, 1996.

———. "Frontiers, Islands, Forests, Stones: Mapping the Geography of a German Identity in the Habsburg Monarchy, 1848–1900." In *The Geography of Identity,* edited by Patricia Yaeger, 382–406. Ann Arbor: University of Michigan Press, 1996.

Jung, Hermann. "'Schubert Reminiszenzen' bei Gustav Mahler." In *Franz Schubert— Werk und Rezeption: Schubert-Jahrbuch 1999: Bericht über den Internationalen Schubert-Kongreß, Duisburg 1997,* edited by Dietrich Berke, Walther Dürr, Walburga Litschauer, and Christiane Schumann, 41–49. Duisburg, Germany: Deutsche Schubert-Gesellschaft e. V., 2001.

Kaes, Anton. "New Historicism and the Study of German Literature." *German Quarterly* 62 (1989): 210–19.

Kahl, Willi. *Verzeichnis des Schrifttums über Franz Schubert, 1828–1928.* Regensburg, Germany: G. Bosse, 1938.

Kalbeck, Max. *Johannes Brahms.* 4 vols. Berlin: Deutsches Brahms-Gesellschaft m. b. H., 1908–22.

Kallberg, Jeffrey. "Sex, Sexuality, and Schubert's Piano Music." In *Historical Musicology: Sources, Methods, Interpretations,* edited by Stephen A. Crist and Roberta Montemorra Marvin, 219–33. Rochester: University of Rochester Press, 2004.

Kallir, Jane. *Egon Schiele: The Complete Works.* New York: Harry N. Abrams, 1990.

Kapner, Gerhardt. *Zur Geschichte der Ringstrassendenkmäler.* Wiesbaden: Franz Steiner, 1973.

Karin, Friedrich. *Festive Culture in Germany and Europe from the Sixteenth to the Twentieth Century.* Lewiston, NY: Edwin Mellen Press, 2000.

Karl, Frederick R. *Modern and Modernism: The Sovereignty of the Artist, 1885–1925.* New York: Atheneum, 1985.

Keegan, Susanne. *The Bride of the Wind: The Life and Times of Alma Mahler-Werfel.* New York: Viking, 1992.

Kehler, George. *The Piano in Concert.* 2 vols. Metuchen, NJ: Scarecrow Press, 1982.

Kern, Stephen. *The Culture of Love: Victorian to Moderns.* Cambridge, MA, and London: Harvard University Press, 1992.

Kimber, Marian Wilson. "The Composer as Other: Gender and Race in the Biography of Felix Mendelssohn." In *The Mendelssohns: Their Music in History,* edited by John Michael Cooper and Julie D. Prandi, 335–51. Oxford and New York: Oxford University Press, 2002.

Kitlitschka, Werner. *Die Malerei der Wiener Ringstrasse.* Wiesbaden: Franz Steiner Verlag, 1981.

Kittler, Friedrich A. *Discourse Networks, 1800/1900.* Translated by Michael Metteer and Chris Cullens. Stanford, CA: Stanford University Press, 1990.

Koch, Franz. *Geschichte deutscher Dichtung.* Hamburg: Hanseatische Verlagsanstalt, 1942.

Köhler, Louis, "Franz Schubert's Leben und Schaffen." Parts 1–4. *Musikalisches Centralblatt* 2, no. 12 (March 23, 1882): 123–25; no. 13 (March 30, 1882): 131–34; no. 14 (April 6, 1882): 141–43; no. 15 (April 13, 1882): 151–52.

Kohut, Adolph. *Das Ewig-Weibliche in der Welt-Kultur und Litteraturgeschichte.* Leipzig: Neupert, 1898.

Kokoschka, Oskar. *Mein Leben.* Munich: Bruchmann, 1971.

Konecny, Elvira. *Die Familie Dumba und ihre Bedeutung für Wien und Österreich.* Vienna: Verband der wissenschaftlichen Gesellschaften Österreichs, 1986.

Koschatzky, Walter. *Viennese Watercolors of the Nineteenth Century.* New York: Harry N. Abrams, 1988.

Koshar, Rudy. *From Monuments to Traces: Artifacts of German Memory, 1870–1990.* Berkeley and Los Angeles: University of California Press, 2000.

Kostlin, Heinrich Adolf. *Geschichte der Musik im Umriss.* 5th ed. Berlin: Reuther and Reichard, 1899.

Kovach, Thomas A. "Hofmannsthal's 'Ein Brief': Chandos and His Crisis." In *A Companion to the Works of Hugo von Hofmannsthal,* edited by Thomas A. Kovach, 85–96. Rochester, NY: Camden House, 2002.

Kowalke, Kim. *Kurt Weill in Europe.* Ann Arbor, MI: UMI Research Press, 1979.

Krafft-Ebing, Richard von. *Psychopathia Sexualis.* Translated by Harry E. Wedeck. New York: G. P. Putnam's Sons, 1965.

Kral, Eduard, ed. *Jahresbericht des Männer-Gesang-Vereines über das 22. Vereinsjahr.* Vienna: Verlag des Wiener Männer-Gesang-Vereines, 1865.

———. *Jahresbericht des Wiener Männer-Gesang-Vereines über das 23. Vereinsjahr.* Vienna: Verlag des Wiener Männer-Gesang-Vereines, 1866.

———. *Jahresbericht des Wiener Männer-Gesang-Vereines über das 24. Vereinsjahr.* Vienna: Verlag des Wiener Männer-Gesang-Vereines, 1867.

———. *Jahresbericht des Wiener Männer-Gesang-Vereines über das 25. Vereinsjahr.* Vienna: Verlag des Wiener Männer-Gesang-Vereines, 1868.

Kralik, Richard von, and Hanns Schlitter. *Wien: Geschichte der Kaiserstadt und ihrer Kultur.* Vienna: A. Holzhausen, 1912.

Kramer, Lawrence. *After the Lovedeath: Sexual Violence and the Making of Culture.* Berkeley and Los Angeles: University of California Press, 1997.

———. "*Carnaval,* Cross-Dressing, and the Woman in the Mirror." In *Musicology and Difference: Gender and Sexuality in Music Scholarship,* edited by Ruth A. Solie, 305–25. Berkeley and Los Angeles: University of California Press, 1993.

———. *Classical Music and Postmodern Knowledge.* Berkeley and Los Angeles: University of California Press, 1995.

———. *Franz Schubert: Sexuality, Subjectivity, Song.* Cambridge: Cambridge University Press, 1998.

———. *Music as Cultural Practice, 1800–1900.* Berkeley and Los Angeles: University of California Press, 1990.

Krasa, Selma. "Sculpture during the Biedermeier Years." In *Vienna in the Biedermeier Era, 1815–1848,* edited by Robert Waissenberger, 191–216. New York: Mallard Press, 1986.

Kraus, Karl. "Die Dankbarkeit des Rudolf Hans Bartsch." *Die Fackel,* nos. 381–83 (September 1913): 26–32.

———. "Die Einakter." *Die Fackel,* no. 1 (April 1899): 24–27.

———. *Frühe Schriften: 1892–1900.* Edited by Johannes J. Braakenburg, 2 vols. Munich: Kosel, 1979.

Kraus, Karl. "Im dreißigsten Kriegsjahr. Gesprochen in der 300. Wiener Vorlesung am 30. November." *Die Fackel*, nos. 800–805 (February 1929): 1–45.
——. *In These Great Times: A Karl Kraus Reader.* Translated and edited by Harry Zohn. Montreal: Engendra Press, 1976.
——. "Die Kenner.—Tina Blau.—Herr Klimt und das revolutionierte Kunstempfinden des Herrn von Dumba." *Die Fackel*, no. 1 (April 1899): 27–28.
——. "Nachruf." *Die Fackel*, nos. 501–7 (January 1919): 1–120.
——. "Schober im Liede." *Die Fackel*, nos. 781–86 (June 1928): 105–21.
Kreissle von Hellborn, Heinrich. *Franz Schubert.* Vienna: Carl Gerold's Sohn, 1865. Reprint, Hildesheim, Germany: Georg Olms, 1978.
——. *Franz Schubert, eine biografische Skizze.* Vienna: Druck und Verlag der typographisch-literarisch-artistischen Anstalt, 1861.
——. *The Life of Franz Schubert.* Translated by Arthur Duke Coleridge. 2 vols. London: Longmans, Green, and Co., 1869.
Krenek, Ernst. "Das Schubert-Jahr ist zu Ende." *Musikblätter des Anbruch* 11 (1929): 11–15.
Kuhn, Reinhard. *Corruption in Paradise: The Child in Western Literature.* Hanover, NH: University Press of New England, 1982.
Kupffer, Elisarion von. *Lieblingminne und Freundesliebe in der Weltliteratur.* Berlin-Neurahnsdorf: Adolf Brand's Verlag, 1900. Reprint, Berlin: Verlag rosa Winkel, 1995.
Kürnberger, Ferdinand. *Literarische Herzenssachen: Reflexionen und Kritiken.* Vienna: L. Rosner, 1877.
Lagercrantz, Olof. *August Strindberg.* Translated by Anselm Hollo. New York: Farrar, Straus, Giroux, 1984.
La Grange, Henry-Louis de. *Gustav Mahler.* 2 vols. Oxford: Oxford University Press, 1995–99.
——. *Mahler.* Vol. 1. Garden City, NJ: Doubleday, 1973.
Laurence, Richard R. "Viennese Literary Intellectuals and the Problem of War and Peace, 1889–1914." In *Focus on Vienna 1900: Change and Continuity in Literature, Music, Art and Intellectual History*, edited by Erika Nielsen, 12–22. Munich: Wilhelm Fink, 1982.
Lawson, Richard H. "Thematic Reflections of the 'Song of Love and Play of Death' in Schnitzler's Fiction." In *Arthur Schnitzler and His Age: Intellectual and Artistic Currents*, edited by Petrus W. Tax and Richard H. Lawson, 70–89. Bonn: Bouvier, 1984.
Leavis, F. R. *The Great Tradition.* Garden City, NJ: Doubleday, 1954.
Leisching, Eduard [E. L.]. "Acht Jahre Sezession." *Kunst und Kunsthandwerk* 9 (1906): 88–90.
Lensing, Leo A. "Peter Altenberg's Fabricated Photographs." In *Vienna 1900: From Altenberg to Wittgenstein*, edited by Edward Timms and Ritchie Robertson, 47–72. Edinburgh: Edinburgh University Press, 1990.
——. "Scribbling Squids and the Giant Octopus: Oskar Kokoschka's Unpublished Portrait of Peter Altenberg." In *Turn-of-the-Century Vienna and Its Legacy: Essays in Honor of Donald G. Daviau*, edited by Jeffrey B. Berlin, Jorun B. Johns, and Richard H. Lawson, 193–220. New York: Edition Atelier, 1993.
Leppert, Richard. *Music and Image: Domesticity, Ideology and Socio-Cultural Formation in Eighteenth-Century England.* Cambridge: Cambridge University Press, 1988.
——. "Sexual Identity, Death, and the Family Piano." *19th-Century Music* 16, no. 2 (Fall 1992): 105–28.
——. *The Sight of Sound: Music, Representation, and the History of the Body.* Berkeley and Los Angeles: University of California Press, 1993.

Le Rider, Jacques. *Modernity and Crises of Identity: Culture and Society in Fin-de-Siècle Vienna.* Translated by Rosemary Morris. New York: Continuum, 1990.

Leskowa, Sylvia. "Das Bild des historischen Künstlers in der Österreichischen Literaur des späten 19. und frühen 20. Jahrhunderts." PhD diss., University of Vienna, 1985.

Leventhal, Jean H. *Echoes in the Text: Musical Citation in German Narratives from Theodor Fontane to Martin Walser.* New York: Peter Lang, 1995.

Lewin, David. "Inversional Balance as an Organizing Force in Schoenberg's Music and Thought." *Perspectives of New Music* 6, no. 2 (Spring–Summer, 1968): 1–21.

———. "A Theory of Segmental Association in Twelve-Tone Music." *Perspectives of New Music* 1, no. 1 (Fall 1962): 89–116.

Lewis, P. B. "Wittgenstein on Words and Music." *British Journal of Aesthetics* 17, no. 2 (Spring 1973): 111–21.

Lindner, Anton. "Schubert im Bilde." *Bühne und Welt* 9, no. 18 (June 1907): 232–35.

Litschauer, Walburga. *Neue Dokumente zum Schubert-Kreis aus Briefen und Tagebüchern seiner Freunde.* Vienna: Musikwissenschaftlicher Verlag Wien, 1986.

Littrow-Bischoff, August. *Aus dem persönlichen Verkehre mit Franz Grillparzer.* Vienna: L. Rosner, 1873.

Lloyd, Genevieve. *The Man of Reason: "Male" and "Female" in Western Philosophy.* Minneapolis: University of Minnesota Press, 1984.

Loesser, Arthur. *Men, Women and Pianos: A Social History.* New York: Simon and Schuster, 1954.

Loos, Adolf. *Spoken into the Void: Collected Essays 1897–1900.* Translated by Jane O. Newman and John H. Smith. Cambridge, MA: MIT Press, 1982.

Lorenz, Dagmar C. G., ed. *A Companion to the Works of Arthur Schnitzler.* Rochester, NY: Camden House, 2003.

Louis, Rudolf. *Die deutsche Musik der Gegenwart.* 2nd ed. Munich: G. Müller, 1912.

Lueger, Karl. *"I Decide Who Is a Jew!" The Papers of Dr. Karl Lueger.* Translated and edited by Richard S. Geehr. Washington, DC: University Press of America, 1982.

Luft, David S. *Eros and Inwardness in Vienna: Weininger, Musil, Doderer.* Chicago: University of Chicago Press, 2003.

Lunzer, Heinz, and Victoria Lunzer-Talos. *Peter Altenberg: Extracte des Lebens.* Salzburg: Residenz Verlag, 2003.

Lüthi, Kurt. *Feminismus und Romantik: Sprache, Gesellschaft, Symbole, Religion.* Vienna: Böhlau, 1985.

Lux, Joseph August. *Grillparzers Liebesroman: Die Schwestern Frölich: Roman aus Wiens klassischer Zeit.* Berlin: R. Bong, 1912.

MacLeod, Catriona. *Embodying Ambiguity: Androgyny and Aesthetics from Winckelmann to Keller.* Detroit: Wayne State University Press, 1998.

Macleod, Diane Sachko. *Art and the Victorian Middle Class.* Cambridge: Cambridge University Press, 1996.

Mahler, Alma. *And the Bridge Is Love.* New York: Harcourt, Brace, 1958.

Mahler-Werfel, Alma. *Diaries 1898–1902.* Translated by Anthony Beaumont. Ithaca, NY: Cornell University Press, 1999.

Mahling, Christoph-Hellmut. "Arrangements d'oeuvres de Schubert aux XIXe et XXe siècles." *Revue de musicologie* 66, no. 1 (1980): 86–89.

———. "Zur Rezeption von Werken Franz Schuberts." In *Zur Aufführungspraxis der Werke Franz Schuberts*, edited by Vera Schwarz, 12–23. Munich-Salzburg: Emil Katzbichler, 1981.

Mandyczewski, Eusebius. "Franz Schubert. Zur Erinnerung an seinen 100. Geburtstag." *Mittheilungen der Musikalienhandlung Breitkopf & Härtel*, no. 48 (January 1897): 1609–10.

Martens, Frederick H. "Schubert and the Eternal Feminine" *Musical Quarterly* 14, no. 4 (October 1928): 539–52.

Mason, John W. *The Dissolution of the Austro-Hungarian Empire, 1867–1918*. 2nd ed. London: Longman, 1997.

Mattl, Siegfried. "Geschlecht und Volkscharakter." *Österreichische Zeitschrift für Geschichtswissenschaften* 7, no. 4 (1996): 499–515.

Mayer, Andreas. "Der Psychoanalytisches Schubert." *Schubert durch die Brille* 9 (1992): 7–31.

Mayer, Jill E. " 'By Drip and by Drop': The Discourse of German Nationalism in the Press of Habsburg Austria—Salzburg, Styria, Vienna: 1877–1897." PhD diss., University of Manitoba, 1993.

McClary, Susan. "Constructions of Subjectivity in Schubert's Music." In *Queering the Pitch: The New Gay and Lesbian Musicology*, edited by Philip Brett, Elizabeth Wood, and Gary C. Thomas, 205–33. New York: Routledge, 1994.

———. *Feminine Endings: Music, Gender and Sexuality*. Minneapolis: University of Minnesota Press, 1991.

McColl, Sandra. "A Model German." *Musical Times* 138 (March 1997): 7–12.

———. *Music Criticism in Vienna, 1896–1897: Critically Moving Forms*. Oxford: Clarendon Press, 1996.

McGrath, William J. *Dionysian Art and Populist Politics in Austria*. New Haven, CT, and London: Yale University Press, 1974.

McGuinness, Brian. *Wittgenstein: A Life*. Berkeley and Los Angeles: University of California Press, 1988.

McKay, Elizabeth Norman. *Franz Schubert: A Biography*. Oxford: Clarendon Press, 1996.

Mellor, Anne K., ed. *Romanticism and Feminism*. Bloomington and Indianapolis: Indiana University Press, 1988.

———. *Romanticism and Gender*. New York and London: Routledge, 1993.

Melman, Billie. "Gender, History and Memory: The Inventions of Women's Past in the Nineteenth and Early Twentieth Centuries." *History and Memory* 5 (1993): 5–41.

Merian, Hans. *Illustrierte Geschichte der Musik von der Renaissance bis auf die Gegenwart*. 3rd ed. Leipzig: O. Spamer, 1913.

Messing, Scott. "Franz Schubert and Viennese Modernity." In *Wien 1897: Kulturgeschichtliches Profil eines Epochenjahres*, edited by Christian Glanz, 173–88. Frankfurt am Main: Peter Lang, 1997.

———. "Klimt's Schubert and the Fin-de-Siècle Imagination." In *Music and Modern Art*, edited by James Leggio, 1–35. New York and London: Routledge, 2002.

———. *Neoclassicism in Music: From the Genesis of the Concept through the Schoenberg/Stravinsky Polemic*. Ann Arbor, MI: UMI Research Press, 1988.

———. "The Vienna Beethoven Centennial Festival of 1870." *Beethoven Newsletter* 6, no. 3 (1991): 57–63.

Metken, Günter. "Schubert am Klavier (Gustav Klimt pinx.)." *Merkur* 41, no. 4 (1987): 349–54.

Meyer, Henry Cord. *"Mitteleuropa" in German Thought and Action, 1815–1945*. The Hague: Martinus Nijhoff, 1955.

Michael, Nancy C. *Elektra and Her Sisters: Three Female Characters in Schnitzler, Freud, and Hofmannsthal*. New York: Peter Lang, 2001.

Milanowski, Anna. "Der Zeitzeuge Tadeusz Rittner und seine polnischen Feuilletons." In *Wien 1897: Kulturgeschichtliches Profil eines Epochenjahres*, edited by Christian Glanz, 133–54. Frankfurt am Main: Peter Lang, 1999.

Millenkovich-Morold, Max. *Die österreichische Tonkunst*. Vienna: Carl Fromme, 1918.

Mitsch, Erwin. *The Art of Egon Schiele*. New York: Hudson Hills Press, 1988.

Moldenhauer, Hans. "A Webern Archive in America." In *Anton von Webern Perspectives*, edited by Demar Irvine, 117–66. Seattle: University of Washington Press, 1966.

Moldenhauer, Hans, and Rosaleen Moldenhauer. *Anton von Webern: A Chronicle of His Life and Work*. New York: Alfred A. Knopf, 1979.

Moll, Albert. *Berühmte Homosexuelle*. Wiesbaden: J. F. Bermann, 1910.

Mollik, Kurt, Hermann Reining, and Rudolf Wurzer. *Planung und Verwirklichung der Wiener Ringstrassezone*. Wiesbaden: Franz Steiner, 1980.

Morgan, Robert P. "Secret Languages: The Root of Musical Modernism." In *Modernism: Challenges and Perspectives*, ed. Monique Chefdor, Ricardo J. Quinones, and Albert Wachtel, 33–53. Urbana: University of Illinois Press, 1986.

Morton, Frederick. *A Nervous Splendor*. Boston: Little, Brown, 1979.

Mosse, George L. *Germans and Jews*. New York: Howard Fertig, 1970.

———. *Nationalism and Sexuality: Respectability and Abnormal Sexuality in Modern Europe*. New York: Howard Fertig, 1985.

Müller, Robert. *Österreich und der Mensch: Eine Mystik des Donau-Alpenmenschen*. Berlin: Fischer, 1916.

Münz, Ludwig, and Gustav Künstler. *Adolf Loos: Pioneer of Modern Architecture*. Translated by Harold Meek. New York: Praeger, 1966.

Munz, Sigmund. *Österreichische Profile und Reminiszenzen*. Vienna: Deutsch-Österreichischer Verlag, 1913.

Musgrave, Michael. "Schoenberg and Brahms: A Study of Schoenberg's Response to Brahms's Music as Revealed in His Didactic Writings and Selected Early Compositions." PhD diss., London University, 1979.

Musil, Robert. *Diaries, 1889–1942*. Translated by Philip Payne and edited by Adolf Frisé and Mark Mirsky. New York: Basic Books, 1998.

———. *Precision and Soul: Essays and Addresses*. Translated and edited by Burton Pike and David S. Luft. Chicago: University of Chicago Press, 1990.

Muxfeldt, Kristina. "Schubert, Platen, and the Myth of Narcissus." *Journal of the American Musicological Society* 49, no. 3 (Fall 1996): 480–527.

Naaff, Anton August. "Die Schubert-Jahrhundertfeier in Wien." *Die Lyra* 20, no. 11 (March 1, 1897): 122–23.

Naumann, Emil. *Deutsche Tondichter von Sebastian Bach bis auf die Gegenwart*. 5th ed. Berlin: R. Oppenheim, 1882.

Nebehay, Christian M. *Gustav Klimt Dokumentation*. Vienna: Nebehay, 1969.

———. *Gustav Klimt: From Drawing to Painting*. Translated by Renée Nebehay-King. New York: Harry N. Abrams, 1994.

———. "Gustav Klimt schreibt an eine Liebe." *Mitteilungen der Österreichischen Galerie* 22/23, nos. 66/67 (1978/1979): 102–18.

———. *Gustav Klimt: Das Skizzenbuch aus dem Besitz von Sonja Krips*. Vienna: Tusch, 1987.

———. *Vienna 1900: Architecture and Painting*. Vienna: Christian Brandstatter, 1984.

Nelson, Robert L. "German Comrades—Slavic Whores: Gender Images in the German Soldier Newspapers of the First World War." In *Home/Front: The Military, War and Gender in Twentieth-Century Germany*, edited by Karen Hagemann and Stefanie Schüler-Springorum, 69–86. Oxford: Berg, 2002.

Nethersole, Reingard. "Viennese Early Postmodernism: Hofmannsthal's 'Prolog zu dem Buch Anatol.'" In *Turn-of-the-Century Vienna and Its Legacy: Essays in Honor of Donald G. Daviau*, edited by Jeffrey B. Berlin, Jorun B. Johns, and Richard H. Lawson, 29–45. New York: Edition Atelier, 1993.

Nettheim, Nigel. "How the Young Schubert Borrowed from Beethoven." *Musical Times* 132 (July 1991): 330–31.

Neubauer, John. *The Fin-de-Siècle Culture of Adolescence*. New Haven, CT, and London: Yale University Press, 1992.

Neu Österreich: Seine Kultur, Bodenschätze, Wirtschaftsleben und Landschaftsbilder. Edited by Eduard Stepan. Amsterdam and Vienna: S. L. van Looy, 1923.

Newbould, Brian. *Schubert: The Music and the Man*. Berkeley and Los Angeles: University of California Press, 1997.

——, ed. *Schubert Studies*. Aldershot, UK: Ashgate, 1998.

Newlin, Dika. *Bruckner, Mahler, Schoenberg*. New York: Norton, 1978.

——. *Schoenberg Remembered*. New York: Pendragon, 1980.

Nielsen, Erika, ed. *Focus on Vienna 1900: Change and Continuity in Literature, Music, Art and Intellectual History*. Munich: Wilhelm Fink, 1982.

Nietzsche, Friedrich. *Human, All Too Human*. Translated by R. J. Hollingdale. Cambridge: Cambridge University Press, 1986.

——. *Sämtliche Werke: Kritische Studienausgabe*. Edited by Girogio Colli and Mazzino Montinari. Vol. 1. Munich: Deutscher Taschenbuch Verlag, 1980.

Niggli, Arnold. *Schubert*. Leipzig: Philipp Reclam, 1889.

——. *Schubert*. Revised ed. Leipzig: Philipp Reclam, 1925.

Nipperdey, Thomas. "Nationalidee und Nationaldenkmal in Deutschland." *Historische Zeitschrift* 206, no. 3 (June 1968): 529–85.

Nordau, Max. *Degeneration*. New York: D. Appleton, 1895.

Notley, Margaret. "Brahms as Liberal: Genre, Style, and Politics in Late 19th-Century Vienna." *19th-Century Music* 17, no. 2 (Fall 1993): 107–23.

Nottebohm, Gustav. *Briefe an Robert Volkmann*. Edited by Hans Clauss. Lüdenscheid, Germany: Rudolf Beucker, 1967.

Novotny, Fritz. "Zu Gustav Klimts 'Schubert am Klavier.'" *Mitteilungen der Österreichische Galerie* 7, no. 51 (1963): 90–101.

Novotny, Fritz, and Johannes Dobai. *Gustav Klimt*. Translated by Karen Olga Philippson. Boston: New York Graphic Society, 1975.

Oesterle, Günter, ed. *Jugend—Ein romantisches Konzept?* Würzburg: Königshausen & Neumann, 1997.

Offizielles Erinnerungsalbum an das 10. Deutsches Sängerbundesfest Wien 1928. Vienna: Lechner, 1928.

Okey, Robin. *The Habsburg Monarchy: From Enlightenment to Eclipse*. New York: St. Martin's Press, 2001.

Olsen, Donald J. *The City as a Work of Art*. New Haven, CT: Yale University Press, 1986.

Oosterhuis, Harry. *Stepchildren of Nature: Krafft-Ebing, Psychiatry, and the Making of Sexual Identity*. Chicago and London: University of Chicago Press, 2000.

Ortner, Sherry B. *Making Gender: The Politics and Erotics of Culture*. Boston: Beacon Press, 1996.

Die österreichisch-ungarische Monarchie in Wort und Bild. Vol. 1. Vienna: Druck und Verlag der kaiserlich-königliche Hof- und Staatsdruckerei, 1886.

Oxaal, Ivar, Michael Pollack, and Gerhard Botz, eds. *Jews, Antisemitism and Culture in Vienna*. London: Routledge and Keegan Paul, 1987.

Panizza, Oskar. "Bayreuth and Homosexuality." Translated by Isolde Vetter. *Wagner* 9, no. 2 (April 1988): 71–75.

———. "Bayreuth und die Homosexualität." *Die Gesellschaft: Monatsschrift für Literatur, Kunst und Socialpolitik* 11 (1895): 88–92.

Parakilas, James, et al. *Piano Roles: Three Hundred Years of Life with the Piano.* New Haven, CT, and London: Yale University Press, 1999.

Partsch, Erich Wolfgang, and Oskar Pausch, eds. *Der vergessene Schubert: Franz Schubert auf der Bühne.* Vienna: Böhlau Verlag, 1997.

Partsch, Susanna. *Gustav Klimt: Painter of Women.* Translated by Michael Robertson. Munich and New York: Prestel, 1994.

Pascall, Robert. "Brahms and Schubert." *Musical Times* 124 (May 1983): 286–91.

Pauley, Bruce F. *From Prejudice to Persecution: A History of Austrian Anti-Semitism.* Chapel Hill: University of North Carolina Press, 1992.

Paupié, Kurt. *Handbuch der österreichischen Pressegeschichte 1848–1959.* 2 vols. Vienna: Wilhelm Braumüller, 1960.

Pederson, Sanna. "Beethoven and Masculinity." In *Beethoven and His World,* edited by Scott Burnham and Michael P. Steinberg, 313–31. Princeton, NJ, and Oxford: Princeton University Press, 2000.

———. "On the Task of the Music Historian: The Myth of the Symphony after Beethoven." *Repercussions* 2 (1993): 5–30.

Pirchan, Emil. *Gustav Klimt.* Vienna: Bergland, 1956.

Placek, Maria. "Die Gestalt Franz Schuberts in der deutschen und österreichischen Literatur des 19. Jahrhunderts 1828–1898." Master's thesis, University of Vienna, 1991.

Plantinga, Leon B. *Schumann as Critic.* New Haven, CT, and London: Yale University Press, 1967.

Portig, Gustav. *Schiller in seinem Verhältnis zur Freundschaft und Liebe sowie in seinem inneren Verhältnis zu Goethe.* Hamburg and Leipzig: Leopold Voss, 1894.

Powell, Nicolas, and Adolf Opel. *The Sacred Spring: The Arts in Vienna, 1898–1918.* New York: New York Graphic Society, 1974.

Price, Renée, ed. *New Worlds: German and Austrian Art, 1890–1940.* New Haven, CT, and London: Yale University Press, 2002.

Pudor, Heinrich. "Männliches und weibliches Empfinden in der Kunst." *Politisch-anthropologische Revue* 1, no. 8 (November 1902): 640–48.

———. "Richard Wagners Bisexualität." *Geschlecht und Gesellschaft* 2, no. 3 (1907): 140–44.

Pulzer, P. G. J. *The Rise of Political Anti-Semitism in Germany and Austria.* New York: John Wiley and Sons, 1964.

Pylleman, Franz. "Die Schubert-Feier in Wien." *Allgemeine musikalische Zeitung* 7, no. 26 (June 26, 1872): 416–21.

Raffalovich, Marc-André. *Uranisme et unisexualité: Étude sur différentes manifestations de l'instinct sexuel.* Lyons: Storck, 1896.

Rath, R. John. *The Viennese Revolution of 1848.* Austin: University of Texas Press, 1957.

Rau, Hans. *Franz Grillparzer und sein Liebesleben.* Berlin: H. Barsdorf, 1904.

Reed, John. *Schubert.* New York: Schirmer Books, 1997.

———. *Schubert: The Final Years.* New York: St. Martin's Press, 1972.

———. *The Schubert Song Companion.* Manchester, UK: Mandolin, 1997.

Regel, Heinrich. *Die Jahreszeiten der Liebe.* Vienna: Universal Edition, 1912.

Reich, Eduard. *Studien über die Frauen.* Jena: H. Costenoble, 1875.

Reich, Willi. *Schoenberg: A Critical Biography.* Translated by Leo Black. New York: Praeger, 1971.

Reissmann, August. *Franz Schubert: Sein Leben und seine Werke*. Berlin, J. Guttentag, 1873.

Rhees, Rush, ed. *Recollections of Wittgenstein*. Oxford: Oxford University Press, 1984.

Riberio, António. "Karl Kraus and Modernism: A Reassessment." In *The Turn of the Century: Le tournant de siècle*, edited by Christian Berg, Frank Durieux, and Geert Lernout, 143–54. Berlin: Walter de Gruyter, 1995.

Robb, Graham. *Strangers: Homosexual Love in the Nineteenth Century*. New York: Norton, 2003.

Robertson, Ritchie. *The "Jewish Question" in German Literature, 1749–1939*. Oxford: Oxford University Press, 1999.

Roe, Ian F., and John Warren, eds. *The Biedermeier and Beyond: Selected Papers from the Symposium held at St. Peter's College, Oxford from 19–21 September 1997*. Bern: Peter Lang, 1999.

Roessler, Arthur. *In Memoriam Gustav Klimt*. Vienna: Officina Vindobonensis, 1926.

Rosario, Vernon A. *The Erotic Imagination: French Histories of Perversity*. New York: Oxford University Press, 1997.

———, ed. *Science and Homosexualities*. New York and London: Routledge, 1997.

Rosen, Charles. *Arnold Schoenberg*. New York: Viking Press, 1975.

———. *The Frontiers of Meaning*. New York: Hill and Wang, 1994.

———. *The Romantic Generation*. Cambridge, MA: Harvard University Press, 1995.

Rossbacher, Karlheinz. *Literatur und Liberalismus: Zur Kultur der Ringstrasse in Wien*. Vienna: J&V, 1992.

Rotenberg, Robert. *Landscape and Power in Vienna*. Baltimore and London: Johns Hopkins University, 1995.

———. *Time and Order in Metropolitan Vienna: A Seizure of Schedules*. Washington, DC, and London: Smithsonian Institution Press, 1992.

Rowbotham, John Frederick. *The Private Life of the Great Composers*. New York: Thomas Whittaker, 1893.

Rowland, David, ed. *The Cambridge Companion to the Piano*. Cambridge: Cambridge University Press, 1998.

Roxenblitt, Marsha L. *The Jews of Vienna, 1867–1914: Assimilation and Identity*. Albany: State University of New York Press, 1983.

Rufer, Joseph. *Composition with Twelve Tones*. Translated by Humphrey Searle. London: Barrie and Rockliff, 1961.

———. *The Works of Arnold Schoenberg*. Translated by Dika Newlin. New York: Free Press of Glencoe, 1962.

Saerchinger, Cesar. *Artur Schnabel: A Biography*. London: Cassell, 1957.

Salten, Felix. "Geistiger Leben in Österreich." *Über Land und Meer* 56 (1914): 232–33.

———. *Wurstelprater*. Vienna: Rosenbaum, 1911. Reprint, Vienna: Molden, 1973.

Sams, Eric. *The Songs of Hugo Wolf*. London: Eulenburg, 1983.

Samson, Jim, ed. *The Cambridge History of Nineteenth-Century Music*. Cambridge: Cambridge University Press, 2001.

Saslaw, Janna K., and James P. Walsh. "Musical Invariance as a Cognitive Structure: 'Multiple Meaning' in the Early Nineteenth Century." In *Music Theory in the Age of Romanticism*, edited by Ian Bent, 211–37. Cambridge: Cambridge University Press, 1996.

Saur, Pamela S. "Peter Altenberg: The 'Radical Bachelor.'" In *Joinings and Disjoinings: The Significance of Marital Status in Literature*, edited by JoAnna Stephens Mink and

Janet Double Ward, 120–31. Bowling Green, OH: Bowling Green University Popular Press, 1991.

Schauffler, Robert Haven. *The Unknown Brahms: His Life, Character and Works.* New York: Dodd, Mead and Company, 1933.

Schaukal, Richard. *Mimi Lynx. Die Sängerin: Novellen (Eine Tragigroteske).* Edited by Ingo Warnke and Andreas Wicke. Siegen, Germany: Carl Böschen Verlag, 1999.

Scheffler, Karl. *Die Frau und die Kunst: Eine Studie.* Berlin: Julius Bard, [1908].

Scheichl, Sigurd Paul, and Wolfgang Duchkowitsch, eds. *Zeitungen im Wiener Fin de Siècle.* Munich: R. Oldenburg, 1997.

Schenker, Heinrich. "Ein Epilog zur Schubertfeier." *Neue Revue* 8, no. 1 (1897): 211–16.

———. *Harmony.* Translated by Elisabeth Mann Borgese and edited by Oswald Jonas. Chicago and London: University of Chicago Press, 1954.

———. *Heinrich Schenker als Essayist und Kritiker: Gesammelte Aufsatze, Rezensionen und kleiner Berichte aus den Jahren 1891–1901.* Edited by Hellmut Federhofer. Hildesheim, Germany: Georg Olms, 1990.

———. *Der Tonwille: Pamphlets in Witness of the Immutable Laws of Music, Offered to a New Generation of Youth.* Translated by Ian Bent, William Drabkin, Joseph Dubiel, Timothy Jackson, Joseph Lubben, and Robert Snarrenberg, and edited by William Drabkin. Vol. 1. Oxford: Oxford University Press, 2004.

———. *Der Tonwille: Pamphlets/Quarterly Publication in Witness of the Immutable Laws of Music, Offered to a New Generation of Youth.* Translated by Ian Bent, William Drabkin, Joseph Dubiel, Joseph Lubben, William Renwick, and Robert Snarrenberg, and edited by William Drabkin. Vol. 2. Oxford: Oxford University Press, 2005.

Schmidt-Dengler, Wendelin. "Literature and Theatre." In *Vienna 1890–1920,* edited by Robert Waissenberger, 241–63. New York: Tabard Press, 1984.

Schmitz, Eugen. *Schuberts Auswirkung aus die deutsche Musik.* Leipzig: Breitkopf & Härtel, 1954.

Schnabel, Artur. *My Life and Music.* New York: St. Martin's Press, 1963.

Schnerich, Alfred. *Der Messen-Typus von Haydn bis Schubert.* Vienna: Im Selbstverlage des Verfassers, 1892.

Schnitzler, Arthur. *Die dramatischen Werke.* 2 vols. Frankfurt am Main: S. Fischer, 1962.

———. *Die erzählenden Schriften.* 2 vols. Frankfurt am Main: S. Fischer, 1961.

———. *The Letters of Arthur Schnitzler to Hermann Bahr.* Edited by Donald G. Daviau. Chapel Hill: University of North Carolina Press, 1978.

———. *Medizinische Schriften.* Edited by Horst Thomé. Vienna: Paul Zsolnay, 1988.

———. *Tagebuch.* 10 vols. Vienna: Verlag der Österreichischen Akademie der Wissenschaften, 1991.

Schoenberg, Arnold. *Fundamentals of Musical Composition.* Edited by Gerald Strang and Leonard Stein. New York: St. Martin's Press, 1967.

———. *Harmonielehre.* 3rd. ed. Vienna: Universal Edition, 1922.

———. "The Relationship to the Text." In Wassily Kandinsky and Franz Marc, eds., *The "Blaue Reiter" Almanac,* translated by Henning Falkenstein, Manug Terzian, and Gertrude Hinderlie, and edited by Klaus Lankheit, 90–102. New York: Viking, 1974.

———. *Structural Functions of Harmony.* Revised and edited by Leonard Stein. London: Faber, 1969.

———. *Style and Idea.* Translated by Leo Black and edited by Leonard Stein. Berkeley and Los Angeles: University of California Press, 1975.

Schoenberg, Arnold. *Theory of Harmony.* Translated by Roy E. Carter. Berkeley and Los Angeles: University of California Press, 1978.
Schoenberg, Barbara Z. "'Woman-Defender' and 'Woman-Offender,' Peter Altenberg and Otto Weininger: Two Literary Stances vis-à-vis Bourgeois Culture in the Viennese 'Belle Epoque.'" *Modern Austrian Literature* 20, no. 2 (1987): 51–69.
Schoenberg Nono, Nuria, ed. *Arnold Schoenberg Self-Portrait.* Pacific Palisades, CA: Belmont, 1988.
Schorske, Carl. *Fin-de-Siècle Vienna: Politics and Culture.* New York: Knopf, 1979.
———. *Thinking with History: Explorations in the Passage to Modernism.* Princeton, NJ: Princeton University Press, 1998.
Schroeder, David P. "Alban Berg and Peter Altenberg: Intimate Art and the Aesthetics of Life." *Journal of the American Musicological Society* 46, no. 2 (Summer 1993): 261–94.
———. "Feminine Voices in Schubert's Early Laments." *Music Review* 55, no. 3 (August 1994): 183–201.
Schroeder, Paul W. "Austro-German Relations: Divergent Views of the Disjoined Partnership." *Central European History* 11, no. 3 (September 1978): 302–12.
Schubert-Ausstellung der Stadt Wien. Vienna: Künstlerhaus, 1897.
Schumann, Robert. "Grosses Duo f. d. Pfte. zu 4 Hdn. Op. 140. und: F. Schubert's allerletzte Composition: Drei grosse Sonaten für Pianoforte." *Neue Zeitschrift für Musik* 8, no. 45 (June 5, 1838): 177–79.
Schwarz, Egon. *On Four Modernists.* Edited by Arthur R. Evans, Jr. Princeton, NJ: Princeton University Press, 1970.
Scott, Joan W. "Gender: A Useful Category of Historical Analysis." *American Historical Review* 91, no. 5 (1986): 1053–75.
Seeba, Hinrich C. "Hofmannsthal and *Wiener Moderne:* The Cultural Context." In *A Companion to the Works of Hugo von Hofmannsthal,* edited by Thomas A. Kovach, 25–44. Rochester, NY: Camden House, 2002.
Segel, Harold B. *The Vienna Coffeehouse Wits: 1890–1938.* West Lafayette, IN: Purdue University Press, 1993.
Sengoopta, Chandak. *Otto Weininger: Sex, Science, and Self in Imperial Vienna.* Chicago: University of Chicago Press, 2000.
Sessions, Roger. "Schoenberg in the United States." *Tempo,* no. 103 (1972): 8–17.
Shedel, James. *Art and Society: The New Art Movement in Vienna, 1897–1914.* Palo Alto, CA: Society for the Promotion of Science and Scholarship, 1981.
Sheehan, James J. *German History, 1770–1866.* Oxford: Clarendon Press, 1989.
Sheppard, Richard. "The Crises of Language." In *Modernism 1890–1930,* edited by Malcolm Bradbury and James McFarlane, 323–36. Harmondsworth, UK: Penguin, 1976.
Siegel, Sandra. "Literature and Degeneration: The Representation of 'Decadence.'" In *Degeneration: The Dark Side of Progress,* edited by J. Edward Chamberlin and Sander L. Gilman, 199–219. New York: Columbia University Press, 1985.
Simmel, Monika. *Erziehung zum Weibe: Mädchenbildung im 19. Jahrhundert.* Frankfurt am Main: Campus Verlag, 1980.
Simpson, Josephine M. N. *Peter Altenberg: A Neglected Writer of the Viennese Jahrhundertwende.* Frankfurt am Main: Peter Lang, 1987.
Sitte, Camillo. *The Art of Building Cities.* Translated by Charles T. Stewart. New York: Reinhold Publishing Corp., 1945.
Sked, Alan. *The Decline and Fall of the Habsburg Empire, 1815–1918.* London: Longman, 1989.

Smith, Joan Allen. *Schoenberg and His Circle.* New York: Schirmer Books, 1986.

Solie, Ruth A., ed. *Musicology and Difference: Gender and Sexuality in Music Scholarship.* Berkeley and Los Angeles: University of California Press, 1993.

Solomon, Maynard. "Franz Schubert and the Peacocks of Benvenuto Cellini." *19th-Century Music* 12, no. 3 (Spring 1989): 193–208.

———. "Franz Schubert's 'My Dream.'" *American Imago* 38, no. 2 (Summer 1981): 137–54.

———. "Schubert and Beethoven." *19th-Century Music* 7, no. 2 (November 1979): 114–25.

———. "Schubert: Some Consequences of Nostalgia." *19th-Century Music* 17, no. 1 (Summer 1993): 34–46.

Spector, Scott. "Marginalizations: Politics and Culture beyond *Fin-de-Siècle Vienna.*" In *Rethinking Vienna 1900,* edited by Steven Beller, 132–53. New York: Berghahn Books, 2001.

Speidel, Ludwig. *Ausgewählte Schriften.* Edited by Sigismund von Radecki. Wedel in Holstein, Germany: Curt Brauns, 1947.

———. *Wiener Frauen und anderes Wienerische.* Vol. 2 of *Ludwig Speidels Schriften.* Berlin: Meyer & Jessen, 1910.

Stackelberg, Roderick, and Sally A. Winkle. *The Nazi Germany Sourcebook: An Anthology of Texts.* London: Routledge, 2002.

Staubach, Carl. "Ein deutsche Liederfürst." *Deutsches Volksblatt* (Morgen-Ausgabe). January 31, 1897, 1–5.

Steakley, James. *The Homosexual Emancipation Movement in Germany.* New York: Arno Press, 1975.

Steblin, Rita. "In Defense of Scholarship and Archival Research: Why Schubert's Brothers Were Allowed to Marry." *Current Musicology,* no. 62 (1998): 7–17.

———. "Neue Forschungsaspekte zu Caroline Esterhazy." *Schubert durch die Brille* 11 (1993): 21–33.

———. "The Peacock's Tale: Schubert's Sexuality Reconsidered." *19th-Century Music* 17, no. 1 (Summer 1993): 5–33.

———. "Schubert's 'Nina' and the True Peacocks." *Musical Times* 138 (March 1997): 13–20.

———. "Schubert's Problematic Relationship with Johann Mayrhofer: New Documentary Evidence." In *Essays on Music and Culture in Honor of Herbert Kellman,* edited by Barbara Haggh, 465–95. Paris: Minerve, 2001.

Steinberg, Michael P. *The Meaning of the Salzburg Festival: Austria as Theater and Ideology, 1890–1938.* Ithaca, NY: Cornell University Press, 1990.

Steinebach, Friedrich. "Immortellenkranz gelegt auf das Grab von Franz Schubert. Als Prolog zur Schubertfeier im Vereine Hesperus am 30. Januar 1858." *Wiener Theaterzeitung* 52, no. 26 (February 2, 1858): 102. Also published in *Thalia. Taschenbuch für 1859* 46 (1859): 214–16.

Stevenson, Edward Prime. [Xavier Mayne, pseud.]. *The Intersexes: A History of Similisexualism as a Problem in Social Life.* 1908. Reprint, New York: Arno Press, 1975.

Steward, Jill. "'Gruss aus Wien': Urban Tourism in Austria-Hungary before the First World War." In *The City in Central Europe: Culture and Society from 1800 to the Present,* edited by Malcolm Gee, Tim Kirk, and Jill Steward, 123–44. Aldershot, UK: Ashgate, 1999.

Stewart, John L. *Ernst Krenek: The Man and His Music.* Berkeley and Los Angeles: University of California Press, 1991.

Stillmark, Alexander. "'Es war alles gut und erfüllt.' Rudolf Hans Bartsch's *Schwammerl* and the Making of the Schubert Myth." In *The Biedermeier and Beyond: Selected Papers from the Symposium held at St. Peter's College, Oxford from 19–21 September 1997*, edited by Ian F. Roe and John Warren, 225–34. Bern: Peter Lang, 1999.

Stooss, Toni, and Christoph Doswald, eds. *Gustav Klimt.* Stuttgart: G. Hatje, 1992.

Storck, Karl. *Geschichte der Musik.* Stuttgart: Muth, 1904.

———. *Geschichte der Musik.* 6th ed. 2 vols. Stuttgart: Metzler, 1926.

Strathausen, Carsten. *The Look of Things: Poetry and Vision around 1900.* Chapel Hill and London: University of North Carolina Press, 2003.

Straus, Joseph N. *Remaking the Past: Musical Modernism and the Influence of the Tonal Tradition.* Cambridge, MA: Harvard University Press, 1990.

Strauss, Richard, and Hugo von Hofmannsthal. *A Working Friendship: The Correspondence between Richard Strauss and Hugo von Hofmannsthal.* Translated by Hanns Hammelmann and Ewald Osers. New York: Vienna House, 1974.

Strelka, Joseph P., ed. *Wir sind aus solchem Zeug wie das zu Träumen: Kritische Beiträge zum Werk Hugo von Hofmannsthals.* Bern: Peter Lang, 1992.

Strindberg, August. *Pre-Inferno Plays.* Translated by Walter Johnson. Seattle: University of Washington Press, 1970.

———. *Strindberg's Letters.* Translated and edited by Michael Robinson. 2 vols. Chicago: University of Chicago Press, 1992.

Strobl, Alice. *Gustav Klimt: Die Zeichnungen, 1878–1903.* Salzburg: Verlag Galerie Welz, 1980.

Strobl, Friedrich. *Jahres-Bericht des Sängerbundes "Dreizehnlinden" in Wien über das I. Vereinsjahr 1896–1897.* Vienna: Verlag des Sängerbundes "Dreizehnlinden," 1897.

Strong, George V. *Seedtime for Fascism: The Disintegration of Austrian Political Culture, 1867–1918.* Armonk, NY: M. E. Sharpe, 1998.

Stuckenschmidt, Hans Heinz. *Arnold Schoenberg: His Life, World and Work.* Translated by Humphrey Searle. New York: Schirmer Books, 1977.

———. *Schönberg: Leben, Umwelt, Werk.* Zürich and Freiburg: Atlantis-Verlag, 1974.

Surette, Thomas Whitney. "Schubert and His Music." *The Chautauquan* 41 (1905): 41–47.

Swales, Martin. *Arthur Schnitzler: A Critical Study.* Oxford: Clarendon Press, 1971.

Swift, Richard. "1-XII-99: Tonal Relations in Schoenberg's *Verklärte Nacht.*" *19th-Century Music* 1, no. 1 (July 1977): 3–14.

Tacke, Charlotte. *Denkmal im sozialen Raum: Nationale Symbole in Deutschland und Frankreich im 19. Jahrhundert.* Göttingen: Vandenhoeck and Ruprecht, 1995.

Tax, Petrus W., and Richard H. Lawson, eds. *Arthur Schnitzler and His Age: Intellectual and Artistic Currents.* Bonn: Bouvier, 1984.

Thieme, Ulrich. *Studien zum Jugendwerk Arnold Schönbergs: Einflüsse und Wandlungen.* Regensburg, Germany: G. Bosse, 1979.

Thomalla, Arianne. *Die "femme fragile": Ein literarischer Frauentypus der Jahrhundertwende.* Düsseldorf: Bertelsmann, 1972.

Thomasberger, Andreas. "Hofmannsthal's Poems and Lyric Dramas." In *A Companion to the Works of Hugo von Hofmannsthal,* edited by Thomas A. Kovach, 47–63. Rochester, NY: Camden House, 2002.

Tietze, Hans. "Gustav Klimts Persönlichkeit: Nach Mitteilung seiner Freunde." *Die bildenden Künste* 2 (1919): 1–14.

Tilly, Margaret. "The Psychoanalytic Approach to the Masculine and Feminine Principles in Music." *American Journal of Psychiatry* 103 (1946–47): 477–83.

Timms, Edward. "The 'Child-Woman': Kraus, Freud, Wittels, and Irma Karczewska." In *Vienna 1900: From Altenberg to Wittgenstein,* edited by Edward Timms and Ritchie Robertson, 87–107. Edinburgh: Edinburgh University Press, 1990.

———. *Karl Kraus, Apocalyptic Satirist: The Post-war Crisis and the Rise of the Swastika.* New Haven, CT, and London: Yale University Press, 2005.

———. "Peter Altenberg—Authenticity or Pose?" In *Fin de Siècle Vienna,* edited by G. J. Carr and Eda Sagarra, 126–42. Dublin: Trinity College, 1985.

Tovey, Donald Francis. *The Forms of Music.* London: Oxford University Press, 1957.

———. *The Main Stream of Music and Other Essays.* New York: Oxford University Press, 1949.

Traum und Wirklichkeit: Wien 1870–1930. Vienna: Eigenverlag der Museen der Stadt Wien, 1985.

Troeltsch, Ernst. "Der Geist der deutschen Kultur." In *Deutschland und der Weltkrieg,* edited by Otto Hintze et al., 74–77. Leipzig: B. G. Teubner, 1916.

Trost, Alois. "Franz Schubert's Bildnisse." *Berichte und Mittheilungen des Alterthums-Vereines zu Wien* 33, no. 2 (1898): 85–95.

Tuana, Nancy. *The Less Noble Sex: Scientific, Religious, and Philosophical Conceptions of Woman's Nature.* Bloomington: Indiana University Press, 1993.

Unowsky, Daniel Louis. "The Pomp and Politics of Patriotism: Imperial Celebrations in Habsburg Austria, 1848–1916." PhD diss., Columbia University, 2000.

Urban, Bernd. "Schnitzler and Freud as Doubles: Poetic Intuition and Early Research on Hysteria." Translated by John Menzies and Peter Nutting. *Psychoanalytic Review* 65, no. 1 (Spring 1978): 131–65.

Urbanitsch, Peter. "Pluralistic Myth and Nationalist Realities: The Dynastic Myth of the Habsburg Monarchy—A Futile Exercise in the Creation of Identity?" *Austrian History Yearbook* 35 (2004): 101–41.

Varnedoe, Kirk. *Vienna 1900: Art, Architecture and Design.* New York: Museum of Modern Art, 1986.

Vergo, Peter. *Art in Vienna, 1898–1918.* London: Phaidon Press, 1975.

Wagner, Manfred. "Egon Schiele as Representative of an Alternative Aestheticism." In *Egon Schiele: Art, Sexuality, and Viennese Modernism,* edited by Patrick Werkner, 79–88. Palo Alto, CA: Society for the Promotion of Science and Scholarship, 1994.

Wagner, Richard. *Richard Wagner's Prose Works.* Translated by William Ashton Ellis. 8 vols. 1893–99. Reprint, St. Clair Shores, MI: Scholarly Press, 1972.

Waidelich, Till Gerrit, et al. *Franz Schubert: Dokumente, 1817–1830.* Vol. 1. Tutzing, Germany: Hans Schneider, 1993.

Waissenberger, Robert, ed. *Vienna, 1890–1920.* New York: Tabard Press, 1984.

———. *Vienna in the Biedermeier Era, 1815–1848.* New York: Mallard Press, 1986.

———. *Wien, 1870–1930: Traum und Wirklichkeit.* Salzburg and Vienna: Residenz, 1984.

Walker, Frank. *Hugo Wolf: A Biography.* New York: Knopf, 1952.

Warren, John. "Eduard von Bauernfeld and the Beginnings of Austrian Social Drama." In *The Biedermeier and Beyond: Selected Papers from the Symposium held at St. Peter's College, Oxford from 19–21 September 1997,* edited by Ian F. Roe and John Warren, 127–45. Bern: Peter Lang, 1999.

Wasserman, Janet. "A Schubert Iconography: Painters, Sculptors, Lithographers, Illustrators, Silhouettists, Engravers, and Others Known or Said to Have Produced a Likeness of Franz Schubert." *Music in Art* 28, nos. 1–2 (2003): 199–241.

Watkins, Glenn. *Soundings: Music in the Twentieth Century.* New York: Schirmer, 1988.

Wawro, Geoffrey. *The Austro-Prussian War.* Cambridge: Cambridge University Press, 1996.

Webern, Anton. *Letters to Hildegard Jone and Josef Humplik.* Edited by Joseph Polnauer. Bryn Mawr, PA: Theodore Presser, 1967.

Webster, James. "Schubert's Sonata Form and Brahms's First Maturity." *19th-Century Music* 2, no. 1 (July 1978): 18–35; 3, no. 1 (July 1979): 52–71.

Weedon, Chris. "Of Madness and Masochism: Sexuality in Women's Writing at the Turn of the Century." In *Taboos in German Literature,* edited by David Jackson, 79–96. Providence, RI: Berghahn Books, 1996.

Weeks, Jeffrey. *Sexuality and Its Discontents: Meanings, Myths, and Modern Sexualities.* London: Routledge, 1985.

Wegs, J. Robert. *Growing Up Working Class: Continuity and Change among Viennese Youth, 1890–1938.* University Park: Pennsylvania State University Press, 1989.

Wehmeyer, Grete. *Max Reger als Liederkomponist.* Regensburg, Germany: Gustav Bosse, 1955.

Weiner, Marc A. *Arthur Schnitzler and the Crisis of Musical Culture.* Heidelberg: C. Winter, 1986.

———. *Richard Wagner and the Anti-Semitic Imagination.* Lincoln and London: University of Nebraska Press, 1995.

Weininger, Ottto. *Genie und Verbrechen.* Edited by Walther Schneider. Graz and Vienna: Stiasny Verlag, 1962.

———. *Geschlecht und Charakter.* 26th ed. Vienna and Leipzig: Wilhelm Braumüller, 1925.

Weinmann, Ignaz. "Franz Schuberts Beziehungen zu Zseliz." Typescript. Musiksammlung, Österreichische Nationalbibliothek, Vienna, 1975.

Weiß, Anton, ed. *Fünfzig Jahre Schubertbund. Chronik des Vereines vom 1. bis 50. Vereinsjahre.* Vienna: Verlag des Schubertbundes, 1913.

Weissenberg, Klaus. "Hofmannsthals Entwicklung des Essays zur inneren Zwangsläfigkeit von Typologie und Form." In *Wir sind aus solchem Zeug wie das zu Träumen: Kritische Beiträge zum Werk Hugo von Hofmannsthals,* edited by Joseph P. Strelka, 81–108. Bern: Peter Lang, 1992.

Werba, Robert. "Schubert und die Nachwelt." *Österreichische Musikzeitschrift* 33, no. 11 (November 1978): 599–604.

———. *Schubert und die Wiener: Der volkstümliche Unbekannte.* Munich: Jugend und Volk, 1978.

Werfel, Franz. *Zwischen Oben und Unten: Prosa. Tagebücher. Aphorismen. Literarische Nachträge.* Munich: Langen-Müller, 1975.

West, Kenyon. "The Centenary of Franz Schubert." *Outlook* 55, no. 6 (February 6, 1897): 401–7.

Whaples, Miriam. "Mahler and Schubert's A Minor Sonata D. 784." *Music & Letters* 65, no. 3 (July 1984): 255–63.

Whiteside, Andrew. *Austrian National Socialism before 1918.* The Hague: M. Nijhoff, 1962.

———. *The Socialism of Fools: Georg Ritter von Schönerer and Austrian Pan-Germanism.* Berkeley and Los Angeles: University of California Press, 1975.

Wickert, Gabriele. "Freud's Heritage: Fathers and Daughters in German Literature (1750–1850)." In *In the Shadow of the Past: Psychology Portrays the Sexes,* edited by Miriam Lewin, 26–38. New York: Columbia University Press, 1984.

"Das Wiener Schubert-Monument und die Preiskonkurrenzen." *Beiblatt zur Zeitschrift für bildende Kunst* 1, no. 20 (September 28, 1866): 129–31.

Wiesner-Hanks, Merry E. *Gender in History.* Malden, MA: Blackwell, 2001.

Wilberforce, Edward. *Franz Schubert: A Musical Biography*. London: Wm. H. Allen & Co., 1866.

Williams, C. E. *The Broken Eagle: The Politics of Austrian Literature from Empire to Anschluss*. London: Paul Elek, 1974.

Willner, A. M., and Heinz Reichert. *Das Dreimäderlhaus: Singspiel in drei Akten*. Leipzig: Ludwig Doblinger (Bernhard Herzmansky), [1912].

Wingfield, Nancy M. "Statues of Emperor Joseph II as Sites of German Identity." In *Staging the Past: The Politics of Commemoration in Habsburg Central Europe, 1848 to the Present*, edited by Maria Bucur and Nancy M. Wingfield, 178–205. West Lafayette, IN: Purdue University Press, 2001.

Winkle, Sally A. *Woman as Bourgeois Ideal: A Study of Sophie von La Roche's "Geschichte des Fräuleins von Sternheim" and Goethe's "Werther."* New York: Peter Lang, 1988.

Wistrich, Robert S. *The Jews of Vienna in the Age of Franz Joseph*. Oxford: Oxford University Press, 1989.

Wittels, Fritz. *Critique of Love*. New York: The Macaulay Company, 1929.

Wittgenstein, Ludwig. *Philosophical Investigations*. 3rd ed. Translated by G. E. M. Anscombe. New York: Macmillan, 1958.

Wittgenstein Familienbriefe. Edited by Brian McGuinness, Maria Concetta Ascher, and Otto Pfersmann. Vienna: Verlag Hölder-Pichler-Tempsky, 1996.

Wolf, Helga Maria, ed. *Franz Schubert in Kunst und Kitsch*. Vienna: Bezirksmuseum, Galerie Alsergrund, 1978.

Wolf, Hugo. *The Music Criticism of Hugo Wolf*. Translated and edited by Henry Pleasants. New York: Holmes & Meier, 1978.

Wunberg, Gotthart, ed. *Das Junge Wien: Österreichische Literatur- und Kunstkritik 1887–1902*. 2 vols. Tübingen, Germany: Max Niemeyer Verlag, 1976.

———. *Die literarische Moderne: Dokumente zum Selbstverständnis der Literatur um die Jahrhundertwende*. Frankfurt am Main: Athenäum, 1971.

———. *Die Wiener Moderne: Literatur, Kunst und Musik zwischen 1890 und 1910*. Stuttgart: Reclam, 1981.

Wurzbach, Constant von. *Biographisches Lexikon des Kaiserthums Oesterreich*. 60 vols. Vienna: K. K. Hof- und Staatsdruckerei, 1856–91.

Yates, W. E. "Hofmannsthal's Comedies." In *A Companion to the Works of Hugo von Hofmannsthal*, edited by Thomas A. Kovach, 139–56. Rochester, NY: Camden House, 2002.

———. *Schnitzler, Hofmannsthal, and the Austrian Theater*. New Haven, CT: Yale University Press, 1992.

Youens, Susan. *Hugo Wolf: The Vocal Music*. Princeton, NJ: Princeton University Press, 1992.

———. "Schubert, Mahler, and the Weight of the Past: 'Lieder eines fahrenden Gesellen' and 'Winterreise.'" *Music & Letters* 67, no. 3 (July 1986): 256–68.

Zenck, Martin. "Entwurf einer Soziologie der musikalischen Rezeption." *Die Musik* 33, no. 3 (1980): 253–79.

———. "Franz Schubert im 19. Jahrhundert." In *Franz Schubert und Gustav Mahler in der Musik der Gegenwart*, edited by Klaus Hinrich Stahmer, 9–24. Mainz: Schott, 1997.

Zenger, Max. *Franz Schuberts Wirken und Erdenwallen*. Langensalza, Germany: Hermann Beyer & Söhne, 1902.

Zuckerkandl, Bertha. *My Life and History*. Translated by John Sommerfield. New York: Knopf, 1939.

Zweig, Stefan. *The World of Yesterday*. Lincoln and London: University of Nebraska Press, 1964.

Index

Esterházy, Marie, 83, 84, 252n23
Eugene, Prince of Savoy, 16, 27, 31, 113
Ewers, Hans Heinz, 147

Die Fackel, 91, 93, 155, 156, 159, 204, 205, 255n47
Fechner, Gustav, 25
Feis, Oswald, 123
femininity, 85, 102, 121, 132; and Altenberg, 112, 146–50, 159, 164; and Austria, 9, 113–14, 116, 119–20, 122, 199, 243n5, 243n7; and Austrian literature, 96, 112, 121, 123, 143, 199; and Beethoven, 157; and Grillparzer, 130–32; and Hofmannsthal, 111, 112; and Schubert, 1–3, 7, 9, 19, 25–27, 93, 96, 100, 103, 106, 110, 115, 118, 123, 125, 133, 136, 137–39, 144, 146, 149–53, 158, 169, 195–96, 198–201, 249n69, 269n2; and sexuality, 118–19, 125, 128, 141–42, 158; and Vienna, 114, 120; and Wagner, 123, 127; and Weininger, 126–27, 134
Fernkorn, Anton, 16
Fessenden, Reginald, 258n72
Fichte, Johann Gottlieb, 29, 127
Fidus, 254n44
fin de siècle, 5, 213n4
Fischer, Wolfgang Georg, 84
Flöge, Emilie, 84–85, 87, 90, 235n39, 235n41
Flöge, Helene, 84
Der Floh, 25, 64, 67–68
Forel, August, 134
Förster, Ludwig, 237n14
Franck, César, 192
Franco-Prussian War, 32, 33
Frankl, Ludwig August, 34–35, 222n70
Franz Joseph I, Emperor of Austria-Hungary, 14, 15, 16, 31, 39, 41, 61, 66, 221n56, 223n5, 230n2; and Schubert exhibition, 37, 53–56, 70–71, 75, 80

Frederick II, "the Great," King of Prussia, 128
Freiheit!, 43
Fremden-Blatt, 71
Freud, Sigmund, 125, 126, 139–41, 160–61, 162, 247n61, 249n73, 255n51; *The Interpretation of Dreams*, 212n1, 248n64
Friedjung, Heinrich, 119–20, 121
Friedländer, Benedikt, 135
friendship between men, 129, 131, 136–37, 142, 143, 245n30, 246n45; cult of, 132, 135; Schubert and, 135, 138, 142, 241n64
Frisch, Walter, 188, 189, 264n41
Fröhlich, Kathi, 85, 130
Fromme's musikalische Welt, 72
Fuchs, Hanns, 127–30, 131, 136, 142
Funder, Friedrich, 224n15
Furtwängler, Wilhelm, 193

Gabillon, Louis, 27, 29, 34
Geiger, Benno: "Deutschlands Sterbegesang," 115
Geiger, Karl Joseph, 73–75
Geisler-Schubert, Karoline, 39
gender, 4, 209n2, 242n3, 249n75; and Altenberg, 147; and Austria, 113, 121; and modernist literature, 96, 119, 121, 199; and Schnitzler, 105; and Schubert, 1–5, 9–10, 48, 58, 118–19, 139, 153, 197–200, 205, 210n3; and Vienna, 114; and Wagner, 139, 157; and Weininger, 134
George, Stefan, 111, 171, 257n64; "Litanei," 266n53
Gerber, Artur, 156
Germany, 32–33, 57, 59, 114; compared to Austria, 113–15, 116–17, 242n67; as masculine nation, 113, 120; Schubert's reception in, 13. *See also* Prussia
Geschlecht und Gesellschaft, 124
Gibbs, Christopher H., 3
Giese, Fritz, 249n75

Eastman Studies in Music

The second volume of *Schubert in the European Imagination* continues the first volume's examination of the historical reception of Franz Schubert in nineteenth- and early twentieth-century Europe, this time concentrating on fin-de-siècle Vienna.

By 1900, Schubert had attained enormous prestige and, in Vienna, a uniquely iconic status as the only renowned composer of serious music who was born, spent his entire life, and died in the capital of the Habsburg Empire. As a result, Vienna's greatest musical son and his works were discussed and portrayed in ways that reflected shifts in nationalist allegiances, particularly when municipal commemorations of his life coincided with larger political events.

In addition, the concept of Schubert as a feminine type—which had begun with Robert Schumann's coining of the term *Mädchencharakter* ("girlish" character) in 1838—had by 1900 become firmly embedded in the popular consciousness. Schubert was now a readily familiar sign for passive innocence.

To many people in literature and the arts, though, passivity was also embodied in the type of young woman whose weakness was fated to be overwhelmed by the increasingly recognized power of sexuality. Thus, the generation that came of age at the turn of the new century used the acquired portrait of Schubert to critique the values that lay behind that very image.

Some of the most original and powerful Viennese figures of the period—including composer Arnold Schoenberg, painter Gustav Klimt, and writers Arthur Schnitzler, Hugo von Hofmannsthal, and Peter Altenberg—refashioned Schubertian hagiography in ways that suited their own creative ends. In so doing, they redefined the Romantic traditions that they inherited, and heralded the turbulent challenges of twentieth-century artistic and cultural modernism.

Scott Messing is Charles A. Dana Professor of Music at Alma College. His book *Neoclassicism in Music* went through three printings with UMI Research Press and then the University of Rochester Press. His articles on music of the nineteenth and twentieth centuries have appeared in major scholarly journals and in the books *Wien 1897: Kulturgeschichtliches Profil eines Epochenjahres* and *Music and Modern Art*.

"This is cultural history at its best—'thick' history that uncovers the multiple, fascinating forces at work between the centennial celebrations of Schubert's birth and death. A dazzling work of reception history, Messing's book illuminates Schubert's role in the politics of gender, race, and cultural identity in fin-de-siècle Vienna. In so doing it provides the long-awaited musical counterpart to Carl Schorske's classic study *Fin-de-siècle Vienna: Politics and Culture.*"
 —Glenn Watkins, Earl V. Moore Professor Emeritus, University of Michigan, and author of *Proof Through the Night: Music and the Great War*

"Franz Schubert as flower or thorn? Musicologist Scott Messing's intriguing sequel to his first volume on Schubert in the nineteenth-century European imagination is a graceful, far-ranging, important study of fin-de-siècle perceptions of the Viennese composer as they affected national politics and cultural self-definition in the early twentieth century. The conceptual legacy of a feminine Schubert is scrutinized through the lens of political history ('masculine' Germany versus 'feminine' Austria), art (Kundmann's statue, Klimt's portrait), literature (Schnitzler, Hofmannsthal, Altenberg), music (Schoenberg), and the inquisitive but choosy new science of sexuality. Proceeding with the contagious tempo of a fine mystery novel, this is 'reception history' at its broadest, yet most exacting, often surprising best."
 —Alessandra Comini, University Distinguished Professor of Art History Emerita, Southern Methodist University